Item Response Theory
for Psychologists

MULTIVARIATE APPLICATIONS BOOKS SERIES

The Multivariate Applications book series was developed to encourage the use of rigorous methodology in the study of meaningful scientific issues, and to describe the applications in easy to understand language. The series is sponsored by the Society of Multivariate Experimental Psychology and welcomes methodological applications from a variety of disciplines, such as psychology, public health, sociology, education, and business. Books can be single authored, multiple authored, or edited volumes. The ideal book for this series would take on one of several approaches: (1) demonstrate the application of a variety of multivariate methods to a single, major area of research; (2) describe a methodological procedure or framework that could be applied to a variety of research areas; or (3) present a variety of perspectives on a controversial topic of interest to applied researchers.

There are currently four books in the series:

1. *What if There Were No Significance Tests?*, co-edited by Lisa L. Harlow, Stanley A. Mulaik, and James H. Steiger (1997).
2. *Structural Equation Modeling with LISREL, PRELIS, and SIMPLIS: Basic Concepts, Applications and Programming*, written by Barbara M. Byrne (1998).
3. *Multivariate Applications in Substance Use Research*, co-edited by Jennifer S. Rose, Laurie Chassin, Clark C. Presson, and Steven J. Sherman (2000).
4. *Item Response Theory for Psychologists*, co-authored by Susan E. Embretson and Steven P. Reise.

Interested persons should contact the editor, Lisa L. Harlow, at: Department of Psychology, University of Rhode Island, 10 Chafee Rd., Suite 8, Kingston, RI 02881-0808; Phone: 401-874-4242; FAX: 401-874-5562; or E-Mail: LHarlow@uri.edu. Information can also be obtained from one of the editorial board members: Leona Aiken (Arizona State University), Gwyneth Boodoo (Educational Testing Service), Barbara Byrne (University of Ottawa), Scott Maxwell (University of Notre Dame), David Rindskopf (City University of New York), or Steve West (Arizona State University).

Item Response Theory
for Psychologists

Susan E. Embretson
University of Kansas

Steven P. Reise
University of California

LEA LAWRENCE ERLBAUM ASSOCIATES, PUBLISHERS
2000 Mahwah, New Jersey London

Lawrence Erlbaum Associates, Inc., Publishers
10 Industrial Avenue
Mahwah, New Jersey 07430-2262

Cover design by Kathryn Houghtaling Lacey

Library of Congress Cataloging-in-Publication Data

Embretson, Susan E.
Item response theory for psychologists / Susan E. Embretson and Steven P. Reise.
p. cm. — (Multivariate applications)
Includes bibliographical references and index.
ISBN 0-8058-2818-4 (cloth : alk. paper) — ISBN 0-8058-2819-2 (pbk. : alk. paper)
1. Item response theory. 2. Psychometrics. I. Reise, Steven P. II. Title. III. Multivariate applications book series.
BF39.E495 2000
150'.28'7—dc21   99-048454
                                                               CIP

Books published by Lawrence Erlbaum Associates are printed on acid-free paper, and their bindings are chosen for strength and durability

Printed in the United States of America
10 9 8 7 6 5 4 3 2

*To Marshall and to the many IRT scholars
who have shaped the field and taught us their insights.*
—Susan

*To my parents, Ben and Ruth,
who provided support and inspiration throughout my pursuit
of higher education.*
—Steve

Contents

PART IV: APPLICATIONS OF IRT MODELS

Preface

The purpose of this book is to explain the new measurement theory to a primarily psychological audience. Item response theory (IRT) is not only the psychometric theory underlying many major tests today, but it has many important research applications. Unfortunately, the few available textbooks are not easily accessible to the audience of psychological researchers and practitioners; the books contain too many equations and derivations and too few familiar concepts. Furthermore, most IRT texts are slanted toward understanding IRT application within the context of large-scale educational assessments, such as analyzing the SAT. Our approach is more geared toward a psychological audience that is familiar with small-scale cognitive and personality measures or that wants to use IRT to analyze scales used in their own research.

Herein, familiar psychological concepts, issues, and examples are used to help explain various principles in IRT. We first seek to develop the reader's intuitive understanding of IRT principles by using graphical displays and analogies to classical measurement theory. Then, the book surveys contemporary IRT models, estimation methods, and computer programs. Because many psychological tests use rating scales, polytomous IRT models are given central coverage. Applications to substantive research problems, as well as to applied testing issues, are described.

The book is intended for psychology professionals and graduate students who are familiar with testing principles and classical test theory (CTT), such as covered in a graduate textbook on psychological testing (e.g., Anastasi & Urbina, 1997). Furthermore, the reader should have had a first-year sequence in graduate statistics, such as required in most psychology graduate programs. The reader need not have further training in either statistics or measurement, however, to read this book. Although equations are necessary to present IRT models and estimation methods, we attempt to define all symbols thoroughly and explain the equations verbally or graphically.

The book is appropriate as a graduate textbook for a measurement course; in fact, drafts of the text have been used at the University of Kansas, University of California, Los Angeles, and the University of Virginia. We wish to thank students in these courses for finding numerous typos and for their comments on principles that have helped us improve the treatment of several topics. Although the book is most appropriate for psychology measurement courses, nothing precludes use in related fields. In fact, it can be used in schools of education, as well as in other social sciences and related areas, such as behavioral medicine and gerontology, where it might be used to explain measurement principles.

The idea for this book emerged during an American Psychological Association meeting in 1996. Susan Embretson had presented a paper on IRT in a session entitled "What Every Psychologist Should Know About Measurement—but Doesn't." In this paper, a foundation for chapter 2 in this book, the lack of an appropriate textbook was cited as one reason why psychologists are largely unfamiliar with IRT. Unintentionally, Susan convinced herself to write it—that is, if she could find the right coauthor. But who? Well, she thought, if Steve Reise were willing, maybe this textbook could be written. A few hours later, Steve appeared at an APA reception. To the point, Susan asked immediately "How about writing a book on IRT for psychologists with me?" "Yeah, good idea," replied Steve in his characteristic low-key manner.

Of course, the path from ideas to products is long. Although the writing was easy enough, many inconsistencies and incomparabilities in the literature and in the computer programs for estimating IRT parameters created difficulty. Developing a clear exposition requires unified concepts and generalities. The book was not finished until Spring 1999.

We think that two important communalities influenced the book. First, we have both taught measurement and IRT in departments of psychology. Thus, we are familiar with the conceptual issues that develop in teaching the psychology audience. Second, we are both Psychology PhDs of the University of Minnesota. Susan finished in 1973, and Steve in 1990. Thus, we share some perspectives on the role of measurement in psychology. However, we also differ in several ways. Susan struggled with IRT principles during the early years of its development. She was interested then, and now, in developing IRT models and methodology to interface cognitive theory and psychometrics. She focused primarily on Rasch-family models for binary data. Steve, in contrast, is a more recent PhD. He was interested in interfacing IRT models with personality measurement. He has concentrated primarily on complex IRT models (i.e., those with discrimination parameters) for rating scale data. These intellectual differences have enabled the book to include greater bredth of coverage and to elaborate differing perspectives on IRT models.

ACKNOWLEDGMENTS

We have relied on many good colleagues for their critiques of the chapters. IRT is not an easy field; the scholarship of our colleagues has been invaluable. We wish to thank the following persons for reading one or more chapters: Terry Ackerman, R. Darrell Bock, Paul DeBoeck, Fritz Drasgow, Niahua Duan, Mathilde Dutoit, Jan-Eric Gustafsson, Mark Haviland, Karen McCollam, Robert Mislevy, Eiji Muraki, Michael Nering, Mark Reckase, Lynne Steinberg, Jurgen Rost, David Thissen, Niels Waller, and Michael Yoes. Of course, these readers are not responsible for any remaining problems in the book. The book departs in many ways from typical treatments; IRT principles are explained in a simple and direct way. However, accomplishing simplicity sometimes requires obscuring issues that some scholars find important. We are very interested in improving the book in later revisions, so we urge the readers to address any comments or problems to us directly.

Last, but not least, we would like to thank those persons close to us. Marshall Picow, Susan's husband, knows what effort it has required to finish this book. He has been most helpful and patient while Susan has chained herself to the computer for days on end. He deserves much thanks for his continuing support. Steve thanks several scholars who have been of tremendous assistance throughout his career as an IRT researcher: David J. Weiss, Auke Tellegen, and his research associates Niels G. Waller and Keith Widaman.

—*Susan E. Embretson*
—*Steven P. Reise*

I

INTRODUCTION

1

Introduction

In an ever-changing world, psychological testing remains the flagship of applied psychology. Although the specific applications and the legal guidelines for using tests have changed, psychological tests have been relatively stable. Many well-known tests, in somewhat revised forms, remain current. Furthermore, although several new tests have been developed in response to contemporary needs in applied psychology, the principles underlying test development have remained constant. Or have they?

In fact, the psychometric basis of tests has changed dramatically. Although classical test theory (CTT) has served test development well over several decades, item response theory (IRT) has rapidly become mainstream as the theoretical basis for measurement. Increasingly, standardized tests are developed from IRT due to the more theoretically justifiable measurement principles and the greater potential to solve practical measurement problems.

This chapter provides a context for IRT principles. The current scope of IRT applications is considered. Then a brief history of IRT is given and its relationship to psychology is discussed. Finally, the purpose of the various sections of the book is described.

SCOPE OF IRT APPLICATIONS

IRT now underlies several major tests. Computerized adaptive testing, in particular, relies on IRT. In computerized adaptive testing, examinees receive items that are optimally selected to measure their potential. Different examinees may receive no common items. IRT principles are involved in both selecting the most appropriate items for an examinee and equating scores across different subsets of items. For example, the Armed Services Vocational Aptitude Battery, the Scholastic Aptitude Test (SAT), and the Graduate Record Examination (GRE) apply IRT to estimate abilities. IRT has also been applied to several individual intelligence tests, including the Differential Ability Scales, the Woodcock-Johnson Psycho-Educational Battery, and the current version of the Stanford-Binet, as well as many smaller volume tests. Furthermore, IRT has been applied to personality trait measurements (see Reise & Waller, 1990), as well as to attitude measurements and behavioral ratings (see Engelhard & Wilson, 1996). Journals such as *Psychological Assessment* now feature applications of IRT to clinical testing issues (e.g., Santor, Ramsey, & Zuroff, 1994).

Many diverse IRT models are now available for application to a wide range of psychological areas. Although early IRT models emphasized dichotomous item formats (e.g., the Rasch model and the three-parameter logistic model), extensions to other item formats has enabled applications in many areas; that is, IRT models have been developed for rating scales (Andrich, 1978b), partial credit scoring (Masters, 1982), and multiple category scoring (Thissen & Steinberg, 1984). Effective computer programs for applying these extended models, such as RUMM, MULTILOG, and PARSCALE, are now available (see chap. 13 for details). Thus, IRT models may now be applied to measure personality traits, moods, behavioral dispositions, situational evaluations, and attitudes as well as cognitive traits.

The early IRT applications involved primarily unidimensional IRT models. However, several multidimensional IRT models have been developed. These models permit traits to be measured by comparisons within tests or within items. Bock, Gibbons, and Muraki (1988) developed a multidimensional IRT model that identifies the dimensions that are needed to fit test data, similar to an exploratory factor analysis. However, a set of confirmatory multidimensional IRT models have also been developed. For example, IRT models for traits that are specified in a design structure (like confirmatory factor analysis) have been developed (Adams, Wilson, & Wang, 1997; Embretson, 1991, 1997; DiBello, Stout, & Roussos, 1995). Thus, person measurements that reflect comparisons on subsets of items, change over time, or the effects of dynamic testing may be specified as the target traits to be measured. Some multidimensional IRT models have been closely connected with cognitive theory variables. For example, person differences in underlying processing components (Embretson, 1984; Whitely, 1980), developmental stages (Wilson, 1985) and qualitative differences between examinees, such as different processing strategies or knowledge structures (Kelderman & Rijkes, 1994; Rost, 1990) may be measured with the special IRT models. Because many of these models also have been generalized to rating scales, applications to personality, attitude, and behavioral self-reports are possible, as well. Thus many measurement goals may be accommodated by the increasingly large family of IRT models.

HISTORY OF IRT

Two separate lines of development in IRT underlie current applications. In the United States, the beginning of IRT is often traced to Lord and Novick's (1968) classic textbook, *Statistical Theories of Mental Test Scores*. This textbook includes four chapters on IRT, written by Allan Birnbaum. Developments in the preceding decade provided the basis for IRT as described in Lord and Novick (1968). These developments include an important paper by Lord (1953) and three U.S. Air Force technical reports (Birnbaum, 1957, 1958a, 1958b). Although the air force technical reports were not widely read at the time, Birnbaum contributed the material from these reports in his chapters in Lord and Novick's (1968) book.

Lord and Novick's (1968) textbook was a milestone in psychometric methods for several reasons. First, these authors provided a rigorous and unified statistical treatment of test theory as compared to other textbooks. In many ways, Lord and Novick (1968) extended Gulliksen's exposition of CTT in *Theory of Mental Tests*, an earlier milestone in psychometrics. However, the extension to IRT, a much more statistical version of test theory, was very significant. Second, the textbook was well connected to testing. Fred Lord, the senior author, was a long-time employee of Educational Testing Service. ETS is responsible for many large-volume tests that have recurring psychometric issues that are readily handled by IRT. Furthermore, the large sample sizes available were especially amendable to statistical approaches. Third, the textbook was well connected to leading and emerging scholars in psychometric methods. Lord and Novick (1968) mentioned an ongoing seminar at ETS that included Allan Birnbaum, Michael W. Browne, Karl Joreskog, Walter Kristof, Michael Levine, William Meredith, Samuel Messick, Roderick McDonald, Melvin Novick, Fumiko Samejima, J. Philip Sutcliffe, and Joseph L. Zinnes in addition to Frederick Lord. These individuals subsequently became well known for their contributions to psychometric methods.

R. Darrell Bock, then at the University of North Carolina, was inspired by the early IRT models, especially those by Samejima. Bock was interested in developing effective algorithms for estimating the parameters of IRT models. Subsequently, Bock and several student collaborators at the University of Chicago, including David Thissen, Eiji Muraki, Richard Gibbons, and Robert Mislevy, developed effective estimation methods and computer programs, such as BILOG, TESTFACT, MULTILOG, and PARSCALE. In conjunction with Murray Aitken (Bock & Aitken, 1981), Bock developed the marginal maximum likelihood method to estimate the parameters, which is now considered state of the art in IRT estimation. An interesting history of IRT, and its historical precursors, was published recently by Bock (1997).

A rather separate line of development in IRT may be traced to Georg Rasch (1960), a Danish mathematician who worked for many years in consulting and teaching statistics. He developed a family of IRT models that were applied to develop measures of reading and to develop tests for use in the Danish military. Rasch (1960) was particularly interested in the scientific properties of measurement models. He noted that person and item parameters were fully separable in his models, a property he elaborated as *specific objectivity*. Andersen (1972), a student of Rasch, consequently elaborated effective estimation methods for the person and item parameters in Rasch's models.

Rasch inspired two other psychometricians who extended his models and taught basic measurement principles. In Europe, Gerhard Fischer (1973) from the University of Vienna, extended the Rasch model for binary data so that it could incorporate psychological considerations into the parameters. Thus stimulus properties of items, treatment conditions given to subjects, and many other variables could be used to define parameters in the linear logistic latent trait model. This model inspired numerous applications and developments throughout Europe. Fischer's (1974) textbook on IRT was influential in Europe but had a restricted scope since it was written in German.

Rasch visited the United States and inspired Benjamin Wright, an American psychometrician, to subsequently teach objective measurement principles and to extend his models. Rasch visited the University of Chicago, where Wright was a professor in education, to give a series of lectures. Wright was particularly inspired by the promise of objective measurement. Subsequently, a large number of doctoral dissertations were devoted to the Rasch model under Wright's direction. Several of these PhDs became known subsequently for their theoretical contributions to Rasch-family models, including David Andrich (1978a), Geoffrey Masters (1982), Graham Douglas (Wright & Douglas, 1977), and Mark Wilson (1989). Many of Wright's students pioneered extended applications in educational assessment and in behavioral medicine. Wright also lectured widely on objective measurement principles and inspired an early testing application by Richard Woodcock in the Woodcock-Johnson Psycho-Educational Battery.

Rather noticeable by its absence, however, is the impact of IRT on psychology. Wright's students, as education PhDs, were employed in education or in applied settings rather than in psychology. Bock's affliation at the University of Chicago also was not primarily psychology, and his students were employed in several areas but rarely psychology.

Instead, a few small pockets of intellectual activity could be found in psychology departments with programs in quantitative methods or psychometrics. The authors are particularly familiar with the impact of IRT on psychology at the University of Minnesota, but similar impact on psychology probably occurred elsewhere. Minnesota had a long history of applied psychological measurement. In the late 1960s and early 1970s, two professors at Minnesota — Rene Dawis and David Weiss — became interested in IRT. Dawis was interested in the objective measurement properties of the Rasch model. Dawis obtained an early version of Wright's computer program through Richard Woodcock, who was applying the Rasch model to his tests. Graduate students such as Merle Ace, Howard Tinsley, and Susan Embretson published early articles on objective measurement properties (Tinsley, 1972; Whitely[1] & Dawis, 1976). Weiss, on the other hand, was interested in developing computerized adaptive tests and the role for complex IRT models to solve the item selection and test equating problems. Graduate students who were involved in this effort included Isaac Bejar, Brad Sympson, and James McBride. Later students of Weiss, including Steve Reise, moved to substantive applications such as personality.

The University of Minnesota PhDs had significant impact on testing subsequently, but their impact on psychological measurement was limited. Probably like other graduate programs in psychology, new PhDs with expertise in IRT were actively recruited by test publishers and the military testing laboratories to implement IRT in large volume tests. Although this career path for the typical IRT student was beneficial to testing, psychology remained basically unaware of the new psychometrics. Although (classical) test theory is routine in the curriculum for applied psychologists and for many theoretically inclined psychologists, IRT has rarely had much coverage. In fact, in the 1970s and 1980s, many psychologists who taught measurement and testing had little or no knowledge of IRT. Thus the teaching of psychological measurement principles became increasingly removed from the psychometric basis of tests.

THE ORGANIZATION OF THIS BOOK

As noted in the brief history given earlier, few psychologists are well acquainted with the principles of IRT. Thus most psychologists' knowledge of the "rules of measurement" is based on CTT. Unfortunately, under IRT many well-known rules of measurement derived from CTT no longer ap-

---

[1]Susan E. Embretson has also published as Susan E. Whitely.

ply. In fact, some new rules of measurement conflict directly with the old rules. IRT is based on fundamentally different principles than CTT. That is, IRT is model-based measurement that controls various confounding factors in score comparisons by a more complete parameterization of the measurement situation.

The two chapters in Part II, "Item Response Theory Principles: Some Contrasts and Comparisons," were written to acquaint the reader with the differences between CTT and IRT. Chapter 2, "The New Rules of Measurement," contrasts 10 principles of CTT that conflict with corresponding principles of IRT. IRT is not a mere refinement of CTT; it is a different foundation for testing. Chapter 3, "Item Response Theory as Model-Based Measurement," presents some reasons why IRT differs fundamentally from CTT. The meaning and functions of measurement models in testing are considered, and a quick overview of estimation in IRT versus CTT is provided. These two chapters, taken together, are designed to provide a quick introduction and an intuitive understanding of IRT principles that many students find difficult.

More extended coverage of IRT models and their estimation is included in Part III, "The Fundamentals of Item Response Theory." Chapter 4, "Binary IRT Models," includes a diverse array of models that are appropriate for dichotomous responses, such as "pass versus fail" and "agree versus disagree." Chapter 5, "Polytomous IRT Models," is devoted to an array of models that are appropriate for rating scales and other items that yield responses in discrete categories. Chapter 6, "The Trait Level Scale: Meaning, Interpretations and Measurement Scale Properties," includes material on the various types of trait level scores that may be obtained from IRT scaling of persons. Also, the meaning of measurement scale level and its relationship to IRT is considered. Chapters 7 and 8, "Measuring Persons: Scoring Examinees with IRT Models" and "Calibrating Items: Estimation," concern procedures involved in obtaining IRT parameter estimates. These procedures differ qualitatively from CTT procedures. The last chapter in this section, "Assessing the Fit of IRT Models" (chap. 9), considers how to decide if a particular IRT model is appropriate for test data.

The last section of the book, "Applications of IRT Models," is intended to provide examples to help guide the reader's own applications. Chapter 10, "IRT Applications: DIF, CAT, and Scale Analysis," concerns how IRT is applied to solve practical testing problems. Chapters 11 and 12, "IRT Applications in Cognitive and Developmental Assessment" and "IRT Applications in Personality and Attitude Assessment," consider how IRT can contribute to substantive issues in measurement. The last chapter of the book, "Computer Programs for IRT Models," gives extended coverage to the required input and the results produced from several selected computer programs.

Although one more chapter originally was planned for the book, we decided not to write it. IRT is now a mainstream psychometric method, and the field is expanding quite rapidly. Our main concern was to acquaint the reader with basic IRT principles rather than to evaluate the current state of knowledge in IRT. Many recurring and emerging issues in IRT are mentioned throughout the book. Perhaps a later edition of this book can include a chapter on the current state and future directions in IRT. For now, we invite readers to explore their own applications and to research issues in IRT that intrigue them.

II

ITEM RESPONSE THEORY PRINCIPLES: SOME CONTRASTS AND COMPARISONS

2

The New Rules of Measurement

Classical test theory (CTT) has been the mainstay of psychological test development for most of the 20th century. Gulliksen's (1950) classic book, which remains in print, is often cited as the defining volume. However, CTT is much older. Many procedures were pioneered by Spearman (1907, 1913). CTT has defined the standard for test development, beginning with the initial explosion of testing in the 1930s.

However, since Lord and Novick's (1968) classic book introduced model-based measurement, a quiet revolution has occurred in test theory. Item response theory (IRT) has rapidly become mainstream as a basis for psychological measurement. IRT, also known as latent trait theory, is model-based measurement in which trait level estimates depend on both persons' responses and on the properties of the items that were administered. Many new or revised tests, particularly ability tests, have been developed from IRT principles. Yet, because most test users are unfamiliar with IRT, test manuals mention its application only in passing or in a technical appendix. Thus test users are largely unaware that the psychometric basis of testing has changed.

Initially, IRT appealed to U.S. test developers because it solved many practical testing problems, such as equating different test forms (see Lord, 1980). More recently, the promise of IRT for substantive issues in psychology has become apparent. Score interpretations may now be related to underlying skills through the conjoint measurement properties of IRT (see Rule 10). Furthermore, the justifiable measurement scale properties for IRT can have significant impact on inferential statistics about group differences (Embretson, 1996a; Maxwell & Delaney, 1985), as well as on test score comparisons within or between persons.

Most psychologists' knowledge of the "rules of measurement" is based on CTT. Test theory is included in the curriculum for applied psychologists and for many theoretically inclined psychologists. In some graduate programs, CTT is presented in a separate course, which is required for applied psychologists and elective for other areas. In other graduate programs, CTT is elaborated in testing methods for courses for clinical, counseling, industrial, and school psychologists.

To provide continuity between the new test theory and the old test theory, Lord and Novick (1968) derived many CTT principles from IRT. On the surface, this seems to be good news for the busy psychologist who knows CTT but not IRT. The existence of the derivations seemingly suggests that the rules of measurement, although rooted in a more sophisticated body of axioms, remain unchanged.

Yet, in the new model-based version of test theory, IRT, some well-known rules of measurement no longer apply. In fact, the new rules of measurement are fundamentally different from the old rules. Many old rules, in fact, must be revised, generalized, or abandoned altogether.

This chapter contrasts several old rules of measurement to the corresponding new rules of measurement to illustrate the depth of the differences between CTT and IRT. These differences are described in their most extreme form in this chapter. Although many extensions of CTT were developed to handle some of the problems noted in this chapter, their application has been limited. We believe that for the many hundreds of small-volume psychological tests, the old rules are valid.

A COMPARISON OF MEASUREMENT RULES

Several old rules of measurement may be gleaned from the principles of CTT or its common extension. Other old rules are implicit in many applied test development procedures. Table 2.1 shows 10 old rules that are reviewed here. The old rules are followed by 10 corresponding new rules, which obviously conflict with the old rules.

We argue that the old rules represent common knowledge or practice among psychologists. These rules have guided the development of many, but certainly not all, published psychological tests. Obvious exceptions include some selection and admissions tests that were developed by large-scale testing corporations and the military. In these cases, non-IRT procedures were developed to circumvent the limitations of some old rules. For example, nonlinear test equating (see Holland & Rubin, 1982) was developed to handle the limitation of Old Rule 3. Also, population-free item indices, such as the delta index used by ETS (see Gulliksen, 1950, p. 368), was developed to counter Old Rule 4, respectively. Last, pro-

TABLE 2.1
Some "Rules" of Measurement

The Old Rules

Rule 1.   The standard error of measurement applies to all scores in a particular population.
Rule 2.   Longer tests are more reliable than shorter tests.
Rule 3.   Comparing test scores across multiple forms is optimal when the forms are parallel.
Rule 4.   Unbiased estimates of item properties depend on having representative samples.
Rule 5.   Test scores obtain meaning by comparing their position in a norm group.
Rule 6.   Interval scale properties are achieved by obtaining normal score distributions.
Rule 7.   Mixed item formats leads to unbalanced impact on test total scores.
Rule 8.   Change scores cannot be meaningfully compared when initial score levels differ.
Rule 9.   Factor analysis on binary items produces artifacts rather than factors.
Rule 10. Item stimulus features are unimportant compared to psychometric properties.

The New Rules

Rule 1.   The standard error of measurement differs across scores (or response patterns), but generalizes across populations.
Rule 2.   Shorter tests can be more reliable than longer tests.
Rule 3.   Comparing test scores across multiple forms is optimal when test difficulty levels vary between persons.
Rule 4.   Unbiased estimates of item properties may be obtained from unrepresentative samples.
Rule 5.   Test scores have meaning when they are compared for distance from items.
Rule 6.   Interval scale properties are achieved by applying justifiable measurement models.
Rule 7.   Mixed item formats can yield optimal test scores.
Rule 8.   Change scores can be meaningfully compared when initial score levels differ.
Rule 9.   Factor analysis on raw item data yields a full information factor analysis.
Rule 10. Item stimulus features can be directly related to psychometric properties.

cedures have been developed to estimate measurement errors at specific score levels (see Feldt & Brennan, 1989) to counter Old Rule 1. However, these techniques are not well known outside large-scale testing programs, hence they are not routinely applied in the development of psychological tests. Thus the old rules characterize substantial practice in test development.

Rule 1: The Standard Error of Measurement

Old Rule 1: The standard error of measurement applies to all scores in a particular population.

New Rule 1: The standard error of measurement differs across scores but generalizes across populations.

These two rules concern the properties of the standard error of measurement. The standard error of measurement describes expected score fluctuations due to error. Not only is the standard error of measurement basic to describing the psychometric quality of a test, it is also critical to individual score interpretations. The confidence intervals defined by the standard error can guide score interpretations in several ways. Differences between two scores, for example, may be interpreted as not significant if their confidence interval bands overlap.

New Rule 1 conflicts with Old Rule 1 in two ways. First, the rules differ in whether the standard error of measurement is constant or variable among scores in the same population. Old Rule 1 specifies constancy, whereas New Rule 1 specifies variability. Second, the rules differ in whether the standard error of measurement is specific or general across populations. Old Rule 1 is population-specific, whereas New Rule 1 is population-general.

The basis of the standard error of measurement differs substantially between CTT and IRT. Thus we elaborate these differences somewhat more here. A more complete elaboration of the IRT standard error of measurement is presented in chapter 7.

In CTT, the standard error of measurement is computed as the square root of 1 minus reliability $(1 - r_{tt})^{1/2}$, times the standard deviation of the test σ as follows:

$$SE_{\text{Msmt}} = (1 - r_{tt})^{1/2}\sigma \qquad (2.1)$$

Confidence intervals are constructed for individual scores under the assumption that measurement error is distributed normally and equally for all score levels.

To illustrate the old rule, item response data were simulated for 3,000 examinees on a 30-item test with a normal difficulty range. The examinees were sampled from a population with a standard normal distribution of trait scores (see Embretson, 1994b, for details). In the upper panel of Fig. 2.1, classical true scores (shown as standard scores) are regressed on raw test scores. A 68% confidence interval, using a standard error of .32 (e.g., from Cronbach's alpha index of internal consistency), is shown by the dotted lines.

Two important points about the old rule may be gleaned from the upper panel of Fig. 2.1. First, the estimated true score is a standard score that is derived as a *linear* transformation of raw score, as noted by the linear regression. Second, the confidence intervals are also represented as straight lines for all scores because the same confidence interval applies to each score. In CTT, both the transformation of raw score to true score and the standard error apply to a particular population because their estimation

Classical Test Theory

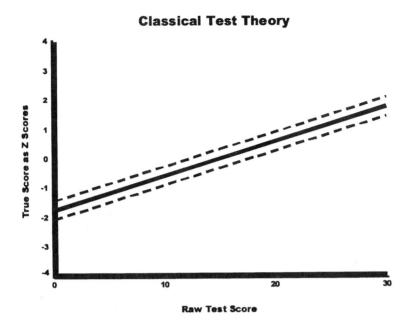

Item Response Theory

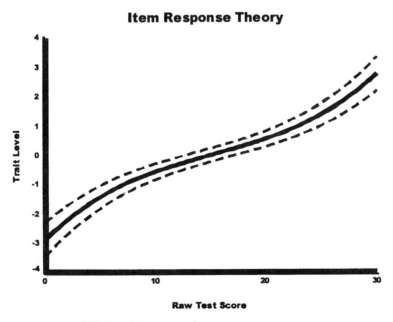

FIG. 2.1.   Regression of true score on raw score.

depends on population statistics. That is, the standard score conversion requires estimating the raw score mean and standard deviation for a population, whereas the standard error requires estimating both the variance and reliability.

To illustrate the new rule, trait scores were estimated using the Rasch IRT model on the simulation data that were described earlier. In the lower panel of Fig. 2.1, IRT trait level scores are regressed on raw scores. The lower panel differs from the upper panel of Fig. 2.1 in two important ways: First, the relationship between trait score and raw score is *nonlinear*; second, the confidence interval band becomes increasingly wide for extreme scores. Unlike CTT, neither the trait score estimates nor their corresponding standard errors depend on population distributions. In IRT models, trait scores are estimated separately for each score or response pattern, controlling for the characteristics (e.g., difficulty) of the items that were administered. Standard errors are smallest when the items are optimally appropriate for a particular trait score level and when item discriminations are high. The details of IRT standard errors are provided in later chapters.

The standard errors from IRT may be averaged to provide a summary index for a population. A composite reliability (see Andrich, 1988b) may be computed for the group by comparing the averaged squared standard errors, σ_θ^2, to the trait score variance, σ^2, as follows:

$$r'_{tt} = 1 - \frac{\sigma_\theta^2}{\sigma^2} \tag{2.2}$$

Obviously, the smaller the standard error at each trait score level, the higher the reliability. In the large normal population of simulated examinees, with a test that was appropriate for its trait level (see Embretson, 1995c), the *average* standard error, across examinees, was .32, the same as the uniform standard error from CTT in the first analysis. However, these standard errors will be similar only in limited circumstances. For example, if test difficulty was not well matched to the sample or if the distribution was not normal, differences would be expected.

Rule 2: Test Length and Reliability

Old Rule 2: Longer tests are more reliable than shorter tests.
New Rule 2: Shorter tests can be more reliable than longer tests.

These two rules contrast directly, and even surprisingly. It is axiomatic in CTT that longer tests are more reliable. In fact, this principle is represented by an equation in CTT; namely, the Spearman–Brown prophesy formula. Specifically, if a test is lengthened by a factor of n parallel parts, true variance increases more rapidly than error variance (Guilford, 1954, presents the classic proof). If r_{tt} is the reliability of the original test, the reliability of the lengthened test r_{nn} may be anticipated as follows:

$$r_{nn} = \frac{n\, r_{tt}}{1 + (n-1)r_{tt}} \qquad (2.3)$$

Equation 2.3 may also be applied to shortened tests. That is, if a test with a reliability of .86 is shortened to two-thirds of the original length ($n = .667$), then the anticipated reliability of the shorter test is .80. Figure 2.2 shows the effect of doubling, tripling, and so on, a test with an initial reliability of .70 with parallel items.

The new rule counters the old rule by asserting that short tests can be more reliable. Figure 2.3 shows the standard error of measurement at various levels of trait score for various lengths and types of tests based on the simulation data. Item discrimination was held constant in all analyses. All results in the lower panel are based on IRT. The two fixed content tests, of 20 and 30 items, respectively, show the characteristic IRT pattern of higher measurement errors for extreme scores. Also notice that the standard errors from the 30-item test are smaller than those from the 20-item test at all trait levels. This pattern is consistent with the *old rule*.

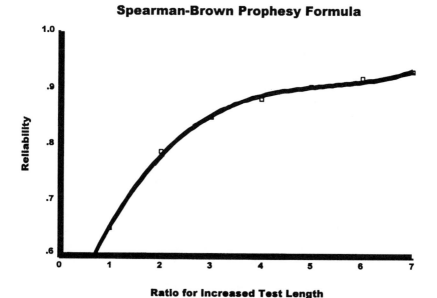

Reliability Under Increased Test Length

Spearman-Brown Prophesy Formula

FIG. 2.2.   Impact of test length in classical test theory.

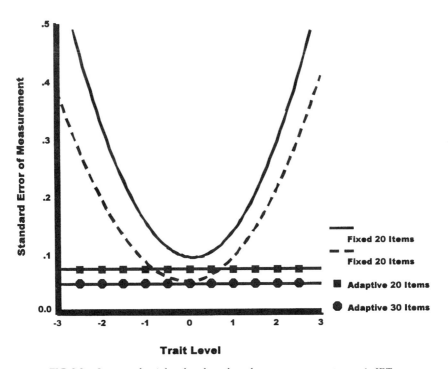

FIG. 2.3.   Impact of trait level and test length on measurement error in IRT.

The standard errors from two adaptive tests also are shown on the lower panel of Fig. 2.3. In adaptive tests, items are selected for each examinee to be most appropriate for their ability level. Thus, examinees at different ability levels will be administered different items. Given sufficient coverage of item difficulty in the item bank, equal standard errors can be obtained for each trait level. In the simulation study, Fig. 2.3 shows that equal standard errors were obtained across trait levels.

The new rule is illustrated by comparing the standard errors between traditional fixed content tests and adaptive tests. Notice that the standard error from the 20-item adaptive test is *lower* for most trait levels than from the 30-item fixed content test. This is a typical pattern for adaptive testing. The implication, of course, is that the shorter test yields less measurement error. Thus, a more reliable "test" has been developed at a shorter length with items of the same quality (i.e., item discriminations are constant). Thus, a composite reliability across trait levels as in Eq. 2.1, would show the shorter (adaptive) test as more reliable than the longer normal range test.

In fairness to CTT, it should be noted that an assumption underlying the Spearman–Brown prophesy formula is that the test is lengthened with parallel parts. An adaptive test, by its nature, fails to meet this assumption. The item difficulties vary substantially in the adaptive tests. However, the point made here is that the old rule about test length and reliability conflicts sharply with current adaptive testing practice, which is based on the new rule from IRT.

Rule 3: Interchangeable Test Forms

Old Rule 3: Comparing test scores across multiple forms is optimal when test forms are parallel.

New Rule 3: Comparing test scores across multiple forms is optimal when test difficulty levels vary between persons.

When examinees receive different test forms, some type of equating is needed before their scores can be compared. Traditionally, CTT relied on test form parallelism to equate scores. Gulliksen (1950) defined strict conditions for test parallelism in his exposition of CTT. The conditions included the equality of means and variances across test forms, as well as equality of covariances with external variables. If test forms meet Gulliksen's statistical conditions for parallelism, then scores may be regarded as comparable across forms.

Practically, however, test form parallelism cannot be met. Test form means and variances often differ somewhat. Furthermore, often score comparisons between rather different tests sometimes are desired. Thus, substantial effort has been devoted to procedures for test equating (see Angoff, 1982; Holland & Rubin, 1982). Comparable scores between test forms are established by techniques such as linear equating and equipercentile equating. In linear equating, for example, scores on one test form are regressed on the other test form. The regression line can then be used to find the comparable scores from one test form to the other.

Although the various equating methods can be applied when the test forms that have different means, variances, and reliabilities; equating error is influenced by differences between the test forms. Equating error is especially influenced by differences in test difficulty level (see Peterson, Marco, & Stewart, 1982). Thus, although scores can be linked between test forms, equating error can be problematic. Test forms with high reliabilities and similar score distributions will be most adequately equated.

The adverse effect of test difficulty differences on equating scores may be illustrated by considering some further results from the simulation study. In the simulation, 3,000 examinees were given two test forms containing the same item discriminations but substantially different item difficulties. Item responses for the easy test and the hard test were generated.

To illustrate the equating problem, consider the regression of the scores from the easy test on scores from a hard test shown in Fig. 2.4. The spread of scores on the easy test is shown at each score on the hard test. The best-fit linear regression between the tests yielded a squared multiple correlation of .67. This correlation is not very high for comparing scores across forms.

Thus the data shown in Fig. 2.4 have two problems for equating. First, a nonlinear regression is needed to fully describe score correspondence. For example, Fig. 2.4 shows that with linear equating, the easy test scores are underestimated at some score levels and overestimated at others. Nonlinear equating is significantly better in this case. The best-fit cubic relationship yielded a squared multiple correlation of .84, which leads to a lower equating error. Second, however, equating error will be substantial even for nonlinear equating. The variance of easy test scores at low scores on the hard test is quite large. For example, for an observed score of zero on the hard test, examinees scores on the easy test range from 0 to 20. The hard test simply does not have the floor to distinguish these examinees, so equating cannot be very satisfactory. Similarly, high scores on the hard test are associated with the same (perfect) score on the easy test. Thus no method of equating will match scores appropriately.

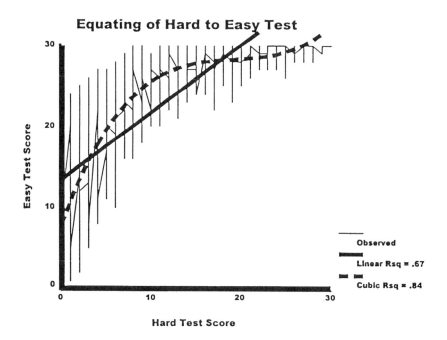

FIG. 2.4. Regression of easy test scores on hard test scores.

Because the scores shown in Fig. 2.4 are based on simulated data, the true trait levels are known. Thus the reliability index for the classical test scores could be computed directly by correlating raw scores with true scores. The upper panel of Fig. 2.5 shows the relationship of the two classical test forms with true trait level (i.e., the generating value in the simulation). Two points are worth noting in the upper panel. First, the relationship of scores on both tests are nonlinearly related to true trait level. That is, the relative distances between true scores are not reflected by the relative distances between raw scores on either test. Second, the squared correlation between true score and raw score is .8666 and .8736, respectively, for the hard test and the easy test. Although this value is high, it is rather low for simulation data based on a unidimensional trait underlying the items.

The lower panel of Fig. 2.5 shows the relationship of true trait level to estimated trait level from a simulated adaptive test of 30 items. In the adaptive test, examinees receive different subsets of items, which vary substantially in item difficulty. In fact, item difficulty is selected to be optimally appropriate for each examinee in an adaptive test. For persons with high trait levels, difficult items will be selected, whereas for persons with low trait levels, easier items will be selected. Trait level is estimated separately for each person using an IRT model that controls for differences in item difficulty. Notice that the squared correlation of the true trait level with the adaptive test score is much higher than for the two classical tests (r^2 = .9695).

In summary, Fig. 2.5 shows the new rule clearly. Better estimation of true trait level is obtained by *nonparallel* test forms. That is, each adaptive test is a separate test form that differs substantially — and deliberately — in difficulty level from other forms. The correlation of estimated trait level with true trait level is substantially higher than the correlations for the classic tests in the upper panel of Fig. 2.5. An explanation of how item difficulty influences measurement error is provided in several chapters, especially chapters 3 and 7.

Rule 4: Unbiased Assessment of Item Properties

Old Rule 4: Unbiased assessment of item properties depends on having representative samples.

New Rule 4: Unbiased estimates of item properties may be obtained from unrepresentative samples.

The CTT statistic for item difficulty is *p*-value, which is computed as the proportion passing. The CTT statistic for item discrimination is item-total correlation (e.g., biserial correlation). Both statistics can differ substantially

Classical Test Scores

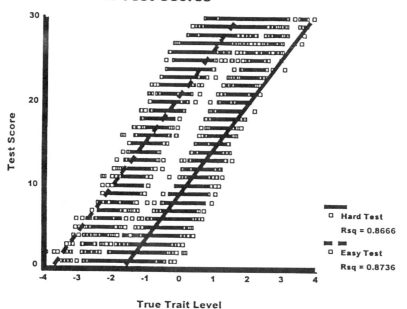

Item Response Theory

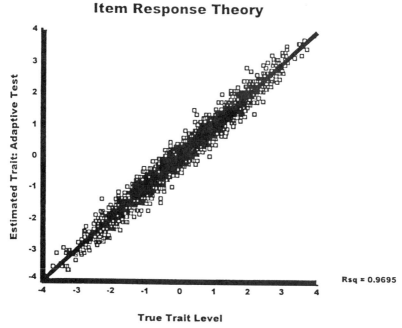

FIG. 2.5. Regression of test scores on true trait level.

across samples if computed from unrepresentative samples. To illustrate the effect, the 3,000 simulated examinees, described earlier, were split at the median into two extreme samples of 1,500 each. The high group had scores above the median, whereas the low group had scores below the median.

In the upper panel of Fig. 2.6, the estimated p-values for items are plotted by the two groups. A linear regression would indicate that the relative intervals between items is maintained. However, notice that the relationship between p-values, although generally monotonic, is not linear. The distances between items with high p-values is greater in the low ability sample, whereas the distances between items with low p-values is greater in the high ability sample. The correlation between p-values is only .800. The biserial correlations (not shown) of items with total score differed even more between groups.

The lower panel of Fig. 2.6 shows the item difficulty values that are obtained by a Rasch model scaling of the same data as shown in the upper panel. In the lower panel, unlike the upper panel, the correspondence of item difficulty values is quite close between the two extreme groups. The correlation between item difficulty values in the lower panel is .997.

Rule 5: Establishing Meaningful Scale Scores

Old Rule 5: Test scores obtain meaning by comparing their position in a norm group.

New Rule 5: Test scores obtain meaning by comparing their distance from items.

The comparison standard for tests that stem from CTT is a relevant group of persons; namely, the norm group. The numerical basis of the comparison is order (i.e., position in the distribution). Standard scores are obtained by linear transformations of raw scores so that scores may be readily compared to positions in a normally distributed population of persons.

To illustrate the differences between the old and the new rule, Fig. 2.7 presents data from the Functional Independence Measurement (FIM) scale. The FIM is a behavioral report on activities of everyday living that often challenge elderly persons. The lower panel shows the items on the scale, ordered by difficulty. The FIM shows high internal consistency, which indicates a common order in the loss of these functions.

The upper panel of Fig. 2.7 shows the classical norm-referenced interpretation of FIM scores. In Fig. 2.7 is a histogram to show the frequencies of various FIM z-scores in a population of persons from age 80 to 89. Expectations from the normal distribution are overlaid. Here, the z-scores for

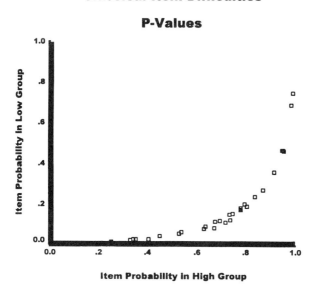

Classical Item Difficulties

P-Values

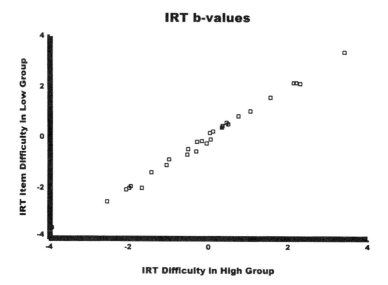

IRT Item Difficulties

IRT b-values

FIG. 2.6.   Relationship between item difficulties obtained from two groups.

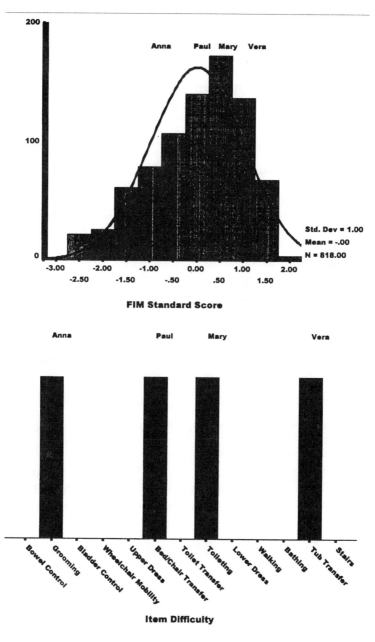

FIG. 2.7. Norm-referenced versus item-referenced meaning for the Functional Independence Measurement Scale.

four persons are projected into the distribution. Anna has a negative z-score, which indicates that her performance in everyday living skills is relatively low compared to her age group. Vera and Mary, in contrast, score relatively higher, while Paul is at the mean. Thus, we would conclude that Paul, Vera, and Mary are functioning relatively well for their age, whereas Anna is not. Score meaning, then, is determined primarily as location in a norm-referenced standard. Of course, as has been argued by proponents of criterion-referenced testing, norm-referenced scores have no meaning for what the person actually can do. That is, scores are not anchored to the skills represented by the items.

In IRT models, trait levels may be compared to items since persons and items are placed on a common scale. The difficulty of items is located on a continuum, typically ranging from –3 to +3, which is similar in magnitude to z-scores. The lower panel of Fig. 2.7 shows the relative location of the FIM items, ranging from most difficult (on the right) to most easy (on the left), as scaled by the Rasch model. The items on the right end are lost relatively early for elderly adults, while the items on the lower end are lost much later. The same four persons now are projected on the item scale. The black bars on the lower panel of Fig. 2.7 represents the location of the four persons with respect to the 13 FIM items.

The difference between a person's trait level and item difficulty has direct meaning for performance. If the person's trait score equals the item's difficulty, then the person is as likely to pass as to fail the item. Thus, items at the person's location in the scale have probability of .50 of being performed successfully. So the probability that Anna successfully completes "Grooming" is .50, while the probability that she completes the more difficult functions is lower than .50. For Paul, the probability that he completes "Bed/Chair Transfer" successfully is .50, but his probability is higher than .50 for all the lower activities, such as "Wheelchair Mobility" and "Grooming." Thus, meaning is referenced to the items.

It should be noted that IRT scaling of ability does not preclude linear transformations to standard scores so that norm-referenced meaning also may be obtained. The meaning of ability for item performance also may be retained by transforming item difficulties by a corresponding linear transformation.

Rule 6: Establishing Scale Properties

Old Rule 6: Interval scale properties are achieved by obtaining normal score distributions.

New Rule 6: Interval scale properties are achieved by applying justifiable measurement models.

Although many test developers probably would not explicate Old Rule 6, the rule is implicit in routine test development procedures. Normal distributions are achieved in two ways. First, for many psychological tests, items are selected to yield normal distributions in a target population. Expositions of CTT typically show how normal score distributions may be achieved by selecting items with proportions passing around .50 (see Gulliksen, 1950). Second, for many other psychological tests, normal distributions are achieved by normalizing procedures. For example, intelligence tests are often scored as composites over several subtests. If the composites are not normally distributed in the target population, then either nonlinear transformations or percentile matching procedures may be applied. In percentile matching, the percentile rank of each raw score in the nonnormal distribution is calculated. Then, the normalized standard score is the z score in the normal distribution that corresponds to the percentile rank of the raw score. Normalizing by percentile matching is a *nonlinear* transformation that changes the relative distances between scores.

The relationship between score distributions and scale levels may be considered by revisiting the regression of easy test scores on hard test scores (i.e., Fig. 2.4). Scores were compressed on opposite ends of the continuum for the two tests. For the hard test, scores were compressed on the low end, while for the easy test, scores were compressed on the high end. Thus, the regression of hard test scores on easy test scores was nonlinear.

Score compression has two effects that are relevant to achieving interval level scales. First, the *relative distances* between scores are not constant under CTT scaling. The upper panel of Fig. 2.8 shows the best nonlinear equating of the easy test to the hard test. Consider a pair of low scores that are 5 points apart, at the score of 5 and 10 (see the reference lines). The distance between the equated scores is still 5 points, although of course now the scores are much higher (i.e., 20 and 25, respectively). Consider another pair of scores that are 5 points apart on the hard test; the scores at 20 and 25. Their equated scores on the easy test are not 5 points apart. Instead, their expected scores differ by less than one point. Failing to maintain constant distances between scores across tests implies that interval scale measurement is not achieved.

The lower panel of Fig. 2.8 shows how equal trait level differences in IRT led to the equal differences in performance expectations for an easy item versus a hard item. Constant differences in trait level imply constant differences in log odds for item success. Regardless of item difficulty level, the same difference in log odds is observed. Second, tests with scale compression have skewed score distributions in the target population. Figure 2.9 shows the frequency distributions for the easy and the hard tests, which are negatively and positively skewed, respectively.

If normal distributions are achieved, what happens to scale properties? Jones (1971) pointed out that under certain assumptions interval scale

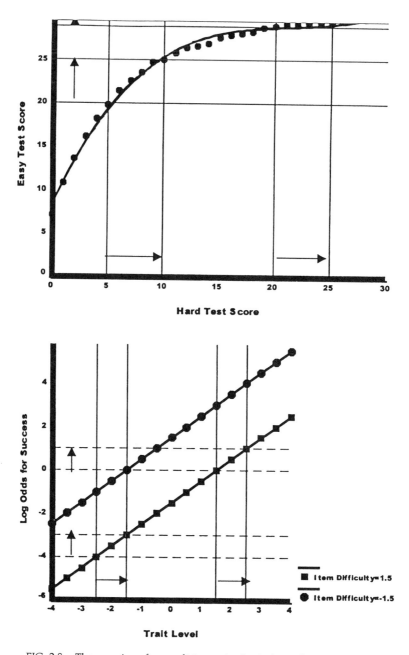

FIG. 2.8. The meaning of score distances in classical test theory versus IRT.

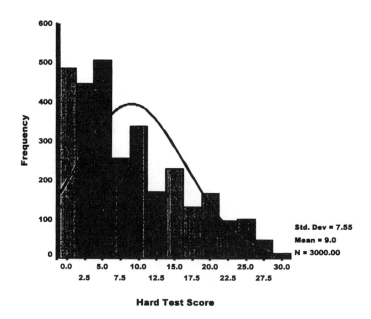

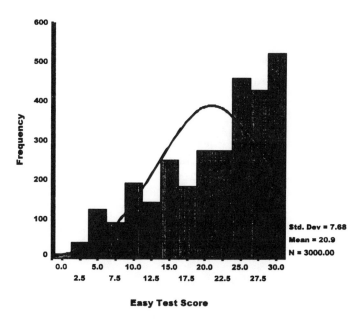

FIG. 2.9.   Histograms for easy and hard tests.

measurement can be justified by achieving normal distributions; specifically, one must assume that true scores have both interval scale properties and a normal distribution in the target population. If these assumptions are met, then achieving a normal test score distribution in the target population leads to interval level measurement. Only linear transformations preserve score intervals as well as distribution shapes (see Davison & Sharma, 1990, for the latter). Thus, if raw scores are normally distributed, then only a linear transformation, such as a standard score conversion, will preserve score intervals to appropriately estimate true score.

Using item selection and score normalization to achieve normal distributions seems most justifiable if item difficulty levels are somewhat arbitrary. That is, a trait may be reflected in responses to a large domain of items; the particular items that appear on the test is somewhat happenstance. Thus the failure to achieve normal distributions can be viewed as a limitation of the particular item set.

Notice that this rationale ties scale properties to a specific population. If the test is applied to a person from another population, can the interval scale properties still be justified? If they cannot, then the scale properties are population-specific. Theoretically, being able to justify measurement scale properties only for a particular population is not very appealing, particularly if the trait is deemed to be widely applicable. In practice, tests are often applied to several different populations. Thus, linking scale properties to population distributions is quite limiting.

For the Rasch model, several papers (e.g., Fischer, 1995; Roskam & Jansen, 1984) show how interval or even ratio scale properties are achieved through justification in the measurement model. Unlike CTT, justification by the measurement model does not depend on having normally distributed trait levels in a target population. Instead, the measurement scale level is based on some principles of fundamental measurement and on invariant comparisons. If test data fit the Rasch model reasonably well, then IRT scaling is a real advantage. For other IRT models, the justification is less clear than for the Rasch model. Nonetheless, a weaker justification of interval level properties is plausible. These developments are reviewed in chapter 6 on the meaning of the trait level scale.

Rule 7: Mixing Item Formats

Old Rule 7: Mixed item formats leads to unbalanced impact on test total scores.
New Rule 7: Mixed item formats can yield optimal test scores.

In CTT, mixing item formats can lead to unequal weighting of items on total score. To illustrate the impact of mixing item formats, consider some data from the Energetic Arousal Scale (Thayer, 1989), which was administered to 818 young adults (Embretson, 1998c). The Energetic Arousal Scale consists of 10 items that have 4-point rating scales. Suppose that the number of categories for the last item is doubled (obtained in this example by multiplying the original response by two) so that it now has categories ranging from 2 to 8. The last item now implicitly receives twice the credit as compared to the other nine items.

Both the original and altered scores on the Energetic Arousal scale were calculated for the sample of 818 young adults. Table 2.2 shows that the mean and standard deviation both increase when the categories for the last item are doubled. Perhaps more crucial, however, is that individual differences also shift. Figure 2.10 shows the regression of the new total score on the original total score. The original total score is not uniquely associated with an altered total score. For example, persons who scored 30 on the original scale now have somewhat varying scores on the altered scale, depending on their original response pattern. In the original scale, with constant item formats, which specific items are endorsed most highly does not matter. However, for the altered scale, endorsing the highest category on the last item leads to a relatively higher altered score.

Various methods to handle unequal categories have been employed with tests developed from CTT. One approach is to compute z scores for each item and then sum z scores across items for a standardized total score. This approach has the disadvantage, however, of depending on the item means and standard deviations in a particular sample. Applications to another sample may not be justified. Another approach to equating the number of categories is to divide by a constant. In the preceding example, the item with the largest number of categories could be divided by two. This approach is successful for the current example because ratings were increased artificially by multiplying by two. However, this approach is inappropriate if persons apply different strategies when more categories are used. That is, persons do not necessarily use a larger number of categories in a manner that is proportional to a smaller number of categories.

In IRT, however, items with different numbers of categories can be combined without difficulty. In IRT analysis for rating scales, such as the generalized partial credit model (Muraki, 1990), item parameters are set to

TABLE 2.2
Descriptive Statistics for Original and Altered
Scores on Energetic Arousal Scale

Test	Mean	Standard Deviation
Original	22.33	8.03
Altered	24.62	8.85

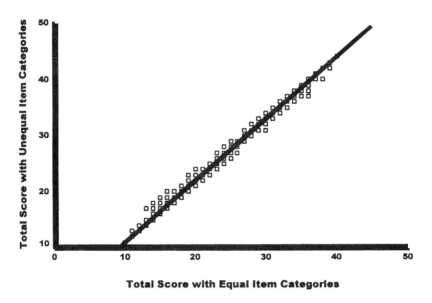

FIG. 2.10.   Regression of tests scored with different numbers of categories on one item.

relate responses to the latent trait. To show how category range is accommodated in IRT, the Energetic Arousal Scale was analyzed under both the original and altered version. Figure 2.11 shows the relationship of category response to trait level for the last item in the two analyses. The upper panel shows the original scale with four categories. For any given trait level, the probability of endorsing each category, represented as 0 to 3, is shown. The trait level at which two adjacent categories intersect is the point at which they are equally likely. Notice how the categories are widely dispersed over trait level when the last item has only four categories. The lower panel shows the altered scale for the last item. Notice that the categories are now much more tightly distributed across trait level. Although the range of categories is greater in the altered scale, the increasing levels of category endorsement for trait level is far less meaningful. Models for polytomous data, such as shown here, are elaborated in chapter 5.

Rule 8: The Meaning of Change Scores

Old Rule 8: Change scores cannot be meaningfully compared when initial score levels differ.

New Rule 8: Change scores can be meaningfully compared when initial score levels differ.

Ex010 I010:   Locn = -0.072   Resid = 2.802   ChiSqProb = 0.548

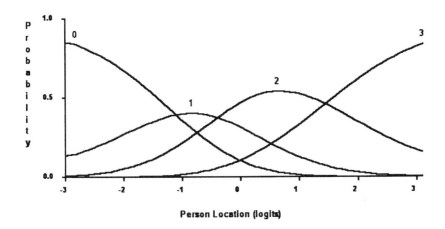

Ex010 I010:   Locn = -0.616   Resid = 7.588   ChiSqProb = 0.000

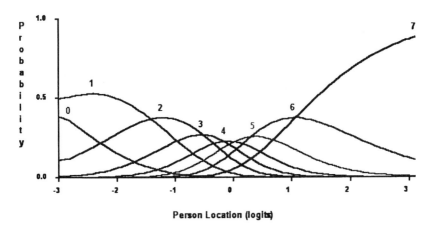

FIG. 2.11.   Relationship of trait level to category endorsement for an item scored with differing numbers of categories.

A change score can be computed as the simple difference between two successive test scores for person j, such as a pretest, X_{j1}, and a posttest, X_{j2}, as follows:

$$X_{j,change} = X_{j2} - X_{j1} \qquad (2.4)$$

Bereiter (1963) noted three fundamental problems with change scores: (a) paradoxical reliabilities, such that the lower the pretest to posttest correlation, the higher the change score reliability; (b) spurious negative correlations between initial status and change (due to the subtraction); and (c) different meaning from different initial levels. For the latter, Bereiter did not have a proof but he suspected that an increase of one point from a moderate score meant less than the same increase from an extreme score. Cronbach and Furby (1970) reviewed the literature on change scores and suggested that they be abandoned if at all possible.

For change measurement to be equal from different initial levels, interval scale level measurement is required. Yet, in CTT, from Rule 6, the interval scale measurement often is not easily justified. If the trait level scale is more compressed at the high end (say, from an easy test as shown on Fig. 2.8), then small changes from a high score means more than a small change from a moderate score.

In contrast, interval level scaling can be justified directly by the IRT measurement model, particularly the Rasch model (see chap. 6). Thus, change measured on IRT trait levels will have constant meaning for performance when measured from different initial levels.

A recent study on cognitive aging (Embretson, 1998b) examined the relationship of simple change scores, $X_{j,change}$, to modifiability (IRT trait level). The multidimensional Rasch model for learning and change (MRMLC; Embretson, 1991) was applied to item response data on a spatial ability test. Figure 2.12 presents the regression of MRMLC modifiability estimates on raw gain for younger versus elderly adults. It can be seen that raw gain is not uniquely associated with a particular modifiability; each raw gain score is associated with several different modifiabilities. Furthermore, raw gain has a nonlinear relationship to modifiability. In MRMLC, the implication of gain for modifiability is adjusted for initial level. Figure 2.12 also shows that the relationship of raw gain to modifiability depends on the age group. Modifiabilities depart more from the fitted regressions for young adults. IRT models for measuring change are considered again in chapters 4 and 11.

Rule 9: Factor Analysis of Binary Items

Old Rule 9: Factor analysis on binary items produces artifacts rather than factors.

New Rule 9: Factor analysis on raw item data yields a full information factor analysis.

Item factor analysis is often applied to binary items to support construct validity. For example, the unidimensionality of a test is supported if a single factor is adequate to reproduce item intercorrelations. It has long been

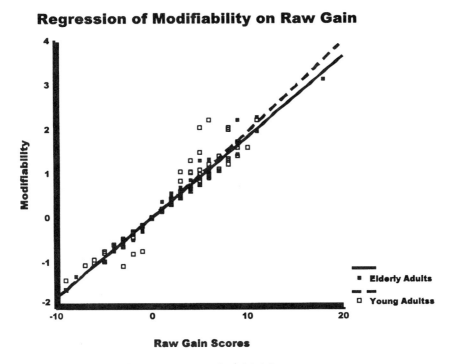

FIG. 2.12.   Regression of modifiability on raw gain.

known that factor analysis of Pearson product–moment correlations can produce difficulty factors (Carroll, 1945). The Pearson product–moment correlation between items, the phi correlation, is restricted in magnitude by the similarity of the item difficulty levels. The maximum phi correlation between two items with sharply different difficulties, measured as p-values (i.e., accuracy rates), will be significantly less than 1.00. Consequently, factor analysis of phi correlations can lead to "difficulty" factors, which are artifacts because they reflect the similarity of item p-values.

Tetrachoric correlations are preferred over phi correlations because they correct for item difficulty effects. However, tetrachoric correlations have several disadvantages. Adjusting a whole matrix of item correlations to tetrachorics sometimes results in a singular correlation matrix, which is not appropriate for factor analysis. Further, the adjustments given by the tetrachoric correlations are quite substantial for extreme p-values. Strong assumptions about normality and linearity are required to justify the adjustments. Last, tetrachoric correlations do not make full use of the data. The adjustments are based on summary statistics about the data.

Full information factor analysis (Bock, Gibbons, & Muraki, 1988) is so named because item response data is modeled directly so that no information in the data is lost. In contrast, only summary statistics, namely correlations or covariances, are modeled in factor analysis so that information from individual responses is not directly modeled. No adjustments to the data are needed in full information factor analysis because the model is directly appropriate for the data. In contrast, special adjustments to the correlations (e.g., tetrachoric correlations) are required for item data in factor analysis.

Full information factor analysis also provides indices of factor strength for each item that are useful psychometrically. That is, IRT item parameters are estimated directly in full information factor analysis. The full information factor analysis model is elaborated in chapter 4, which presents models for binary data. Applications of full information factor analysis are considered in both chapters 11 and 12.

Rule 10: Importance of Item Stimulus Features

Old Rule 10: Item stimulus features are unimportant compared to psychometric properties.

New Rule 10: Item stimulus features can be directly related to psychometric properties.

Item stimulus features usually are not precisely specified in test development. Even for achievement tests, which rely on content validity for meaning, the most detailed specifications still do not prescribe item content precisely. As noted by Cronbach (1988), it is doubtful that two different groups of item writers would develop the same items even from the most detailed specifications. For trait tests, which rely on construct validity for meaning, item specifications are much less rigorous and sometimes rather informal. Even when item specifications do exist, the features that are specified are quite global. For example, "abstract" versus "concrete" content is a specification that appears in many ability tests. This global distinction may be reliably discerned for many item types, but it certainly does not precisely specify item features. Item features are sometimes further specified by content constraints (e.g., science vs. literature). Again, however, the exact item features that fulfill this constraint is diverse. For some tests, items are further screened for special content problems. For example, gender or ethnicity bias in item features is an important consideration for tests that are used for selection.

Beyond the initial item specifications and screening for special content problems, the stimulus features of items typically have little role in the remaining test development process. Item selection typically is guided mainly by the psychometric properties of items, such as difficulty levels and correlations with total scores. Item writers often have access to the psychometric properties of the items that have been composed. However, rarely do the psychometric results indicate how item features influence the psychometric properties.

In IRT, several models are now available to relate item stimulus features to psychometric properties and to trait levels. These models are reviewed as "confirmatory" IRT models in chapter 4. Applications are presented in chapter 11 to show item features may be manipulated to influence psychometric properties.

SUMMARY

Rules of measurement are principles by which tests and measures of individual differences are developed. This chapter elaborated 10 rules of measurement that differ substantially between CTT and IRT. These rules differ somewhat in scope and importance. For example, the impact of test length on measurement error is a very important rule of measurement that applies to all tests. The new rule is based on a different underlying principle and sometimes conflicts with the old rule about the most appropriate test length. On the other hand, the rule about mixed item formats applies to many, but not all, tests.

The sharp differences in rules of measurement shows that IRT is not just a refinement of CTT. In fact, many extensions of CTT were derived to resolve its inherent limitations as a foundation for measurement. For example, methods for test equating emerged because the CTT constraint of parallel test forms could not be met in practice. The primary limitation of CTT for score equating, however, is the omission of item properties in the CTT model of true and error scores.

The rules of measurement that were compared in this chapter show that IRT is a different set of principles than CTT. Although CTT principles can be derived as special cases from IRT, the reverse is not true. IRT is a more general foundation for psychometric methods. Many CTT principles are unnecessary or even inappropriate.

Perhaps the main reason for contrasting the rules of measurement in this chapter was to generate interest in IRT. Although we attempt to make IRT as intuitively clear as possible, it is still more difficult to understand than CTT. Few readers would want to understand IRT solely for its psychometric elegance; however, both the practical advantages and substantive advantages of IRT for measurement are quite substantial. These advantages are highlighted in chapters 10, 11, and 12. Furthermore, because increasingly more tests are based on IRT, it is important for psychologists to understand the basis of these tests and measures. The contrasts between the rules of measurement were presented to show that an understanding of IRT is necessary for correct intuitions about contemporary psychological measurement.

3

Item Response Theory as Model-Based Measurement

In item response theory (IRT), a person's trait level is estimated from responses to test items. An IRT model specifies how both trait level and item properties are related to a person's item responses. Trait level is estimated in the context of an IRT model; thus, IRT is model-based measurement.

This chapter elaborates some key features of IRT in two main sections. First, IRT is contrasted to classical test theory (CTT) as model-based measurement. We show that IRT provides more complete rationale for model-based measurement than CTT. Second, the process for estimating a person's IRT trait level is explicated. Estimating an IRT trait level contrasts sharply with CTT. In CTT, true scores estimates typically are obtained by summing responses across items. In IRT, estimating trait levels involves a search process for optimal estimates to model behavior. More details on the estimation process for measuring persons are presented in chapter 7. Estimation of item characteristics is explicated in chapter 8.

MODELS IN MEASUREMENT

Psychological constructs are usually conceptualized as latent variables that underlie behavior. Latent variables are unobservable entities that influence observable (or manifest) variables such as test scores or item responses. The particular item response or test score is an indicator of a person's standing on the latent variable, but it does not completely define the latent variable.

Measurements of psychological constructs are usually indirect; latent variables are measured by observing behavior on relevant tasks or items. The properties of both persons and items on a psychological dimension are inferred from behavior. Thus, a measurement theory in psychology must provide a rationale for relating behaviors to the psychological construct.

Typically, a measurement theory rationale includes a model of behavior. Both CTT and IRT provide rationales for behaviorally based measurement. However, these rationales differ substantially. In this section, CTT and IRT are compared as model-based systems for measurement.

Definition of Models

Models are commonly used in psychology to relate behavior to constructs or experimental manipulations. The term *model* has many meanings in psychology (see Gentner, 1985). For example, in cognitive psychology, a model may be a concrete replica, such as a plaster model of the brain, or it may be an abstraction of a system of dynamic relations, such as a flow chart of information processing. However, for psychological measurement the most relevant meaning is a mathematical model in which independent variables are combined numerically to optimally predict a dependent variable.

Several features define a particular mathematical model. First, the model specifies the scale for the observations, which is the *dependent variable*. The dependent variable may be a score, or item responses or a matrix of relationships among items or responses. Second, a mathematical model specifies one or more design variables, which are the *independent variables*. Like dependent variables, the independent variables may be scores, item responses, matrices, and so forth. Third, a mathematical model specifies how the independent variables are *combined numerically* to predict the dependent variable. The model may specify a simple additive combination of variables that directly predicts the dependent variable, as in a linear regression model. The weights for the design variables, or independent variables, are the parameters of the model, or the model may specify a more complex relationship. For example, the independent variables may combine interactively or occur within a distributional function (e.g., cumulative normal distribution, logistic distribution) to relate the independent variables to the dependent variable.

Figure 3.1 shows two versions of how a latent variable relates to behavior. In the upper panel, the observed variables are scores on alternative test forms, while the independent variables are the latent variable and error. These diagrammed relationships may be converted into mathematical models, for example, as in structural equation modeling. If the latent variable represents the true score, then the upper panel of Fig. 3.1 represents the CTT model. In the lower panel of Fig. 3.1, the observed variables are

LATENT VARIABLE TO BEHAVIOR RELATIONSHIPS

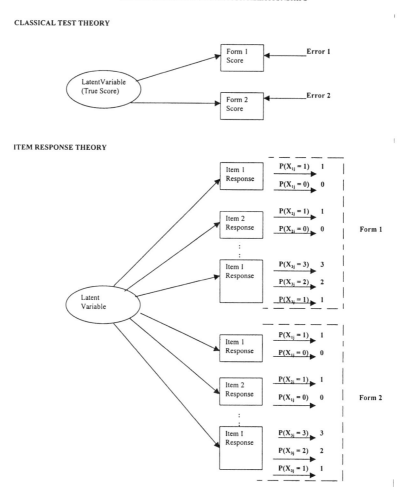

FIG. 3.1.   Models of latent variables and measuring tasks.

responses (e.g., 0 or 1) to specific items. The latent variable influences the probabilities of the responses to the items (shown as $P(X_{is} = 1)$, etc.). Notice that the number of response options varies across items. This representation corresponds to the mathematical models of IRT.

CTT Model

Model and Assumptions

The CTT model is simple; the dependent variable is the total test score for a particular person (i.e., X_{Os}). The independent variables are the person's true score on the trait, X_{Ts}, and the person's error on the testing occasion, X_{Es}. The independent variables combine *additively* and *directly* to predict the dependent variable, as follows:

$$X_{Os} = X_{Ts} + X_{Es} \qquad (3.1)$$

Several assumptions are made about error for the CTT model. The basic assumptions are (a) the expected value for error over persons is zero, (b) error is not related to other variables (e.g., true score, other error scores and other true scores). Additional assumptions about error are required for interpreting various indices that are typically derived from the CTT model. For example, to interpret the standard error of measurement, errors are assumed to be normally distributed within persons and homogeneously distributed across persons.

Evaluation

The CTT model is limited in several ways. First, X_{Ts} applies to items on a specific test or to items on test with equivalent item properties. That is, since no provision for possibly varying item parameters are included in the CTT model, they must be regarded as fixed on a particular test. If more than one set of items may reasonably measure the same trait, the generality of true score depends on test parallelism (see Gulliksen's, 1950, definition) or on test equating (see Holland & Rubin's, 1982, survey of methods). Second, although the model specifies two separate independent variables for a person, these independent variables are not really separable for an individual score. Instead, the model is used to justify estimates of population statistics. When combined with other assumptions (e.g., error distributions), Eq. 3.1 provides a rationale for estimating true variance and error variance. Although true and error components may be further decomposed under extensions of CTT (see Cronbach, Gleser, Nanda, & Rajaratman, 1972), multiple observations under varying conditions are required. Third, item properties are not linked to behavior in Eq. 3.1. That is, the omission of item properties from the model requires that they be justified outside the mathematical model for CTT. Thus, using item difficulty and discrimination to select items is justified by their impact on various test statistics, such as variances and reliabilities.

Item Response Theory Models

IRT is known as a "strong" modeling method because strong assumptions must be met. Before introducing some models, these assumptions are described. Then, two unidimensional IRT models that are appropriate for tests that measure a single latent trait are described. Models that are appropriate for multidimensional tests or for complex dependencies among items are described in chapter 4. IRT models also are appropriate for rating scale and other polytomous item formats. These IRT models are described in chapter 5. To simplify the presentation in this chapter, however, only dichotomously scored items are described.

Basic Data Matrix

The target of an IRT model is the encounter of a person with a particular item. The person's response pattern to a particular set of items provides the basis for estimating trait level.

It is instructive to conceptualize measurement data with a basic data matrix. Rasch (1960) formulated his pioneering IRT models to summarize measurement data such as shown in Table 3.1. Rasch (1960) studied the measurement properties of cognitive ability test items. Table 3.1 presents item response data for a large sample on 16 dichotomous items from a subtest of the Danish military aptitude battery. The columns represent groups of persons who have the same total score on items. The rows represent blocks of items with similar difficulty levels (i.e., p-values). The item blocks are ordered from easy to hard. The cells contain the probabilities that items in a particular row are passed by persons with the total score corresponding to the column. To assure adequate sample sizes for estimating each probability, some items and some score categories were combined by Rasch (1960).

Table 3.1 shows that the probabilities increase as the total score category increases (from .92 to 1.00 for Items 1 and 2). Furthermore, for each score category the probabilities decrease as the items become more difficult, across the ordered item blocks.

Figure 3.2 plots the probabilities, across score categories (shown as raw score), for each item block. Some interesting features in the item response

TABLE 3.1
Basic Data Matrix for Ability Test Item Responses

Item Set	\multicolumn{11}{c}{Raw Score and Sample Size}
	3 (49)	4 (112)	5 (82)	6 (76)	7 (82)	8 (102)	9 (119)	10 (133)	11 (123)	12 (94)	13–16 (88)
1–2	.92	.98	.98	.99	.98	.99	.99	1.00	1.00	1.00	1.00
3–4	.48	.84	.84	.86	.86	.90	.95	.96	.98	.99	1.00
5–6	.06	.11	.40	.70	.70	.79	.84	.88	.94	.95	.98
7–9	.01	.04	.12	.21	.42	.62	.73	.83	.90	.93	.99
10–11	.00	.02	.07	.07	.24	.28	.45	.59	.76	.87	.92
12–13	.01	.00	.04	.05	.09	.09	.16	.28	.39	.66	.82
14–16	.00	.00	.00	.00	.02	.01	.02	.03	.06	.09	.31

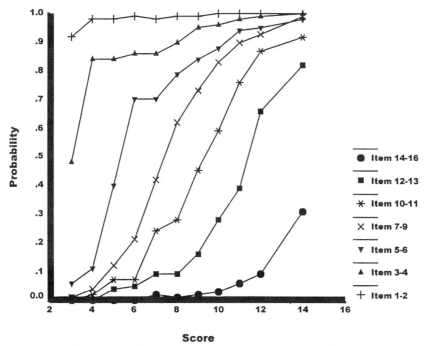

Score

FIG. 3.2.   Item by score category probabilities for an ability test.

data emerge in this plot. First, the probabilities for the easy items climb much sooner than those for the hard items. That is, moderate to high probabilities are observed even for persons with low total scores. Second, the probabilities show a nonlinear relationship to total score. That is, as often found for test data, item response probabilities have an S-shaped regression on total score. Third, the item curves in Fig. 3.2 do not cross. This implies that the items maintain their difficulty order across score categories. Rasch (1960) developed his one-parameter logistic model, shown next, to optimally scale item response data with these properties.

It should be noted that the item response curves do cross for many tests. In such cases, Rasch's (1960) simple model will not be adequate to characterize the data. Either a more complex IRT model (e.g., models with discrimination parameters) is required or, if the Rasch model is retained, items with curves that cross should be deleted from the test.

Assumptions for IRT Models

Item response theory (IRT) models involve two key assumptions: (a) the item characteristic curves (ICCs) have a specified form, and (b) local independence has been obtained. These will be elaborated in turn.

The *form* of an ICC describes how changes in trait level relate to changes in the probability of a specified response. For dichotomous items, in which a specified response is considered "correct" or in "agreement" with an item, the ICC regresses the probability of item success on trait level. For polytomous items, such as rating scales, the ICC regresses the probability of responses in each category on trait level.

Figure 3.3 shows ICCs for three dichotomous items from an IRT model that is appropriate for test data in which the relative ordering of item difficulty is constant across score levels (e.g., the data in Fig. 3.2). Several features of ICCs may be observed. First, each ICC shown in Fig. 3.3 is S-shaped, which plots the probability of a correct response as a monotonic and increasing function of trait level. Further, in the middle of the curve, small changes in trait level imply large changes in item solving probabilities. At the extremes, large changes in trait level lead to very small changes in the probabilities. The general shape of the ICC is specified by a function that relates the person and item parameters to the probabilities. Although many different monotonically increasing relationships can be specified, logistic functions (e.g., in the Rasch model) and normal ogive functions (i.e., cumulative normal distribution) are very prevalent. Second, although all three ICCs have the same general shape, they differ in location.

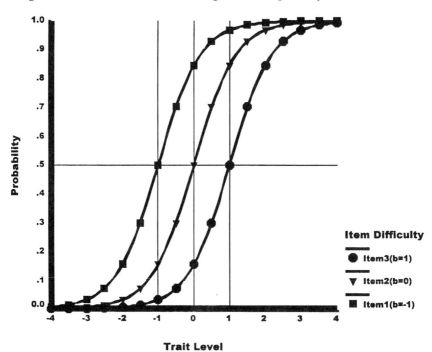

FIG. 3.3.   Item characteristics curves for three items from the Rasch model.

Location corresponds to item difficulty in the models shown in Fig. 3.3. Location describes the extent to which items differ in probabilities across trait levels. For example, the trait level associated with a probability of .50 is much lower for Item 1 than for Item 2 or Item 3. Thus, Item 1 is easier.

Figure 3.4 shows ICCs that differ in several ways. These items differ in slope and lower asymptote, as well as in location. Slope corresponds to item discrimination. It describes how rapidly the probabilities change with trait level. For Item 2, the change is much slower than for Item 1 or Item 3. Thus, Item 2 is less discriminating than the other two items because the item response probabilities are relatively less responsive to changes in trait level. The item–total score correlations from CTT may be derived from item regression slopes (see Lord & Novick, 1968) under certain assumptions. The asymptotes of the ICCs are the upper and lower bounds. For two items shown in Fig. 3.4, the item response probabilities range from .00 to 1.00. In some IRT models, however, a more restricted range of probabilities is specified. For example, items that can be "solved" by guessing are accommodated by an ICC with the lower asymptote greater than zero. For Item 3 on Fig. 3.4, the probably that the item is solved never falls to zero, no matter how low the trait level.

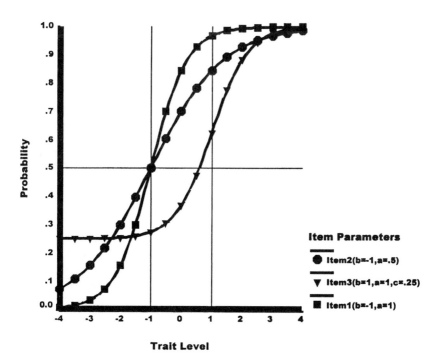

FIG. 3.4.   Item characteristics curves for items with varying slopes and asymptotes.

Local independence pertains to the sufficiency of an IRT model for the data. Essentially, local independence is obtained when the relationships among items (or persons) is fully characterized by the IRT model. For example, the high intercorrelations among test items is expected to be fully accounted for by their parameter differences (e.g., location, slope, etc.) and by the person parameters, as specified in the IRT model. Stated more precisely, local independence is obtained when the probability of solving any item i ($\mathrm{Prob}(X_{is} = 1)$) is independent of the outcome of any other item i' ($X_{i's} = 1$), controlling for person parameters (θ_s) and item parameters (ξ_i), as follows:

$$\mathrm{Prob}(X_{is} = 1|X_{i's} = 1,\xi_k,\theta_s) = \mathrm{Prob}(X_{is} = 1|\xi_k,\theta_s) \qquad (3.2)$$

Notice that Eq. 3.2 states that the probability of solving item i, conditional on the outcome of item i', is the same as the probability of solving item i.

At first glance, the conditional independence of items seems to conflict with the CTT principle of internal consistency. That is, highly correlated items provide more reliable measures. Local independence seems to call for uncorrelated items. However, the key to this apparent conflict is the conditioning of item responses on persons' trait levels, as well as on item difficulties, in Eq. 3.2. That is, the principle of local independence states that no further relationships remain between items when the model parameters are controlled.

Local independence is also related to the number of different latent variables (traits) that underlie item performance. That is, local independence is evidence for unidimensionality if the IRT model contains person parameters on only one dimension. However, local independence also can be achieved for multidimensional data if the model contains person parameters for each dimension. Furthermore, local independence can be achieved even for data with complex dependencies among items (linked items, interactions, etc.). In this case, the definition of an "item" is extended to include the interactive effects or linkages.

A Simple IRT Model: The Rasch Model

Item response theory now contains a large family of models. The simplest model is the Rasch (1960) model (although Rasch developed more than one IRT model), which is also known as the one-parameter logistic model (1PL). For the simple Rasch model, the dependent variable is the dichotomous response (i.e., success/failure or reject/accept) for a particular person to a specified item. The independent variables are the person's trait score, θ_s, and the item's difficulty level, β_i. The independent variables combine additively, and the item's difficulty is subtracted from the person's ability, θ_s. The relationship of this difference to item responses depends on which dependent variable is modeled, log odds or probabilities.

In the log odds version of the Rasch (1960) model, the dependent variable is the natural logarithm of the odds of passing an item. Odds are expressed as a ratio of the number of successes to the number of failures. For example, if the odds that a person passes an item is 4/1, then out of five chances, four successes and one failure are expected. Alternatively, odds are the probability of success divided by the probability of failure, which would be .80/.20 in this example.

For the Rasch model, the natural logarithm of the odds ratio is modeled by the simple difference between person s's trait score, θ_s, and the item's difficulty, β_i. That is, the ratio of the probability of success for person s on item i, P_{is}, to the probability of failure, $1 - P_{is}$, is modeled as follows:

$$\ln[P_{is}/(1 - P_{is})] = \theta_s - \beta_i \tag{3.3}$$

If the trait level equals item difficulty (e.g., $\theta_s = \beta_i = .70$), then the *log* odds of success will be zero. Taking the antilog of zero yields an odds of 1.0 (or .50/.50), which means that the person is as likely to succeed as to fail on this particular item.

Figure 3.5 shows the implications of several item difficulties on the log odds for three persons with different trait scores. Notice that when item difficulty increases, log odds decrease. Furthermore, when item difficulty equals the trait level, the log odds are zero. If the trait level exceeds item difficulty, then the person is more likely to succeed than to fail. On the other hand, if item difficulty exceeds the trait score, the person is more likely to fail than to pass.

The simple Rasch model has several desirable features that may be inferred from Eq. 3.3. First, a trait level estimate may be applied to any item for which difficulty is known. That is, for a given trait level, the log odds of success can be given for any calibrated item. The simple Rasch model given by Eq. 3.3 includes item difficulty in relating relationship to performance. Other item properties, such as discrimination, guessing, the nature of the alternatives, and even substantive features of items, are included as independent variables in more complex IRT models. Second, both item properties and trait levels are linked to behavior. Thus, IRT provides a full model of behavior because separate parameters are included for both persons and items. Third, trait level and item properties are independent variables that may be estimated separately. The separability of these parameters is essential for an important property in measurement theory, namely, specific objectivity, which will be discussed later in this chapter. Fourth, the conjoint scaling of trait level and item difficulty is shown in Eq. 3.3. That is, response probabilities are increased in the same way by

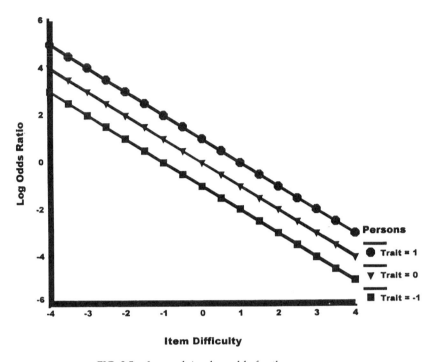

FIG. 3.5. Item solving log odds for three persons.

adding a constant amount to trait level or by subtracting the same constant from item difficulty.

In the second version of the Rasch model, the dependent variable is the simple probability that person s passes item i, $P(X_{is} = 1)$. Although the independent variables, person trait score and item difficulty, still combine additively, linking the dependent variable to the independent variables requires a nonlinear function. In this case, the logistic function provides the prediction as follows:

$$P(X_{is} = 1 \mid \theta_s, \beta_i) = \frac{\exp(\theta_s - \beta_i)}{1 + \exp(\theta_s - \beta_i)} \tag{3.4}$$

where θ_s and β_i are defined as before. The term $\exp(\theta_s - \beta_i)$ indicates to take the natural antilog of the difference between the person parameter and the item parameter. This also may be written as $e^{(\theta_s - \beta_i)}$.

This version of the Rasch model differs from Eq. 3.3 because the dependent variable is predicted as a probability rather than as a log odds. Equation 3.4 is also known as the one-parameter logistic (1PL) measurement model, due to its exponential form in predicting probabilities and to the inclusion of only one item parameter (i.e., difficulty) to represent item differences.

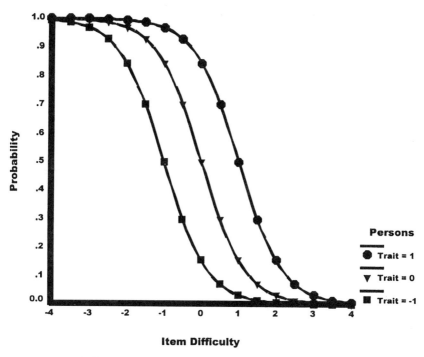

FIG. 3.6.   Item solving probabilities for three persons.

One advantage of the presentation of the Rasch model in Eq. 3.4 is that probabilities are a more familiar dependent variable than log odds ratios. However, a slight complication of Eq. 3.4 is that the relationship of the response outcome to trait level and item difficulty is nonlinear. Figure 3.6 shows the relationship between item difficulty and the probability of item success for the same three persons, as shown in Fig. 3.4. In these S-shaped curves, the greatest impact of changes in item difficulty on item-solving success occurs around the person's trait level. For Person 1, for example, with a trait level of –1, the probability of item success decreases greatly as item difficulty increases from –1 to 0. Increases of item difficulty beyond 2, however, have less impact on probabilities for Person 1 because the probabilities are already low. For Person 3, with a higher trait level, increases of item difficulty beyond 2 still affect the probabilities.

A More Complex IRT Model: The 2PL

In the two-parameter logistic model (2PL), item discrimination is included in the measurement model. The model includes two parameters to represent item properties. Both item difficulty, β_i, and item discrimination, α_i, are included in the exponential form of the logistic model, as follows:

$$P(X_{is} = 1 \mid \theta_s, \beta_i, \alpha_i) = \frac{\exp(\alpha_i(\theta - \beta_i))}{1 + \exp(\alpha_i(\theta_s \quad \beta))} \tag{3.5}$$

Notice that item discrimination is a multiplier of the dif′ ⎯⎯ ⎯ce between trait level and item difficulty. Item discriminations are related to the biserial correlations between item responses and total scores. For Eq. 3.5, then, the impact of the difference between trait level and item difficulty depends on the discriminating power of the item. Specifically, the difference between trait level and item difficulty has greater impact on the probabilities of highly discriminating items.

Figure 3.7 shows the item characteristics curves for four items from the 2PL model. The four items have discriminations of .5, 1, 3, and 1, respectively. Items 2 and 4, which have the same discrimination value, have equal slopes and hence never cross. Although Items 2 and 4 have different item difficulties, changes in trait level have equal impact on the probabilities of item solving. The discrimination value for Item 1 is relatively low and thus changes in trait level have less impact on the probabilities. This item provides less information about the latent trait because trait level is less relevant to changes in success. By contrast, Item 3 has a high discrimination, so changes in trait level have a much greater impact on probabilities.

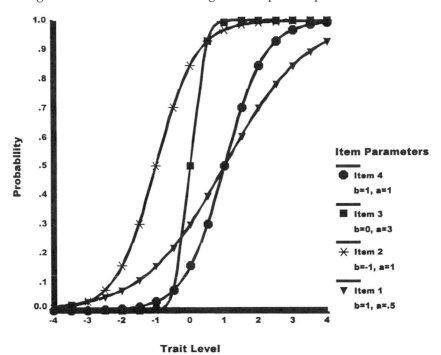

FIG. 3.7.   Item characteristics curves for varying discriminations.

When item discrimination is included in an IRT model, trait level estimates depend on the specific pattern of successes and failures in the item set. Two response patterns with the *same* total score can have *different* trait level estimates. Succeeding on highly discriminating items and failing on poorly discriminating items leads to the highest trait level estimate, as demonstrated in the next section. Thus, in the 2PL model items do not have equal weight in estimating trait levels.

Model-Based Measurement: A Comparison

IRT differs substantially from CTT as a model-based system of measurement. Unlike IRT, CTT does not include item properties in the basic model, which has several implications. First, *true score* has meaning only for a fixed set of item properties in CTT. By not including item properties in the model, true score can apply only to a particular set of items or their equivalent. By contrast, IRT trait levels have meaning for any set of calibrated items because IRT models include item properties. Second, the properties of items are not explicitly linked to behavior in CTT. The relative impact of difficult items on trait level estimates and item responses is known only from an IRT model. Third, separate estimates for the independent variables are not feasible in CTT without additional observations. That is, a person's true and error score may not be decomposed from a single test administration. In an IRT model, the independent variables are trait level and item properties. Later, we show how separate estimates may be obtained.

ESTIMATING TRAIT LEVEL

So far, we have examined the implications of a person's trait level for performance, given that the trait level is already *known*. Of course, the very purpose of giving a test is to determine a person's trait level from his or her responses to the items. Thus, the trait level is *unknown*. In this section, the IRT process of estimating trait level is described and contrasted with CTT.

IRT: Item Responses as Symptoms

The relationship between item responses and trait level is fundamentally different in IRT and CTT. Under CTT, trait levels are scored by combining responses across items. Typically, responses are summed into a total score and then converted into a standard score. However, in IRT, determining the person's trait level is *not* a question of how to add up the item responses. Instead, a somewhat different question is asked.

In a sense, the IRT process of estimating trait levels is analogous to the clinical inference process. In models of the clinical inference process, a potential diagnosis or inference is evaluated for plausibility. That is, given the presenting behaviors (including test behaviors), how plausible is a certain diagnosis (e.g., Tyler, 1972). Thus, the behaviors (and test responses) are symptoms of a latent variable that must be inferred. Given the limited context in which the person's behavior can be observed by the clinician and knowledge of how behaviors are influenced by a latent syndrome, what diagnosis is most likely to explain the presenting behaviors? The IRT process is akin to clinical inference; given the properties of the items and knowledge of how item properties influence behavior (i.e., an IRT model), what trait level is most likely to explain the person's responses?

Now, suppose we know that a person received very hard items and succeeded on nearly all of them. This response pattern is not very likely if a person has a low trait level. The likelihood that a person with a moderate trait level could pass all the items is somewhat higher, but, of course, the likelihood of the response pattern is even higher for a person who has a high trait level.

Finding the IRT trait level for a response pattern requires a search process rather than a scoring procedure. That is, the trait level that yields the highest likelihood for the responses is sought. In some cases, collateral information may be incorporated into the estimation process (e.g., trait distribution in the relevant population) so that more information than the response pattern is available. In IRT, trait levels are estimated in a model (e.g., Eq. 3.4) for a person's responses, controlling for the characteristics of the items. Typically, trait levels are estimated by a maximum likelihood method; specifically, the estimated trait level for person s maximizes the likelihood of his or her response pattern given the item properties. Thus, to find the appropriate trait level, one must (a) represent the likelihoods of a response pattern under various trait levels and (b) conduct a search process that yields the trait level that gives the highest likelihood.

Computing Likelihoods for Response Patterns

To find the most likely trait score, first the likelihood of the person's response pattern must be expressed in the model that contains the properties of the items that were administered. Once so expressed, the likelihood of the person's response pattern may be computed for any hypothetical trait level. Then, the likelihoods may be plotted by trait level so that the trait level with the highest likelihood can be observed.

To illustrate, suppose that a test with five items was administered. Assume that item difficulties are $(-2, -1, 0, 1, 2)$. The vector of responses for any person s will be noted as $\underline{X}_s$. Suppose further that a person passed the first four items and failed the last item; the response pattern for person s is $(\underline{X}_s = 1, 1, 1, 1, 0)$. Now, because the first four items are passed, the probability can be computed directly from Eq. 3.4 for these items as P_{1s}, P_{2s}, P_{3s}, and P_{4s}, respectively. The person fails the last item, however, so the probability of failure, which is 1 minus the probability of success (i.e., $1 - P_{5s}$), is included in the model. So, the likelihood of person s's responses, $L(\underline{X}_s)$, taken across all five items, is the product of the probabilities for their item responses, as follows:

$$L(\underline{X}_s) = P_{1s}P_{2s}P_{3s}P_{4s}(1 - P_{5s}) \tag{3.6}$$

If the trait level and the item difficulties are known for person s, a probability can be calculated for each item P_{is} from Eq. 3.4. These probabilities then are multiplied in Eq. 3.6 to give the probability of the observed response pattern, $L(\underline{X}_s)$. Table 3.2 shows the computation of the probabilities of response pattern of person s under two hypothetical trait levels ($\theta_s = -1$ and $\theta_s = 2$). The response pattern and the appropriate probabilities to be computed are shown in the columns. The last row contains the likelihoods for the response pattern for the two trait levels, which is the product of the individual item probabilities. Intuitively, since four of five items are passed, the higher trait level should be more likely. Notice that the computed likelihood for $\theta_s = 2$ is much higher than for $\theta_s = -1$.

Searching for Trait Level: Maximum Likelihood by Brute Force

The maximum likelihood method may be illustrated by a simple brute-force estimation method. The trait level is not known, but the im-

TABLE 3.2
Computation of Likelihoods for Response Pattern (1, 1, 1, 1, 0)
for Two Hypothetical Trait Levels

				Trait Levels	
Item	Difficulty	$\underline{X}_s$	Term	$\theta_1 = -1$	$\theta_2 = 2$
1	-2	1	P_{1j}	.73[a]	.98
2	-1	1	P_{2j}	.50	.95
3	0	1	P_{3j}	.27	.88
4	1	1	P_{4j}	.12	.73
5	2	0	$1 - P_{5j}$	.95	.50[b]
Likelihood				.73*.50*.27*.12*.95 = .01	.98*.95*.88*.73*.50 = .30
				$L(\underline{X}_s\,\|\,\theta_s = -1) = .01$	$L(\underline{X}_s\,\|\,\theta_s = 2) = .30$

[a]$P_{11} = \dfrac{\exp(-1-(-2))}{1+\exp(-1-(-2))}$ [b]$P_{52} = \dfrac{\exp(2-2)}{1+\exp(2-2)}$

pact of any hypothetical trait level on the likelihood of the response pattern can be computed as shown earlier. The brute-force method involves trying out many estimates and examining their impact on the likelihood of the response pattern. The goal is to find the trait score for which the likelihood is highest. Suppose that the likelihoods for 22 different hypothetical trait levels are computed in the range of −3.5 to 7 at intervals of .5.

In Figure 3.8, the likelihoods for each trait level computed from Eq. 3.6, the Rasch model for the response pattern elaborated earlier ($\underline{X}_s$ = 1, 1, 1, 1, 0) is shown as Pattern 1. For the trait levels that were computed, it can be seen that the highest likelihood occurs at a trait level of 2.0. However, although this likelihood is higher than the likelihoods of the adjacent trait levels of 1.5 and 2.5, it is not necessarily the trait level that gives the highest likelihood. If the interval size were .1, for example, then several higher likelihoods than likelihood computed at the trait level of 2.0 may have been found (i.e., 2.1, 2.2, etc.). Decreasing the interval size increases precision in estimating trait level. Unfortunately, this process rapidly becomes computationally burdensome. The greater the precision desired, the more calculations are required under the brute force method. Methods for numerical analysis, however, may be applied to search more efficiently for the point of maximum likelihood (this is reviewed in chap. 7). Numerical

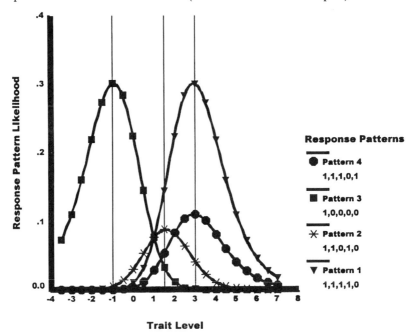

FIG. 3.8.   Brute force estimation of trait level for items with uniform discriminations.

analysis involves evaluating the relative changes in likelihoods so that calculations can be selectively focused at the most promising trait levels.

Figure 3.8 also shows the likelihood for three other response patterns. It can be seen that the likelihoods for the various trait levels varies between the response patterns. For Pattern 3, for example, only one item, the easiest item, is solved. For this pattern, the high trait level scores are quite unlikely. The maximum likelihood was calculated for the trait level of –2.0. In Pattern 2, three items were solved. Notice that the maximum likelihood was calculated for –.5, which is higher than the trait level estimated for Pattern 3 and lower than the trait level estimated for Pattern 1. Pattern 4, which has the same total score as Pattern 1, reaches the highest calculated likelihood at the same point (i.e., 2.0), as well.

Two other points are worth noting from Fig. 3.8. First, Patterns 1 and 4, which have the same total score, also have the highest calculated likelihood at the same value, namely, 2.0. Thus, different response patterns with the same total score have the same point at which the relatively greatest likelihood occurs. In the Rasch model, from which the likelihoods were calculated, total score is a *sufficient statistic* for estimating trait level. For a sufficient statistic, no additional information is required from the data for estimation. Thus, the specific items that were passed provide no additional information about trait level in the Rasch model. Each total score has only one associated trait level in the Rasch model, regardless of which items are passed or failed. In other IRT models, such as the 2PL, total score is *not* a sufficient statistic. Second, the height of the likelihood curve for Patterns 4 and 2 is generally lower than the height of the other two curves. Patterns 2 and 4 are somewhat inconsistent response patterns. In Pattern 4, the fifth item is passed, whereas the fourth item is failed. Yet, the fifth item is harder than the fourth item. Similarly, in Pattern 2, the relatively easier third item is failed rather than the harder fourth item. Response inconsistency lowers the likelihood of all trait levels for the response pattern. This information is important in evaluating the interpretability of the person's response (see chap. 9).

For the 2PL model, the likelihoods for the various trait levels depends on which items were passed. Suppose that five items had the same relative difficulties (–2, –1, 0, 1, 2), but varying discriminations (1, 3, 1, 3, 3), respectively. The second, fourth, and fifth items are more discriminating for trait level than the first and third items. Now consider two response patterns with total scores of 3. In the first response pattern (1, 1, 1, 0, 0), the person passes the three easiest items, which includes the two items with lower discriminations. In the second response pattern, (1, 1, 0, 1, 0), the person passes the harder but more discriminating fourth item rather than the third item.

Figure 3.9 shows the likelihoods computed from the 2PL model in Eq. 3.5, multiplied across items for the two response patterns. Here Pattern 2

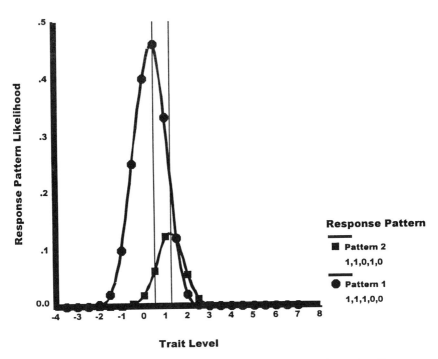

FIG. 3.9.   Brute force estimation of trait level for items with varying discriminations.

shows generally smaller likelihoods at all trait levels. The decreased likelihood results from some inconsistencies in the response pattern; specifically, a harder item is passed, and an easier item is failed. Most significantly, however, the trait level that gives the maximum likelihood differs
between response patterns even though they have the same total score.
The higher trait levels yield higher likelihoods for Pattern 2 because the
harder item that was passed had a higher discrimination value. That is,
the peak of the calculated likelihoods are shifted toward the more discriminating items that are passed.

Estimating Trait Level from Different Tests

An important feature of IRT models is that trait level estimates with invariant meaning may be obtained from any set of items. That is, given the
item parameters, trait level may be estimated for a person's response pattern from any set of items. The meaning of the response patterns for estimating trait scores is adjusted explicitly by including item properties in
the model.

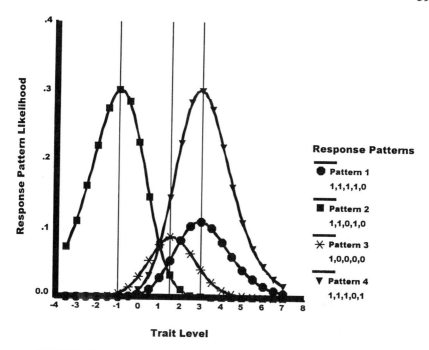

FIG. 3.10. Brute force estimation of trait level for items with different difficulty levels.

To illustrate, suppose that the same four response patterns were observed, as shown earlier, but on a harder test. Specifically, the item difficulties are higher (–1, 0, 1, 2, 3). Intuitively, a higher trait level is required to pass hard items than to pass easier items. Like clinical inference, observations of positive behavioral indicators under more stringent conditions leads to a more extreme hypotheses about the latent variable.

Figure 3.10 shows the likelihood curves for the four response patterns that were shown in Fig. 3.8. For Pattern 3, the trait level with the highest likelihood is now –1. In contrast, in Fig. 3.8 the highest likelihood for Pattern 3 was –2. The most likely trait level for Pattern 1 is higher in Fig. 3.10 because the items are more difficult. Similarly, higher trait levels are estimated for the other three patterns as well.

Trait Level Estimation in IRT: Summary

Unlike CTT, the trait level that corresponds to a response pattern is determined from a search process rather than from a simple computation. The brute-force method, although computationally burdensome and imprecise, illustrates the concept of a search process. Various trait levels were examined for their impact on the likelihood of a given response pattern. A person's response pattern is "scored" by finding the trait level that gives the maximum likelihood. In practical applications of IRT models, computer programs are used to estimate trait levels. The brute-force method, although illustrative, may not be practical due to the many computations required. Instead, efficient search algorithms are employed to find the trait level at the maximum for a particular response pattern (see chap. 7).

Whether or not response patterns with the same total score are estimated to have the same trait level depends on the IRT model. For the Rasch model, total score is a sufficient statistic. Thus, the same trait level estimate is received regardless of which items are passed or failed. For the 2PL model, which contains item discriminations, the trait level estimate depends on exactly which items are passed or failed. Passing relatively more discriminating items leads to higher trait level estimates.

Last, trait level estimates are implicitly adjusted for item difficulty in the IRT estimation process. The most likely trait level for passing four out of five hard items is higher than the trait level for passing four out of five easier items.

SUMMARY

Psychological measurement is indirect. A person's standing on a latent trait must be inferred from his or her behavior on measuring tasks. A model is needed to describe how the latent-trait construct relates to behavior. The CTT model is simple; namely, observed score is the sum of true score and error. This model is limited in several ways: (a) true score applies only to a specific set of items or their equivalent, (b) item properties are not directly linked to test behavior, and (c) the independent variables are not separately estimable.

An IRT model is introduced by showing Georg Rasch's target data, a basic data matrix of item response probabilities. The relationship between item probabilities and score level is predicted by an IRT model. The Rasch model predicts item probabilities from two independent variables, trait level and item difficulty. The Rasch model is presented in two forms, a model for probabilities and a model for log odds.

IRT models require two basic assumptions. First, the item characteristics curves specified by an IRT model must fit the test data. That is, the IRT model specifies how changes in trait level are related to changes in item-response probabilities. Second, the local independence assumption requires that the item parameters and person parameters fully account for interrelationships between items and persons. Local independence means that, given the model parameters, no further relationships exist in data.

The IRT model has several advantages: (a) an IRT trait level estimate can be derived from any item for which properties are known, (b) item properties are directly linked to test behavior, and (c) the independent variables, trait level and item properties, can be estimated separately without additional data. The IRT model compares very favorably to the CTT model, which did not have these properties.

The estimation process in IRT differs greatly from CTT. IRT trait levels are derived by maximizing the likelihood of a person's observed response pattern in a model of test behavior. The model includes the properties of the items on the test. Estimating IRT trait levels is analogous to a clinical inference process in which behaviors are symptoms of a latent syndrome. In IRT, the observed behaviors are item responses, and the latent variable is trait level. Finding the trait level that was most likely to have generated the response pattern requires a search process. The search process involves comparing likelihoods of a particular response pattern under various trait levels. A worked-out example shows the computation of response pattern likelihoods.

A search process is illustrated by a brute-force method used to estimate trait level for various response patterns. A distribution of response pattern likelihoods under many possible trait levels is calculated. The goal is to find the trait level that yields the highest likelihood.

Trait level estimates are shown to depend on the specific item properties included in the IRT model. Analogous to the clinical inference process, the meaning of behavior for the latent syndrome is adjusted for observational opportunities. That is, the trait level that yields the highest likelihood depends on the specific properties of the items that were administered.

III

THE FUNDAMENTALS OF ITEM REPONSE THEORY

4

Binary IRT Models

This chapter presents IRT models that are appropriate for binary data. In binary data, item responses are scored into two categories to represent success (1) or failure (0). Two features of such data should be noted. First, although ability or achievement items are the prototypic binary data (i.e., Right vs. Wrong), many other types of data are also appropriate. For example, personality self-reports (True vs. Not True), attitude endorsements (Agree vs. Disagree) and behavioral rating scales (Yes vs. No) are also binary data. Second, in some cases, multicategory responses can be reduced to a binary format. For example, a four-category rating scale can be reduced to binary format by combining the categories at each end. This is appropriate only if no information about the latent trait is lost (see Jansen & Roskam, 1986; Andrich, 1996). If information about the latent trait is lost by binary scoring, a polytomous model should be considered (see chap. 5).

This chapter is divided into two major sections: (a) unidimensional IRT models, in which a single trait level represents person differences; and (b) multidimensional IRT models, in which two or more trait levels represent person differences. Although many new IRT models have been proposed in the last two decades, this chapter covers only a few major models of each type. The interested reader should see van der Linden and Hambleton's (1996) book, which contains chapters written by the original authors of several IRT models using common notation and common topical outlines.

UNIDIMENSIONAL IRT MODELS FOR BINARY
DATA

In unidimensional IRT models, a single latent trait is deemed sufficient to characterize person differences. A unidimensional IRT model is appropriate for data in which a single common factor underlies item response. Sometimes unidimensional IRT models are appropriate for items with two or more underlying factors; for example, a unidimensional IRT model will fit the data when all items involve the same combination of each factor (see Reckase, 1979). However, unidimensional IRT models are not appropriate for data in which (a) two or more latent traits have differing impact on the items and (b) persons differ systematically in the strategies, knowledge structures, or interpretations that they apply to the items. In these cases, a multidimensional IRT model is more appropriate.

In the unidimensional models presented in this chapter, the following symbols will be used:

X_{is} = response of person s to item i (0 or 1)

θ_s = trait level for person s

β_i = difficulty of item i

α_i = discrimination for item i

γ_i = lower asymptote (guessing) for item i

The IRT parameters from the three logistic unidimensional IRT models are illustrated with a large data set. The IRT item parameters are estimated by marginal maximum likelihood, using a computer program called BILOG (see chap. 13). The data set consists of 30 items from the Abstract Reasoning Test (ART; Embretson, 1998), which was administered to a sample of 787 young adults. Table 4.1 shows the classical item statistics for ART. It can be seen that item difficulty, given as percentage correct, ranges widely across the items. Also, the biserial correlations are all positive, and only a few fall below .30.

Traditional Logistic Models

The logistic IRT models are based on the logistic distribution, which gives the probability of a response in a simple expression. Specifically, if w_{is} represents the combination of person and item parameters in the model, then the probability is given as follows:

$$P(X_{is} = 1 \mid w_{is}) = \frac{\exp(w_{is})}{1 + \exp(w_{is})} \tag{4.1}$$

TABLE 4.1
Classical Item Statistics for 30 Items from the Abstract Reasoning Test

Item	Number Passing	Percentage Correct	Biserial Correlation
1	746	.948	.582
2	439	.558	.483
3	662	.841	.407
4	519	.659	.465
5	634	.806	.539
6	647	.822	.384
7	683	.868	.629
8	547	.695	.546
9	511	.649	.465
10	646	.821	.726
11	585	.743	.587
12	352	.447	.363
13	612	.778	.636
14	355	.451	.525
15	368	.468	.417
16	588	.747	.542
17	285	.362	.368
18	296	.376	.408
19	346	.440	.512
20	439	.558	.505
21	367	.466	.468
22	188	.239	.174
23	468	.595	.452
24	207	.263	.333
25	164	.208	.200
26	255	.324	.464
27	534	.679	.225
28	555	.705	.339
29	311	.395	.337
30	334	.424	.249

where $\exp(w_{is})$ (also written as $e^{w_{is}}$) is the natural log base (2.718) raised to the power w_{is}. The probability of success is computed by taking the antilog of w_{is}, according to Eq. 4.1.

One Parameter Logistic Model (1PL) or Rasch Model

The Rasch model predicts the probability of success for person s on item i (i.e., $P(X_{is} = 1)$), as follows:

$$P(X_{is} = 1 \mid \theta_s, \beta_i) = \frac{\exp(\theta_s - \beta_i)}{1 + \exp(\theta_s - \beta_i)} \quad (4.2)$$

The logit of Eq. 4.2, $\theta_s - \beta_i$, is the simple difference of trait level and item difficulty, which replaces w_{is} in Eq. 4.1. The Rasch model is also described

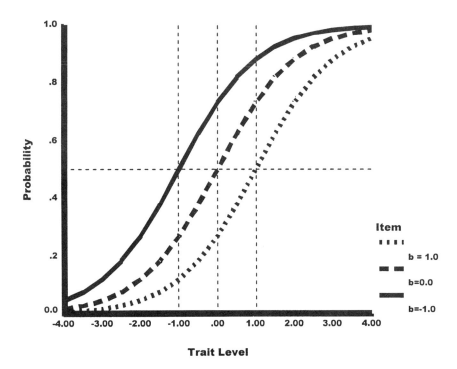

FIG. 4.1. Item characteristics curves from the one-parameter logistic model.

as the one-parameter logistic (1PL) model because it contains one item parameter.

Figure 4.1 shows item characteristic curves (ICCs) for three items from
the Rasch model. There are several general features of the ICC in the
Rasch model. First, the probabilities gradually increase with trait level for
each item. Second, items differ only in difficulty. The slopes of the curves
are equal. The curves converge, but they do not cross. Third, the point of
inflection of the ICC, where the rate of change shifts from accelerating increases to decelerating increases, occurs when the probability of passing
an item is .50. Reference lines from trait level to each ICC are shown. The
reference lines are drawn from the trait level that equals the item's difficulty when they cross the ICC at a probability of .50. This relationship
makes trait level interpretable as a threshold level for item difficulty; that
is, trait level indicates the difficulty level at which the person is as likely to
pass as to fail an item. For example, for the item with a difficulty of 1.00,
the probability that a person with a trait level of 1.00 passes the item is .50.

Equation 4.2 is the typical form of the Rasch model. However, the 1PL
model also may be written with a constant item discrimination value, α, as
follows:

$$P(X_{is} = 1 \mid \theta_s, \beta_i) = \frac{\exp(\alpha(\theta_s - \beta_i))}{1 + \exp(\alpha(\theta_s - \beta_i))} \qquad (4.3)$$

In Eq. 4.3, the constant value for item discrimination is freely estimated. In contrast, in Eq. 4.2 the value of the constant item discriminations are assumed to be 1.0. The choice of scaling for the constant (1.0 or freely estimated) has implications for the other parameters in the model, which will be reviewed in chapter 6. However, given the appropriate scaling of all parameters, Eqs. 4.2 and 4.3 give identical predictions.

Table 4.2 presents the item difficulties, β_i and their standard errors, σ_β, that were obtained for ART. The items are scaled so that Eq. 4.2 gives the

TABLE 4.2
Rasch and 2PL Model Item Parameters for the Abstract Reasoning Test

Item	Rasch Model		2PL Model			
	β	σ_β	α	β	σ_α	σ_β
1	−2.826	.172	1.578	−2.118	.240	.238
2	.188	.081	1.154	.032	.118	.072
3	−1.479	.104	.958	−1.723	.132	.237
4	−.318	.084	1.067	−.466	.115	.099
5	−1.200	.101	1.290	−1.114	.139	.127
6	−1.325	.100	.910	−1.639	.119	.228
7	−1.72	.119	1.686	−1.278	.191	.124
8	−.509	.088	1.281	−.541	.127	.090
9	−.265	.083	1.086	−.407	.116	.090
10	−1.315	.109	2.154	−.858	.200	.073
11	−.788	.094	1.446	−.700	.142	.088
12	.712	.078	.791	.579	.098	.101
13	−1.006	.099	1.628	−.796	.169	.085
14	.694	.082	1.334	.474	.131	.065
15	.615	.079	.942	.441	.102	.084
16	−.812	.092	1.236	−.820	.129	.105
17	1.127	.081	.816	1.061	.103	.125
18	1.057	.081	.932	.910	.108	.102
19	.748	.082	1.227	.531	.121	.070
20	.188	.081	1.179	.035	.123	.072
21	.621	.08	1.052	.435	.115	.076
22	1.809	.086	.476	2.815	.087	.470
23	.009	.081	.998	−.175	.111	.089
24	1.663	.087	.777	1.750	.106	.199
25	2.008	.09	.499	3.073	.098	.538
26	1.324	.085	1.144	1.070	.117	.096
27	−.419	.079	.496	−1.303	.085	.294
28	−.566	.084	.692	−1.097	.097	.203
29	.963	.079	.715	.933	.094	.129
30	.821	.076	.524	.893	.085	.167

| −2 log Likelihood = 25924.52 | −2 log Likelihood = 25659.39 |

predicted probabilities. It can be seen that the item difficulties range from
–2.826 to 2.008. The standard errors for the item difficulties differ across
items. In general, more extreme item difficulties have larger standard errors. The standard errors can be used to set confidence intervals around
the estimated item difficulties. More information on the standard errors
for item parameters is presented in chapter 8.

Two-Parameter Logistic Model (2PL)

The 2PL model adds item discrimination parameters. In this case, the
probability that person s solves item i is given as follows:

$$P(X_{is} = 1 \mid \theta_s, \beta_i, \alpha_i) = \frac{\exp[\alpha_i(\theta_s - \beta_i)]}{1 + \exp[\alpha_i(\theta_s - \beta_i)]} \tag{4.4}$$

Comparing Eq. 4.4 to Eq. 4.3 shows a subtle but important difference: The
item discrimination parameter contains a subscript, α_i, that represents
item differences in discrimination. Thus, the 2PL model is appropriate for
measures in which items are not equally related to the latent trait. Or,
stated from another perspective, the items are not equally indicative of a
person's standing on the latent trait.

Figure 4.2 shows item characteristic curves for three items under the
2PL model. Although these items have the same difficulties as those described earlier, the item discriminations differ. Notice that the item characteristic curve for Item 2 crosses the curves for Item 1 and Item 3. Also
notice that item difficulty in the 2PL model still indicates the trait level at
which the probability is .50 for success.

Table 4.2 also presents the item parameters for the 2PL model on ART.
The item discriminations and difficulties were scaled to be comparable to
the Rasch model. The 2PL model item difficulties differ somewhat from
the Rasch model item difficulties. The estimated slopes vary substantially,
ranging from .476 to 2.154, which indicates that a constant item discrimination may not fit the data well. The 2PL model item difficulties are somewhat different from the Rasch model item difficulties due to the varying
item discriminations. Item difficulty becomes more extreme as item discriminations decrease. For Item 22, which has the lowest discrimination,
item difficulty is more extreme in the 2PL model than in the Rasch model.

Three-Parameter Logistic Model (3PL)

The 3PL model adds a parameter to represent an item characteristics
curve that does not fall to zero. For example, when an item can be solved
by guessing, as in multiple choice cognitive items, the probability of success is substantially greater than zero, even for low trait levels. The 3PL

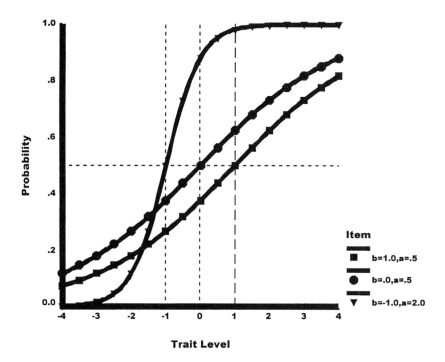

FIG. 4.2.   Item characteristics curves from the two-parameter logistic model.

model accommodates guessing by adding a lower-asymptote parameter, γ_i, as follows:

$$P(X_{is} = 1 \mid \theta_s, \beta_i, \alpha_i, \gamma_i) = \gamma_i + (1 - \gamma_i) \frac{\exp[\alpha_i(\theta_s - \beta_i)]}{1 + \exp[\alpha_i(\theta_s - \beta_i)]} \qquad (4.5)$$

Figure 4.3 shows three items with equal difficulties and discriminations but with different lower asymptotes. For even the lowest trait level, the probability of item success is greater than zero. For the item with γ_i equal to .25, the probability of success is at least .25 for even the lowest trait levels. Such a prediction is plausible if the probability of guessing correctly is not zero. For items with four alternatives, the probability of success from random guessing is .25. However, estimates of lower asymptote from the 3PL model often differ from the random guessing probability. For example, if examinees can systematically eliminate implausible distractors, selecting the correct answer from the remaining alternatives will have a higher probability than random guessing.

The 3PL model with unique lower asymptotes for each item can lead to estimation problems (see chap. 8). To avoid such estimation problems, a common lower asymptote is often estimated for all items or for groups of similar items.

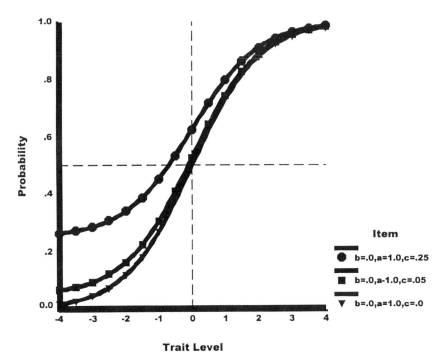

FIG. 4.3.   Item characteristics curves from the three-parameter logistic model.

Last, it should be noted that *item difficulty* has a different meaning in the 3PL model. Although item difficulty still occurs at the point of inflection in the ICC, it is no longer the trait level at which the probability of success is .50. The inflection point is shifted by the lower asymptote. To illustrate, Fig. 4.3 shows three items with different lower asymptotes but the same difficulty level of .00, which is indicated by the vertical line. Notice that item difficulty is associated with a much higher probability than .50 for the item with a lower asymptote of .25.

Table 4.3 presents the 3PL item parameter estimates, and the associated standard errors, for ART. The lower asymptote estimates are somewhat greater than zero, ranging from .095 to .226. The item difficulty and discrimination estimates given in Table 4.3 differ somewhat from the 2PL model, due to the varying lower asymptotes.

Which Model?

Several criteria can be applied to determine which model is the best. These criteria include (a) the weights of items for scoring (equal vs. unequal), (b) the desired scale properties for the measure (chap. 8 reviews

TABLE 4.3
3PL Item Parameters for the Abstract Reasoning Test

	3PL Item Parameters			Standard Errors		
Item	α	β	γ	σ_α	σ_β	σ_γ
1	1.286	-2.807	.192	.200	.320	.086
2	1.203	.136	.162	.196	.171	.056
3	.814	-2.033	.196	.122	.364	.087
4	.941	-.557	.142	.126	.218	.063
5	1.083	-1.461	.153	.133	.227	.070
6	.752	-1.979	.182	.107	.364	.082
7	1.363	-1.785	.146	.172	.204	.068
8	1.083	-.776	.118	.127	.176	.054
9	1.149	-.239	.214	.191	.224	.070
10	1.837	-1.247	.132	.201	.135	.057
11	1.269	-.917	.153	.159	.184	.064
12	.783	.819	.129	.142	.223	.053
13	1.501	-.963	.196	.213	.188	.073
14	1.417	.526	.118	.228	.116	.039
15	.949	.577	.126	.156	.178	.049
16	1.150	-.882	.204	.163	.238	.077
17	.846	1.303	.112	.166	.204	.044
18	.986	1.090	.113	.183	.168	.043
19	1.295	.597	.115	.215	.123	.039
20	1.065	-.017	.110	.145	.158	.048
21	.948	.470	.095	.140	.156	.042
22	1.150	2.609	.170	.436	.433	.029
23	.928	-.110	.155	.143	.227	.065
24	.934	1.957	.103	.225	.246	.035
25	.728	3.461	.128	.264	.743	.036
26	1.452	1.144	.107	.281	.113	.030
27	.460	-.793	.226	.091	.589	.094
28	.609	-1.018	.192	.099	.409	.084
29	.779	1.291	.142	.167	.238	.052
30	.576	1.607	.178	.144	.399	.066

-2 log Likelihood = 25650.60

these properties), (c) fit to the data, and (d) the purpose for estimating the parameters. For example, if items are to be equally weighted and if the strongest justification for scale properties is desired, then the Rasch model is favored. However, if fit to the existing set of items or highly accurate parameter estimates are needed, the 2PL or 3PL models may be favored.

At the bottom of Tables 4.2 and 4.3 are values useful for evaluating model fit. In maximum likelihood estimation, -2 times the log likelihood of the data indicates the degree of departure of the data from the model. Model differences in these values may be evaluated as chi-square statistics to evaluate the improvements made by the successively more complex models. Specifically, the improvement made by the 2PL over the Rasch model is evaluated as follows:

$$\chi^2 = -2 \log \text{Likelihood}_{\text{Rasch}} - (-2 \log \text{Likelihood}_{\text{2PL}})$$
$$= 25924.52 - 25659.39$$
$$= 265.13 \qquad\qquad (4.6)$$

The degrees of freedom for χ^2 are the number of increased parameters for the more complex model. The 2PL adds 30 item discrimination parameters as compared to the Rasch model. At 30 degrees of freedom, the χ^2 of 265.13 is very unlikely. Thus, the 2PL model fits significantly better than the Rasch model. Similarly, the difference between the 3PL and the 2PL models can be evaluated ($\chi^2 = 25659.39 - 25650.60$). The resulting value of 8.79 is not significant at 30 degrees of freedom; therefore, the 3PL model does not fit significantly better than the 2PL model.

If the purpose for estimating the parameters is understanding the basis of item difficulty, then these estimates should be compared directly between the models. Figure 4.4 presents a plot of the 2PL and 3PL item diffi-

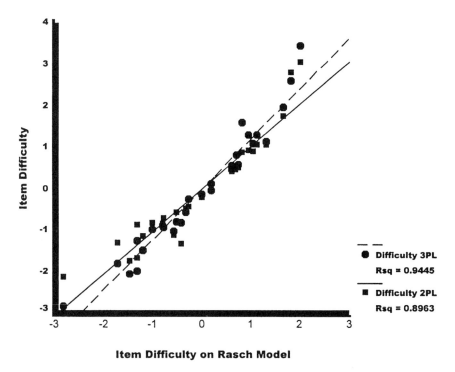

FIG. 4.4.   Regression of item difficulties from two- and three-parameter logistic models on the Rasch model.

culties by the Rasch model item difficulties. It can be seen that the item difficulties differ somewhat between 2PL and the Rasch model. For ART, the relationship of item difficulty to cognitive design principles was a primary interest (Embretson, 1998a). Using the 2PL instead of the Rasch model item difficulties could lead to somewhat different interpretations in this case.

If the primary purpose is accurately estimating trait level, these estimates should be compared between models. Figure 4.5 presents a plot of the 2PL trait levels on the Rasch model trait levels. Although the correlations is high ($R^2 = .98$), it can be seen that the 2PL estimates scatter around the Rasch model estimates. The importance of this scatter depends on the decision that is made from the trait level estimates.

In summary, the relative values of the various criteria determines which model is best for a particular application. No single criterion can be recommended as sufficient. If the primary concern is fitting an IRT model to the existing data, the 2PL model is favored in the ART example. If the item parameter estimates must be very accurate, the 2PL model is also favored. However, if items are equally important or if a highly justifiable scaling is

FIG. 4.5.   Regression of two-parameter logistic abilities on Rasch model abilities.

desired, the Rasch model may be selected. In fact, it may be possible to fit the Rasch model by eliminating a few items with extreme discriminations.

Traditional Normal Ogive Models

As for logistic models, normal ogive models are named for the number of item parameters than they contain. Normal ogive models contain the same parameters as their corresponding logistic models; however, the item characteristic curve is produced by a different function. The function is more complex than the logistic model because the probability of success is given by the cumulative proportion of cases in the normal distribution. Thus, a normal ogive model gives the ICC as the proportion of cases below a certain standard score, z_{is}, as follows:

$$P(X_{is} = 1) = \int_{-\infty}^{z_{is}} \frac{1}{(2\pi)^{1/2}} \exp(-t^2/2)\,dt \qquad (4.7)$$

where

$\int_{-\infty}^{z_{is}} dt =$ integral notation for the area in the distribution from $-\infty$ to z_{is}

$\pi =$ the constant 3.14

Thus, Eq. 4.7 contains the normal density function and the integral notation means to find the cumulative proportion of cases to z_{is}. The standard score, z_{is}, contains the parameters of the IRT model.

Both the two-parameter and the three-parameter normal ogive model have been applied frequently. The parameter structures of these two models are identical to the 2PL and 3PL models, respectively. A one-parameter normal ogive model could be given, but it does not have the same theoretical appeal or practical application as the 1PL. Thus, only the two- and three-parameter normal ogive models are presented.

Two-Parameter Normal Ogive Model

The two-parameter normal ogive model contains the same parameter structure as the 2PL model. That is, z_{is} is given as follows:

$$z_{is} = \alpha_i(\theta_s - \beta_i) \qquad (4.8)$$

The value of the parameter, z_{is}, functions as a standard score so that the cumulative proportion of cases to z_{is} gives the probability of a correct response, as follows:

$$P(X_{is} = 1 \mid \theta_s, \beta_i, \alpha_i) = \int_{-\infty}^{\alpha_i(\theta_s - \beta_i)} \frac{1}{(2\pi)^{1/2}} \exp(-t^2/2) dt \qquad (4.9)$$

For example, if $\alpha_i = 1.0$, $\theta_s = 2.00$ and $\beta_i = 1.00$, then the value of z_{is} can be computed from Eq. 4.8 as 1.00. The proportion below a z_{is} of 1.00 in the normal distribution is .8413; thus, the probability given by 4.9 for item success is .8413. To give another example, if the combination of parameters results in a z_{is} of −1.50, the probability from the cumulative normal distribution is .0668.

If trait level is normally distributed and the two-parameter normal ogive model fits the data, Lord and Novick (1968) show that the item parameters of the normal ogive model have some interesting relationships to classical test theory indices when trait level is normally distributed. First, the biserial correlation, r_{bis}, of an item with total score is directly related to the IRT item discrimination parameter, as follows:

$$\alpha_i \cong r_{bis}/(1 - r_{bis}^2)^{1/2} \qquad (4.10)$$

Since item discrimination increases monotonically with the biserial correlation, selecting items by IRT item discriminations is comparable to selecting items by biserial correlations.

Second, the IRT item difficulty parameter, β_i, is related to p-value, p_i, but it also depends on the biserial correlation of the item with total score. This relationship can be easily shown if p_i is converted into a normal deviate, z_i, such that p_i is the area *above* z_i (e.g., if $p_i = .84$, then $z_i = −1.00$). Then, the IRT item difficulty parameter, β_i, is approximately equal to z_i divided by the biserial correlation, r_{bis}, as follows:

$$\beta_i \cong z_i/r_{bis} \qquad (4.11)$$

Thus, p-values orders items somewhat differently than IRT item difficulty. Consequently, using the IRT item difficulties can lead to selecting different items than classical test theory p-values. For other differences in selecting items by IRT, see chapter 10 on test construction.

Three-Parameter Normal Ogive Model

Analogous to the 3PL model, a lower asymptote may be added to the normal ogive model to accommodate item response data with guessing. The three-parameter normal ogive model is given as follows:

$$P(X_{is} = 1 \mid \theta_s, \beta_i, \alpha_i, \gamma_i) = \gamma_i + (1 - \gamma_i) \int_{-\infty}^{\alpha_i(\theta_s - \beta_i)} \frac{1}{(2\pi)^{1/2}} \exp(-t^2/2) dt \qquad (4.12)$$

As for the 3PL model, the item difficulty parameter represents the point of inflection for the ICC, but it is not the .50 threshold value of trait level.

Comparison of Logistic and Normal Ogive Models

The logistic and normal ogive models predict very similar probabilities. Consider again the two examples presented earlier to illustrate the two-parameter normal ogive model, where $z_{is} = 1.0$ (Item 1; $\alpha_i = 1.0$, $\theta_s = 2.00$, $\beta_i = 1.00$), and $z_{is} = -1.5$ (Item 2; $\alpha_i = 1.5$, $\theta_s = 2.00$, $\beta_i = 3.00$). To compute corresponding probabilities from the 2PL model, the multiplier 1.7 must be included in the exponent (see chap. 6 on the trait level scale). For Item 1, the 2PL model with the multiplier 1.7 gives the probability as .8455, which is very close to the normal ogive model prediction of .8413. For Item 2, the 2PL model gives the probability as .0724, which is close to the normal ogive model prediction of .0668.

In fact, the whole item characteristics curves generated by logistic and normal ogive models with corresponding parameter structures are virtually indistinguishable. Figure 4.6 shows the ICCs produced by the two-parameter logistic and normal ogive models for a single item. The

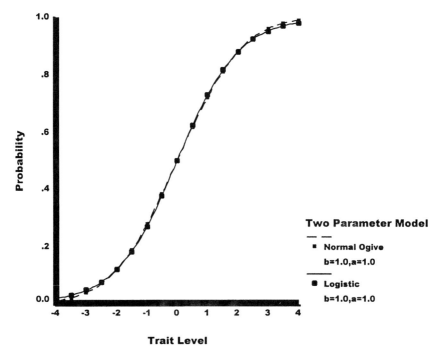

FIG. 4.6.   Comparison of logistic and normal ogive item characteristics curves.

ICCs are nearly completely overlaid. The greatest differences between the models occur at the extreme trait levels.

Should the logistic or normal ogive model be selected for a particular measure? Since the logistic and normal ogive models predict nearly identical ICCs, few differences in either model fit or parameter estimates are expected. However, logistic models are now more prevalent than normal ogive models, due to their computational simplicity. The normal ogive model is complex because integration over a distribution is required. Normal ogive models, however, remain interesting due to their relationship to classical test theory.

Other Unidimensional Models

Although a complete description of other binary response items is beyond the scope of this introductory chapter, a few models should be mentioned. Some applications may be found in chapter 11.

Models With Restrictions on the Parameter Structure

The linear logistic latent trait model (LLTM; Fischer, 1973) was developed to incorporate item content into the prediction of item success. If appropriate content factors can be specified for each item, then parameters to reflect impact on item difficulty can be estimated directly, as follows:

$$P(X_{is} = 1 \mid \theta_s, \tau_k) = \frac{\exp(\theta_s - \Sigma_k \tau_k q_{ik})}{1 + \exp(\theta_s - \Sigma_k \tau_k q_{ik})} \tag{4.13}$$

where

q_{ik} = value of stimulus factor k in item i

τ_k = weight of stimulus factor k in item difficulty

Suppose, for example, that paragraph comprehension items were known to be influenced by five factors: vocabulary level, syntactic complexity and the density of three basic types of propositions. If the involvement of each factor can be specified numerically for each item, then LLTM can be applied to estimate the weights of each factor in item difficulty. Thus, the difficulty of an item is characterized by influence of each underlying stimulus factor. Some applications of LLTM are given in chapter 11.

A special case for LLTM is the measurement of change. In this case, the parameter structure for an item also represents the occasion under which it is presented. If an item is presented to a person after a condition that changes average trait levels, then a constant is added to reflect the administration condition for the item. More detailed presentations of LLTM are available in Fischer (1973).

Models for Combining Speed and Accuracy

For many tests, a person's performance level depends on both accuracy and speed. For such tests, time limits may be imposed or evaluated to estimate trait level. For cognitive tests with tight time limits, for example, mental ability may be regarded as a combination of power and speed.

Several models have been proposed to incorporate speed and accuracy into the estimation of trait level. The probability of a correct response depends partly on the time involved in answering the item. Roskam (1997) and Verhelst, Verstralen and Jansen (1997) present various models which incorporate item response time into the prediction of item success. For some variants of these models, the only additional observation that is required is average or total item response time.

Single Items With Multiple Attempts

In single item data with multiple attempts, the same task is repeated several times. For example, in psychomotor tasks or sports, a person attempts the same task (e.g., throwing a basketball) over again and it can be scored for accuracy (i.e., making the basket). Or, perhaps the task is an affective task (e.g., appropriate social responses) that is observed repeatedly. In either case, an "item" is a particular attempt, and trait level is determined from the number of successes. Appropriate models for multiple attempt single item data are presented by Masters (1992) as well as Spray (1997). For example, Spray (1997) describes three appropriate models: a binomial model, a Poisson model, and an inverse binomial model. Interesting applications to motor behavior are described by Safrit, Costa and Cohen (1989).

Models With Special Forms for ICC

If the probability of an item response decreases with the *absolute* distance from the person's trait level, then a different form for the ICC is required. For example, in attitude data, the probability that a person endorses a certain statement may decrease if the item is higher *or* lower than a person's trait level. Andrich (1997) shows that endorsing a statement "I think capital punishment is necessary but I wish it were not" is highest for a moderate attitude toward capital punishment. Persons at higher or lower levels for favorableness are less likely to endorse the item. Appropriate models for this type of data include Andrich's (1997) hyperbolic cosine IRT model and Hoijtink's (1991) parallelogram IRT model.

The various IRT models described above assume that the ICC is adequately characterized by the form specified in the model. For some measures, assuming a single function for the ICC may be too restrictive. More complex functions may be needed to characterize the changes in item responses with increasing trait level. The form of the ICC can be estimated from the data by a nonparametric approach to IRT models. Ramsey's (1991) nonparametric approach to IRT applies a kernel smoothing approach to estimate the ICCs for each item.

Figure 4.7 shows three ICCs that can be fit by Ramsey's approach but not by the parametric IRT models, such as the logistic models and normal ogive models. Notice that one ICC does not have a lower asymptote of .00. Nonparametric IRT can fit data that is fit by the 3PL. However, ICCs that would not be fit by any parametric model also can be accommodated. At some score levels on Figure 4.7, the probability of success changes little or even dips over certain score levels for the three items. Such data would not fit the 3PL but would be fit by nonparametric IRT. Of course, the greater flexibility in fit of the nonparametric models is offset by the greater complexity of the model. Each item may require a different function.

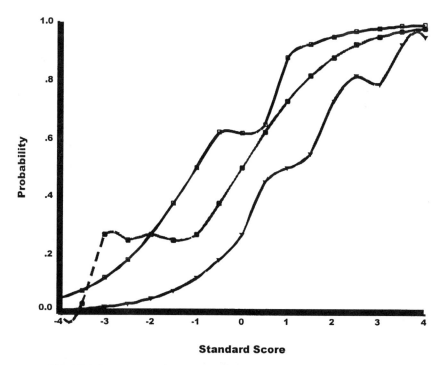

FIG. 4.7. Comparison of nonparametric item characteristics curve to the three-parameter normal ogive model.

MULTIDIMENSIONAL MODELS

Multidimensional IRT models contain two or more parameters to represent each person. Multiple dimensions provide increased fit for item response data when persons differ systematically in which items are hard or easy. In many multidimensional models, multiple item discrimination parameters represent the impact of the dimensions on specific items. In this section, the following parameters will be used to express the models:

X_{is} = response of person s to item i (0 or 1)

θ_{sm} = trait level for person s on dimension m

β_i = difficulty of item i

δ_i = easiness intercept for item i

α_{im} = discrimination for item i on dimension m

γ_i = lower asymptote (guessing) for item i

It should be noted that item easiness, δ_i, is typically used in multidimensional models rather than item difficulty. However, item difficulty may be obtained directly from item easiness, as noted later.

The multidimensional models will be reviewed in two categories: exploratory models and confirmatory models. Analogous to factor analysis, an exploratory multidimensional IRT involves estimating item and person parameters on more than one dimension to improve the fit of the model to the data. Theories about the substantive nature of the factors does not determine the estimation process or the required number of factors. In contrast, confirmatory multidimensional IRT involves estimating parameters for specified dimensions. Analogous to factor analysis, a confirmatory analysis involves specifying the relationship of the items to the dimensions.

In the following sections, the multidimensional models will be overviewed only. Since these models are relatively newer than the unidimensional models, they have been applied less extensively. Illustrative applications may be found in chapters 11 and 12.

EXPLORATORY MULTIDIMENSIONAL MODELS
FOR BINARY DATA

Factor analysis of binary items has become increasingly similar to multidimensional IRT models. In fact, under certain assumptions, it can be proved that they are the same model (Takane & de Leeuw, 1988). McDonald's (1967) non-linear factor analysis model can be considered a unifying foundation for factor analysis, classical test theory and item response theory. Recently, Reckase (1997) notes that extensions of exploratory factor analysis to handle binary item data became increasing similar to IRT models. The exploratory multidimensional models reviewed in this section are highly related to factor analysis. A person's potential on an item is a weighted combination of their standing on the underlying trait dimensions.

To date, multidimensional IRT models have been mainly employed in the construct development phase of test development. That is, the constructs in the items are explicated by the IRT model that fits the data. The number of latent traits required to obtain fit, and the substantive nature of the dimensions, explicates the constructs in the items. The resulting IRT item parameters are particularly useful for selecting items to measure targeted traits. That is, items with split trait dependencies can be eliminated or balanced so that a single targeted trait is measured.

However, several traits may be estimated simultaneously for a person in a multidimensional IRT model. If success on an item depends on more than one latent trait, then the person's response provides information about two or more traits simultaneously. With future developments, multidimensional IRT may be applied more routinely for estimating multiple trait levels from adaptive testing. When traits are correlated or when items depend on two or more traits, a person's item responses provide information on the non-targeted trait. Thus, an adaptive testing (see chap. 10) of the non-targeted trait can begin at a level that is more appropriate for the person and hence will require fewer items to be administered.

Multidimensional Logistic Models

Multidimensional Rasch Model

McKinley and Reckase (1982) describe the multidimensional Rasch model as follows:

$$P(X_{is} = 1 \mid \underline{\theta}_s, \delta_i) = \frac{\exp(\Sigma_m \theta_{sm} + \delta_i)}{1 + \exp(\Sigma_m \theta_{sm} + \delta_i)} \tag{4.14}$$

In Eq. 4.14, as compared to the simple Rasch model above, the unidimensional trait level θ_s is replaced by a composite of equally weighted traits. As Reckase (1978) points out, when the multiple dimensions are equally weighted in each item, a unidimensional Rasch model fits the data. Further, with equal weights, there is no pattern of item responses that can indicate the person's *differential* standing on the various dimensions. Thus, the different trait levels cannot be separately estimated and the model is thus not identified.

Stegelmann (1983) proposed a multidimensional Rasch model that can estimate different trait levels. However, the model has a serious restriction; the items must be equally difficult. Thus, Stegelmann's (1983) model is not practical for most applications.

Multidimensional Extension of the Two Parameter Logistic Model

In this model, a discrimination parameter is given for each item on each dimension, as follows:

$$P(X_{is} = 1 \mid \underline{\theta}_s, \delta_i, \underline{\alpha}_i) = \frac{\exp(\Sigma_m \alpha_{im} \theta_{sm} + \delta_i)}{1 + \exp(\Sigma_m \alpha_{im} \theta_{sm} + \delta_i)} \tag{4.15}$$

In Eq. 4.15, the potential of the person on the item is reflected by a sum of several weighted traits rather than a single trait as in Eq. 4.4. The higher the weight, (i.e., α_{im}, the item discrimination), the more important the trait is in item success. Reckase (1997) describes how this model can be identified under minimal restrictions on the parameters, such as fixing the trait means and standard deviations.

Figure 4.8 is a three-dimensional plot of the probability of success on an item that is governed by two latent traits. It can be seen that individual differences in Trait Level 1 are more important for item success because the probability surface climbs more rapidly with changes in trait level. This reflects the higher discrimination value for Trait Level 1 in this item. Individual differences in Trait Level 2, although still important for item success, have less impact on the probability of item success.

Multidimensional Extension of Three Parameter Logistic Model

A multidimensional extension of the three parameter logistic model also can be described. Here, a lower asymptote is added to Equation 4.15 to accommodate guessing, as follows:

$$P(X_{is} = 1 \mid \underline{\theta}_s, \delta_i, \underline{\alpha}_i, \gamma_i) = \gamma_i + (1 - \gamma_i) \frac{\exp(\Sigma_m \alpha_{im} \theta_{sm} + \delta_i)}{1 + \exp(\Sigma_m \alpha_{im} \theta_{sm} + \delta_i)} \tag{4.16}$$

The three-dimensional probability surfaces that would correspond to this model would be similar to Fig. 4.8, except that the probability surface would not begin on the floor. That is, the probability would be higher than zero for all combinations of trait levels.

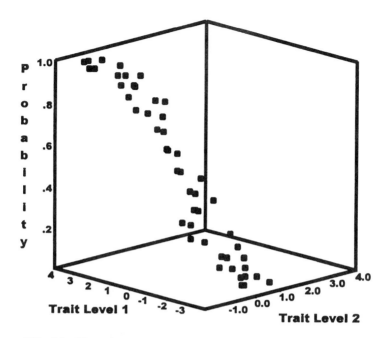

FIG. 4.8. Three-dimensional plot from the multidimensional logistic model.

Normal Ogive Models

Multidimensional Extension of Two Parameter Normal Ogive Model

Bock, Gibbons and Muraki (1988) elaborated a multidimensional normal ogive IRT model. Bock et al. (1988) describe this model as a factor analysis model with full information. Unlike factor analysis which models correlations, the item responses are modeled directly. The Bock et al. (1988) model is an extension of the two parameter normal ogive model to accommodate two or more dimensions. The model can be formulated with the potential of person s on item i, z_{is}, from a weighted combination of the multiple trait levels, θ_{sm}, as follows:

$$z_{is} = \Sigma_m \alpha_{im}\theta_{sm} + \delta_i \qquad (4.17)$$

The item discrimination parameters, α_{im}, give the weight of each dimension m in performance on item i and δ_i is the intercept (as easiness) for item i. The normal ogive model gives the probability of an observation exceeding the person's item potential from the cumulative normal distribution as follows:

$$P(X_{is} = 1 | \underline{\theta}_s, \delta_i, \underline{\alpha}_i) = \int_{-z_{is}}^{\infty} \frac{1}{(2\pi)^{\frac{1}{2}}} \exp(-t^2/2) dt \tag{4.18}$$

Factor loadings, λ_{im}, and standard item difficulty, δ_i, may be calculated from the model parameters in Eq. 4.18 as follows:

$$\lambda_{im} = \alpha_{im}/g_i \qquad \text{and} \qquad \beta_i = \delta_i/g_i \tag{4.19}$$

where

$$g_i = \sqrt{1 + \Sigma_m \alpha_{im}^2}$$

Multidimensional Normal Ogive Model With Guessing

The Bock et al. (1988) model may be readily formulated to accommodate items with guessing, such as multiple choice items, by adding a lower asymptote parameter, γ_i, as follows:

$$P(X_{is} = 1 | \underline{\theta}_s, \beta_i, \underline{\alpha}_i, \gamma_i) = \gamma_i + (1 - \gamma_i) \int_{-z_{is}}^{\infty} \frac{1}{(2\pi)^{1/2}} \exp(-t^2/2) dt \tag{4.20}$$

As for the three-parameter normal ogive model, the lower asymptote can be constrained to a constant value across items or subsets of items.

CONFIRMATORY MULTIDIMENSIONAL MODELS

Confirmatory multidimensional items contain design structures or mathematical models to link items to specified traits. These models are appropriate for items or measuring tasks in which prior research or theory has explicated the processes that underlie item performance. Examples are found in chapter 11.

In this section, only a few models will be presented. IRT modeling is a rapidly expanding area, as new models are increasingly proposed to handle special types of psychological measurement data. This section cannot review all these developments, but several models should be at least mentioned.

Models for Noncompensatory Dimensions

The multicomponent latent trait model (MLTM; Whitely,[1] 1980) was proposed to measure multiple processing components that underlie item solving. MLTM combines a mathematical model of the response process with an IRT model. Both component trait levels and component item difficulties are estimated. In MLTM, it is assumed that item success or endorsement depends on the success of several components. If any component is failed, then the item is not successfully solved. Thus, MLTM gives the probability of success for person s on item i, X_{isT}, as the product of success on each underlying component, X_{ism}, as follows:

$$P(X_{isT} = 1 \mid \underline{\theta}_s, \underline{\beta}_i) = \Pi_m \frac{\exp(\theta_{sm} - \beta_{im})}{1 + \exp(\theta_{sm} - \beta_{im})} \qquad (4.21)$$

where

$\underline{\theta}_s$ = the trait levels of person j on the M components

$\underline{\beta}_i$ = the difficulty of item i on the M components

θ_{sm} = the trait level of person j on component m

β_{im} = the difficulty of item i on component m

Notice that the right side of Eq. 4.21 is a Rasch model for the probability of success on a component. The product of the component probabilities gives the overall probability of success on the item. Other parameters, such as guessing, may be incorporated into MLTM as well (see Embretson, 1985).

A generalization of MLTM, the general component latent trait model (GLTM, Embretson, 1984), incorporates a mathematical model of component item difficulty. Like LLTM, item difficulty is given by the weighted sum of underlying stimulus factors, q_{ikm}, as follows:

$$P(X_{isT} = 1 \mid \underline{\theta}_s, \underline{\beta}_i) = \Pi_m \frac{\exp(\theta_{sm} - \Sigma_k \tau_{km} q_{ikm})}{1 + \exp(\theta_{sm} - \Sigma_k \tau_{km} q_{ikm})} \qquad (4.22)$$

where

τ_{km} = the weight of stimulus factor k in component m

q_{ikm} = the score of stimulus factor k on component m for item i

Originally, both MLTM and GLTM required component responses, as well as the total item response, to estimate the component parameters. Component responses could be observed, for example, by administering

---

[1]Susan Embretson has published under the name Susan Whitely.

subtasks from the total item. However, a recent development in estimation (Maris, 1995) can be applied to a generalization to GLTM to permit component estimation without subtasks. In items or measurement tasks for which mathematical models strongly predict item difficulty, constraints may be set to identify the component parameters.

Some of the advantages of GLTM and MLTM include 1) controlling the measured construct by selecting items for specified patterns of component difficulty and 2) measuring persons on covert processing components.

Models for Learning and Change

The multidimensional Rasch model for learning and change (MRMLC; Embretson, 1991) was developed to solve psychometric problems in the measurement of change (see chap. 11). In a design that is appropriate for MRMLC, a person is observed under two or more conditions or occasions (e.g., pretest and posttest) that facilitate or hinder performance. MRMLC treats modifiabilities as separate dimensions. A Wiener process structure defines involvement of the dimensions, θ_m, in a particular condition, C_k. In a Wiener process structure, each new occasion involves a new dimensions. For four measurements, the following structure would be given:

$$\Lambda_{kXm} = \begin{array}{c} \\ C_1 \\ C_2 \\ C_3 \\ C_4 \end{array} \begin{array}{|cccc} \underline{\theta}_1 & \underline{\theta}_2 & \underline{\theta}_3 & \underline{\theta}_4 \\ 1 & 0 & 0 & 0 \\ 1 & 1 & 0 & 0 \\ 1 & 1 & 1 & 0 \\ 1 & 1 & 1 & 1 \end{array} \qquad (4.23)$$

where

θ_1 = initial trait level

$\theta_2, \ldots, \theta_M$ = modifiability from preceding measurement

The columns represent the traits and the rows represent the conditions (occasions) under which items are observed. The zero values denote conditions in which a particular dimension is not involved in performance. As shown in Equation 4.23 above, the initial trait level is involved in all occasions. The second trait level is a modifiability that represents the change from the first to the second occasion. The third trait level is a modifiability that represents change from the second to the third occasion, and so on. The Wiener process structure is appropriate for data in which variances are increasing across conditions, since successively more traits are involved. Complex cognitive data often have increasing variances over time (see Embretson, 1991).

The design structure may be embedded in a Rasch model as follows:

$$P(X_{i(k)s} = 1 \mid \underline{\theta}_s, \beta_i) = \frac{\exp(\Sigma_m^k \theta_{sm} - \beta_i)}{1 + \exp(\Sigma_m^k \theta_{sm} - \beta_i)} \qquad (4.24)$$

where

θ_{sm} = level on trait m for person j

β_i = difficulty for item i

The summation sign, Σ_m^k, controls the involvement of the appropriate modifiabilities on condition k. Since MRMLC is estimated as a multidimensional model, standard errors are available for both initial ability and the several modifiabilities.

Under certain conditions, it is possible to extend unidimensional IRT models for measuring change dimensions. For example, Fischer (1997) extends the LLTM model to the multidimensional case by defining "technical persons". That is, a person becomes technically two or more different persons to characterize his or her trait levels in each condition. It should be noted, however, LLTM is not a multidimensional IRT model and standard errors for individual trait level changes are not routinely available.

Models With Specified Trait Level Structures

When items are presented under varying conditions or occasions, the trait levels that are involved may vary systematically as well. Design structures may be incorporated into the IRT trait level structure to define which traits are involved in a particular condition. From another perspective, the design structure also determines the substantive nature of trait level as well, because trait level results from a specified comparison of performance over conditions. Several IRT models with design structures have been proposed. The general structured latent trait model (SLTM; Embretson, 1995; 1997) was proposed to include many ability design structures, including those with unequal item discriminations and interactions of items with conditions. Wang, Wilson and Adams (1997) present a similar structured model in which each dimension forms a Rasch model. Adams, Wilson, and Wang (1997) show that their model is quite general and can incorporate many design structures, including some SLTM structures. A computer program, MATS (Wu, Adams, & Wilson, 1995) is available for these models. Similarly, DiBello, Stout, & Roussos (1995) presented a unified model with ability and item design structures. The DiBello et al. (1995) model is more general, however, since it is not restricted to Rasch-type models with a constant item discrimination.

To illustrate models with design structures, consider SLTM. In SLTM, a trait level design structure is incorporated as follows:

$$P(X_{i(k)s} = 1 \mid \underline{\theta}_s, \beta_i, \lambda_{i(k)m}) = \frac{\exp(\Sigma_m \lambda_{i(k)m} \theta_{sm} - \Sigma_k \beta_{ik})}{1 + \exp(\Sigma_m \lambda_{i(k)m} \theta_{sm} - \Sigma_k \beta_{ik})} \qquad (4.25)$$

where

θ_{sm} = level on trait m for person s

β_{ik} = difficulty contribution of condition k on item i

$\lambda_{i(k)m}$ = specified weight of trait m in item i under condition k

An important feature of SLTM, in contrast to the multidimensional logistic model in Eq. 4.15, is that weights may be fixed to zero rather than estimated. Thus, SLTM is analogous to a confirmatory factor model rather than an exploratory factor model. For example, the MRMLC design matrix could be specified as a special case of SLTM. However, SLTM also permits differing item discriminations, like 2PL models. Unlike an exploratory multidimensional IRT models, SLTM permits constraints on the discrimination parameters. Thus, a slight generalization of the MRMLC design structure is the following marix, Λ_{kXm}:

$$\Lambda_{kXm} = \begin{matrix} \lambda_{11} & 0 & 0 & 0 \\ \lambda_{21} & \lambda_{22} & 0 & 0 \\ \lambda_{31} & \lambda_{32} & \lambda_{33} & 0 \\ \lambda_{41} & \lambda_{42} & \lambda_{43} & \lambda_{44} \end{matrix} \qquad (4.26)$$

where

$\underline{\lambda}_{km}$ = the discriminations of items in condition k on dimension m

Two types of constraints on item discriminations are contained in this model. First, some item discriminations are forced to be zero, as in MRMLC. For example, for all items in condition 1, the discrimination on Dimension 2 is zero. Second, non-zero item discriminations must be equal across conditions. Although item discriminations vary between items within a condition, the discriminations are constrained to be equal across conditions. Specifically, the discrimination of item i on dimension m is constant across conditions. Several other design structures are possible for SLTM, as it is a quite general model.

Models for Distinct Classes of Persons

IRT models are available to define latent classes which are not observable by any external variable. The classes are identified by systematic differences in response patterns. These models contain both class and trait parameters to predict item responses. Although these models technically contain only one trait level for each person, they are classified as multidimensional because 1) the person's response probability is predicted with class membership parameters, in addition to trait level and the item parameters and 2) item difficulty orders vary across persons, as in multidimensional models.

The SALTUS model (*saltus* means "to leap" in Latin) was proposed for developmental or mastery data (Wilson, 1985). Such data often fails to fit a traditional IRT model because reaching a certain stage implies a sudden transition in success on an entire class of items. For example, some developmental tasks, such as the balance task, involve distinctly different types of rules. Children vary in acquistion of rules so that when certain rules are mastered, the probabilities for solving items that involve those rules shifts dramatically. Other items, however, remain unaffected because they do not involve those rules.

As in other IRT models, SALTUS predicts gradual increases in item success with increasing trait level. However, for some types of items, the probabilities increase drastically when a person reaches a certain stage. Items that have the same pattern of influence across developmental stages belong to the same type. Further, persons belong to stages (which is related to trait level). To model the increased probability for success on items that are influenced by a particular stage, a parameter is added as follows:

$$P(X_{is} = 1 \mid \theta_s, \beta_i) = \Pi_m \frac{\exp(\theta_s - \beta_i + \zeta_{h(s)k(i)})}{1 + \exp(\theta_s - \beta_i + \zeta_{h(s)k(i)})} \tag{4.27}$$

where

$\zeta_{h(s)k(i)}$ = increased success for item type k in stage h

An important implication of the SALTUS model is that the ICC depends on the developmental stage.

However, distinct classes may exist even for data that are not developmental. For example, in a spatial ability test, items often may be solved by either a spatial or a verbal strategy. Or, for another example, certain groups of persons may define certain self-report or attitude items differently from other groups. In both cases, what distinguishes the groups is a different pattern of item difficulties or endorsements.

Rost (1990) presents a mixed population Rasch model (MIRA) that combines IRT with latent class analysis. The IRT part of the model belongs to the unidimensional Rasch model family in which only one trait level characterizes a person. However, the meaning of the trait level depends on the class to which the person belongs. Item difficulties are scaled (and ordered) differently within the latent classes. The classes are regarded as mixed in the observed sample, according to a proportion, γ_h, for each latent class. The sum of proportions equals one. Thus, the following model may be given for the item response:

$$P(X_{is} = 1 \mid \theta_s, \beta_i) = \Sigma_h \gamma_h \frac{\exp(\theta_{sh} - \beta_{ih})}{1 + \exp(\theta_{sh} - \beta_{ih})} \qquad (4.28)$$

A computer program to estimate the model, WINMIRA (von Davier, 1997), gives the item difficulties within each latent class and the class proportion. Further, post hoc estimates of the probability that each person belongs to each class are also given. Class membership probabilities are determined from the relative likelihood of the person's response pattern within the various latent classes.

To give an example, some spatial items may be relatively easier under a verbal strategy than under a spatial strategy. Thus, item difficulty values depend on the latent class. Further, the relative likelihood of a person's response pattern under the two classes determines the probability that the person belongs to the verbal versus spatial strategy class. The meaning of trait level (i.e., spatial ability versus verbal ability on spatial tasks) depends on the class. Rost (1991) also generalizes his models to polytomous item formats (see chap. 5).

Yamamoto (1987) developed a model that also defines latent classes, but the classes are structured. That is, the model distinguishes valid response patterns that fit the IRT model from random response patterns (i.e., guessing). One implication of this model is that the difficulty of hard items, which are relatively more likely to be solved by guessing than easy items, may be calibrated as too easy if the class of random guessers is included.

SUMMARY

This chapter presents a diverse array of IRT models that are appropriate for binary data. In binary data, item responses are scored for only two outcomes, success versus failure. Both unidimensional and multidimensional IRT models are available for binary data.

The unidimensional IRT models define a single trait level for each person. These models are appropriate for items that involve a single underlying trait or a combination of traits that is constant across items. The most popular unidimensional models are the logistic IRT models due to their computationally simple form. These include the one-parameter logistic model (1PL or Rasch model), the two-parameter logistic model (2PL) and the three-parameter logistic model (3PL). The models are named for the number of item parameters that are included. The item parameters, in order of successive inclusion in the models, are item difficulty, item discrimination, and guessing. Corresponding normal ogive models for the 2PL and 3PL models are also available for unidimensional data. These models are based on the cumulative normal distribution. However, the normal ogive models are currently less popular due to their computationally more complex form. The normal ogive and the logistic model are appropriate for the same type of data. The item characteristics curves of the normal ogive model are virtually indistinguishable from the logistic model under appropriate scaling of trait level.

Some special IRT models for unidimensional data were also described. The linear logistic latent trait model was developed to relate item stimulus features to item difficulty. Models have also been developed for combining speed and accuracy data, as well as for data consisting of multiple attempts for on a single item. Last, models have been developed for data with item characteristics curves that differ sharply from the logistic and normal ogive models. Nonparametric IRT models are particularly flexible; the item characteristics curves need not be strictly increasing nor have a constant form across items.

The multidimensional IRT models contain two or more parameters to represesnt each person. The models are appropriate for data in which more than one trait or quality contributes to item responses. The multidimensional models were considered in two separate categories, exploratory and confirmatory. The exploratory multidimensional IRT models specify two or more dimensions that are combined to predict the item responses. In exploratory IRT models with compensatory dimensions, persons' potentials to solve items are obtained by summing their trait levels across dimensions. Exploratory multidimensional IRT models are sometimes described as full information factor analysis. The goal is similar to factor analysis; namely, to determine the number and the nature of the factors that underlie item performance. Like factor analysis, the nature of the dimensions is interpreted by the relative pattern of discriminations across the items. However, unlike factor analysis, item response level data is modeled in IRT so that full information is extracted from the data. In contrast, factor analysis models correlations rather than response level data. Both logistic and normal ogive multidimensional IRT models are available.

The confirmatory multidimensional IRT models contain design structures to link items to hypothesized traits or processes. These models are useful when item differences have theoretical meaning. Some confirmatory IRT models are compensatory. In this case, the confirmatory IRT models are analogous to confirmatory factor analysis in which dimensions are specified to explain the pattern of relationships between the items. Several different models are available to incorporate diverse confirmatory item structures. Further, IRT models with some special design structures have been developed to measure change and learning effects.

Other confirmatory IRT models are appropriate for individual differences that have more complex effects on item solving. The multicomponent latent trait model, for example, is appropriate for binary items in which successful outcome depends on success on a series of underlying components. This model has been useful for ability items. IRT models have also been proposed for data in which qualitative distinct classes of persons exist. For example, the SALTUS model is appropriate for item types that are mastered at different developmental stages. Parameters to represent developmental stages and the impact of stages on items are included in the model. For another example, the mixed Rasch model is appropriate for data in which classes of persons differ systematically in the basis of their responses. Different knowledge structures or different strategies may produce distinct patterns of item difficulties in these classes. The mixed Rasch model estimates trait level and class membership for each person.

Research on IRT models for binary data remains an active area in psychometric methods. The scope of applicability for IRT is extended by these active developments.

5

Polytomous IRT Models

The IRT models for representing the relation between a continuous latent trait variable and a dichotomous item response presented in chapter 4 are limited in that many response formats commonly employed by psychologists cannot be scored as true versus false or right versus wrong. Numerous measurement instruments, especially in the attitude and personality assessment domains, include items with multiple ordered-response categories. Researchers employ these formats for a variety of reasons but mainly because they are more informative and reliable than dichotomously scored items. For these multiple-category types of item-response data, polytomous IRT models are needed to represent the nonlinear relation between examinee trait level and the probability of responding in a particular category.

In this chapter we present an overview of IRT models for describing polytomous item response data. Many polytomous IRT models are available, and new models are proposed yearly. We do not provide a comprehensive summary of extant models. Rather, we provide basic descriptions of the psychometric properties of six fairly well-known polytomous models. Readers interested in a wider variety of models and more technical details pertaining to item parameter estimation and fit assessment are directed to van der Linden and Hambleton (1996).

We begin by describing the homogeneous case of the graded response model (GRM; Samejima, 1969) that is an extension of the 2PL model discussed in the previous chapter. We then describe Muraki's (1992) modification of the graded response model for use with questionnaires that have a common rating scale format (e.g., all item responses scored on a five-point scale). These first two models are considered as "indirect" models because a two-step process is needed to determine the conditional probability of an examinee responding in a particular category. The remaining models to be described are considered "direct" IRT models because only a single equation is needed to describe the relationship between examinee trait level and the probability of responding in a particular category. Specifically, we cover two polytomous models that are extensions of the Rasch 1PL: the partial credit model (PCM; Masters, 1982) and the rating scale model (RSM; Andrich, 1978a; 1978b). We also describe Muraki's (1990) modification of the PCM to include an item slope parameter. Finally, we introduce a general model called the nominal response model (NRM; Bock, 1972) that is appropriate when item responses cannot necessarily be classified into ordered categories. We conclude by briefly summarizing several alternative models and with discussion of how researchers may select between competing models.

To illustrate model application, we use the responses of 350 undergraduates to the 12 items on the Neuroticism scale of the Neuroticism Extraversion Openness Five-Factor Inventory (NEO-FFI) (Costa & Mc-Crae, 1992). In Table 5.1 for each item is displayed a brief description of the item content, the observed response frequencies within each category, and the item mean score when scored on a 0 to 4 scale. The item means do not demonstrate a wide spread, however, within items the response frequencies across the categories are quite variable. In Table 5.2 is displayed a listing of the raw score means by response category and item-test

TABLE 5.1
Content of the 12 NEO–FFI Neuroticism Items,
Response Frequencies, and Item Means ($N = 350$)

		Category					
	Content	0	1	2	3	4	M
1	Is not a worrier (R)[a]	29	55	50	137	79	2.52
2	Feels inferior to others	35	120	100	72	23	1.70
3	Feels like going to pieces under stress	25	72	43	141	69	2.45
4	Rarely feels lonely, blue (R)	20	90	68	125	47	2.25
5	Feels tense and jittery	17	111	97	101	24	2.01
6	Sometimes feels worthless	72	89	52	94	43	1.85
7	Rarely feels fearful or anxious (R)	11	95	79	130	35	2.24
8	Gets angry with way treated by others	22	98	92	109	29	2.07
9	Feels discouraged, like giving up	27	128	66	95	34	1.96
10	Is seldom sad, depressed (R)	22	105	79	107	37	2.09
11	Often feels helpless, needy	56	129	68	73	24	1.66
12	Experiences shame	30	88	55	118	59	2.25

Note. 0 = strongly disagree; 1 = disagree; 2 = neutral; 3 = agree; 4 = strongly agree.
[a]All items have already been reverse coded.

TABLE 5.2
The Mean Raw Total Scores as a Function of Response Category
for the 12 NEO–FFI Neuroticism Items ($N = 350$)

Item	Mean Raw Scores					
	1	2	3	4	5	6
0	23.2	15.8	14.8	17.7	14.0	17.0
1	19.5	25.7	19.1	18.4	20.4	21.6
2	21.2	26.0	21.9	23.8	25.7	25.9
3	25.2	31.0	27.4	28.8	29.3	29.8
4	32.0	34.7	32.3	33.1	34.6	34.6
R_{ps}	.43	.61	.64	.64	.59	.70

Item	Mean Raw Scores					
	7	8	9	10	11	12
0	16.4	18.0	14.3	18.5	16.2	16.9
1	19.8	21.4	20.3	19.7	22.5	20.5
2	22.9	25.1	26.0	24.3	27.1	23.9
3	28.9	28.7	30.1	29.5	31.1	27.7
4	32.7	29.4	36.0	33.1	35.7	32.1
R_{ps}	.56	.42	.72	.58	.67	.56

Note. Item responses are scored on a 0 to 4 scale.

polyserial correlations for each item. These values demonstrate substantial differences among the NEO-FFI items in terms of their relationship with the total test score and ultimately their capacity to discriminate among examinees. In all analyses to follow, we assume that the NEO-FFI item responses form a unidimensional scale and are locally independent. In practice, these assumptions would need to be supported by empirical evidence.

THE GRADED-RESPONSE MODEL

The graded-response model (GRM; Samejima, 1969; 1996) is appropriate to use when item responses can be characterized as ordered categorical responses such as exist in Likert rating scales. The GRM is a generalization of the 2PL model described in chapter 4 and falls under the "difference model" rubric (Thissen & Steinberg, 1986). Difference models can be considered as "indirect" IRT models because computing the conditional probability for an examinee responding in a particular category requires a two-step process. To fit the GRM within a measure the items need not have the same number of response categories; no complications arise in item parameter estimation or the subsequent parameter interpretation as a result of a measure having items with different response formats. This is not true for the rating scale model to be described in a later section.

In the GRM, each scale item (i) is described by one item slope parameter (α_i) and $j = 1 \ldots m_i$ between category "threshold" parameters (β_{ij}). We denote $m_i + 1 = K_i$ to be equal to the number of item response categories within an item. There are two stages to computing the category response probabilities in the GRM. To understand these stages, consider a test item with $K = 5$ response options where examinees receive item scores of $x = 0$ $\ldots 4$. With five response options, there are $m_i = 4$ thresholds ($j = 1 \ldots 4$) between the response options as shown in the drawing below. One goal of fitting the GRM is to determine the location of these thresholds on the latent trait continuum.

Question: *I enjoy attending large noisy fraternity parties?*

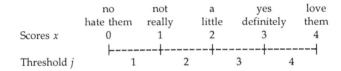

	no hate them	not really	a little	yes definitely	love them
Scores x	0	1	2	3	4
Threshold j	1	2	3	4	

The first step in estimating response probabilities in the GRM involves the computation of m_i curves for each item of the form given in Eq. 5.1, which is simply the 2PL function described in chapter 4. Each curve shown in Eq. 5.1 represents the probability of an examinee's raw item response (x) falling in or above a given category threshold ($j = 1 \ldots m_i$) conditional on trait level (θ) (for convenience we are dropping the subscript s after θ).

$$P_{ix}^{*}(\theta) = \frac{\exp[\alpha_i(\theta - \beta_{ij})]}{1 + \exp[\alpha_i(\theta - \beta_{ij})]} \tag{5.1}$$

where

$x = j = 1, \ldots, m_i.$

We refer to the $P_{ix}^{*}(\theta)$ curves as "operating characteristic curves." In the GRM, one operating characteristic curve must be estimated for each between category threshold, and hence for a graded response item with five categories, four β_{ij} parameters are estimated and one common item slope (α_i) parameter. The β_{ij} parameters have a simple interpretation; namely, their value represents the trait level necessary to respond above threshold

j with .50 probability. Essentially, what occurs in the GRM is that the item is treated as a series of $m_i = K - 1$ dichotomies (i.e., 0 vs. 1, 2, 3, 4; 0, 1 vs. 2, 3, 4; 0, 1, 2 vs. 3, 4; 0, 1, 2, 3, vs. 4) and 2PL models are estimated for each dichotomy with the constraint that the slopes of the operating characteristic curves are equal within an item. Once these 2PL operating characteristic curves are estimated (i.e., the $P_{ix}^{*}(\theta)$ are estimated), computing the actual category response probabilities for $x = 0 \ldots 4$ is done by subtraction as shown in Eq. 5.2:

$$P_{ix}(\theta) = P_{ix}^{*}(\theta) - P_{i(x+1)}^{*}(\theta) \tag{5.2}$$

By definition, the probability of responding in or above the lowest category is $P_{i0}^{*}(\theta) = 1.0$, and the probability of responding above the highest category is $P_{i5}^{*}(\theta) = 0.0$. Keeping with the present example, the probability of responding in each of the five categories is as follows:

$$P_{i0}(\theta) = 1.0 - P_{i1}^{*}(\theta)$$
$$P_{i1}(\theta) = P_{i1}^{*}(\theta) - P_{i2}^{*}(\theta)$$
$$P_{i2}(\theta) = P_{i2}^{*}(\theta) - P_{i3}^{*}(\theta)$$
$$P_{i3}(\theta) = P_{i3}^{*}(\theta) - P_{i4}^{*}(\theta)$$
$$P_{i4}(\theta) = P_{i4}^{*}(\theta) - 0$$

We call these curves *category response curves* (CRCs), and they represent the probability of an examinee responding in a particular category conditional on trait level. For illustrative purposes, in Fig. 5.1 is shown the four operating characteristic curves, $P_{ix}^{*}(\theta)$, for a graded response item with five categories and $\alpha_i = 1.5$, $\beta_{i1} = -1.5$, $\beta_{i2} = -0.5$, $\beta_{i3} = 0.5$, and $\beta_{i4} = 1.5$. From this figure, it is evident that the between category threshold parameters represent the point along the latent trait scale at which examinees have a .50 probability of responding above a category threshold. Equivalently, the β_{ij} parameters represent the point on the latent trait scale where examinees have a .50 probability of responding in or above category $j = x$. In Fig. 5.2 are shown the category response curves for this item. These curves represent the probability of responding in each category ($x = 0 \ldots 4$) conditional on examinee trait level. Observe that for any fixed value of θ, the sum of the response probabilities is equal to 1.0.

The item parameters in the GRM dictate the shape and location of the category response curves and operating characteristic curves. In general, the higher the slope parameters (α_i), the steeper the operating characteristic curves (Fig. 5.1) and the more narrow and peaked the category response curves (Fig. 5.2) indicating that the response categories differentiate among trait levels fairly well. The between category threshold parameters (β_{ij}) determine the location of the operating characteristic

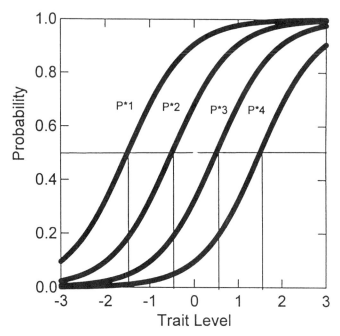

FIG. 5.1. Operating characteristic curves for five-category example item under the graded response model.

curves (Fig. 5.1) and where each of the category response curves (Fig. 5.2) for the middle response options peaks. Specifically, the category response curves peak in the middle of two adjacent threshold parameters. Other examples of item parameter estimates for the GRM based on real data can be found in Koch (1983), Reise, Widaman, & Pugh (1993), and Steinberg & Thissen (1995).

In Table 5.3 are shown the estimated item parameters for the 12 NEO-FFI neuroticism items using the program MULTILOG (Thissen, 1991). The between category threshold parameters appear to be fairly well spread out over the trait range. For some items the first and last category threshold parameters are not estimated well (e.g., Items 1 and 8). This occurs because few examinees select the extreme options for this item as shown in Table 5.1 and these items are not highly related to the latent trait. Notice that within each item, the between category threshold parameters are ordered. This must occur in the GRM. As demonstrated shortly, however, the property of ordered threshold parameters is not a requirement in the partial credit or generalized partial credit models.

Item 9 ("feels discouraged, like giving up") and Item 6 ("sometimes feels worthless") have the largest slope parameters while Item 8 ("gets angry with way others treat them") and Item 1 ("is not a worrier") have the

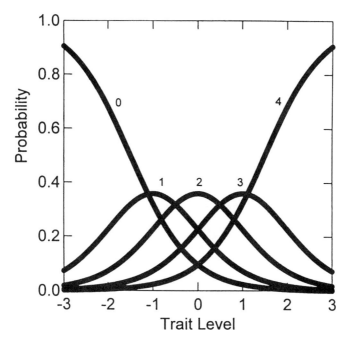

FIG. 5.2   Category response curves for five-category example item under the graded response model.

TABLE 5.3
Estimated Item Parameters for the Graded Response Model and the
Observed Minus Expected Proportion of Responses within Each Category

	α (SE)	β1 (SE)	β2 (SE)	β3 (SE)	β4 (SE)
1	0.70 (0.13)	−3.80 (0.84)	−1.93 (0.43)	−0.87 (0.28)	1.88 (0.39)
2	1.42 (0.15)	−2.07 (0.25)	−0.22 (0.12)	0.93 (0.15)	2.42 (0.26)
3	1.43 (0.15)	−2.37 (0.28)	−0.93 (0.14)	−0.39 (0.13)	1.34 (0.17)
4	1.31 (0.15)	−2.72 (0.36)	−0.81 (0.15)	0.04 (0.13)	1.85 (0.24)
5	1.14 (0.14)	−3.14 (0.42)	−0.60 (0.16)	0.64 (0.15)	2.72 (0.39)
6	1.84 (0.19)	−1.15 (0.14)	−0.15 (0.10)	0.37 (0.10)	1.60 (0.18)
7	1.06 (0.13)	−3.75 (0.57)	−0.99 (0.20)	0.11 (0.16)	2.47 (0.37)
8	0.65 (0.12)	−4.43 (0.90)	−1.08 (0.31)	0.75 (0.28)	3.96 (0.79)
9	2.09 (0.20)	−1.93 (0.18)	−0.20 (0.09)	0.42 (0.09)	1.70 (0.17)
10	1.18 (0.14)	−2.81 (0.39)	−0.64 (0.16)	0.37 (0.15)	2.24 (0.32)
11	1.69 (0.18)	−1.46 (0.17)	0.08 (0.10)	0.81 (0.12)	2.13 (0.23)
12	1.15 (0.14)	−2.52 (0.35)	−0.76 (0.16)	−0.04 (0.14)	1.71 (0.24)

Note.   0 = strongly disagree; 1 = disagree; 2 = neutral; 3 = agree; 4 = strongly agree.

smallest slope parameters. As will be explained in more detail shortly, in polytomous IRT models these values should not be interpreted directly as item discriminations. To directly assess the amount of discrimination these items provide a researcher needs to compute item information curves (IICs), as detailed in chapter 7.

As to be described in chapter 9, the quality of a particular model application may be examined in many ways. In this regard, a useful feature of MULTILOG is that for each item the program provides both the observed proportion of responses in each category and model predicted values (i.e., predicted by the item parameters and the estimated latent trait distribution). The difference in these values indicate how well the model predicts the actual item responses. In the present case, the estimated model parameters do an outstanding job in predicting the observed response proportions — no residual is greater than .01, and most are zero. However, these residual values would be expected to increase when the model is applied in a new sample of examinees not included in the calibration. Also, one fit index is seldom satisfactory in judging the complex issue of model-fit in IRT, and in practice, several approaches should be used.

THE MODIFIED GRADED RESPONSE MODEL

Muraki (1990) developed a modification of the GRM that facilitates the use of this model in the analysis of questionnaires with rating-scale type response formats (e.g., an attitude questionnaire where all the items have the same number of response categories). Herein we refer to this model as the "modified" graded response model (M-GRM). Note that Muraki and others refer to this model as a "rating scale model." We will not use this nomenclature because we believe that it might confuse readers into thinking that the M-GRM is equivalent to the Andrich rating scale model to be described shortly. In fact, the M-GRM is a restricted case of Samejima's (1969) GRM described in the previous section. Like the GRM, the M-GRM allows the item-slope parameters to vary across items and is indirect (i.e., computing response probabilities requires a two-step process). However, in the M-GRM the between category threshold parameters (β_{ij}) of the GRM are partitioned into two terms, namely, a location parameter (b_i) for each item, and a set of category threshold parameters (c_j) for the entire scale. That is, $\beta_{ij} = b_i - c_j$.

The operating characteristic curves for the M-GRM model can be written as:

$$P_{ix}^{*}(\theta) = \frac{\exp[\alpha_i(\theta - (b_i - c_j))]}{1 + \exp[\alpha_i(\theta - (b_i - c_j))]} \qquad (5.3)$$

or equivalently,

$$P_{ix}^*(\theta) = \frac{\exp[\alpha_i(\theta - b_i + c_j)}{1 + \exp[\alpha_i(\theta - b_i + c_j)}$$ (5.4)

and therefore the probability of responding in a particular category is:

$$P_{ix}(\theta) = P_{ix}^* - P_{i(x+1)}^*$$ (5.5)

where, just as with the GRM,

$$P_{i(x=0)}^*(\theta) = 1.0 \qquad \text{and} \qquad P_{i(x=m+1)}^*(\theta) = 0.0$$

Equation 5.3 shows the probability of responding in a given category ($x = 1, \ldots, m_i$) or higher and is analogous to Eq. 5.1. The slope parameter in the M-GRM is analogous to that in the GRM; it indicates how quickly the expected item scores change as a function of trait level. The difference between the GRM and M-GRM is that in the GRM one set of category threshold parameters (β_{ij}) is estimated for each scale item, whereas in the M-GRM one set of category threshold parameters (c_j) is estimated for the entire scale, and one location parameter (b_i) is estimated for each item. As can be seen from Eq. 5.3 the item location parameter serves to move the category threshold parameters within an item up and down the trait continuum. These location parameters thus indicate the "difficulty," or scale value, of a particular item. Few examinees are expected to score in the highest response categories on an item with a large positive b_i value, and conversely, few examinees are expected to score low on an item with a large negative b_i value. In sum, the M-GRM is "restricted" because the model assumes that the category boundaries are equally distant from each other across scale items, whereas in the GRM they are free to vary across items. As a consequence, the M-GRM requires fewer parameters estimates than the GRM.

The motivation for the M-GRM model was to describe responses to Likert format attitude scales (Muraki, 1990). One advantage of the M-GRM, relative to the GRM, is that it allows separation of the estimation of item location and category threshold parameters. However, note that there is an arbitrariness to the scale of the category threshold parameters (c_j). If a measurement instrument contains items with different response formats, then the GRM is much easier to implement in practice relative to the M-GRM. If the M-GRM were to be estimated for items with different numbers of response categories, then items with similar formats would have to be treated as a "block" and category and item parameters estimated within blocks. In this case, the item parameters (α_i and b_i) within a block could not be directly compared to item parameters in other blocks because of the indeterminacy of the scale for the c_j parameters. To compare item parameters across blocks, a researcher would have to place the item parameters onto a common metric using some form of scale linking. On the other hand, if a set of scale items has a common set of response options, the M-GRM may provide advantages over the GRM in that the item locations and the category threshold parameters can be estimated separately. One advantage of this is that the item location parameters (b_i) can be used to order the items according to their difficulty (or scale value). Also, the category threshold parameters (c_j) provide an estimate of the psychological distance between the scale points independent of the item parameters (Muraki, 1990). These properties combined make the M-GRM analogous to Thurstone's method of successive categories.

The neuroticism item parameters (i.e., slope and location) under the M-GRM are shown in the first two columns of Table 5.4. These estimates were derived using PARSCALE (Muraki, 1993) and all twelve items were treated as a single block. [Note that when the analysis was conducted treating each item as its own block, parameter estimates were almost exactly the same as for the GRM estimated with MULTILOG.] Thus, any differences in the parameters given in Tables 5.3 and 5.4 are due solely to the estimation of a "common" set of category thresholds in the G-RSM. On the bottom of Table 5.4 is shown the category threshold parameters (c_j) for the entire scale. Notice that these thresholds in the M-GRM add up to zero

TABLE 5.4
Estimated Item Parameters for the Modified Graded
Response Model and Item Chi–Square Fit Statistics

	Slope (SE)	Location (SE)	Item Fit	CHI	DF
1	0.93 (0.05)	−0.96 (0.10)	20.66	12	0.055
2	1.45 (0.07)	0.28 (0.06)	14.67	13	0.328
3	1.13 (0.06)	−0.73 (0.08)	21.15	12	0.048
4	1.33 (0.07)	−0.39 (0.07)	6.90	11	0.808
5	1.58 (0.08)	−0.02 (0.06)	8.37	12	0.756
6	0.98 (0.05)	0.25 (0.09)	36.90	13	0.000
7	1.51 (0.08)	−0.35 (0.06)	11.10	10	0.349
8	1.19 (0.06)	−0.09 (0.08)	18.47	13	0.140
9	1.50 (0.08)	0.06 (0.06)	21.37	13	0.060
10	1.33 (0.07)	−0.15 (0.07)	7.97	13	0.847
11	1.30 (0.07)	0.51 (0.07)	36.64	12	0.000
12	1.03 (0.05)	−0.42 (0.09)	8.28	13	0.825

M–GRM category thresholds = 2.266 (.04) 0.431 (.02) −0.451 (.02) −2.254 (.04)

Note. Taking the location (b_i) minus the category thresholds (c_j) roughly yields the β_{ij} parameters in the graded response model. They are not exactly the same because the two models make different assumptions.

and are ordered. The slope parameters in the M-GRM tend to be less variable than the slope estimates under the GRM. Even a relatively poor functioning item such as Item 1 has a slope parameter of 0.93. To conclude this section, in the last set of columns in Table 5.4 is shown the chi-square fit statistics (see chap. 9) as output from PARSCALE. These statistics indicate that 3 of the 12 items are not well represented by the estimated M-GRM item parameters ($p < .05$).

THE PARTIAL CREDIT MODEL

The partial credit model (PCM; Masters, 1982) was originally developed for analyzing test items that require multiple steps and for which it is important to assign partial credit for completing several steps in the solution process. Thus, the PCM model lends itself naturally to describing item responses to achievement tests (e.g., math problems) where partially correct answers are possible. The PCM is also perfectly appropriate for analyzing attitude or personality scale responses where subjects rate their beliefs, or respond to statements on a multi-point scale (see Masters & Wright, 1996).

In contrast to the GRM and M-GRM just described, the partial credit model is a divide-by-total (Thissen & Steinberg, 1986) or as we term it, a "direct" IRT model. This means that the probability of responding in a particular category will be written directly as an exponential divided by the sum of exponentials. The PCM can be considered as an extension of the 1PL model described in chapter 4, and it has all the standard Rasch model features such as separability of person and item parameters (see chap. 8 for details). Assume as before that item i is scored $x = 0, \ldots, m_i$ for an item with $K_i = m_i + 1$ response categories. For $x = j$ the category response curves for the PCM can be written as:

$$P_{ix}(\theta) = \frac{\exp\left[\sum_{j=0}^{x}(\theta - \delta_{ij})\right]}{\sum_{r=0}^{m_i}\left[\exp\sum_{j=0}^{r}(\theta - \delta_{ij})\right]} \tag{5.6}$$

where

$$\sum_{j=0}^{0}(\theta - \delta_{ij}) \equiv 0$$

The δ_{ij} ($j = 1, \ldots, m_i$) term is sometimes called the item *step difficulty* associated with a category score of j; the higher the value of a particular δ_{ij}, the more difficult a particular step is relative to other steps within an item.

A δ_{ij} term can also be directly interpreted as the point on the latent trait scale at which two consecutive category response curves intersect. For this reason, herein we refer to the δ_{ij} parameters of the PCM as *category intersections*. In the PCM all items are assumed to have equal slopes and thus this term disappears from the model. Equation 5.6 states that the probability of an examinee responding in category x on an m_i step item is a function of the difference between an examinee's trait level and a category intersection parameter. In other words, the δ_{ij} intersection parameters can be considered as step "difficulties" associated with the transition from one category to the next, and there are m_i step difficulties (intersections) for an item with $m_i + 1$ response categories.

To understand the PCM model, consider the following graphical representation of a four-category attitude-type item:

```
        0----------1----------2----------3
    not at all    a little   moderately   agree
             step 1      step 2     step 3
```

In this item, an examinee must complete three steps in order to respond in the highest category, that is, they have to decide between not at all and a little (Step 1), between a little and moderately (Step 2), and between moderately and agree (Step 3). The δ_{ij} parameters in polytomous Rasch models, such as the PCM, do not represent a point along the latent trait continuum at which an examinee has a .50 probability of responding above a category threshold, as the β_{ij} parameters do in the GRM. Rather, in the PCM the δ_{ij} parameters represent the relative difficulty of each step. Within an item some steps (category intersections) may be relatively easier or more difficult than others. Furthermore, the δ_{ij} parameters indicate where on the latent-trait continuum the category response curves intersect and hence indicate where on the latent-trait scale the response of one category becomes relatively more likely than the previous category.

To illustrate the PCM, Fig. 5.3 shows the category response curves for a three-category item (2 steps) taken from Masters (1985, p. 76). For this item, the δ_{ij} parameters are $\delta_{i1} = -0.29$ and $\delta_{i2} = 0.95$, respectively. Observe how these points represent where on the latent-trait continuum the category response curves intersect (i.e., their transitions). At these points, the completion of another step becomes relatively more likely than noncompletion given that an examinee has already completed the previous step(s). Furthermore, these category response curves can be used to compute the most likely response for examinees at various points along the trait continuum. For example, judging from Fig. 5.3 the most likely response for an examinee with a trait level of –2.0 would be to complete 0 steps (score 0), whereas the most likely response for an examinee with a trait level of 1.5 would be to complete 2 steps (Score 2). Other examples

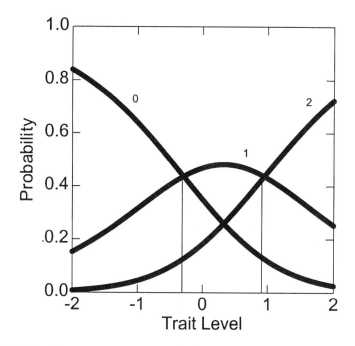

FIG. 5.3.   Category response curves for the example items under the partial credit model.

and analyses of the partial credit model may be found in Masters (1984) and Wright and Masters (1982).

A second way to describe the relationship between examinee trait level and item responses is to use the PCM item parameters to graph the expected score (sometimes called a true score) on an item for all latent trait levels. This can be done by using Eq. 5.7. Such curves represent the expected raw item score for examinees at a particular trait level. If these curves are added together over items, then the resulting curve would represent the expected raw score for examinees at a particular trait level. Use of these curves will be illustrated shortly.

$$E(X) = \sum_{x=0}^{m_i} xP_x(\theta) \qquad (5.7)$$

A particularly attractive feature of the PCM, as with any Rasch model, is that the raw scale score is a sufficient statistic for estimating examinee trait level; examinees with the same raw score on a set of items that fit the PCM are estimated to have equivalent positions on the latent trait. The drawback, of course, is that all items must be equally related to the underlying latent trait, a property sometimes hard to produce in practice. In the present case with the 12 neuroticism items, we do not expect a good fit to the PCM because of the large variation in the item slope parameters found with the GRM (Table 5.3).

In Table 5.5 are shown the estimated category intersection parameters for the 12 neuroticism items. These parameters were estimated using PARSCALE (Muraki, 1993). The first observation to be drawn is that the δ_{ij} parameters are not necessarily ordered as they were for the GRM (Table 5.3). When the intersection parameters are not ordered, this phenomena is known as a "reversal" (Dodd & Koch, 1987). To illustrate what happens when there is a reversal the CRCs for Item 3 ("feels like going to pieces under stress") is displayed in Fig. 5.4. In this item the relative order of the intersections (step difficulty) is: Step 1, Step 3, Step 2, and Step 4. In fact, what these values indicate is that going from a raw score of 0 to 1 (Step 1) or from 2 to 3 (Step 3) are relatively easy transitions for examinees to make. Notice how the PCM nicely accounts for the fact that on Item 3 category two is sel-

TABLE 5.5
Estimated Item Parameters for the Partial
Credit Model and Item-Fit Statistics

	$\delta 1$	$\delta 2$	$\delta 3$	$\delta 4$	χ^2	DF	Probability
1	−1.400	−0.279	−1,017	0.923	38.78	10	0.000
	(.23)	(.19)	(.16)	(14)			
2	−1.763	0.080	0.622	1.830	11.36	11	0.413
	(.19)	(.14)	(.15)	(.24)			
3	−1.800	0.167	−1.168	1.117	9.36	10	0.498
	(.23)	(.19)	(.17)	(.15)			
4	−2.205	−0.003	−0.507	1.471	8.82	11	0.639
	(.25)	(.16)	(.15)	(.17)			
5	−2.519	−0.063	0.170	2.055	9.90	10	0.450
	(.26)	(.14)	(.14)	(.23)			
6	−0.686	0.431	−0.354	1.376	5.74	10	0.837
	(.16)	(.17)	(.17)	(.19)			
7	−2.890	−0.105	−0.383	1.835	13.86	10	0.179
	(.32)	(.15)	(.14)	(.19)			
8	−2.143	−0.154	0.011	1.907	29.31	10	0.001
	(.24)	(.15)	(.14)	(.21)			
9	−2.132	0.505	−0.139	1.636	7.53	11	0.755
	(.21)	(.15)	(.16)	(.20)			
10	−2.206	0.065	−0.134	1.623	13.35	10	0.204
	(.24)	(.15)	(.15)	(.19)			
11	−1.281	0.600	0.264	1.823	22.29	11	0.022
	(.16)	(.15)	(.17)	(.24)			
12	−1.738	0.203	−0.666	1.166	20.02	10	0.029
	(.21)	(.17)	(.16)	(.16)			
					190.38	124	0.000

Note.   −2 log likelihood = 11,553.011.

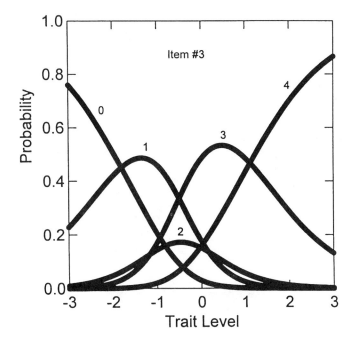

FIG. 5.4. Category response curves for Item 3 (reversal) under the partial credit model.

dom selected and responses in category three are relatively frequent (see Table 5.1).

In contrast, Fig. 5.5 shows the CRCs for Item 5 ("feels tense and jittery"). This item has ordered intersection parameters and most examinees responded in either category one, two, or three (see Table 5.1). As a rule, if the category intersection parameters are ordered within an item, then there is at least one trait level where every response option is most likely. If there is a "reversal" in intersection parameters, this guarantees that there will be at least one category that is never the most likely option conditional on trait level (Andrich, 1988).

In the last set of columns in Table 5.5 is shown the likelihood-ratio chi-square fit statistics (see chap. 9) as output from PARSCALE. These statistics indicate that 4 of the 12 items are not well represented by the estimated PCM item parameters. These chi-square statistics are additive across items and the resulting chi-square of 190.39 on 124 degrees of freedom also indicates that the overall model does not fit well. The –2 times the log-likelihood value is 11,553.011. This statistic cannot be used to assess model-fit, nevertheless it will serve a useful purpose in comparing the PCM with the generalized partial credit model described in the next section.

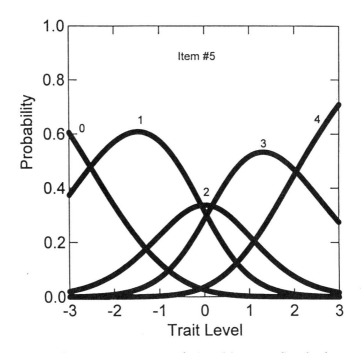

FIG. 5.5.   Category response curves for Item 5 (no reversal) under the partial credit model.

Finally, as mentioned before, Eq. 5.7 shows how an examinee's predicted item response (sometimes called an item true score) changes as a function of trait level. Because the PCM is a Rasch model, and all items have the same slope (1.0), these curves are highly similar across items. These item "true-score" curves are also additive across items, and Fig. 5.6 shows the aggregation of the 12 neuroticism true-score curves. This curve displays how the expected raw score changes as a function of trait level. Apparently, examinees who are around zero on the latent-trait variable are expected to score roughly around 24 raw score points. Inspection of such curves is one way to study the quality of a measurement instrument in terms of assessing a latent-trait variable. The curve in Fig. 5.6, which shows a nonlinear relationship between observed scores and trait levels, should be contrasted with the CTT perspective, which assumes a linear relationship.

THE GENERALIZED PARTIAL CREDIT MODEL

Muraki (1992; 1993) developed a generalization of the PCM that allows the items within a scale to differ in slope parameter. In this chapter his model will be referred to as the generalized partial credit model (G-PCM).

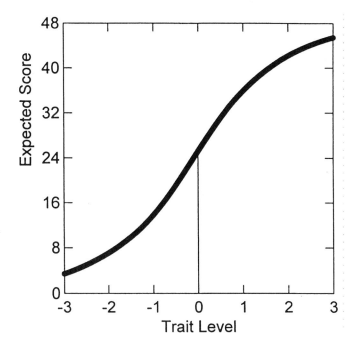

FIG. 5.6. True score curve for the neuroticism scale under the partial credit model.

Parameters for this model can be estimated using the program PARSCALE (Muraki, 1993). In Eq. 5.8 we have written the G-PCM by substituting a slope parameter into Eq. 5.6.

$$P_{ix}(\theta) = \frac{\exp \sum_{j=0}^{x} \alpha_i(\theta - \delta_{ij})}{\sum_{r=0}^{M} \left[\exp \sum_{j=0}^{r} \alpha_i(\theta - \delta_{ij}) \right]} \tag{5.8}$$

where

$$\sum_{j=0}^{0} \alpha_i(\theta - \delta_{ij}) \equiv 0$$

The category intersection parameters (δ_{ij}) in this model are interpreted in the same way as in the PCM, that is, as the intersection point of two adjacent category response curves. They are the points on the latent-trait scale where one category response becomes relatively more likely than the preceding response, given that the examinee has completed previous steps. However, the slope (α_i) parameters are not interpreted in the same way as they are in dichotomous IRT models. The reason is because in polytomous models the item discrimination depends on a combination of the slope parameter and the spread of the category thresholds (in GRM or M-GRM) or category intersections (in PCM and G-PCM). In the G-PCM the slope parameters "indicate the degree to which categorical responses vary among items as θ level changes" (Muraki, 1992, p. 162). As the slope parameter in Eq. 5.8 becomes smaller than 1.0 the CRCs flatten out relative to the PCM, while as the slope parameter becomes larger than 1.0 the CRCs tend to become more peaked relative to the PCM.

Note that in the previous and following PARSCALE analyses, we specified that the 12 NEO–FFI neuroticism items each formed their own "block" (see chap. 13 for details). Consequently, a separate set of category intersection parameters is estimated for each item. The G-PCM item slope and intersection estimates for the neuroticism items are shown in Table 5.6. First, notice that there is quite a large degree of variation among the

TABLE 5.6
Estimated Item Parameters for the Generalized
Partial Credit Model and Item-Fit Statistics

	α	$\delta 1$	$\delta 2$	$\delta 3$	$\delta 4$	χ^2	DF	$Probability$
1	0.261	−2.937	0.121	−3.857	2.328	36.29	13	0.001
	(.03)	(.87)	(.74)	(.63)	(.54)			
2	0.877	−2.130	0.070	0.755	2.197	8.71	13	0.795
	(.07)	(.22)	(.16)	(.18)	(.28)			
3	0.797	−2.295	0.197	−1.462	1.399	9.29	14	0.813
	(.06)	(.30)	(.24)	(.22)	(.19)			
4	0.735	−2.923	0.028	−0.703	1.919	3.02	13	0.998
	(.06)	(.34)	(.22)	(.20)	(.23)			
5	0.683	−3.513	−0.041	0.182	2.808	9.29	12	0.678
	(.05)	(.38)	(.20)	(.21)	(.33)			
6	1.073	−0.873	0.358	−0.226	1.547	8.71	11	0.650
	(.09)	(.15)	(.16)	(.16)	(.18)			
7	0.583	−4.493	−0.004	−0.732	2.792	16.93	11	0.109
	(.05)	(.55)	(.26)	(.24)	(.33)			
8	0.345	−4.815	0.012	−0.362	4.256	11.58	14	0.640
	(.03)	(.68)	(.42)	(.41)	(.60)			
9	1.499	−1.997	0.210	0.103	1.627	4.93	11	0.934
	(.11)	(.15)	(.10)	(.11)	(.14)			
10	0.631	−3.215	0.195	−0.292	2.299	15.07	13	0.302
	(.05)	(.37)	(.24)	(.23)	(.30)			
11	1.059	−1.440	0.551	0.397	2.039	22.12	11	0.023
	(.09)	(.16)	(.15)	(.16)	(.23)			
12	0.565	−2.628	0.534	−1.241	1.720	9.65	13	0.723
	(.05)	(.37)	(.30)	(.29)	(.28)			
						155.64	149	0.338

Note. −2 log Likelihood = 11,384.921.

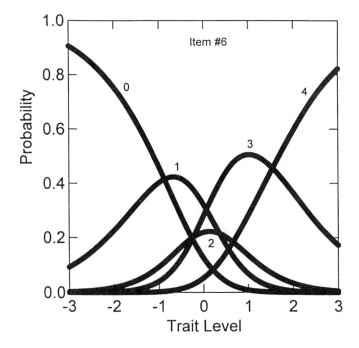

FIG. 5.7. Category response curves for Item 6 under the generalized partial credit model.

slope parameters. Generally speaking, the item ordering by slope in the G-PCM is equivalent to that observed in the GRM. To illustrate model features, we show the CRCs for three items. Figure 5.7 shows the CRCs for Item 6 ("sometimes feel worthless"). This item has a slope estimate around 1.0 and thus can be considered a baseline for comparison to other curves. Figure 5.8 displays the CRCs for Item 5 ("feels tense and jittery"), which has a relatively low slope value. Notice again how these curves do a great job of capturing the fact that most of the responses to this item occur in categories one and three. Finally, to illustrate an item with a large slope in Figure 5.9 is shown the CRCs for Item 9 ("feels discouraged, like giving up"). Observe how peaked the curves are relative to Item 5.

To conclude this section, the last set of columns in Table 5.6 shows the chi-square fit statistics output from PARSCALE. In contrast to the results with the PCM (Table 5.5), these statistics indicate a pretty good fit in that only 2 of the 12 items are not well represented by the estimated G-PCM item parameters. These chi-square statistics are additive across items and the resulting chi-square of 155.64 on 149 degrees of freedom ($p = .33$) indicates that the overall fit is adequate. The -2 times log-likelihood value is 11,553.011. Finally, the change in chi-square in going from the PCM to the

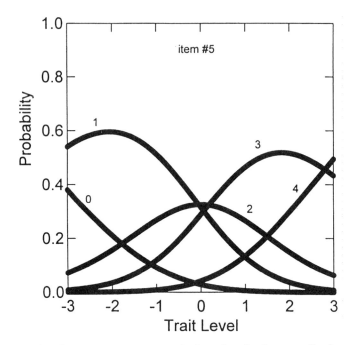

FIG. 5.8.   Category response curves for Item 5 under the generalized partial credit model.

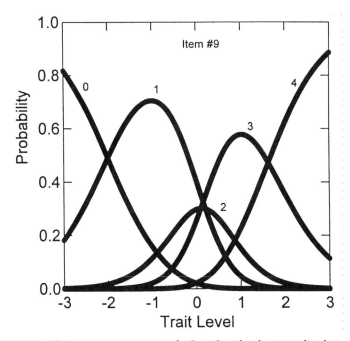

FIG. 5.9.   Category response curves for Item 9 under the generalized partial credit model.

G-PCM is thus 168.08 on 12 degrees of freedom ($p < .001$), which means that the G-PCM is a significant improvement over the PCM.

RATING SCALE MODEL

Before describing the model in this section, it is important to note that the literature on the "rating scale model" can be a little confusing because there are several versions of this model that vary in complexity and are formulated in different ways by different authors (see Andersen, 1995, p. 273). Thus, what is presented in this section is just one way of conceptualizing and writing a rating scale model. With this in mind, although the rating scale model (RSM; Andrich, 1978a; 1978b) can be derived from the PCM (Masters & Wright, 1984) there is a crucial distinction. For items with the same response format, in the RSM each item is described by a single scale location parameter, λ_i, which reflects the relative easiness or difficulty of the particular item. Furthermore each of the $J = K - 1$ category thresholds, taken over all items in the measure, is described by a category intersection parameter (δ_j). In other words, response categories are assigned intersection parameters that are considered equal across items, and an item's location is described by only a single λ_i parameter (Dodd, 1990). As with the PCM described earlier, the rating scale model assumes all items to be equally discriminating, and the raw scale score is a sufficient statistic for estimating examinee trait level.

The PCM and RSM differ in that the PCM makes no assumptions about the relative difficulties of the steps (intersections) within any item. That is, the spread of the category intersection parameters can differ across different items. In contrast, with a rating scale item format where the anchors are the same across items, it is easy to assume that the relative difficulties of the steps within items should vary little. Thus in the RSM, a common set of δ_j parameters are estimated. To make this more concrete, with a set of math items that require multiple steps for completion, it makes sense that within and between items, some steps will be relatively easy while others are more difficult. However, when working with a rating scale attitude measure with common anchors, such as 1 = disagree, 2 = modestly agree, and 3 = agree completely, the relative difficulties of the steps within each item would not be expected to change much across items.

In the RSM model, the step difficulties (intersections) of the PCM (Eq. 5.6) are decomposed into two components, namely, λ_i and δ_j, where $\delta_{ij} = (\lambda_i + \delta_j)$. The λ_i is the location of the item on the latent scale, and the δ_j are the category intersection parameters. Dodd (1990) writes the RSM as Eq. 5.9.

$$P_x(\theta) = \frac{\exp\left\{\sum_{j=0}^{x}\left[\theta - (\lambda_i + \delta_i)\right]\right\}}{\sum_{x=0}^{M}\exp\left\{\sum_{j=0}^{x}\left[\theta - (\lambda_i + \delta_j)\right]\right\}} \qquad (5.9)$$

where

$$\sum_{j=0}^{0}\left[\theta - (\lambda_i + \delta_j)\right] = 0$$

Alternatively, some authors (Dodd, DeAyala, & Koch, 1995; Rost, 1988) express the RSM in a slightly different, but equivalent, form:

$$P_x(\theta) = \frac{\exp\left[\psi_x + x(\theta - \lambda_i)\right]}{\sum_{x=0}^{M}\exp\left[\psi_x + x(\theta - \lambda_i)\right]} \qquad (5.10)$$

where

$$\psi_x = -\sum_{j=0}^{x}\delta_j$$
$$\psi_0 = \psi_m = 0$$

The RSM assumes that a fixed set of rating points are used for the entire item set. If the items within a scale have different formats, the rating scale model is not an appropriate choice. With a program like RUMM (Sheridan, Andrich, & Luo, 1996) however, it would be possible to estimate the parameters of groups of items with similar numbers of response categories within a single block. The measure may consists of two or three blocks of RSM items with different formats. The problem in such an analysis lies in trying to equate the item parameters across the different blocks. This is a problem for comparing items across blocks and not a problem for predicting responses, however.

In the first column of Table 5.7 are shown the estimated RSM location parameters (λ_i) for the example data set as estimated by RUMM (Sheridan, Andrich, & Luo, 1996). The location parameters in Table 5.7 indicate the "difficulty" of the item, and notice that the ordering corresponds perfectly with the item means shown in Table 5.1. That is, Item 2 has the small mean indicating that few examinees score high and Item 1 has a large mean indicating that few examinees score low on this item. Observe in Table 5.7 that Item 2 has a high location ($\lambda_2 = 0.30$), and Item 1 has a low location ($\lambda_2 = -0.44$).

On the bottom of Table 5.7 are shown the four estimated category intersection (δ_j) parameters. These values are constant across all 12 items and sum to 0. This latter feature is a scale identification constraint imposed by the program. To illustrate the effect of the location parameter, in Figs. 5.10 and 5.11 is shown the CRCs for Items 1 and 2, respectively. Notice how the

TABLE 5.7
Estimated Item Parameters for the Rating Scale Model and
Item–Fit Chi–Square Statistics Output from RUMM

	Location (SE)		Item Fit	CHI	DF	Probability
1	-0.44	(0.05)	7.492	9.199	1	0.031
2	0.30	(0.05)	-1.943	2.492	1	0.648
3	-0.39	(0.05)	1.008	4.470	1	0.329
4	-0.16	(0.05)	-0.934	0.960	1	0.913
5	0.08	(0.05)	-2.356	5.728	1	0.200
6	0.27	(0.05)	1.631	28.309	1	0.000
7	-0.14	(0.05)	-0.695	6.234	1	0.160
8	0.21	(0.05)	3.838	20.313	1	0.000
9	0.15	(0.05)	-3.502	7.524	1	0.087
10	0.00	(0.05)	0.010	1.318	1	0.855
11	0.47	(0.05)	-1.107	11.022	1	0.000
12	-0.17	(0.05)	3.800	1.392	1	0.841

Note. RSM intersections = -1.600, 0.224, -0.184, and 1.560.

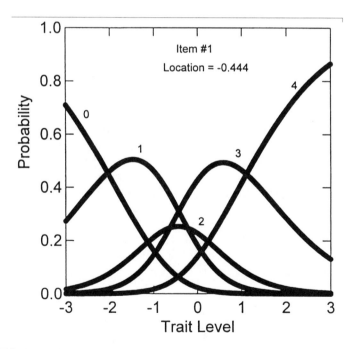

FIG. 5.10. Category response curves for Item 1 under the rating scale model.

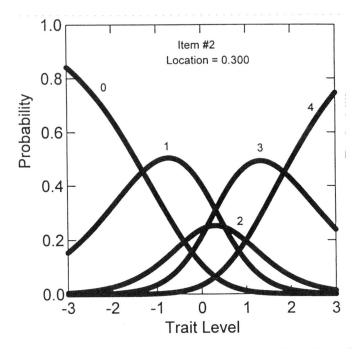

FIG. 5.11. Category response curves for Item 2 under the rating scale model.

general shape is the same but the curves for Item 2 are shifted to the right relative to Item 1. The location parameter represents an average difficulty for a particular item relative to the category intersections.

Finally, for each item and person the RUMM program computes an item-fit statistic. In the first set of columns in Table 5.6 are shown the item-fit values, their 1 degree of freedom chi-square values and the associated probabilities for the RSM. These values indicate that around half (5) of the 12 items do not fit this model ($p < .05$). We might have suspected that the RSM would yield a rather poor fit at the item level because our previous analysis with the G-PCM and GRM showed us that the items differ in slope. Simply stated, the NEO-FFI items probably do not form a rating scale as assumed by the RSM.

SCORE COMPARISONS

At this point, we thought it interesting to step back and examine what the examinee's latent trait scores look like under the various models described thus far. This process was facilitated because each of the programs used (i.e., RUMM and PARSCALE) provides for examinee scoring. All latent-trait scores reported here are maximum likelihood estimates with the exception of the M-GRM in which we used EAP scoring and the GRM in which we used MAP scoring. These latter two scoring methods differ from ML primarily in their use of priors (see chap. 7 for details). There are six scores to be compared in these analyses: the raw scale score (RAW), and the latent trait estimates under the GRM, PCM, G-PCM, RSM, and M-GRM.

In Table 5.8 are shown the descriptive statistics for each of the scores estimated in the present study. These values differ across IRT models indicating the differing metrics that are used. Importantly, all latent trait scores are highly correlated (i.e., $r > .97$), and in turn, each is highly correlated with raw scores. In fact, the lowest correlation was $r = .97$ between raw scores and the G-PCM. These results are visually summarized by means of a scatterplot matrix (SPLOM) in Fig. 5.12. Of particular note here is that in the PCM and RSM the trait level estimates are a non-linear transformation of the raw scores (i.e., raw score is a sufficient statistic for trait level). This property does not hold true in any of the other models that contain a slope parameter.

The pattern of results shown in Fig. 5.12 should not be taken to mean that IRT modeling is therefore no better than simply computing a raw scale score. For a relative ordering of examinees, this may be true. However, the IRT models are optimal scalings of examinee trait levels and as described throughout this book, the IRT model parameters enable numerous psychometric advantages. For example, linking (equating) test scales, exploring differential item functioning, computing person-fit statistics, computerized adaptive testing, and allowing the standard error to change as a function of trait level are just some of psychometric advantages to the IRT modeling.

THE NOMINAL RESPONSE MODEL

Bock (1972) proposed a general divide-by-total or direct IRT model that can be used to characterize item responses when responses are not necessarily ordered along the trait continuum. In fact, all the divide-by-total or direct models described above are special cases of the nominal response model (Thissen & Steinberg, 1986). The original motivation for developing

TABLE 5.8
Descriptive Statistics for Raw Scores and Latent Trait Scores

	RAW	GRM	PCM	G-PCM	RSM	M-GRM
Mean	25.13	0.00	0.00	−0.01	0.11	0.00
SD	8.30	0.95	0.80	1.13	0.76	0.93
Skew	−0.13	−0.11	−0.16	−0.28	−0.15	−0.47
Kurtosis	−0.59	−0.07	0.31	0.88	0.27	−0.03

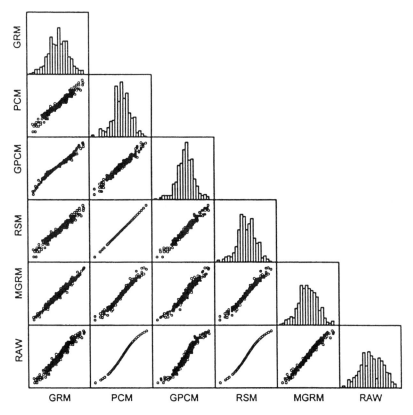

FIG. 5.12. SPLOM of trait level estimates under the various polytomous models.

the NRM was to allow the distracters in multiple-choice tests to be characterized by trace lines. Nevertheless, the NRM may be used for any items
with multiple response options, which includes applications in personality and attitude assessment (see Thissen, 1993).

In the NRM, the probability of an examinee responding in category x ($x = 0 \ldots m_i$) can be written as

$$P_{ix}(\theta) = \frac{\exp(\alpha_{ix}\theta + c_{ix})}{\displaystyle\sum_{x=0}^{m} \exp(\alpha_{ix}\theta + c_{ix})} \qquad (5.11)$$

To identify the model (i.e., to estimate parameters), the constraint must
be set that $\Sigma\,\alpha_{ix} = \Sigma\,c_{ix} = 0$, or in some cases, that the parameters for the lowest response category $\alpha_{i1} = c_{i1} = 0$. In this model, one α_{ix} and c_{ix} parameter

must be estimated for each of the $m_i + 1$ response categories within an item. The α_{ix} are related to the slope of the trace lines (i.e., the discrimination) for category x, and the c_{ix} is an intercept parameter for category x.

To illustrate, we borrow from an example given in Thissen (1993, p. 91). In this example, the items measure the presence or risk for bulimia. Most items within the scale contained sensible multiple ordered response categories. However, there was an item that had no obvious ordering of categories. Specifically, the item asked examinees to respond to the stem, "I prefer to eat:" with option choices of: (a) at home alone, (b) at home with others, (c) in a public restaurant, (d) at a friend's house, and (e) doesn't matter.

Thissen estimated the parameters of the nominal response model for this item and found $\alpha_a = -0.39$, $\alpha_b = -0.39$, $\alpha_c = 0.24$, $\alpha_d = -0.39$ $\alpha_e = 0.93$, and $c_a = 2.02$, $c_b = -1.49$, $c_c = -0.26$, $c_d = 0.57$, and $c_e = -0.83$. Figure 5.13 displays the response probabilities for this item. As evident in this figure, it is only response option (a), "at home alone," that is associated with increased risk for bulimia. Other examples of application of the nominal response model to psychological data may be found in Bock (1972) and in Thissen and Steinberg (1988).

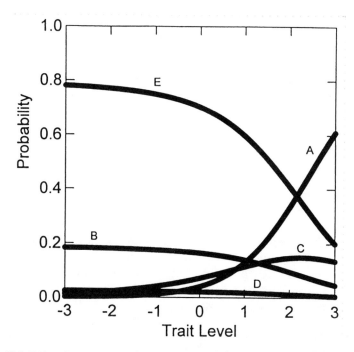

FIG. 5.13. Category response curves for the example under the nominal response model.

CONTINUOUS RESPONSE MODELS

Very rarely, researchers in the social sciences have made use of continuous response formats. For example, a researcher interested in attitudes may ask a subject to describe their views on a 1 to 100 scale, or a subject may be asked to indicate their views by marking on a line that is anchored from high to low. Furthermore, even the responses to Likert-type item formats can be viewed as approximations to a continuous scale. There is good reason for staying away from continuous self-report rating scales and multipoint Likert ratings in personality and attitude assessment; namely, they beg response bias due to the increased subjectivity of the expanded scale.

Nevertheless, as Mellenbergh (1994b) has pointed out, continuous response can be readily handled by IRT models by treating them as observed manifestations of a latent variable. In this case, factor analytic models may be used to understand item responses (see Thissen, Steinberg, Pyszczynski, & Greenberg, 1983). Working under this general framework, we note that Mellenbergh (1994b) has derived a latent-trait model for understanding continuous item responses and has demonstrated an application of the model in understanding a continuously rated adjective measure of neuroticism. Although we will not detail this model, we wish to alert readers to its existence and comment that it provides a framework for understanding IRT models and factor models as being among a variety of models falling under the umbrella of generalized linear item response models (Mellenbergh, 1994a).

MODELS NOT DESCRIBED

Due to space considerations, several potentially important models are not described in this chapter. However, we wish to mention these models so that interested readers can go to the original citations. For example, the multiple choice model (Thissen & Steinberg, 1984) may be used to characterize multiple choice test data, the successive intervals model (Rost, 1988) combines features of both the PCM and RSM, and Wilson's (1992) ordered-partitioned model, like the NRM, can handle test items where the response categories are not completely ordered. Finally, multidimensional extensions of polytomous IRT models have not been described, but see Kelderman and Rijkes (1994) for a log-linear multidimensional IRT parameterization, or Muraki and Carlson (1995) for a full-information item-factor analysis approach. Furthermore, it should be noted that several of the multidimensional models described in chapter 4 have polytomous generalizations (see original citations).

HOW MANY SUBJECTS?

Students and colleagues frequently ask how many subjects are needed to estimate IRT model parameters? There is no pat answer to this question because it depends on many factors, such as how discriminating the items are and how many item parameters are being estimated. In an attempt to resolve the number-of-subjects issue, some researchers have conducted Monte Carlo simulation studies. For example, Reise and Yu (1990) have shown that the GRM can be estimated with MULTILOG with as few as 250 examinees, but they recommend around 500. Yet simulation studies are useful only if the data matches the simulated data. An alternative approach is to recommend that a researcher have enough subjects to make the standard errors of parameter estimates reasonably small. The definition of "reasonably small," of course, depends on the researcher's measurement goals; the impact of item parameter estimates on trait level estimates is the ultimate issue for many researchers. As shown by the results here, some of the category threshold parameters were not well estimated in the GRM with 350 examinees.

There are some special considerations in estimating polytomous IRT models that researchers should note, and these are highly relevant to the number of subjects issue. First, it is highly recommended that a researcher estimate parameters based on a heterogeneous sample. Doing so should circumvent a second problem in fitting polytomous models, namely, a researcher must have item responses in each response category. If a response category has zero or few responses, a program to estimate parameters will not be able to estimate a good between category threshold or intersection. We have seen many samples where respondents do not choose a particular item category, possibly due to the quasi categorical nature of the trait. Of course, one way to circumvent this problem is to collapse across categories, or better, to rewrite the item to have fewer categories. However, see Andrich (1995) for some special considerations when collapsing categories.

MODEL COMPARISONS

Given the number of existing models for potential application, it is important to ask how a researcher should go about selecting a model to fit a real data set. Of course, one primary consideration is the type of data that a researcher is working with. Obviously, if response categories are not ordered, then the NRM is the only choice that is appropriate. If the items are suspected to have differing discriminations, as might be revealed through a preliminary factor analysis, then the GRM or one of the Muraki (1990;

1992) models is automatically more appropriate then any of the Rasch-based models such as the RSM or PCM. Also, if the measure does not use the same rating scale for each item, then the RSM is not applicable (unless blocks of items are analyzed separately).

As the reader will see in chapter 9, the science of statistical model comparison in IRT is deficit, especially when compared to structural equation models. Some researchers have used the log-likelihood of model-data fit as a vehicle for comparing different IRT models (e.g., Rost, 1988). Levine et al. (1992) presented an "ideal-observer" statistical technique that offers much promise for deciding if two models really differ in fit to real data. In applications of the ideal-observer technique to real polytomous data, Maydeu-Olivares, Drasgow, and Mead (1994) found very little difference in fit between the GRM and the Thissen and Steinberg (1986) extension of the PCM model.

If there is no readily available statistical magic wand to guide our choice of model selection, we are left to decide amongst models on the basis of more practical concerns. The first is the number of parameter estimates, models with fewer parameters are better than more parameters because, generally speaking, sample size needed for estimation will be smaller. Also, ease of scoring may be a concern. In Rasch models, like the PCM, the raw scale score is a sufficient statistic for examine trait level, assuming all examinees have received the same items. Finally, one's philosophy may dictate model use. For some researchers, it is not appropriate to demand that test items have equal discrimination, and they will use the GRM as opposed to one of the Rasch models. Others researchers may prefer to have scale difficulties such as in the RSM model. In fact, attitude researchers may find the RSM very attractive. Also, it goes without saying that models will only be fit if appropriate and usable programs are readily available.

6

The Trait Level Measurement Scale: Meaning, Interpretations, and Measurement-Scale Properties

In this chapter some intuitions about (a) the meaning of item response theory (IRT) trait levels and (b) the accomplishment of desirable measurement-scale properties by IRT models are developed. This chapter begins by considering how scale score meaning is achieved. It is shown that classical test theory and IRT are based on fundamentally different principles in establishing scale meaning. Furthermore, the numerical magnitude of IRT trait levels also depends on the type of scale unit that is selected and on how the estimation process is anchored. Then, measurement scale properties are reviewed for relationship to trait measurement. Some special relationships between IRT models and fundamental measurement properties are considered. Last, some practical implications of measurement scale properties for score comparisons and statistical inferences are considered.

THE MEANING OF TRAIT LEVEL

The trait level scores presented in various examples in the preceding chapters did not have a familiar basis for interpretation. Although they appeared to approximate z-scores in magnitude, their interpretation is different in several respects. In this section, the meaning of trait level scores is explored. IRT trait levels differ qualitatively from classical test theory (CTT) scores in the basis of comparison.

Comparisons: Standards and Numerical Basis

In measurement theory, the meaning of a measurement, including a test score, requires specifying a comparison (e.g., see Michel, 1990, p. 63). For example, a measurement of height involves comparing the length of a person to the length of a measure, such as a ruler. If the ratio of the person's length to the ruler's length is 5.7, then the measured height is 5.7 feet. Thus, a comparison has two features that must be specified: (a) the standard to which a score is compared and (b) the numerical basis of the comparison (order, difference, ratio, etc.). For height measurement, then, the standard to which a person is compared is a ruler and the numerical basis is a ratio. Item response theory differs from classical test theory in both the standard and the numerical basis of comparisons.

Classical Test Theory

In CTT, the meaning of a score results from comparing its position on a standard, namely a norm group. Comparisons between two different scores exhibit ordinal properties. That is, the position of one score is greater than the other on the norms. Furthermore, regardless of the norm group, the order relationship between the scores will hold.

The norm-referenced interpretation for score meaning can be illustrated with data from the Energetic Arousal Scale (Thayer, 1989). The 10 adjectives that were administered in a binary format ("yes" vs. "no") are listed in Table 6.1. Figure 6.1 presents the meaning of raw scores for standard scores (T-scores, with a mean of 50 and standard deviation of 10) in three different norm groups. The three norm groups were young adults, elderly adults, and adults in a manic phase of an affective disorder. For the young and elderly adult norm groups, raw scores were distributed normally. The raw score–to–standard score conversion is a simple linear relationship in this case. The young adults had a higher mean than elderly adults; hence, the standard score equivalent of any raw score is lower on the young adult norms. For the norm group of adults in manic phase, the

TABLE 6.1
Item Difficulties for Energetic Arousal Scale

Variable	p-value	Logit β_i	Odds ε_i
Energetic Arousal			
Active	.36	1.84	6.30
Energetic	.48	.90	2.45
Vigorous	.69	–.74	.48
Lively	.52	.61	1.84
Full-of-pep	.63	–.22	.80
Sleepy (–)	.73	–1.02	.36
Tired (–)	.76	–1.34	.26
Drowsy (–)	.71	–.94	.39
Wide-awake	.53	.50	1.65
Wakeful	.55	.40	1.49

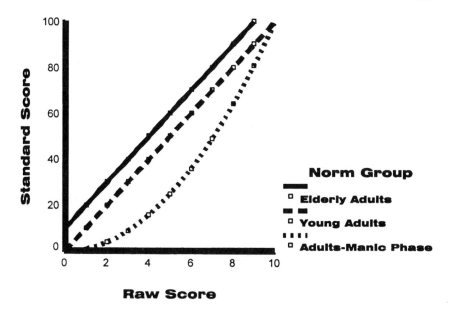

FIG. 6.1. Conversion of Energetic Arousal scores to standard scores in three norm groups.

raw score distribution is negatively skewed. Like many tests, the standard score equivalents of raw scores in this distribution were obtained by normalizing (Anastasi & Urbina, 1997). Normalized standard scores can be computed by finding the standard normal distribution score that corresponds to the observed percentile rank of a raw score. Figure 6.1 shows that normalized standard score equivalent for the manic norm group. Notice that the relationship of raw score to standard score is nonlinear, which is characteristic of normalizing. Thus, the relative distances between scores are changed by normalizing.

In summary, in CTT the standard for score comparisons is other people (i.e., score distributions). The numerical basis of the comparison is order.

Item Response Theory

In IRT, trait levels have meaning in comparison to items. Persons and items are placed on a *common scale* in IRT models. The numerical basis of the comparison is a difference or a ratio, depending on the scale units in the model. Figure 6.2 shows a common scale measurement of persons and items. In Fig. 6.2, all 10 items and 4 persons have been located on the same continuum.

In Fig. 6.2, the difference between a person's trait level and the item's difficulty has direct meaning for the probability of endorsement. For scal-

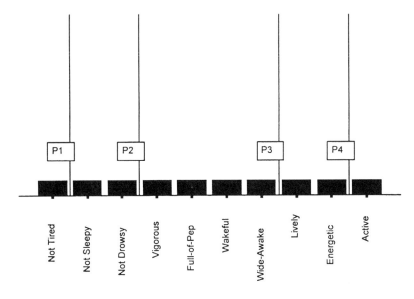

FIG. 6.2.   Person-to-item comparisons.

ing by the Rasch or 2PL model, if item difficulty equals a person's trait level, the probability of endorsing equals .50. The trait level for Person 4 is .90. The item that corresponds to this trait level is "Energetic" (i.e., β_i = .90); thus, the probability that Person 4 endorses "Energetic" is .50. A large positive difference between trait level and item difficulty means that the person is very likely to endorse the item. Thus, Person 4 is increasingly likely to endorse the easier items. The probability that Person 4 endorses "Not Drowsy" (β_i = −.94), for example, is .87.

To understand how comparing a person's performance to items yields direct score interpretations, consider an analogy to psychophysical measurement. In the classic design for measuring hearing, auditory stimuli are presented in varying intensity over multiple trials. For stimuli with high intensities, a person is very likely to respond accurately on a trial. For stimuli with low intensities, a person is much less likely to respond accurately. The *threshold level* is the *stimulus intensity* at which the person has a probability of .50 for accurate detection.

In IRT, item difficulty is analogous to stimulus intensity in psychophysical measurement. Items at a person's trait level may be interpreted as threshold values. Like psychophysical thresholds, IRT items at a person's trait level have a probability of .50 for endorsement or success. (IRT models with lower asymptotes, such as 3PL, complicate this relationship slightly). Thus, a person's trait level has meaning by explicating the items that fall at his or her threshold. In the Energetic Arousal example, Fig. 6.2 shows that Person 2's state is characterized by "Not Drowsy," for example, and Person 4's state is characterized by "Energetic."

Thus, in IRT, trait levels may be interpreted with direct reference to the items. If these items are further structured by type, substantive meaning can be given by making comparisons to the items (see chap. 11 on cognitive applications). Other interpretations of IRT trait levels, including normative ones, are also possible and will be elaborated later in this chapter.

INTERPRETING TRAIT LEVELS

The scale units for IRT trait levels differ substantially from the standard scores from CTT scores because they need not be based on a normal distribution. In this section, the various IRT scale units are reviewed, and some sample interpretations are given.

Types of Scale Units

The numerical values of IRT trait levels can differ substantially in magnitude. IRT trait levels differ in magnitude due to two major decisions in scaling: (a) the anchoring system and (b) the scale type. Thus, to interpret any particular trait level, both must be known.

Anchoring

Setting the Mean and Variance. IRT parameters may be anchored to either items or persons. Anchoring influences the mean and the standard deviation of both trait level and the item parameter estimates. In typical IRT applications, two sets of unknowns must be calibrated; both item properties and trait levels are calibrated from the same data. Because both sets are unknown, either set may provide the anchoring points; anchoring one set is sufficient to identify the model parameters.

In the simple Rasch model, the same log odds may be predicted from infinitely many combinations of trait level and item difficulty; that is, the *difference* between the two sets of parameters makes the prediction. So, for example, suppose that a log odds of 1.5 is to be predicted from the logit of the Rasch model, with a constant slope α, as follows:

$$\ln(P_{is}/1 - P_{is}) = \alpha(\theta_s - \beta_i)$$
$$1.5 = 1(3 - 1.5)$$
$$1.5 = 1(2 - .5)$$
$$1.5 = 1(1 - (-.5))$$
$$1.5 = 2(1 - .25). \tag{6.1}$$

All of these solutions yield the same prediction. Because both item properties and trait levels are known, one may choose any anchoring point that
yields the same predictions. Where is the zero point to be set? Furthermore, what is the constant value of the multiplier, α? Although the value
of α is usually 1.0 for a Rasch model, other values are possible. For more
complex models, such as the 2PL model with varying item discriminations, the mean of item discriminations, α, can be set to any value.

Anchoring the solution provides an initial referent for trait levels.
Whether a trait level is high or low with respect to the anchoring standard
may be readily determined. However, no matter how the solution is anchored, trait levels still have direct meaning for passing particular items.
That is, the probability that a person passes an item, given the item's parameters, may still be predicted from the IRT model.

If the solution is anchored to items, trait levels are most readily interpreted for item performance. For the Rasch model, the mean item difficulty is often set to zero ($\mu_\beta = 0$) and the constant item discrimination set to
one ($\alpha = 1.0$). The anchoring standard may be the whole item domain
(such that the mean difficulty in the item domain is zero), the items on a
particular test, or a subset of items selected to represent a standard. Trait
level may then be interpreted directly with reference to the anchoring set
of items. For example, if a person's trait level (logit scale) is greater than
zero, items are more likely to be passed or endorsed. Conversely, if a person's trait level is less than zero, items are more likely to be failed or not
endorsed. If a person's trait level is zero, then his or her performance is at
the average level of the items.

Like criterion-referenced scores, then, trait levels anchored on items
have readily understood meaning for item performance. However, trait
levels that are anchored to items do not have direct reference to score distributions. The mean and standard deviation are free to vary under item
anchoring. Anchoring IRT solutions to items has been particularly popular in Europe, due to greater emphasis on fundamental measurement
properties and the substantive meaning of items.

Anchoring the solution to persons, in contrast, emphasizes score distributions for trait level meaning. That is, the mean and standard deviation
of trait level are set to zero and one, respectively. Trait levels have initial
meaning, like a z-score in this case; positive values imply above-average
performance, and negative values imply below-average performance.
With person anchoring, the mean-item difficulty and the item discriminations are free to vary. Person anchoring has been popular in the United
States, where IRT has been closely associated with large-scale testing.
Also, anchoring to persons is somewhat easier for the more complex models that include several item parameters (i.e., varying slopes, intercepts,
etc.).

In a sense, however, the impact of anchoring method on score interpretations is trivial. It should be remembered that IRT conjointly scales persons and items. Thus, regardless of anchoring method, persons can be compared to specific items to find threshold levels. Furthermore, regardless of anchoring method, means and standard deviations can be calculated to describe trait level. The anchoring method influences only initial intuitions about trait level meaning.

Setting the Metric with a Multiplier. An additional source of variability in trait levels is the logistic versus normal score metric. A multiplier of 1.7 appears in the logit of the normal metric for the logistic model. Compare the following models:

Log Metric

$$\ln(P(X_{is})/(1 - P(X_{is})) = \alpha(\theta_1 - \beta_i) \tag{6.2}$$

Normal Metric

$$\ln(P(X_{is})/(1 - P(X_{is})) = 1.7\alpha(\theta_1 - \beta_i)$$

The normal metric is often used in theoretical studies because the probabilities predicted by the model may be approximated by the cumulative normal distribution. Furthermore, applications in which the parameters are anchored to a trait distribution often employ the normal metric. Trait level values in this metric are like z-scores in magnitude, particularly if they are anchored to a trait distribution with a mean and standard deviation of zero and one, respectively.

Scale Type

Three different types of scale units are popular in IRT applications: (a) logit units, (b) odds units, and (c) proportion true scores. The type of scale unit determines the type of score comparisons that can be justified in the IRT model. The logit units and odds units are linked to justifiable score comparisons. Proportion true scores, in contrast, have interesting relationships to classical test scores but have similar limitations for score comparisons. These limitations will be discussed more fully in the section on measurement-scale properties.

Values for the three scale types for a measure of Energetic Arousal are shown in Tables 6.1 and 6.2. Table 6.1 shows item difficulties on the three scale types that were obtained from a large sample of young adults. Table 6.2 shows trait levels for five persons on each scale type.

TABLE 6.2
Variations of IRT Trait Level Scores for Energetic Arousal

Person	Logit Scale θ_s	Odds Scale ξ_s	Proportion True Score		
			Test 1	Test 2	Domain
Person 1	-2.20	.11 (1to9)	.13	.06	.18
Person 2	-1.10	.33 (1to3)	.28	.14	.28
Person 3	.00	1.00 (1to1)	.50	.30	.50
Person 4	1.10	3.00 (3to1)	.71	.52	.72
Person 5	2.20	9.02 (9to1)	.87	.73	.85

Logit Scale.   The *logit* scale, the trait level expressed in the exponent form of IRT models, is the most popular type of scale unit. In this scale unit, differences between persons or items have the same meaning, regardless of overall level. Equations 6.1 and 6.2 show trait level expressed on the logit scale. Logit scale values often range between −3 and 3, as shown in Tables 6.1 and 6.2.

Odds Ratio Scale.   For the *odds* ratio scale, scores have a ratio meaning in comparison to items or persons. The odds scale is the antilog of the logit scale. Specifically,

$$\xi_s = e^{\theta_s}$$

$$\varepsilon_i = e^{\beta_i} \tag{6.3}$$

Notice in Table 6.1 that the values for items are never negative for the odds scale. For the first item, the log odds of 6.30 is obtained from the antilog of the logit scale (i.e., $\varepsilon_1 = e^{1.84}$). Table 6.2 shows the odds scale values for five persons. So, for the preceding example, Person 1 and Person 2 have odds trait levels of .11 ($\xi_1 = e^{-2.20}$) and .33 ($\xi_2 = e^{-1.10}$), respectively.

It can be shown that in this scale, the odds for solving an item is trait level divided by item difficulty, as follows:

$$P_{is}/(1 - P_{is}) = \xi_s/\varepsilon_i \tag{6.4}$$

Suppose that items were anchored to a mean difficulty of zero on the logit scale ($\mu_\beta = 0$). The odds ratio scale value that corresponds to this anchor is 1 ($e^0 = 1$). Trait level expressed in the odds ratio scale gives the odds that a person passes an item on the test. For example, if trait level is 2, then the odds that an item on the test is passed are 2 to 1. Notice in Tables 6.1

and 6.2 that odds ratios are always positive and have a wider range compared to the logit scale.

Proportion True Score.   The proportion true score is the expected proportion of items solved or endorsed based on a person's IRT trait level and the calibrated item properties. Obviously, for a particular test, the actual proportion of items solved is known. However, there are two advantages to the IRT proportion true score: (a) the IRT proportion can be less sensitive to random errors in the person's item responses, as it is based on calibrated values, and (b) expectations about performance on tests that were not administered can be anticipated. For the latter, an expected proportion of items solved can be given for any set of calibrated items.

To illustrate computation, proportion true score, P_{ts}, is simply the mean probability of item solving expected from the IRT model divided by the number of items I, as follows:

$$P_{ts} = \Sigma_i P(X_{is} = 1)/I \tag{6.5}$$

Behind the item probabilities are the trait level estimated for the person from a particular test and the calibrated item properties for the test or item bank. Proportion true scores can be calculated from any appropriate IRT model for binary data.

In Table 6.2, proportion true scores are shown for two tests and for the item domain. The expected proportion of passed or endorsed items depends on item difficulty on the test. For example, fewer endorsed items are expected for Test 2 than for Test 1 because Test 2 has more difficult items. For Person 3, for example, although the expected endorsement probability is .50 for Test 1, it is only .30 for Test 2. Also shown in Table 6.2 are the expected endorsement probabilities for the whole item domain, in which item difficulties are normally distributed with a mean β_i of zero. Notice that the differences between proportion true scores depend on the item set. Person 1 and Person 2 differ more on Test 1, the easy test, than on Test 2 or the item domain. The varying person differences across different item sets in computing proportion true score is a disadvantage. The implication is that proportion true score does not yield an interval level scale. Scale level will be elaborated more fully later in this chapter.

Sample Interpretations of IRT Trait Level

Trait levels may be interpreted by several different comparisons: (a) compared to items, (b) compared to other trait levels, and (c) compared to a particular trait level, such as a mean or a standard. Similarly, item difficulties may be compared to each other or to a standard. For these sample interpretations, the Energetic Arousal scale was calibrated by the Rasch model using the logistic metric. The item difficulty (logit scale) and the odds ratio scale, as well a the *p*-values, for the 10 items are all shown in Table 6.1.

Comparing Persons to Items.   The trait level scores given in Table 6.2 may be compared to items by predicting odds ratios or probabilities for a person. The odds may be predicted for any calibrated item in an item bank, regardless of whether the item was actually administered to the person. Figure 6.3 shows two person–characteristic curves that are reported as odds for endorsing each item. Items are ordered by difficulty. For convenience in graphing, the spacing between items is shown as equal. Person 4 has generally higher odds of endorsing any item on the scale, due to a higher trait level. However, notice that their odds differ substantially for the easy items and much less for the harder items. That is, the odds ratio scale is not linearly related to trait level if measured by θ on the logit scale.

Comparing Persons to Fixed Standards.   A person characteristic curve also can be compared to a fixed standard. The standard is defined as a target response to the items. The target could be derived from the item content or from the responses of a target group. Figure 6.4 shows a standard defined on item content; namely, indifference is defined as an odds ratio of 50/50 for endorsing or not endorsing. Person 3's characteristic curve is shown as close to indifference on many items.

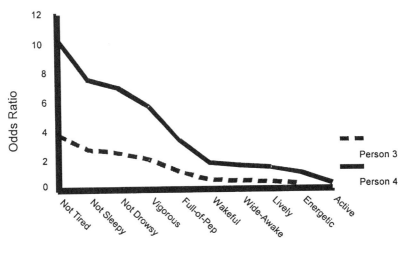

FIG. 6.3.   Comparing persons to items: odds for two persons.

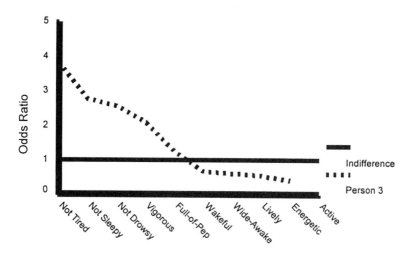

Energetic Arousal Level

FIG. 6.4. Comparing to a standard: indifference.

Comparing Persons to Both Norms and Items. As in CTT, IRT trait levels may also be compared to target population norms. Because trait levels are linked to items, a two-level chart allows the trait level distribution to be compared to the item difficulty distribution. The upper level of Fig. 6.5 shows the frequency distribution of persons in logit units. This distribution is rather rectangular. The lower level of Fig. 6.5 shows the distribution of item difficulties in logit units. Although only 10 items were administered, most items were appropriate for persons near the center of the trait level distribution. The range of item distribution is somewhat restricted because extreme difficulties were not observed.

MEASUREMENT-SCALE PROPERTIES

Test theory concerns assigning numbers to individuals to represent some psychological quality, such as a trait or behavioral disposition. The measurement-scale properties of test scores are important because a wide array of arithmetic operations are routinely applied. That is, arithmetic operations such as summing, subtracting, and squaring are involved in estimating norm distributional parameters, such as the mean and standard deviation. Moreover, in CTT, the norms are essential for estimating an individual's trait level. Trait level is reported as a standard score, which is a linear transformation of raw score. The standard scores (e.g., z score) is computed by subtracting the mean and dividing by the standard devia-

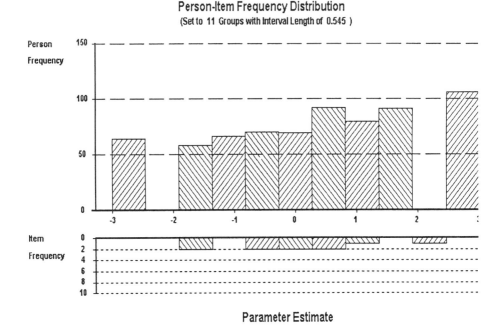

FIG. 6.5.   Person–item frequency distribution.

tion. Furthermore, individual interpretations of scores often involve comparing a person's scores on two different tests. To what extent do total scores possess the numerical properties that would justify these arithmetic operations?

Measurement theory concerns how the properties of numbers are fulfilled in quantitative variables, which includes test scores. Many test scores exhibit only limited numerical properties. For example, suppose numerical scores were assigned to individuals from a diagnosis of abnormal personality types. Abnormal personality types represent discrete categories. Although the scores would be expressed as numbers, the numbers would not represent differences in magnitudes on a psychological construct. Although persons whose scores differ numerically are diagnosed with different personality syndromes, the person with the higher score does not necessarily have any greater or lesser degree of deviancy. In contrast, physical constructs such as length and height more fully exhibit the properties of numbers. For example, rods with different numbers not only differ in length, but the rod with the greater numerical value is longer by a known ratio.

Although psychological test scores usually exhibit greater numerical properties than the scores in the typological example given earlier (i.e., they may be ordered for magnitude), they fall short of the properties exhibited by physical measures. Consequently, comparisons of psychological test scores can be limited by failure to achieve fundamental measurement properties.

In this section, measurement-scale properties are considered. First, some general measurement theory for the social sciences is presented. It is shown that fundamental scaling may be derived from ordinal relationships under certain conditions. Second, the justification of scale level for a measure is examined. In this section, the application of fundamental measurement theory to psychological traits is examined. Two IRT models, Rasch and 2PL, are considered for fulfilling the conditions for conjoint measurement. Third, the scale properties of IRT trait levels are compared to classical test scores.

Some Measurement Theory Principles

In the representational theory of measurement, which is most widely accepted in the philosophy of science (see Michell, 1990), the role of numbers is to represent. That is, numbers are assigned to objects (or persons) so that the relationship between the numbers represents the empirical relationships between the objects. So if the relationship between objects is determined by the magnitude of a property (or perhaps by some trait), then the object that possesses relatively greater magnitude of the property must have the higher numerical value. For example, if the property is weight, then the numerical values of weight must reflect the relationships (e.g., differences) between a set of objects on that property.

What properties of the numerical system may be reflected in comparisons between objects? The properties are distinctiveness, order, additivity, and ratio. Several arithmetic relationships define each of these categories.

Scale Levels

The varying properties of score comparisons are reflected in Stevens' (1946) classic distinction between four levels of measurement, which consists of nominal, ordinal, interval, and ratio measurement. Stevens (1946) distinguished between four scale levels to extend measurement theory to the social sciences. Stevens' (1946) lowest scale of measurement (nominal) even includes simple classification as measurement. Major implications of scale level are the permissible comparisons between scores and appropriate statistics to summarize scores. Both score comparisons and statistics involve arithmetic operations on scores. Which comparisons and combinations are appropriate depends on which properties of numbers are achieved by the test scores. That is, while numbers may be ordered, added, subtracted, multiplied, and so forth, these operations may be inappropriate for scores from a particular test if the appropriate scale level has not been achieved.

The distinction Stevens (1946) made between scale levels has generated considerable controversy in psychology. Some have questioned the logic of the distinctions (e.g., Rozeboom, 1966), but the issue of permissible statistics has been the most controversial aspect. The necessity of achieving the higher scale levels to apply parametric statistics has been viewed as unduly restrictive by some researchers (e.g., Lord, 1953, 1969; Davison & Sharma, 1990) and as essential by others (e.g., Townsend, 1984). More extended discussions of the numerical properties of scale types may be found in Michell (1990).

Nominal Scales.   In nominal measurement, numbers are assigned to represent the class membership of objects or persons. The specific number assigned to the category is merely a label. Membership in a class represents equivalency on some property or trait. For example, a personality typology, as mentioned earlier, represents distinct classes. To provide a measurement system, the classes should be exhaustive and mutually exclusive.

The numerical properties that define order, addition, and ratio are not achieved in nominal measurement. Thus, any transformation that preserves the distinctiveness of the classes is permissible. In Table 6.3, the scale values from Score 1 have been randomly reassigned to create Score 2. No loss of information about class membership is entailed because each class is described by a distinct number. However, Score 3 entails significant loss of information because several different classes now have the same score.

TABLE 6.3
Nominal Measurement of Personality Disorders

Type	Score 1	Score 2	Score 3
Paranoid	1	11	1
Schizoid	2	3	1
Schizotypal	3	4	1
Histrionic	4	9	2
Narcissistic	5	10	2
Antisocial	6	2	3
Borderline	7	5	3
Avoidant	8	6	3
Dependent	9	7	4
Compulsive	10	8	4
Passive-Aggressive	11	1	4

Numerical operations that involve ordering or adding numbers are not appropriate for nominal-level data. Thus, only statistics for categorical data, such as the mode (for central tendency), the contingency coefficient (for relationships), and frequency distributions are appropriate for nominal data.

Ordinal Scales. In ordinal scales, the numbers represent a rank ordering of persons on the measured property. Ordinal scale data fulfill all the properties of nominal data, such as distinctiveness, but additionally the numbers represent an ordering of persons on a trait. However, the relative differences between persons are not meaningful.

Permissible transformations must preserve both distinctness and order. A transformation that preserves both order and distinctiveness is monotonic. Scores could be squared, logged, or placed in some function that has a curvilinear relationship to the original scores.

Consider the Energetic Arousal measurements given in Table 6.4. Scale 1 (X_i) is the raw score on the test. Notice that the difference between the first and second person $(X_2 - X_1 = 2)$ equals the difference between the fourth and fifth person $(X_5 - X_4 = 2)$. Scale 2 is a linear transformation (which, of course, is monotonic) of $.5X_i + 50$. Not only are order and distinctiveness preserved, but the relative score differences are the same. The difference between the first and the second person still equals the differences between the fourth and fifth person, although now the difference is now 1 rather than 2. However, applying another monotonic transformation in Scale 3 (X_i^2) changes the relative differences between scores. Now the difference between the first and second person is much smaller than the difference between the fourth and the fifth person. The Scale 3 trans-

TABLE 6.4
Linear and Nonlinear Transformations of Energetic Arousal Scores

Person	Scale 1 (Raw Score)	Scale 2 ((.5 × Raw) + 50)	Scale 3 ((Raw)²)
1	2	51	4
2	4	52	16
3	10	55	100
4	6	53	36
5	8	54	64
6	2	51	4
7	10	55	100
8	8	54	64
9	6	53	36
Mean	6.22	53.11	47.11
Standard Deviation	3.07	1.53	37.24

formation is nonlinear; it produces a curvilinear relationship between the original scores and the transformed scores. The nonlinear transformation is permissible for ordinal data because the initial score distances were not meaningful.

Because ordering does exist among the persons on the property, statistics such as the median, rank-order correlation, and interquartile range are appropriate. Furthermore, the nominal scale statistics also remain appropriate.

Interval Scales.   In an interval scale, the distances between scores are meaningful. The only permissible transformation is linear, such that scores may be multiplied by a constant and/or have a constant added (i.e., $aX_i + b$). That is, if the Energetic Arousal scores from Scale 1 in Table 6.4 were justifiable as an interval scale, then only Scale 2 would be a permissible transformation. That is, the relative differences between persons in Scale 1 is preserved in Scale 2 but not in Scale 3. In addition to the ordinal scale properties of distinctiveness and order, interval scales also achieve additivity by fulfilling additional arithmetic properties (see Michell, 1990).

Parametric statistics are appropriate for interval scale measurements, including the mean, standard deviation and product moment correlation. If a linear transformation is applied to Scale 1, such as Scale 2, the Scale 1 mean and standard deviation may be obtained by applying the *reverse* transformation to statistics obtained from Scale 2. For the mean

$$(\text{Mean}(X_1) = [\text{Mean}(X_2) - 50] \times 2 = [(53.11 - 50) \times 2] = 6.22$$

which is the Scale 1 mean. When non-linear transformations are applied, as in Scale 3, the *reverse* transformation by taking the square root $(\text{Mean}(X_3)^{1/2} = 6.86)$ is *not* the Scale 1 mean.

Ratio Scales.   In a ratio scale, the ratios of scores are meaningful (i.e., a score of 6 represents twice as much as a score of 3 on the property). The only permissible transformation is multiplication by a constant, which perserves the score ratios. Additional arithmetic properties must be established to justify ratio comparisons among the specific values. Further explanation of these properties is given by Michell (1990).

Permissible statistics include all statistics for the lower-level scales, as well as those that involve ratio comparisons. For example, the coefficient of variation is the ratio of the mean to the standard deviation. In experimental contexts, the coefficient of variation sometimes represents a signal-to-noise ratio (i.e., the mean is the "signal" and the standard deviation is the "noise").

Justifying Scale Level

Some basic measurement theory is needed to understand how scale levels may be justified. According to the representational theory of measurement (see Narens & Luce, 1986), numbers are assigned to observations to represent empirical relationships between them. Scale level depends on which properties of numbers are exhibited by the relationships between observations. Applied to test theory, what kind of comparisons between persons are justified with a certain assignment of numbers to represent trait level?

Fundamental Interval and Ratio Scales

For physical attributes, objects are *fundamentally measurable* because the numerical properties of order and addition have a physical analogue. For example, one rod may be observed to be longer than another to establish order. Furthermore, objects may be concatenated to reflect additivity. Two rods of the same length are "added" by stacking them end to end. If their composite length equals a longer rod, then the numerical value for the length of the longer must be twice the length of the shorter rods.

However, no physical analogue of order and addition is available to justify the scale level of psychological measures. The theory of conjoint measurement (Luce & Tukey, 1964) specifies conditions that can establish the required properties of order and additivity for interval-scale measurement. Basically, conjoint measurement is obtained when an outcome variable is an additive function of two other variables, assuming that all three variables may be ordered for magnitude. Additivity may apply directly or to a monotonic transformation of the measured variables.

Conjoint measurement theory is general; even the scale level of physical variables may be justified by it. For example, conjoint measurement may be applied to Rasch's (1960) favorite example of objective measurement, the classical mechanics relationship between acceleration, force, and mass. Objects may be ordered for magnitude on each of these variables, as required by conjoint measurement theory. A multiplicative relationship holds between them, as follows:

$$\text{Acceleration} = \text{Force}/\text{Mass} \tag{6.6}$$

However, taking the logarithms of both sides of the equations, which is a monotonic transformation, leads to the simple additive relationship, as follows:

$$\log(\text{Acceleration}) = \log(\text{Force}) - \log(\text{Mass}) \tag{6.7}$$

Thus, conjoint measurement has been obtained. In fact, Force and Mass have been placed on a *common scale* by their additive impact on Acceleration.

Rasch (1960) formulated his one-parameter IRT model to achieve the same type of additivity as shown by Eq. 6.7. That is, item performance, scaled as log odds, is an additive combination of log trait level, θ_s, and log item difficulty, β_i, as follows:

$$\log(\text{Item Odds}) = \log(\text{Trait Level}) - \log(\text{Item Difficulty}) \qquad (6.8)$$

For other IRT models, such as 2PL and 3PL, additivity of trait level and item difficulty is also achieved, but the relationship is complicated by additional item parameters, such as slope and asymptotes. These points will be reviewed more thoroughly later in this chapter.

Justifying Scale Level in Item Response Theory

Measuring psychological constructs differs substantially from physical measurement, however, because measurements are inferred from persons' behavior on a set of measuring tasks. Because many different measuring tasks may be used to observe behavior, a psychological construct is a latent variable (see chap. 3). Thus, it is useful to distinguish the latent variable (i.e., the construct) from the manifest variable (i.e., observed test performance).

As latent variables, constructs are theoretical entities whose properties, including numerical properties, must be postulated. Thus, one must specify the numerical properties of scores on the latent construct. The scale level for the latent variable can be specified by the kind of score comparisons that are desired. For example, are scores to be compared as differences or as ratios? Are scores to have an invariant meaning across items? Once the properties of the latent variable are specified, psychometric procedures are applied to achieve test scores that have the desired properties.

Justifying scale properties with IRT models depends on both fitting a specific model and on the scale units that are employed. Several different cases will be considered here and related to fundamental measurement properties.

Fundamental Measurement and the Rasch Model

Successful applications of the Rasch model to the manifest data (i.e., the model fits) can be shown to fulfill several desired features. That is, the Rasch model can be derived from several desired conditions for scores, including the sufficiency of the unweighted total score (Fischer, 1995), the consistency of ordering persons and items (Roskam & Jansen, 1984), additivity (Andrich, 1988) and the principle of specific objectivity (Rasch, 1977). The condition of *specific objectivity* is perhaps the most interesting. Rasch (1977) developed the concept of specific objectivity as a general scientific principle; namely, comparisons between objects must be generalizable beyond the specific conditions under which they were observed. Such conditions include the specific experiment or the specific measuring instrument. In the context of psychological measurement, Rasch (1960, 1967) believed that achieving specific objectivity yields two types of invariant comparisons: (a) comparisons between persons are invariant over the specific items used to measure them, and (b) comparisons between items are invariant over the specific persons used to calibrate them. These comparisons are elaborated here.

Invariant-Person Comparisons. Consider first the meaning of invariant-person comparisons in the Rasch model. In this context, *invariant-person comparisons* means that the same differences are observed regardless of the items. To illustrate this point graphically, Fig. 6.6 shows the regression of log odds for an easy ($\beta_i = -1.5$) and a hard item ($\beta_i = 1.5$) on trait level. The regression lines were obtained directly by applying Eq. 3.3 to the various trait levels to each item. Scores for several persons are indicated on Fig. 6.6. It can be seen that the same performance difference between any two persons is expected on both items. For Person 1 (P1) and Person 2 (P2), for example, it can be seen that the same difference in performance, measured as log odds, is expected for both the hard and the easy item.

Another point about scale properties may also be observed from Fig. 6.6. Trait levels on the logit scale have interval scale properties if the *distances* between persons have invariant meaning for behavior, regardless of initial trait level. That is, if the difference between two pairs of persons is equal, then the same difference in log odds for responses to any item is expected. In Fig. 6.6, the trait level distance between Person 1 and Person 2 equals the distance between Person 3 (P3) and Person 4 (P4). Notice that the same difference in log odds for these two pairs are observed on both items. With Rasch-model scaling, the relative performance differentials between pairs of persons are maintained across items or whole tests regardless of difficulty.

A demonstration of invariant person comparisons also may be shown by equations, following Rasch (1960). Consider the Rasch model predictions for log odds ratio, from Equation 3.3, for the two persons with low trait levels, where $\theta_1 = -2.20$ and $\theta_2 = -1.10$ for an item with difficulty β_i, as follows:

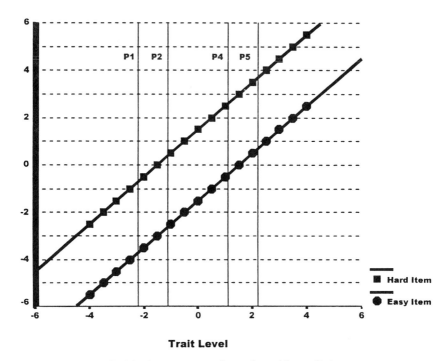

Trait Level

FIG. 6.6.   Item response theory log odds prediction.

$$\ln\{P(X_{i1})/[1 - P(X_{i1})]\} = \theta_1 - \beta_i$$
$$\ln\{P(X_{i2})/[1 - P(X_{i2})]\} = \theta_2 - \beta_i \tag{6.9}$$

Subtracting the differences between the predictions, yields the following:

$$\ln \frac{P(X_{i1})}{1 - P(X_{i1})} - \ln \frac{P(X_{i2})}{1 - P(X_{i2})} = (\theta_1 - \beta_i) - (\theta_2 - \beta_i)$$
$$= \theta_1 - \theta_2$$
$$= -2.20 - (-1.10)$$
$$= -1.10 \tag{6.10}$$

Thus, the difference in log odds for any item is simply the difference between the two trait scores, which is −1.10.

The comparison of trait levels shows how trait level has invariant meaning across items. Equation 6.10 shows that the particular item involved in the comparison is immaterial; the item difficulty β_i dropped out of the equation. That is, the same differences in performance between the two persons is expected, regardless of item difficulty.

Now, similarly for the two persons at the high end, where $\theta_4 = 1.10$ and $\theta_5 = 2.20$:

$$\ln\left\{P(X_{i4})/[1-P(X_{i4})]\right\} - \ln\left\{P(X_{i5})/[1-P(X_{i5})]\right\} = (\theta_4 - \beta_i) - (\theta_5 - \beta_i)$$
$$= \theta_4 - \theta_5$$
$$= 1.10 - 2.20$$
$$= -1.10 \qquad (6.11)$$

Thus, the difference in performance between the two persons is simply the difference between their trait levels.

Also notice that initial score level made no difference in expectations in Eq. 6.10 or 6.11. These demonstrations are one way to show that, in the logit form of the Rasch model, persons are measured on an interval scale. That is, the score differences have invariant meaning for performance, regardless of score level.

Invariant-Item Comparisons. Invariant-item comparisons may be shown in the same manner as invariant-person comparisons for the Rasch model. Invariant-item comparisons means that the differences between items do not depend on the particular persons used to compare them. A graph comparable to Fig. 6.6 could plot log odds for two different persons as a function of item difficulty level. It would be seen that the performance differences between pairs of items is the same for both persons.

Rather than present this figure, however, consider the following two equations for the log odds of two items, Item 1 and Item 2, for any subject s,

$$\ln \frac{P(X_{1s})}{1 - P(X_{1s})} = \theta_s - \beta_1$$

$$\ln \frac{P(X_{2s})}{1 - P(X_{2s})} = \theta_s - \beta_2 \qquad (6.12)$$

The difference between the log odds for Item 1 and Item 2 may be obtained by combining these equations, which are similar to Eq. 6.11 for persons, as follows:

$$\ln \frac{P(X_{1s})}{1 - P(X_{1s})} - \ln \frac{P(X_{2s})}{1 - P(X_{2s})} = (\theta_s - \beta_1) - (\theta_s - \beta_2)$$
$$= -(\beta_1 - \beta_2) \qquad (6.13)$$

Notice that trait level falls out of the comparisons, which means that the expected performance difference, at any trait level, is the difference between the item difficulties.

Item comparisons in the 2PL or 3PL model more clearly fail to meet the same quality of invariance as in the Rasch model. Unlike the Rasch model, the relative ordering of item likelihoods in the 2PL or 3PL model depends on the trait level. The item characteristic curves are not parallel and, in the trait level range of interest, may even cross. Thus, for a pair of items, their relative likelihoods may be reversed at different trait levels. Eq. 6.14 presents the item comparisons for the 2PL model, similar to the comparison for the Rasch model in Eq. 6.13. The difference in log likelihoods for two items that is expected for a person with trait level θ_s is given as follows:

$$\ln\{P(X_{1s})/[1-P(X_{1s})]\} - \ln\{P(X_{2s})/[1-P(X_{2s})]\} = \alpha_1(\theta_s - \beta_1) - \alpha_2(\theta_s - \beta_2)$$
$$= \theta_s(\alpha_1 - \alpha_2) - (\alpha_1\beta_1 - \alpha_2\beta_2) \qquad (6.14)$$

Notice that the difference does not depend only on item difficulty. First, item potential depends on item difficulty weighted by item discrimination (e.g., $\alpha_1\beta_1$). Second, the specific trait level, weighted by the differences in item discrimination, also influences the differences in log likelihoods between items. Essentially, these factors produce ICC's that cross over and hence do not produce a constant ordering of item likelihoods.

A Caveat. The term *invariant comparisons* means that the parameters have invariant meaning. This property allows trait levels to be equated across nonoverlapping item sets, as in adaptive testing where each person receives items tailored to his or her trait level. Also, it can be shown that item parameter estimates are not much influenced by the trait distribution in the calibration sample (see Whitely & Dawis, 1974 for a demonstration). However, the property of invariant comparisons does not mean that the estimates from test data will have identical properties over either items or over persons. For example, the accuracy of estimating two different trait levels from test data differs between item sets. If the item set is easy, a low trait level will be more accurately estimated than a high trait level. Similarly, if the calibration sample has relatively low trait levels, the difficulty of easy items will be more accurately estimated than hard items. Although estimates can be equated over these conditions, the standard errors are influenced. Chapters 7, 8, and 9 cover estimation and equating more fully.

Fundamental Measurement of Persons in More Complex Models

If an IRT model contains an item discrimination parameter, the relationship of performance to person differences on the trait is more complex. In the 2PL model, the meaning of trait level differences between persons depends on the item's discrimination value. Using the same example in Eq. 6.11,

$$\ln\frac{P(X_{i1})}{1-P(X_{i1})} - \ln\frac{P(X_{i2})}{1-P(X_{i2})} = \alpha_i(\theta_1 - \beta_i) - \alpha_i(\theta_2 - \beta_i)$$
$$= \alpha_i(\theta_1 - \theta_2)$$
$$= \alpha_i(-2.20 - (-1.10)) \qquad (6.15)$$

However, as for the Rasch model, trait level differences between pairs of persons has the same meaning for performance, regardless of trait level. For example, the difference in trait level between Person 1 and Person 2 equals the difference between Person 3 and Person 4 (i.e., the difference is −1.10). But, unlike the Rasch model, the expected difference in item performance is not the simple difference between trait levels. The expected difference in performance is *proportional* to their difference in trait level. The proportion for a particular item is α_i.

Fundamental Measurement and Scale Type

The preceding demonstrations showed how the logit scale of the Rasch model yielded invariant meaning for score differences. Thus, the scores can be justified as achieving equal intervals. What if invariant score *ratios* were specified for the latent variable? The logit scale trait levels have meaning as differences, not ratios.

If invariant meaning for score ratios is desired, the simple odds scale of the Rasch model has the desired properties. In this version of the Rasch model, the odds that a person passes an item is given by the ratio of trait level to item difficulty. As noted earlier, the parameters of this model are the antilogs of the logit model values ($\xi_s = \exp(\theta_s)$ and $\varepsilon_i = \exp(\beta_i)$). For two persons, the following odds of item success would be given for any item as follows:

$$\frac{P_{i1}}{(1 - P_{i1})} = \xi_1 / \varepsilon_i$$

$$\frac{P_{i2}}{(1 - P_{i2})} = \xi_2 / \varepsilon_i \qquad (6.16)$$

The ratio of the odds that Person 1 solves item i to Person 2 can be given as follows:

$$\frac{P_{i1} / (1 - P_{i1})}{P_{i2} / (1 - P_{i2})} = \frac{\xi_1 / \varepsilon_i}{\xi_2 / \varepsilon_i} = \frac{\xi_1}{\xi_2} \qquad (6.17)$$

Notice again how item difficulty cancels out of the equation. Thus, the relative odds between that any item is solved for the two persons is simply the ratio of their trait levels. Thus, the ratio of trait levels on this scaling has an invariant meaning for item performance.

Evaluating Psychological Data
for Fundamental Scalability

Of course, in psychology theories are not as explicit as the relationship between acceleration, force, and mass. For observations of psychological variables, can the possibility of additive relationships be evaluated? Luce and Tukey (1964) outline several conditions that must be obtained to support additivity. Two conditions are rather technical (solvability and the Archmidean condition) in that they specify that the comparisons are bounded by the natural number system. The third condition, double cancellation, is of greatest interest here because it defines a pattern in the data that supports additivity. Michell (1990) shows how the double cancellation condition establishes that two parameters are additively related to a third variable.

Consider the Rasch model, in log odds form, which achieves additive decomposition; that is, the third variable (log odds that a person passes an item) is an additive function of trait level, θ_s, and the item's difficulty, β_i, as follows:

$$\ln \frac{(P_{is})}{(1 - P_{is})} = \theta_s - \beta_i \tag{6.18}$$

Equation 6.18 is directly comparable to the physical example in Eq. 6.7. Thus, data that fit the Rasch model have the additivity property, which justifies interval-level measurement. However, measurement data typically is presented as probabilities rather than log odds. Could additivity be detected in the patterns of these probabilities from the condition of double cancellation?

Table 6.5 shows the probabilities calculated from the Rasch model (see Eq. 3.4) for several trait levels and item difficulties. Both items and persons are ordered by level on the trait. A first condition for conjoint meas-

TABLE 6.5
Probabilities Generated by the Rasch Model:
The Principle of Double Cancellation

Item Difficulty	Ability				
	−1.00	.00	1.00	1.25	1.50
−1.00	.50	.73	.88	.91	.92
.00	.27	.50	.73	.78	.82
.25	.22	.44	.68	.73	.78
1.00	.12	.27	.50	.56	.62

urement is single cancellation. That is, the relative order of probabilities for any two items is the *same*, regardless of the ability column. This is shown by the vertical arrow before the first two rows of Table 6.5. Also, the relative probabilities for persons is the same, regardless of which item row is selected. The horizontal arrow shows this relationship. Importantly, the double-cancellation principle implies that the third variable increases as both the other two variables increase. The diagonal arrows show the increasing probabilities everywhere on the table.

Do real test data show the double-cancellation pattern? Table 6.5 contains only the predicted probabilities from the Rasch model, not the observed probabilities in the data. Consider again the classic ability test data observed by Rasch (1960). Table 6.6 shows the probability of persons at various raw score levels for solving certain blocks of items. The diagonal arrows show the ordering required by the criterion of double cancellation. With only minor exceptions, these data generally correspond to the double-cancellation pattern.

The double-cancellation pattern is also related to the form of the item characteristics curves. Figure 6.7 is Fig. 3.1 with overlaid diagonal arrows. Double cancellation is shown by the diagonal arrows. That is, double cancellation is equivalent to stating that the ICCs do not cross.

More complex IRT models, such as 2PL, clearly do not meet the double-cancellation conditions. The 2PL model adds an item discrimination parameter in predicting the probabilities. In Table 6.7, the probabilities predicted from the 2PL model clearly violate double cancellation, as shown by the diagonal arrows. The probabilities sometimes decrease, rather than increase, on the diagonal. This is the effect of the varying item discriminations in the 2PL model. The probabilities do not increase as rapidly when items have low discriminations.

Thus, only the Rasch model fulfills the conjoint measurement conditions fully, and so it is often preferred in applications where measurement-scale

TABLE 6.6
Basic Data Matrix Revisited

Item Set	Raw Score										
	3	4	5	6	7	8	9	10	11	12	13–16
1–2	.92	.98	.98	.99	.98	.99	.99	1.00	1.00	1.00	1.00
3–4	.48	.84	.84	.86	.86	.90	.95	.96	.98	.99	1.00
5–6	.06	.11	.40	.70	.70	.79	.84	.88	.94	.95	.98
7–9	.01	.04	.12	.21	.42	.62	.73	.83	.90	.93	.99
10–11	.00	.02	.07	.07	.24	.28	.45	.59	.76	.87	.92
12–13	.01	.00	.04	.05	.09	.09	.16	.28	.39	.66	.82
14–16	.00	.00	.00	.00	.02	.01	.02	.03	.06	.09	.31

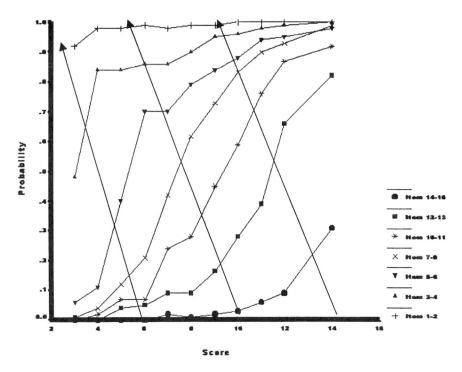

FIG. 6.7.   Figure 3.1 revisited.

properties are deemed very important. However, conjoint measurement theory is only one view of scale level. The 2PL model may be more favorably evaluated under other views of scale level. As discussed earlier, additivity is obtained in the 2PL model if a calibrator value (namely, item discrimination α_i) is added to the model. This property may be crucial in justifying scale properties under a different view of scale level.

It also should be noted that the double cancellation pattern establishes data as appropriate for interval scaling, but it does not specify the

TABLE 6.7
Probabilities Generated from the 2PL Model: Double Cancellation?

Item Difficulty	Item Discrimination	Ability				
		−1.00	.00	1.00	1.25	1.50
−1.00	1.00	.50	.73	.88	.91	.92
.00	1.50	.38	.50	.62	.65	.68
.25	.50	.13	.41	.76	.82	.87
1.00	1.00	.12	.27	.50	.56	.62

metric. The metric for the Rasch model depends on its logistic form. Several papers (e.g., Fischer, 1995; Roskam & Jansen, 1984) outline prove of the special nature of the metric from the Rasch model for interval-level scaling.

Last, the reader should be aware that comparisons between the Rasch model and the more complex IRT models is a recurring topic in the literature. Because only the Rasch model can be justified by conjoint additivity and other fundamental measurement properties, many psychometricians reject the other IRT models as not providing objective measurement. However, proponents of the more complex models often point out that the Rasch model fails to fit important psychological data.

We cannot do justice to this debate in an introductory text, nor can we resolve it in any case. However, we believe that the reader should be aware of the special features of the Rasch model. If the data are reasonably appropriate (i.e., approximately equal item discriminations), then applying the Rasch model has many advantages. But, for some psychological measures, varying item discriminations may be unavoidable. For these measures, the reader should consider the more complex models rather than to change the construct by deleting important items. For example, if a measure is based on a faceted design structure, it may be preferable to use a more complex model than to eliminate a poorly discriminating facet.

Justifying Scale Level in Classical Test Theory

In classical test theory, the difficulty level of the test influences the relative differences between pairs of scores directly. For example, if a very easy test is administered, persons with high trait levels will differ little in total score; they will pass most items. However, if a hard test is administered, performance differences at high trait levels will emerge. That is, persons at the highest levels will pass many more items than persons at somewhat lower levels. A similar relationship holds for trait levels at the low end when tests are too hard. If the items are much too hard, many persons will have very low scores. However, if easier items were administered, a range of low scores would be observed. Thus, the meaning of score differences clearly depends on the test and its item properties. CTT cannot justify interval level measurement in the same way as IRT.

It was noted in chapter 2, interval-level measurement can be justified in CTT if two conditions hold: (a) the true trait level, measured on an interval scale, is normally distributed, and (b) observed scores have a normal distribution. The first condition is a matter of assumption. If, in fact, normal distributions are not reasonably assumed for the trait, then this type of justification for interval level measurement is not appropriate. The second condition may be obtained in two ways. First, items can be selected to yield normal distributions by choosing difficulty levels that are appropriate for the norm group. That is, items with accuracies between .40 and .60 are favored in CTT (see Guilford, 1954). Second, non–normally distributed observed scores can be normalized. Observed scores are mapped to standard or z scores by percentile ranks. Normalizing changes the relative distances between scores.

Consider again the implications of different norm groups for the Energetic Arousal scale that was shown in Fig. 6.1. Consider four persons, with raw scores of 2, 3, 6, and 7, respectively. In all three norm groups, the relative order for these four persons is maintained. The raw score distances between the first and second person equal the distance between the third and fourth person. In the young adult and elderly adult norm groups, the linear conversion relationship implies that the relative distances between the four persons is also maintained. A difference of 1 raw-score unit implies 10 standard-score units. However, for the manic-phase norm group, the equal raw-score differences no longer imply equal standard-score differences. The standard-score distance between the first and second person is 5, while the distance between the third and fourth person is 13.

Figure 6.1 illustrates the complexity of justifying interval-level measurement by obtaining a target distribution of scores. The relative distances between the scores depends on the specific norm group. It might be argued that non–normally distributed norm groups should be excluded. However, for the Energetic Arousal scale, the manic norm group may be a meaningful comparison for some test uses. In fact, items could be selected to yield a normal distribution within this group; however, then the other reference groups would not be normally distributed. If each norm group were normalized, a somewhat chaotic situation results; namely, the distances between scores would depend on the norm group from which they are obtained.

In summary, CTT relies on target distributions for the latent construct. When multiple norm groups exist, it is difficult to justify scaling level on the basis of achieving a certain distribution of scores (i.e., normal distribution). Thus, justifying interval-scale levels for CTT tests is often difficult.

PRACTICAL IMPORTANCE OF SCALE LEVEL

The scale levels are ordered for how many properties of numbers are applicable for score comparisons. Parametric statistics that involve means, standard deviations, and correlations can be justified only as interval- and ratio-scale measures. Unfortunately, for many psychological measures, no justification of interval- or ratio-scale properties is available.

Applying parametric statistics to data that is of only ordinal level is another recurring topic in psychometrics and psychological statistics. To understand what this literature may hold, consider the following points. Under certain restricted conditions, relationships that are found for manifest variables will also hold for the latent variables (Davison & Sharma, 1990). Thus, spurious inferences from the manifest variable may be avoided. However, the same error levels and power may not apply. From another point of view, some researchers may be interested only in the manifest variable (i.e., scores on a particular measure for a particular population), and applying parametric statistics in this case may be justifiable (see Lord, 1969). But, more often, researchers want to generalize their results by reference to latent constructs. Thus, the relationship of the manifest variable to the latent variable is again important. Last, statisticians often point out that important assumptions of parametric statistical methods, such as normal distributions, may be met by monotonic transformations of ordinal data.

Although the implications of measurement level for statistics is often debated theoretically, practically speaking, the results from all kinds of studies are influenced by relative distances between scores. Several studies show that failing to achieve interval-level measurement influences inferential statistics. Biased comparisons may be observed if the data do not achieve interval level properties. For example, Maxwell and Delaney (1985) show how a t-test for group differences can be misleading if interval-level measurement is not achieved. That is, two groups with equal true means can differ significantly on observed means if the observed scores are not linearly related to true scores. Different-shaped distributions, coupled with inappropriate test difficulty levels, creates this effect.

Furthermore, significant interactions can be observed from raw scores in factorial ANOVA designs (Embretson, 1997) when no interaction exists in the true scores. That is, if the raw scores are only ordinally related to the true trait level, spurious interactions can occur. Similar to Maxwell and Delaney (1985), inappropriate test difficulty levels and skewed population distributions on raw scores contribute to this effect. Estimates of growth and learning curves (Embretson, 1994b), repeated measures comparisons and even regression coefficients (Embretson, 1996a) also have been shown to depend on the scale level reached for observed scores.

An implication of these results is that CTT scores and IRT trait levels, calculated on the same data, can lead to different statistical conclusions. IRT trait levels have a nonlinear relationship to proportion correct (which is a CTT score). Figure 6.8 shows the mapping of Rasch trait levels into proportion-correct scores for a test with a constant difficulty level. For convenience, like Maxwell and Delaney (1985), item difficulty was assumed to be a constant of 1.5. As expected for a nonlinear transformation, Fig. 6.8 shows that pairs of scores that are equidistant on the IRT ability

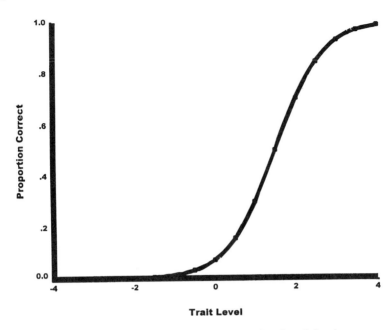

FIG. 6.8.   Mapping proportion correct to Rasch trait levels.

scale are not equal on the accuracy scale. If IRT trait levels are inter-val-level scores, then proportion correct is not.

To illustrate the impact of scale differences on means, a 3 × 2 factorial design was simulated with 300 cases per group. Each group was ran-domly sampled from a distribution with a variance of 1.0. The means var-ied according to the 3 × 2 design. Means for the control groups were −1, .0, and 1.0 for the low, moderate, and high populations, respectively. Means for the treatment groups were specified as .5 higher than the control group means. Thus, the generating values specify two main effects (population and treatment) but no interactions. The generated values were taken as the IRT trait levels. The means obtained for IRT trait level are shown for the six groups in the upper panel of Fig. 6.9. The trait level means clearly show no interactions. The proportion-correct scores for the generated sub-jects were determined from their IRT trait levels, using the correspon-dence shown in Fig. 6.8. The proportion-correct means are plotted in the lower panel of Fig. 6.9. It can be seen that the difference between treatment and control is greatest for the high-level population. Since no interaction appears on the IRT trait level scale, the interaction observed for propor-tion-correct scores is spurious. The interaction resulted from test difficulty level, which was hard. In general, the greatest differences between condi-tions will be found for the population for which the level of test difficulty is most appropriate (see Embretson, 1996a).

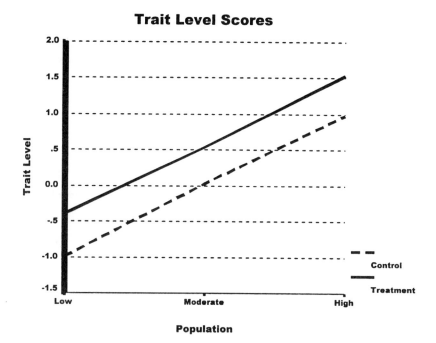

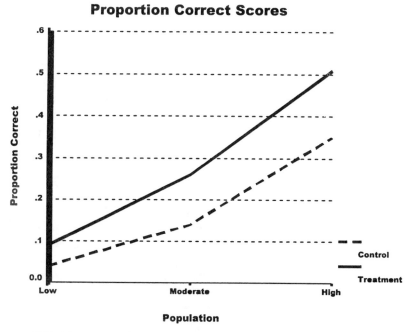

FIG. 6.9. Means of control and treatment groups for three populations.

In summary, several studies show that the fundamental statistics for the general linear model (means, standard deviations, and correlations) are all influenced by measurement scale. Thus, scale level has a practical impact on the inferences that are made from psychological data.

SUMMARY

This chapter examined the meaning, interpretations, and measurement scale properties of IRT trait levels. To illustrate the various scale levels and interpretations, a 10-item measure of Energetic Arousal is presented.

First, the meaning of IRT trait level was contrasted to CTT. Scale meaning requires specifies a standard and a numerical basis for comparison. In CTT, the trait scores are compared to a group of persons for order. It was shown that a norm group can define the score intervals and multiple norm groups can create paradoxes in justifying interval scale properties. In IRT, trait levels are compared to items for differences (in the logit metric) or ratios (in the odds metric). Persons and items can be placed on a common scale. The relative difference between the location of the person and an item has direct meaning for item response probabilities. Furthermore, the IRT trait level scale is analogous to a psychophysical threshold in meaning.

The numerical values of IRT trait levels depends on the types of scale units and on the basis for anchoring. Three different types of scale units often are reported for IRT trait levels. The logit metric is the exponential form that is typically estimated in the IRT model. The odds metric is the antilog of the logic metric, and it gives the relative odds for success or endorsement. The proportion true score metric gives the *expected* accuracy on a set of calibrated items. Anchoring also influences the magnitude of the scale. The mean and variance must be set because two sets of unknowns are estimated. Typically, during an initial calibration, the mean and variance of *persons* can be set to some specified values (e.g., 0 and 1, respectively) *or* the mean and variance of *items* can be set to some specified values (e.g., often also 0 and 1, respectively). If the anchoring is set to persons, then the item mean and variance are free to be estimated. Or, if the anchoring is set to items, then the person mean and variance are free to be estimated. Furthermore, a scaling factor also may be included in the model to determine if the IRT trait levels correspond to a logistic or a normal ogive metric.

Three types of interpretations may be given for IRT trait levels. First, IRT trait levels may interpreted as expectations for responses to all calibrated items. Person characteristics curves show these expectations. Second, IRT trait levels may be compared to a fixed standard for item responses. The standard may be represented on a graph of person characteristic curves. Third, IRT trait levels may be compared to norms. For the latter, since IRT trait level is also linked to items, a two-level distribution provides information about the item difficulty distribution and its match to the trait-level distribution.

The measurement-scale properties of IRT trait levels were examined in the context of more general measurement theory. First, the conditions for conjoint measurement (including persons and items) were explored. Second, the meaning of *scale level* was defined for nominal, ordinal, interval, and ratio scales. Third, it was shown how one IRT model (i.e., the Rasch model) fulfills basic conditions for fundamental measurement.

Last, the practical importance of scale level for measurement and statistics was explored. Studies that show the impact of using CTT-scaled data rather than IRT-scaled data on statistical inferences were reviewed. The literature suggests that inferences about simple group mean differences, standard deviations, interactions in ANOVA, and correlations can all be biased. A Monte Carlo study was presented to show the impact on scale level on the means for a 3 × 2 factorial design. It was seen that the treatment groups did not interact in the IRT trait level scale but did interact on the proportion-correct scale. This spurious interaction resulted from using a test difficulty level that was more appropriate for groups with higher scores. Thus, scale level, although theoretically much debated, can exert influence on inferences from psychological data.

7

Measuring Persons: Scoring Examinees with IRT Models

In this chapter we describe how IRT models are used to score examinees on a latent-trait variable. The discussion is limited to the scoring of dichotomous unidimensional IRT models. The topics addressed include an introduction to the variety of IRT-based scoring algorithms and their relative strengths and weaknesses. Second, by means of examples we illustrate how examinees' latent-trait scores and standard errors are affected by specific item characteristics. Finally, we discuss how IRT-based latent-trait scores are interpreted, how they may be transformed, and how they differ from traditional raw scale scores.

All IRT-based scoring strategies attempt to estimate an examinee's location on a latent-trait continuum by using an examinee's pattern of item responses in conjunction with estimated item parameters. In this chapter we describe three of these strategies for the scoring of dichotomous items: (a) maximum likelihood (ML), (b) maximum *a posteriori* (MAP), and (c) estimated *a posteriori* (EAP). Almost all of the available computer programs for IRT parameter estimation (see chap. 13) provide these scoring methods as standard options. Although we limit the discussion to the scoring of dichotomous items, most of the scoring algorithms illustrated here are readily extended to the case of polytomous response models (see chap. 5). Also, in this chapter the 1PL and 2PL models will be used as a basis for illustration. Of course, scoring depends on the particular IRT model applied, but the logic of the scoring algorithms stays constant regardless of the particular IRT model used.

Several basic working assumptions are important to keep in mind for full appreciation of this chapter. First, as with covariance structure models, the metric of the latent variable in IRT modeling is arbitrary, as noted previously. Researchers often resolve this by assuming that the latent-trait distribution is normal and then fixing the mean of the latent-trait distribution to zero and the standard deviation to 1.0 for some norming sample during item calibration. Item parameters are then estimated assuming that this latent trait distribution is true. In terms of what follows, the example item parameter and latent-trait estimates should be interpreted with this convention in mind. That is, θ_s of -1.0 means that the examinee is one standard deviation below the mean on the latent-variable metric and a β_i parameter of 1.5 would indicate a relatively difficult scale item.

We use two short example tests to illustrate several points in this chapter. The example tests consist of two 10-item tests called Test A and Test B. In Test A, items vary in difficulty but not discrimination (so it is a Rasch-type test). Test A is used to illustrate how responding to items that differ in item difficulty but not discrimination effects scores. Specifically, all items in Test A have item-discrimination parameters of $\alpha_i = 1.50$, and the difficulty parameters are symmetric with: $\beta_i =$ [-2.0, -1.5, -1.0, -0.5, 0.0, 0.0, 0.5, 1.0, 1.5, 2.0]. In Test B, items vary in item discrimination but not difficulty. Specifically, items in Test B have constant difficulty parameters of $\beta_i = 0.0$, and the discrimination parameters increase in 0.10 increments: $\alpha_i =$ [1.0, 1.1, 1.2, 1.3, 1.4, 1.5, 1.6, 1.7, 1.8 1.9]. This test illustrates the effects of endorsing items that vary in their relationship with the latent trait. Finally, we assume logistic models throughout this chapter and that $D = 1.7$ has already been absorbed into the item discrimination parameters — if you are scoring at home, don't include the $D = 1.7$ to verify the findings here.

MAXIMUM LIKELIHOOD SCORING

As its name implies, maximum-likelihood (ML) scoring is a search process (see chap. 3) based on finding the value of θ that maximizes the likelihood of an examinee's item response pattern. Another way of phrasing this is to ask, given the examinee's pattern of 0 (not endorsed) and 1 (endorsed) responses to a set of items, with assumed known item parameter values, what is the examinee's most likely position on the latent-trait continuum? One way to think of the ML estimate of trait level is to realize that for every position on the latent-trait continuum, from positive to negative infinity, a likelihood value can be computed for a particular item response pattern. It is convenient to picture a graph of a function, called the likelihood function, relating θ values on the x-axis with likelihoods of a response pattern on the y-axis. Once these likelihoods have been computed for all pos-

sible θ values, a researcher can then select the value of θ that maximizes
these likelihoods.

    More specifically, an ML estimate of trait level is determined by sum-
ming the likelihood (in log units) of each observed item response (u_{si}) conditional on the value of θ. Then, the maximum (i.e., the mode) of the likelihood function is determined using numerical methods, and this value is
taken as the θ. Before giving more details, we step back and illustrate the
notion of likelihood.

THE LIKELIHOOD FUNCTION

Consider a simple three-item test that has been calibrated under the 2PL
model shown in Equation 7.1:

$$P_i(u_{si} = 1 \mid \theta_s) = \frac{1}{\left[1 + \exp(-\alpha_i(\theta_s - \beta_i))\right]} \tag{7.1}$$

The item discrimination parameters are $\alpha_i = 1.0$, 1.5, and 2.0 for Items 1, 2,
and 3, respectively, and the corresponding item difficulties are $\beta_i = -1.5$,
0.0, and 1.5, respectively. Plugging these parameter values into the formula for the 2PL model, the three resulting item-response curves (IRCs)
are shown in Fig. 7.1a. Observe that the IRCs give the probability of en-
dorsing the item. Call this $P_i(\theta_s)$, and if we take $Q_i(\theta_s) = 1 - P_i(\theta_s)$, we then
know the probability of not endorsing an item for any trait level value.

    By definition, the IRCs provide estimates of long-run relative frequen-
cies. When a long-run relative frequency is computed before the fact, it is
called a *probability*, and when it is computed after the fact it is called a *likelihood*. With this in mind, we can use the IRCs to compute the conditional
(on θ) likelihood of any particular item response, once the item response
pattern is observed. For example, if an examinee endorses Item 1 ($u_{s1} = 1$),
then the likelihood of that occurring, conditional on θ, equals the $P_1(\theta)$
curve evaluated at θ for Item 1. If the examinee does not endorse Item 2
($u_{s2} = 0$), then the likelihood of that particular response is equal to $1 - Q_2(\theta)$
evaluated at θ, and so on.

    Yet, it is not very informative to find the conditional likelihoods of par-
ticular item responses. Rather, as stated earlier, researchers need some
method to compute the likelihood for an item response pattern. It is here
that the assumption of local-item independence, which is central to IRT
modeling, comes into play. As is well known, the probability of independent events is found by multiplying the probabilities of the individual
events. In the current situation, the probabilities of the events are locally
independent. Although item responses are correlated across items, this
correlation is due to the fact that examinees are heterogeneous on the la-

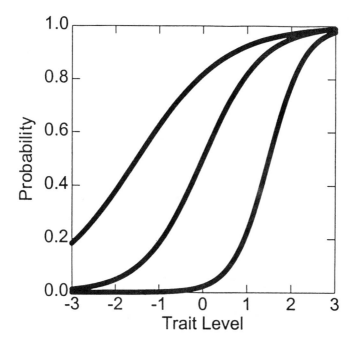

FIG. 7.1A.   Item response curves for the three example items.

tent trait. Conditional on each trait level, however, responses are independent. Stated another way, controlling for the latent trait variable, responses are independent and uncorrelated.

To find the likelihood for an item response pattern, all a researcher needs to do is multiply the appropriate IRCs together. For example, if an examinee responds 1, 1, 0 (endorse, endorse, not endorse) to the three items described earlier, the conditional likelihood would be found by multiplying together the IRCs $P_1(\theta)$, $P_2(\theta)$, and $Q_3(\theta)$. The results of this product over varying hypothetical trait level values is shown in Fig. 7.1B. Now to find the maximum likelihood trait level estimate, a researcher simply locates where the likelihood function is a maximum. By eyeball, it appears that $\theta = 0.90$ is best, but values around that range are almost as equally likely. In general, the conditional likelihood of a response pattern can be computed by Eq. 7.2 where the serial product is computed across all administered items.

$$L(u_{s1}, u_{s2} \ldots , u_{sI} | \theta_s) = \prod_{i=1}^{I} P_i(\theta_s)^{u_{si}} Q_i(\theta_s)^{1-u_{si}} \qquad (7.2)$$

Readers may have noticed problems here with maximum likelihood estimation. First, no trait level estimate (i.e., maximum of the function) would

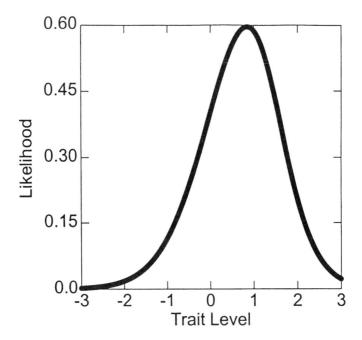

FIG. 7.1B.   The Likelihood Function for the three-item test.

be available until the examinee has endorsed or not endorsed at least one item. An all-endorsed response pattern yields a monotonically increasing likelihood function with a maximum at positive infinity, and an all–not-endorsed response pattern yields a monotonically decreasing likelihood function with negative infinity as the maximum. A second problem is that as IRCs that contain values between zero and one are multiplied together in Eq. 7.2, the conditional likelihoods are going to become very small quickly. In fact, they can become so small that computers lose precision.

To overcome the latter problem, researchers almost always work with log-likelihoods rather than raw likelihoods. Log-likelihoods are found by taking the natural logarithm of the IRC. Note that logarithms of numbers between zero and 1.0 are negative, and large negative numbers yield relatively low probabilities, and small negative numbers represent relatively high probabilities. For example, the natural (base e) log of 0.10 is -2.30, the log of 0.50 is -0.693, and the log of 0.90 is -0.105. In short, a trait level estimate associated with a log-likelihood of -100 is more likely than a trait level estimate associated with a log-likelihood of -200.

The implication of the log-likelihood transformation is this. The log-likelihood function is found by adding together the IRCs rather than multiplying them. Remember the following rule: if numbers are multiplied, we can take the logs and add them. Thus, in the real world, researchers try to find the trait-level estimate that maximizes the log-likelihood function. The θ value that maximizes the likelihood function in Eq. 7.2 will be exactly equal to the trait-level estimate that maximizes the log-likelihood function (Log-L) shown in Eq. 7.3. The log-likelihood function for the three-item example is shown in Fig. 7.1C. Notice that it has exactly the same maximum as the raw likelihood function shown in Fig. 7.1B.

$$\log - L(u_{s1}, u_{s2}, \ldots, u_{sI} | \theta) = \sum_{i=1}^{I} u_{si} \log[P_i(\theta)] + (1 - u_{si}) \log[Q_i(\theta)] \quad (7.3)$$

With a short test it might be possible to add the log-likelihood functions for each item response together and then get a rough eyeball estimate of an examinee's trait level. However, in the real world, where a data set may consist of thousands of examinees who responded to 50 items each, researchers need numerical methods to pinpoint what exactly the maximum of the log-likelihood function is given a particular pattern of item responses. One popular way to find the maximum of the log-likelihood function is to use an iterative Newton–Raphson procedure. This algorithm is used to find the mode (rather than the mean) of each examinee's log-likelihood function. Note that the function in Fig. 7.1C is actually a distribution. Next, we provide a step-by-step description of the Newton–Raphson procedure.

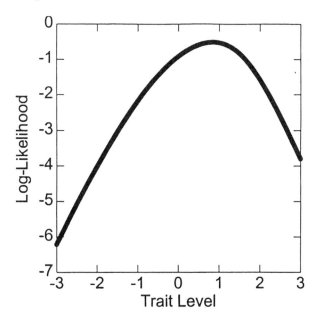

FIG. 7.1C.   The log-likelihood function for the three-item test.

MAXIMIZING THE LIKELIHOOD FUNCTION

Given a vector of estimated item parameters and a vector of item responses, the first step in the Newton–Raphson scoring algorithm is to
specify a starting value for θ. This starting value represents a guess at
what an examinee's trait level may be. In this chapter we use a starting
value of $\theta = 0$ for the examples. Given this tentative estimated value of θ,
we then compute the first and second derivatives of the log-likelihood
function (Eq. 7.3) at this θ value. These values for the 2PL model are
shown in Eqs. 7.4 and 7.5, respectively.

$$\text{First Derivative} \qquad (\theta) = \sum_{i=1}^{I} (\alpha_i (u_{si} - P(\theta_s))) \qquad (7.4)$$

$$\text{Second Derivative} \qquad (\theta) = \sum_{i=1}^{I} \alpha_i^2 (1 - P_i(\theta))(- P_i(\theta)) \qquad (7.5)$$

Given these values, we then compute their ratio, ε, which equals the first
derivative divided by the second derivative. Finally, this ratio is used to
generate a new updated trait level estimate by taking the old estimate minus ε. Using the updated trait level estimate, the iterative procedure is repeated until ε is less than some small value. In our case, we cease the iterations when the ratio is less than 0.001.

The logic of the Newton–Raphson procedure may not be immediately
obvious. To clarify, in Fig. 7.2, we show the log-likelihood function and
the first and second derivatives of that function for a hypothetical
examinee that endorsed the first five and failed to endorse the second five
items in Test A. Recall that this was the test with equal discriminations
and varying difficulties. Now the first derivative of the log-likelihood
function represents its slope. Thus, the maximum of the log-likelihood
function will be located where the first derivative is zero. Essentially, we
need to find where the first derivative of the log-likelihood function is
zero. The second derivative is the slope of the first derivative evaluated
across the trait range, which is always negative (see Eq. 7.5).

It is instructive to work through the process. Sticking with the current
example test and examinee, let's start off by assuming his trait level is
-1.0. Note that in reality, the ML trait level for this examinee is zero 0.0. In
Table 7.1 it is shown that at $\theta = -1.0$, the first derivative is 3.211, the second
derivative is -2.920, and the ratio is thus -1.09. Notice how when we un-
derestimate the true trait level value, the first derivative is positive, and
thus the ratio of the first to the second derivative will be negative because
the second derivative is always negative. Taking -1.00 minus -1.09 yields
a new trait level estimate of 0.09. In the second iteration the first derivative

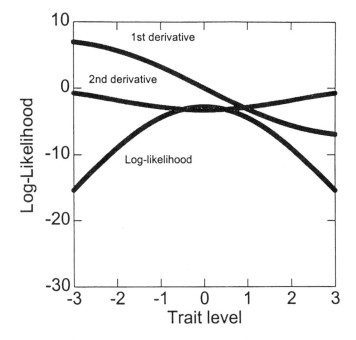

FIG. 7.2.   Illustration of the log-likelihood function and the first and second derivatives of that function.

is now −0.303, the second is now −3.364 and the ratio is 0.090. The updated
trait level estimate is now 0.00, and at this value the first derivative is 0.00
and consequently the iterations stop right here. We take, correctly, a trait
level value of 0.0 as being the ML estimate.

For the sake of illustration, say the starting value for the search was a
trait level value of +1.5 rather than −1.0. The bottom portion of Table 7.1
shows what happens. Although four iterations are now needed, as op-

TABLE 7.1
Examples of Newton–Raphson Iterations to Find
the Maximum Likelihood Trait Level Estimate

Start At	First Derivative	Second Derivative	Change
−1.00	3.211	−2.920	−1.090
0.09	−0.303	−3.364	0.090
0.00	0.000	−3.368	stop
1.500	−4.560	−2.455	1.875
−0.357	1.205	−3.303	−0.364
0.070	−0.236	−3.366	0.070
0.000	0.000	−3.368	stop

posed to three in the previous example, the Newton–Raphson procedure quickly converges on the maximum likelihood estimate. The bottom line of the results presented in Table 7.1 is the following. When trait level is underestimated, the first derivative is positive, and the second derivative is negative. Taking the ratio and then subtracting this value from the old estimate yields a new estimate that is closer to an examinee's correct ML trait-level estimate. Conversely, if we have overestimated trait level, then the first and second derivatives are negative, and taking the ratio and subtracting it from the old estimate yields a new estimate that is closer to the correct ML trait-level estimate. In either case, eventually the first derivative approaches zero, the ratio of the first to second derivatives approaches zero, and we have found the maximal height (mode) of the log-likelihood function.

Also, note that the absolute value of the second derivative is equal to the expected test information (see the Technical Appendix at the end of this chapter for details) provided by the set of items. The higher this value is, the more peaked the log-likelihood function and the more confidence we would have in its maximum. In fact, as will be illustrated shortly, taking the square root of the test information yields the standard error of estimate. The test information, of course, tends to become larger as the number of items are increased.

The ML trait level estimator has several positive asymptotic (large-sample) features. First, it is not biased; that is, the expected value of θ always equals the true θ. Furthermore, it is an efficient estimator, and its errors are normally distributed. However, the ML estimator has some problems. No ML estimate can be obtained from perfect all-endorsed or not-endorsed response vectors. Also, the good statistical properties are only asymptotically true, and they depend on the assumption that the responses fit the model (Bock & Mislevy, 1982). Under conditions of response aberrance and finite test lengths, there is no guarantee that the positive statistical properties will be achieved. Finally, with a short test (e.g., less than 20 items) calibrated under the 3PL model, some response vectors may yield local minima, and the ML algorithm may not converge on the proper solution.

EXAMPLES OF MAXIMUM LIKELIHOOD SCORING

To illustrate maximum likelihood scoring, in the first set of columns in Table 7.2 is displayed a variety of response patterns as scored under Test A, and in the second set of columns is displayed these same patterns as scored under Test B. For each pattern, we display θ and the corresponding standard error of estimate. The standard errors may be computed by taking 1 over the square root of the test information. The test information

TABLE 7.2
Maximum Likelihood Trait Level Estimates and
Standard Errors When Scored Under Test A and Test B

Examinee	Pattern	Test A θ	Test A SE	Test B θ	Test B SE
1	1 1 1 1 1 0 0 0 0 0	0.00	0.54	−0.23	0.43
2	0 1 1 1 1 1 0 0 0 0	0.00	0.54	−0.13	0.43
3	0 0 1 1 1 1 1 0 0 0	0.00	0.54	−0.04	0.42
4	0 0 0 1 1 1 1 1 0 0	0.00	0.54	−0.04	0.42
5	0 0 0 0 1 1 1 1 1 0	0.00	0.54	0.13	0.43
6	0 0 0 0 0 1 1 1 1 1	0.00	0.54	0.23	0.43
7	1 1 1 0 0 0 0 0 0 0	−0.92	0.57	−0.82	0.51
8	0 1 1 1 0 0 0 0 0 0	−0.92	0.57	−0.74	0.50
9	0 0 1 1 1 0 0 0 0 0	−0.92	0.57	−0.66	0.48
10	0 0 0 1 1 1 0 0 0 0	−0.92	0.57	−0.59	0.47
11	0 0 0 0 1 1 1 0 0 0	−0.92	0.57	−0.53	0.46
12	0 0 0 0 0 1 1 1 0 0	−0.92	0.57	−0.46	0.45
13	0 0 0 0 0 0 1 1 1 0	−0.92	0.57	−0.40	0.45
14	0 0 0 0 0 0 0 1 1 1	−0.92	0.57	−0.34	0.44
15	1 0 0 0 0 0 0 0 0 0	−2.20	0.78	−1.80	0.88
16	1 1 0 0 0 0 0 0 0 0	−1.47	0.63	−1.20	0.62
17	1 1 1 0 0 0 0 0 0 0	−0.92	0.57	−0.82	0.51
18	1 1 1 1 0 0 0 0 0 0	−0.45	0.55	−0.51	0.46
19	1 1 1 1 1 0 0 0 0 0	0.00	0.54	−0.23	0.43
20	1 1 1 1 1 1 0 0 0 0	0.45	0.55	0.04	0.42
21	1 1 1 1 1 1 1 0 0 0	0.92	0.57	0.34	0.44
22	1 1 1 1 1 1 1 1 0 0	1.47	0.63	0.71	0.49
23	1 1 1 1 1 1 1 1 1 0	2.20	0.78	1.28	0.65

curves for Tests A and B are shown in Fig. 7.3. Conditional standard errors derived from these curves are shown in Fig. 7.4. Observe that with these short tests, a researcher would not have much confidence in any of the scores, especially at the extremes, because of the limited amount of test information available. That is, regardless of trait level, the standard errors are rather large (i.e., the asymptotic principle has not been satisfied).

In Table 7.2 the first six examinees illustrate different ways of obtaining a raw score of 5. These patterns are ordered by their consistency, or Guttman scalability. That is, the first examinee endorses the five easiest items and doesn't endorse the five most difficult items. The sixth examinee has just the opposite, where he or she has endorsed the five most difficult and failed to endorse the five easiest. Despite these differences, when the Test A item parameters are used, all these examinees receive exactly the same trait level estimate and standard error. The next nine examinees illustrate the same phenomena, but this time with a raw score of three rather than five.

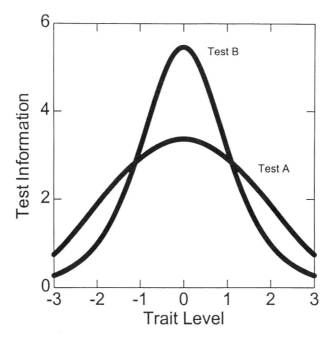

FIG. 7.3.   Test information curves for example tests A and B.

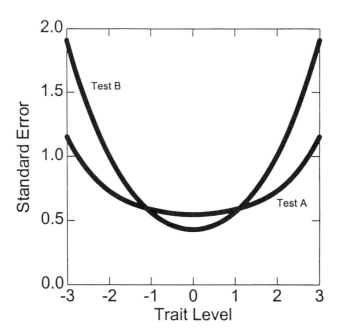

FIG. 7.4.   Standard error curves for example tests A and B.

These results reveal a number of interesting properties of ML scoring. First, when the items are equally discriminating as for the Rasch-like Test A, all examinees with the same raw score receive the same trait level score and standard error. In fact, as illustrated by the last nine examinees in Table 7.2 (i.e., 15–23), with a 10-item dichotomously scored test there are only nine possible trait level scores and standard errors. Under this Rasch model, ML scoring is insensitive to the consistency of an examinee's response pattern. That is, regardless of how the examinee gets to a particular raw score, a specific raw score always yields the same trait level estimate and standard error. Equivalently, the difficulty of the items endorsed and not endorsed plays no role in influencing standard errors. In a Rasch model, examinee raw score is a sufficient statistic for estimating examinee trait level.

In the second set of columns in Table 7.2 are shown the same response patterns when scored under the Test B item parameters. Recall that Test B has discriminations that go from 1.0 to 1.9 and constant difficulty parameters of 0.0. Clearly, examinees who have the same raw score now have different trait level estimates depending on their item response patterns. Specifically, examinees who endorse the most discriminating items receive the highest trait level estimates. For example, Examinee 1 endorsed the least discriminating items and received a trait level estimate of –0.23, and Examinee 6 endorsed the most disciminating and received a trait level score of 0.23. Note that this is exactly the same "scoring philosophy" used in ordinary factor analysis, where scores on the latent variable are determined by the pattern of loadings.

These results reveal more properties of the ML trait level estimate. First, in the 2PL model, trait level estimates are increased according to the discrimination parameters of the endorsed items. In the 2PL model, the sufficient statistic for trait level is the sum of the item discriminations squared times the raw response. The implication is that examinee scores are determined by endorsing highly discriminating items, not items that are highly difficult. Furthermore, when items vary in discrimination, as they do in a test that fits the 2PL model (Test B), it is quite possible for an examinee to have a higher raw score than another examinee but receive a lower trait level estimate. This can be seen in Table 7.2, where Examinee 18 endorsed 4 items and receives a trait level estimate of –0.51, whereas Examinee 14 endorses only 3 items but receives a trait level estimate of –0.34. The preceding discussion is not to be taken to imply that the item difficulty parameter plays no role. In fact, the item difficulty plays a major role because it determines the location of an item's log-likelihood function, which as illustrated previously, ultimately determines where the function is maximized.

Finally, in Table 7.3 we explore the effects of increasing and decreasing the item discrimination parameter values. Table 7.3 shows the same re-

TABLE 7.3
Maximum Likelihood Trait Level Estimates and Standard
Errors When Scored Under Test A with the Item
Discriminations Set at 1.0, 2.0, and 2.5

Examinee	Pattern	α = 1.0		α = 2.0		α = 2.5	
		θ	SE	θ	SE	θ	SE
1	1 1 1 1 1 0 0 0 0 0	0.00	0.73	0.00	0.45	-0.00	0.39
2	0 1 1 1 1 1 0 0 0 0	0.00	0.73	0.00	0.45	-.0.00	0.39
3	0 0 1 1 1 1 1 0 0 0	0.00	0.73	0.00	0.45	-0.00	0.39
4	0 0 0 1 1 1 1 1 0 0	0.00	0.73	0.00	0.45	-0.00	0.39
5	0 0 0 0 1 1 1 1 1 0	0.00	0.73	0.00	0.45	-0.00	0.39
6	0 0 0 0 0 1 1 1 1 1	0.00	0.73	0.00	0.45	-0.00	0.39
7	1 1 1 0 0 0 0 0 0 0	-1.11	0.78	-0.85	0.48	-0.81	0.42
8	0 1 1 1 0 0 0 0 0 0	-1.11	0.78	-0.85	0.48	-0.81	0.42
9	0 0 1 1 1 0 0 0 0 0	-1.11	0.78	-0.85	0.48	-0.81	0.42
10	0 0 0 1 1 1 0 0 0 0	-1.11	0.78	-0.85	0.48	-0.81	0.42
11	0 0 0 0 1 1 1 0 0 0	-1.11	0.78	-0.85	0.48	-0.81	0.42
12	0 0 0 0 0 1 1 1 0 0	-1.11	0.78	-0.85	0.48	-0.81	0.42
13	0 0 0 0 0 0 1 1 1 0	-1.11	0.78	-0.85	0.48	-0.81	0.42
14	0 0 0 0 0 0 0 1 1 1	-1.11	0.78	-0.85	0.48	-0.81	0.42
15	1 0 0 0 0 0 0 0 0 0	-2.73	1.11	-1.98	0.62	-1.88	0.52
16	1 1 0 0 0 0 0 0 0 0	-1.79	0.87	-1.35	0.52	-1.30	0.45
17	1 1 1 0 0 0 0 0 0 0	-1.11	0.78	-0.85	0.48	-0.81	0.42
18	1 1 1 1 0 0 0 0 0 0	-0.54	0.74	-0.41	0.45	-0.39	0.40
19	1 1 1 1 1 0 0 0 0 0	0.00	0.73	-0.00	0.45	-0.00	0.39
20	1 1 1 1 1 1 0 0 0 0	0.54	0.74	0.41	0.45	0.39	0.40
21	1 1 1 1 1 1 1 0 0 0	1.11	0.78	0.85	0.48	0.81	0.42
22	1 1 1 1 1 1 1 1 0 0	1.79	0.87	1.35	0.52	1.30	0.45
23	1 1 1 1 1 1 1 1 1 0	2.73	1.11	1.98	0.62	1.88	0.52

sponse patterns as Table 7.2, but here they are scored only under the parameters of Test A. The first set of columns in Table 7.3 shows the
trait-level scores and standard errors when 0.50 is subtracted from the
item-discrimination parameters of Test A (i.e., all $\alpha_i = 1.0$). Two things are
of note here. First, the trait levels in the first column of Table 7.3 are not
equal to the scores in Table 7.2. In fact, they are more spread out around a
trait-level value of zero. This is because there is less information resulting
from the lower item discrimination parameters, and hence scores are
spread out. Second, the standard errors are much larger now. In the second and third sets of columns, the discrimination parameters from Test A
were increased 0.5 and 1.0, respectively. These results depict the opposite
of the first column results. Namely, as the item discrimination parameters
increase, the trait-level scores tend to get closer to zero and the standard
errors decrease. To illustrate the effects of item discrimination on the standard errors, Fig. 7.5 shows the likelihood function for an examinee who

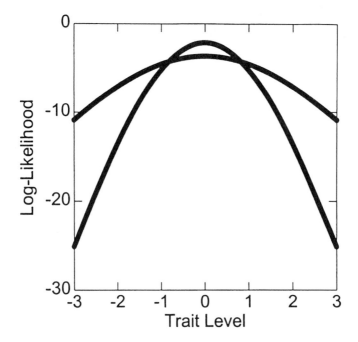

FIG. 7.5. Examples of log-likelihood functions when item discriminations vary in size.

endorsed the first five items for Test A when the discriminations were set to 1.0 and 2.5, respectively. The steeper function in Fig. 7.5 is the log-likelihood when the item discriminations are all equal to 2.5. Clearly, this examinee is measured with more precision; a smaller range of trait level values appear reasonable.

MAXIMUM A POSTERIORI

As observed in the preceding section, a critical problem with the ML estimate is that no trait level can be estimated for examinees with all-endorsed or all–not-endorsed response vectors. Although conceptually this makes sense, it certainly is a limitation in practice. Also, ML methods are asymptotic in nature, and they work best with large samples. In the case of trait level estimation, *samples* refers to items and thus ML estimation is most valuable when a researcher has many test items (e.g., a 50-item test).

As many researchers have pointed out, the limitations of ML procedures can be addressed by incorporating prior information, in the form of a prior distribution, into the log-likelihood function. As reviewed in chapters 8 and 13, many IRT estimation software packages use all types of prior distributions. For example, programs such as XCALIBRE (Assessment Systems, 1996), BILOG (Mislevy & Bock, 1990), and MULTILOG (Thissen, 1991) allow researchers to place prior distributions on the item parameters. The benefit is that if a researcher is willing to assume that a parameter falls within a given range of values, priors allow for more efficient estimation. Prior distributions also protect against outliers or influential data points that may have undue influence on item- or person-parameter estimation.

Analogous to item parameter estimation, a prior distribution can be specified in estimating an examinee's trait level as well. When prior distributions are used in the estimation of examinee trait level, we refer to this procedure as the maximum a posteriori (MAP) scoring strategy. MAP estimation is a Bayesian estimation method in that a researcher makes use of prior information about a parameter value in conjunction with the observed log-likelihood function to derive a trait level estimate based on maximizing a posterior distribution.

There are several key concepts in understanding MAP estimation. The first is the notion of a prior distribution. The prior distribution is nothing more than a hypothetical probability distribution from which a researcher assumes that the examinees are a random sample. The most common prior distribution in IRT trait level estimation is the standard normal distribution. That is, researchers assume that examinees are sampled from a distribution with a mean of zero and a variance of 1.0. In theory, any of a wide variety of forms can be assumed for the prior distribution, however the normal distribution often seems like a reasonable choice.

A second important concept is the log-likelihood function. This topic was extensively covered in the preceding section and will not be reviewed here. Finally, the third important concept is that of a posterior distribution. A posterior distribution is easy to define because it is simply the likelihood function multiplied by the prior distribution function. Technically speaking, in the present context a posterior distribution is the log-likelihood function with the log of the prior distribution added in. The objective of MAP scoring, therefore, is to find the value of θ that maximizes the posterior distribution. The value of θ that maximizes the posterior will equal the mode, and this is why the procedure is sometimes called Bayes modal estimation.

In this chapter, we illustrate MAP scoring by specifying a standard normal distribution as the prior. This prior distribution is shown in Fig. 7.6. To estimate examinee trait levels, we used exactly the same steps as described in the preceding section. Namely, we start off with a guess at what θ is and then, using a particular response pattern and item parameters, we compute the log-likelihood and the first and second derivatives of that

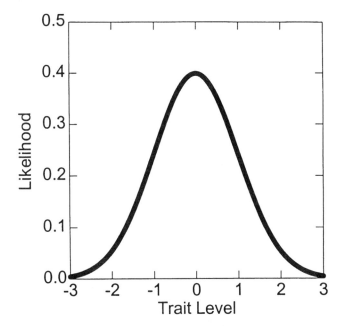

FIG. 7.6.   The normal distribution function.

likelihood function. However, before taking the ratio of the first to second derivative (ε), we incorporate the prior distribution by adjusting the first and second derivatives. For interested readers, this topic is described in more detail in Baker (1993, p. 210). After adjusting the first and second derivatives, we then compute ε and update the trait-level estimate accordingly. Clearly, the shorter the test, the more the prior will affect trait-level estimates. In long tests, on the other hand, the prior distribution will be overwhelmed by the likelihood function and will have little if any effect on trait-level estimation.

To demonstrate the effects of using a prior distribution, in Table 7.4 are shown some examples using the same response vectors as used in the previous tables. In the first set of columns in Table 7.4 are shown the examinees' trait level estimates under the parameters of Test A and in the second set of columns are shown the same examinees' scores under the parameters of Test B. Comparison with Table 7.2 demonstrates that the prior distribution pulls examinee trait level estimates toward the mean of the prior (i.e., toward zero) and to lower the standard error estimates. The reason the standard errors are lower is because there is more information now about examinees. Specifically, we know what distribution they are being sampled from. Is this fair? It is scientifically defensible to the extent to which the prior is valid.

TABLE 7.4
Maximum *a Posterori* Trait Level Estimates and Standard
Errors When Scored Under Test A and Test B

Examinee	Pattern	Test A		Test B	
		θ	SE	θ	SE
1	1 1 1 1 1 0 0 0 0 0	0.00	0.47	−0.19	0.39
2	0 1 1 1 1 1 0 0 0 0	0.00	0.47	−0.11	0.39
3	0 0 1 1 1 1 1 0 0 0	0.00	0.47	−0.03	0.39
4	0 0 0 1 1 1 1 1 0 0	0.00	0.47	0.03	0.39
5	0 0 0 0 1 1 1 1 1 0	0.00	0.47	0.11	0.39
6	0 0 0 0 0 1 1 1 1 1	0.00	0.47	0.19	0.39
7	1 1 1 0 0 0 0 0 0 0	−0.70	0.49	−0.65	0.43
8	0 1 1 1 0 0 0 0 0 0	−0.70	0.49	−0.59	0.42
9	0 0 1 1 1 0 0 0 0 0	−0.70	0.49	−0.54	0.42
10	0 0 0 1 1 1 0 0 0 0	−0.70	0.49	−0.49	0.41
11	0 0 0 0 1 1 1 0 0 0	−0.70	0.49	−0.44	0.41
12	0 0 0 0 0 1 1 1 0 0	−0.70	0.49	−0.38	0.40
13	0 0 0 0 0 0 1 1 1 0	−0.70	0.49	−0.33	0.40
14	0 0 0 0 0 0 0 1 1 1	−0.70	0.49	−0.29	0.40
15	1 0 0 0 0 0 0 0 0 0	−1.48	0.53	−1.17	0.52
16	1 1 0 0 0 0 0 0 0 0	−1.07	0.50	−0.90	0.47
17	1 1 1 0 0 0 0 0 0 0	−0.70	0.49	−0.65	0.43
18	1 1 1 1 0 0 0 0 0 0	−0.34	0.48	−0.42	0.41
19	1 1 1 1 1 0 0 0 0 0	0.00	0.47	−0.19	0.39
20	1 1 1 1 1 1 0 0 0 0	0.34	0.48	0.03	0.39
21	1 1 1 1 1 1 1 0 0 0	0.70	0.49	0.29	0.40
22	1 1 1 1 1 1 1 1 0 0	1.07	0.50	0.58	0.42
23	1 1 1 1 1 1 1 1 1 0	1.48	0.53	0.94	0.48

Smaller standard errors and the trait level estimates being pulled toward the mean of the prior exemplifies the strengths and weaknesses of
the MAP scoring strategy. The strength is that a trait level estimate will be
computable for all examinees, even for perfect all-endorsed and
not-endorsed response patterns. A second strength is the increased precision of trait level estimation brought about by incorporating prior information. On the other hand, a problem is that the MAP scores are biased,
especially when the number of items is small (e.g., <20). That is, the expected value of the MAP estimate does not equal the true parameter
value. Furthermore, we have to assume a particular form for the prior distribution. If the wrong prior is used, scores can be seriously biased and
misleading.

In Table 7.5 we replicate the results of Table 7.3 using a normal prior,
whereas previously no prior was used. That is, the three sets of columns in
Table 7.5 represent the examinees scored by means of the Test A item parameters with the item discriminations all being equal to 1.0, 2.0, and 2.5,

TABLE 7.5
Maximum *a Posteriori* Trait Level Estimates and Standard
Errors When Scored Under Test A with the Item
Discriminations Set at 1.0, 2.0, and 2.5

		$\alpha = 1.0$		$\alpha = 2.0$		$\alpha = 2.5$	
Examinee	Pattern	θ	SE	θ	SE	θ	SE
1	1 1 1 1 1 0 0 0 0 0	0.00	0.59	0.00	0.41	−0.00	0.36
2	0 1 1 1 1 1 0 0 0 0	0.00	0.59	0.00	0.41	−.0.00	0.36
3	0 0 1 1 1 1 1 0 0 0	0.00	0.59	0.00	0.41	−0.00	0.36
4	0 0 0 1 1 1 1 1 0 0	0.00	0.59	0.00	0.41	−0.00	0.36
5	0 0 0 0 1 1 1 1 1 0	0.00	0.59	0.00	0.41	−0.00	0.36
6	0 0 0 0 0 1 1 1 1 1	0.00	0.59	0,00	0.41	−0.00	0.36
7	1 1 1 0 0 0 0 0 0 0	−0.70	0.60	−0.69	0.41	−0.69	0.38
8	0 1 1 1 0 0 0 0 0 0	−0.70	0.60	−0.69	0.42	−0.69	0.38
9	0 0 1 1 1 0 0 0 0 0	−0.70	0.60	−0.69	0.42	−0.69	0.38
10	0 0 0 1 1 1 0 0 0 0	−0.70	0.60	−0.69	0.42	−0.69	0.38
11	0 0 0 0 1 1 1 0 0 0	−0.70	0.60	−0.69	0.42	−0.69	0.38
12	0 0 0 0 0 1 1 1 0 0	−0.70	0.60	−0.69	0.42	−0.69	0.38
13	0 0 0 0 0 0 1 1 1 0	−0.70	0.60	−0.69	0.42	−0.69	0.38
14	0 0 0 0 0 0 0 1 1 1	−0.70	0.60	−0.69	0.42	−0.69	0.38
15	1 0 0 0 0 0 0 0 0 0	−1.46	0.63	−1.49˙	0.47	−1.51	0.42
16	1 1 0 0 0 0 0 0 0 0	−1.07	0.61	−1.07	0.44	−1.08	0.40
17	1 1 1 0 0 0 0 0 0 0	−0.70	0.60	−0.69	0.42	−0.69	0.38
18	1 1 1 1 0 0 0 0 0 0	−0.34	0.59	−0.34	0.41	−0.33	0.37
19	1 1 1 1 1 0 0 0 0 0	0.00	0.59	−0.00	0.41	−0.00	0.36
20	1 1 1 1 1 1 0 0 0 0	0.34	0.59	0.34	0.41	0.33	0.37
21	1 1 1 1 1 1 1 0 0 0	0.70	0.60	0.69	0.42	0.69	0.38
22	1 1 1 1 1 1 1 1 0 0	1.07	0.61	1.07	0.44	1.08	0.40
23	1 1 1 1 1 1 1 1 1 0	1.46	0.63	1.49	0.47	1.51	0.42

respectively. Again, the same phenomena occurs in that all examinees'
scores are pulled in toward the mean. However, notice that the effect is
much larger for the test with the smallest item discrimination parameters.

Consider the examinee who scored 9 out of 10. In the test with the constant item discriminations of 1.0, the trait level estimate goes from 2.73 before the prior (Table 7.3) to 1.46 after. For this same pattern, when the item
discriminations are 2.5, the trait level estimates go from 1.88 (Table 7.3) to
1.51 after the prior is introduced. This phenomena is due to there being
less psychometric information in the test when the item discriminations
are low, and therefore the prior distribution becomes more important and
has a greater effect on examinee trait level estimates. To visually capture
this, in Fig. 7.7 is displayed the likelihood function and posterior distribution for an examinee who responds $u_{si} = [1,1,1,1,1,0,0,0,0,0]$ to Test A when
the item discriminations are a constant 1.0. In contrast, Fig. 7.8 displays
these same values for the same examinee response pattern, but this time,

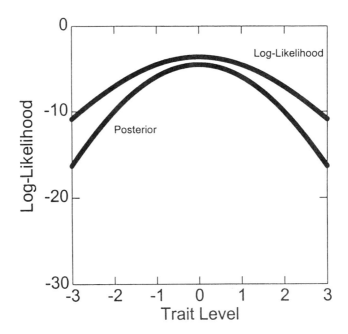

FIG. 7.7. The log-likelihood and posterior distribution for an examinee when the item discriminations are all 1.0.

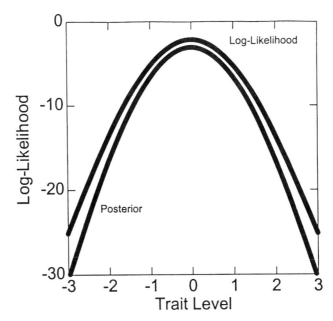

FIG. 7.8. The log-likelihood and posterior distribution for an examinee when the item discriminations are all 2.5.

the item discriminations are a constant of 2.5. Clearly, the prior is having a greater influence in Fig. 7.7 than in Fig. 7.8.

EXPECTED A POSTERIORI SCORING

In contrast to the ML and MAP estimators, the expected a posteriori (EAP; Bock & Mislevy, 1982) estimation of trait level is a noniterative procedure. Contrary to ML estimation, EAP provides a finite trait level estimate for all response patterns — even all-endorsed and not-endorsed response patterns. The EAP is a Bayesian estimator derived from finding the mean, as opposed to the mode, of the posterior distribution. The logic of the EAP scoring strategy is as follows.

For each set of scale items (i.e., a test) a set of probability "densities," or weights, are computed at a fixed number of specified θ values. In turn, the finite number of specified θ values are called *quadrature nodes*. Typically, the densities or weights are taken from a standard normal distribution as shown in Eq. 7.6:

$$F(\theta) = \left[\frac{1}{\sqrt{2 \times 3.14}}\right] \exp(-\theta^2/2) \qquad (7.6)$$

In the analyses conducted in this chapter, we set up 61 quadrature nodes that ranged from $\theta = -3.0$ to 3.0 in 0.10 increments. The densities at each quadrature node (Q_r) are called *weights* $W(Q_r)$, and the weights are transformed so that their sum equaled 1.0. The weights serve as a discrete, as opposed to continuous, prior distribution. Once the quadrature nodes and weights are established, an EAP trait level estimate is derived using Eq. 7.7 (Bock & Mislevy, 1982):

$$\theta = \sum_{r=1}^{61} [Q_r \times L(Q_r) \times W(Q_r)] / \left\{\sum_{r=1}^{61} [L(Q_r) \times W(Q_r)]\right\} \qquad (7.7)$$

In Eq. 7.7, the Q_r values represent the θ values of the 61 quadrature nodes and the $W(Q_r)$ are the weights at each quadrature. The $L(Q_r)$ represents the exponent of the log-likelihood function evaluated at each of the 61 quadrature nodes. The summation in Eq. 7.7 is performed over the 61 quadrature points, and the resulting trait level estimate represents the mean of the posterior distribution. The standard error of the EAP trait level estimate is derived by computing the posterior standard deviation as shown in Eq. 7.8:

$$SE = \sqrt{\frac{\sum_{r=1}^{61}(Q_r - \theta) \times L(Q_r) \times W(Q_r)}{\sum_{r=1}^{61}L(Q_r) \times W(Q_r)}} \tag{7.8}$$

Table 7.6 shows a set of response patterns scored under the EAP method using the item parameters from Test A and Test B, respectively. By contrasting these values with Table 7.4 it is clear that the EAP estimator yields trait level estimates and standard errors that are similar to the MAP estimator. After all, both use prior information, and the only real difference is that one finds the mode of the posterior distribution (MAP), whereas the other locates the mean of the posterior distribution (EAP). However, one of the advantages of EAP over MAP is that it is noniterative and thus computationally faster. This may be important in computerized adaptive testing contexts. Related to this, a researcher does not have to

TABLE 7.6
Expected *a Posterori* Trait Level Estimates and Standard
Errors When Scored Under Test A and Test B

Examinee	Pattern	Test A		Test B	
		θ	SE	θ	SE
1	1 1 1 1 1 0 0 0 0 0	0.00	0.48	−0.21	0.41
2	0 1 1 1 1 1 0 0 0 0	0.00	0.48	−0.13	0.41
3	0 0 1 1 1 1 1 0 0 0	0.00	0.48	−0.04	0.41
4	0 0 0 1 1 1 1 1 0 0	0.00	0.48	0.04	0.41
5	0 0 0 0 1 1 1 1 1 0	0.00	0.48	0.13	0.41
6	0 0 0 0 0 1 1 1 1 1	0.00	0.48	0.21	0.41
7	1 1 1 0 0 0 0 0 0 0	−0.72	0.50	−0.71	0.46
8	0 1 1 1 0 0 0 0 0 0	−0.72	0.50	−0.65	0.45
9	0 0 1 1 1 0 0 0 0 0	−0.72	0.50	−0.59	0.44
10	0 0 0 1 1 1 0 0 0 0	−0.72	0.50	−0.53	0.44
11	0 0 0 0 1 1 1 0 0 0	−0.72	0.50	−0.48	0.43
12	0 0 0 0 0 1 1 1 0 0	−0.72	0.50	−0.42	0.43
13	0 0 0 0 0 0 1 1 1 0	−0.72	0.50	−0.37	0.42
14	0 0 0 0 0 0 0 1 1 1	−0.72	0.50	−0.31	0.42
15	1 0 0 0 0 0 0 0 0 0	−1.52	0.54	−1.27	0.54
16	1 1 0 0 0 0 0 0 0 0	−1.10	0.52	−0.98	0.49
17	1 1 1 0 0 0 0 0 0 0	−0.72	0.50	−0.71	0.46
18	1 1 1 1 0 0 0 0 0 0	−0.35	0.49	−0.46	0.43
19	1 1 1 1 1 0 0 0 0 0	0.00	0.48	−0.21	0.41
20	1 1 1 1 1 1 0 0 0 0	0.35	0.49	0.04	0.41
21	1 1 1 1 1 1 1 0 0 0	0.72	0.50	0.31	0.42
22	1 1 1 1 1 1 1 1 0 0	1.10	0.52	0.63	0.45
23	1 1 1 1 1 1 1 1 1 0	1.52	0.54	1.03	0.50

know the derivatives associated with a particular IRT model to compute the EAP. Consequently, it is very easy to conduct EAP scoring for any dichotomous or polytomous IRT model. This is not true with ML or MAP estimation.

Bock and Mislevy (1982, p. 439) stated "the EAP estimator has minimum mean square error over the population of ability and, in terms of average accuracy, cannot be improved upon." This property applies only when the prior is correct, however (Wainer & Thissen, 1987). The EAP estimator is biased when there is a finite number of items. The type of bias is that the trait level estimates are regressed toward the mean unless the number of items is large (Wainer & Thissen, 1987); how large is unknown. The advantages of the EAP estimator over the ML are that it is noniterative, easily calculated, a minimum mean square estimator, and yields finite trait level estimates for all response patterns.

ALLOWABLE TRANSFORMATIONS AND SCORE INTERPRETATIONS

In the typical application of IRT, marginal maximum likelihood estimation is used to calibrate the item parameters, and a normal distribution of examinee latent-trait scores is assumed. This leads rather directly to the estimated latent-trait scores (θ) being interpreted in the same manner as z-scores. In some contexts, however, this scale is inconvenient or theoretically unappealing, and the researcher prefers some other metric. Generally speaking, this is not a problem in IRT as long as the researcher remembers to transform the item parameters. That is, if the scale of examinee latent-trait scores is changed, the researcher must transform the item parameters to maintain the invariance property.

For example, let's say that the researcher desires a metric with a mean of 500 and a standard deviation of 100. In this case, we have a new trait level estimate (θ^*) as shown in Eq. 7.9:

$$\theta^* = 100(\theta) + 500 \tag{7.9}$$

The appropriate transformations for the parameters of the 3PL model are:

$$\alpha^* = \alpha/100 \tag{7.10}$$

$$\beta^* = \beta + 500 \tag{7.11}$$

$$c^* = c \tag{7.12}$$

In Eqs. 7.10–7.12, the asterisks indicate the value of the transformed parameter.

As alluded to previously, in Rasch models the basic IRT model is often set up a little differently, which in turn affects test-score interpretation. Specifically, it is fairly common in applications of Rasch models that the difficulty parameters have been scaled so that their mean equals zero. The corresponding distribution of latent-trait scores can be anything depending on the trait being assessed. After calibrating a set of items, if a transformation is performed to center the difficulty parameters, then a transformation must also be performed on the latent trait scores to maintain invariance. Specifically, the mean of the item difficulties must be subtracted from the latent trait scores.

One of the really nice aspects of centering the item difficulties around zero is that it calls attention to how test score interpretation under an IRT framework may differ from a CTT framework. Specifically, in traditional CTT score analysis, researchers often use norms, and thus test scores are compared relative to the mean and standard deviation of a norm group. In contrast, IRT scores do not need to be interpreted relative to norms, but rather can be interpreted relative to the item difficulties. This is because the item difficulties and latent-trait scores are on the same metric in IRT modeling.

For example, given the IRT modeling of a math test with the difficulties centered as described earlier, assume that an examinee has a score of $\theta = 0.05$. Without making reference to any latent-trait distribution, a researcher can state that this examinee has a greater than 50% chance of solving any problem of average and below-average difficulty. In turn, his or her probability of solving a problem that is above-average in difficulty is low. Of course, for this kind of interpretation to be meaningful, a researcher must know the content and the psychological processes involved in the types of items that have low, medium, and high difficulty parameters. We note that this approach to test score interpretation has not been considered in the realm of typical performance constructs such as personality traits. Such application, however, may prove revealing.

Beyond the different approaches to test score interpretation, IRT methods differ from traditional methods in other ways. Herein we focus on just two of these. The first difference lies in comparing examinees who have taken different tests of the same construct. In traditional approaches, to compare test scores from two different measures, or from the same measure administered twice as in a longitudinal study, the tests must be "equated," or they have to be parallel forms. In other words, a raw score from Test A can only be compared to a raw score from Test B if the two tests are psychometrically equivalent. Several books have been written on test equating, and we will not attempt a summary here.

Under an IRT framework, test scores can be compared when the metrics have been "linked." Linking is the IRT analogue of CTT equating methods, yet there are crucial differences. Equating methods are based on sample-dependent statistics, which adds a whole realm of complexity to the problem. IRT linking methods, on the other hand, are based on sample-invariant statistics (within a transformation) and are thus easier to pursue. Again, the literature on linking is large, and we will not review it here. However, we would like to indicate briefly that the scales from two different tests can be linked rather easily if the item parameters are calibrated onto a common scale.

Calibrating item parameters from two different tests onto a common scale can be fairly straightforward if a researcher has a set of "anchor items" that were responded to by a common set of examinees. For example, consider Test A and Test B, which are each 30 items long. If one group of examinees responds to Test A and the first 10 items of Test B and then another group of examinees responds to Test B and the last 10 items of Test A, we could then form an "anchor" test. The anchor would consist of the last 10 items of Test A and the first 10 items of Test B. Given this anchor test, it is now easy to calibrate the anchor test so that the item parameters from the remaining items of Test A and B are on a common metric. Once done, then scores from Test A and Test B are directly comparable, and latent-trait estimates from any subset of items from Test A or Test B (as in computerized adaptive testing) are also directly comparable because they are on the same metric.

A second main difference between traditional test score interpretation and IRT latent-trait score interpretation is that the IRT approach avails itself to more creative and potentially more informative communications. Allow us to explain. Consider the likelihood function discussed throughout this chapter. This likelihood function (or take the exponent of the log-likelihood) provides a researcher with the probability of any particular trait level estimate. Of course, because the latent trait scale is continuous, the probability on any particular score is extremely low. Nevertheless, for any particular examinee, the likelihood function can be used to communicate just how relatively likely a certain position on the latent trait continuum is in comparison to another position on the latent trait continuum.

That is, instead of simply reporting a raw score and unconditional standard error, which is assumed equal for all examinees under a CTT framework, the IRT likelihood function can be used (by integration) to state exactly what the probability of a particular score range is (e.g., what is the probability of the examinee's trait level being greater than −1.0 and less than 1.0). These probabilities will be a function of the psychometric properties of the test, and in fact would reveal a lot about the quality of the measure. Furthermore, the IRT likelihood function allows a researcher to provide likelihood ratios for any two points or areas along the trait continuum. For example, a researcher could state the relative likelihood of an examinee having a trait level of +2.0 versus having a trait level of 0.0. In fact, in some testing contexts (e.g., a clinical context), a researcher might want to administer only enough items so that the relative likelihood of an examinee being at a certain trait level is either very high or low, depending on the testing context. In sum, although IRT latent trait level estimation is many times more complex than computing a raw scale score, the IRT approach allows for certain interpretations that would otherwise be difficult to achieve.

SUMMARY

In this chapter, three IRT-based scoring strategies were described: ML, MAP, and EAP. Each approach has strengths and weaknesses. The ML estimator is asymptotically efficient and unbiased, but it requires large item pools and cannot be used for examinees with all-endorsed or all–not-endorsed response patterns. Also, under certain conditions in the 3PL model, an ML estimate may not be computable. The MAP estimator incorporates prior information and a unique trait level estimate exists for all possible response patterns. The problems with MAP is that it may be biased with short tests, especially if the prior used is incorrect. EAP is similar to MAP estimation in that prior information is used, but there are critical differences. Namely, EAP estimation uses a discrete prior as opposed to a continuous prior, is noniterative, and does not require the researcher to know the first and second derivatives of the likelihood function. Therefore, EAP is perhaps the most easily implemented scoring strategy across a range of IRT models and testing contexts.

In this chapter we also described how examinee trait level scores and their associated standard errors are affected by characteristics of the test. In Rasch models, when the item discrimination is constant across items, all examinees with the same raw score receive the same trait level estimate and standard error, regardless of their pattern of responses. In turn, when item discriminations vary across a test, an examinee's score is affected by their particular pattern of item responses. Specifically, endorsing items with higher discriminations has a larger impact on scores. As we discussed, this is analogous to factor analysis, where the factor scores are a function of a person's scores on the variables and the weights for each variable (i.e., factor loadings). Finally, the more discriminating a test, or equivalently, the more psychometric information a test provides across the trait range, the less trait level scores are spread out around the mean, and standard errors are smaller.

Finally, we described appropriate transformations to item and person parameters under IRT models and discussed ways in which test score interpretation differs between IRT and more traditional CTT approaches. One of the main differences is that traditional tests are usually interpreted in terms of norms. Norm-based interpretation is certainly possible using IRT, but IRT also facilitates interpreting trait level scores relative to item content. The reason for this is that examinee trait levels and item difficulties are on the same scale and are thus comparable. IRT-based scoring, through the process of metric linking, also facilitates comparison of scores from examinees who have taken different versions of a test or who have responded to different sets of items at different times. Through the creative use of the likelihood function, IRT scoring also can provide alternative ways of reporting an individual's position on the trait continuum. For example, a researcher might provide a probability of a score being within a certain range or give the likelihood ratio of an examinee's score being at one trait level versus another.

TECHNICAL APPENDIX:
ITEM AND TEST INFORMATION
AND STANDARD ERRORS OF MEASUREMENT

Dichotomous IRT Models

The concept of psychometric information is a fundamental feature of IRT measurement models, both for binary and polytomous item-response formats. It can be shown that an item-response curve (IRC) from any dichotomous IRT model (chap. 4) or the category response curves from polytomous IRT model (chap. 5), can be transformed into an item information curve (IIC). An IIC indicates the amount of psychometric (Fisher) information an item contains at all points along the latent-trait continuum. For a dichotomous item, we can write a general formula for an IIC as follows:

$$I(\theta) = \frac{P_i^*(\theta)^2}{P_i(\theta)(1 - P_i(\theta))} \tag{7A.1}$$

In Eq. 7A.1, $P_i(\Theta)$ is the conditional probability of endorsing an item (i.e., the IRC) as determined from the estimated parameters of some dichotomous IRT model, and the $P_i^*(\Theta)$ term represents the first derivative of the item response curve evaluated at a particular trait level. For computational purposes, Eq. 7A.1 can be rewritten as follows:

$$I(\theta) = \left[\alpha_i^2 \frac{1 - P_i(\theta)}{P_i(\theta)}\right] \left[\frac{(P_i(\theta) - c_i)^2}{(1 - c_i)^2}\right] \tag{7A.2}$$

This equation allows a researcher to compute the conditional item information in the 3PL model. If $c = 0.0$ (i.e., as in the 2PL), then the formula reduces to:

$$I(\theta) = \alpha_i^2 P_i(\theta)(1 - P_i(\theta)) \tag{7A.3}$$

and in the 1PL, item information is simply:

$$I(\theta) = P_i(\theta)(1 - P_i(\theta)) \tag{7A.4}$$

It should be noted that each of these formulas assumes that the $D = 1.7$ scaling factor has already been absorbed into the item-discrimination parameter. The implications of these formulas can be summarized in a few rules. First, in the 1PL and 2PL models, the amount of information an item provides is maximized around the item-difficulty parameter. Consequently, items that are matched in difficulty to examinee ability are maximally informative. In the 3PL model, the maximum amount of item information occurs at a trait level slightly below the item-difficulty parameter. Generally speaking, the effect of the Quessing (c) parameter is to lower the amount of psychometric information an item provides. All else being equal, a 1PL or 2PL item will be more informative than a 3PL item.

A second principle is that the amount of information an item provides is determined by the item-discrimination parameter—the higher the item discrimination, the more psychometric information an item will provide around the difficulty parameter. It is often said that highly discriminating items have "peaked" information curves in that they provide a lot of information in a narrow range of trait values, whereas a low discriminating item has a flatter and more spread-out information curve.

One of the most important features of item information curves is that they are additive across items that are calibrated onto a common latent-trait scale. Therefore, Eq. 7A.5 can be used to determine how well an entire set of items is functioning as a latent-trait measure:

$$TI(\theta) = \sum_{i=1}^{I} I(\theta) \tag{7A.5}$$

The reason test information is critically important in determining how well a test is performing is because it has an exact relationship with an examinee's standard error of measurement under ML scoring. Specifically, an examinee's standard error can be written as

$$SE(\theta) = \frac{1}{\sqrt{TI(\theta)}} \qquad (7A.6)$$

Thus, once a researcher knows a test's information function, which can be established as soon as item parameters are estimated, how precise that test is at various ranges of the latent trait can be determined. Observe that the test information value, unlike a CTT reliability coefficient, is completely independent of the particular examinee sample taking the test. Furthermore, observe that the standard error in IRT, which changes as a function of examinee trait level (unless the test information curve is perfectly flat), is in sharp contrast to the CTT standard error that is assumed constant regardless of examinee raw score.

Item and test information have many uses in IRT. For example, as we describe in chapter 10, item information is used to determine which particular item in a computerized adaptive test is administered to a particular examinee. Also, item information is used in basic test design (e.g., to select which items to include in a measure), and test information can be used to compare two competing measures of a construct.

Polytomous IRT Models

The basic logic of item and test information can be extended to the case of polytomous response formats and the corresponding polytomous IRT models (chap. 5). By this we mean that for each item, it is possible to transform the category-response curves into item-information curves. These item information curves then can be added together to form a test information curve. In the polytomous case, the general form of the item information curve can be written as Eq. 7A.7 (Dodd, DeAyala, & Koch, 1995):

$$I_i(\theta) = \sum_{x=0}^{m} \frac{P_{ix}^*(\theta)^2}{P_{ix}(\theta)} \qquad (7A.7)$$

The rules regarding what factors influence item information are much more complex in polytomous models. For example, in several of the polytomous models the amount of information a particular item provides depends on both the size of the slope parameter and the spread of the category thresholds or intersection parameters. Furthermore, in models such as the partial credit model, the shape of the item information curve depends on the number of reversals in the intersection parameters. More specific insight regarding information in polytomous models can be found in original sources such as Dodd and Koch (1987), Dodd and De Ayala (1994), and Muraki (1993a). A SAS-based computer program is available to compute item information in polytomous models (Fitzpatrick et al., 1994).

8

Calibrating Items: Estimation

In this chapter, methods for estimating IRT item parameters will be introduced. The preceding chapter explores methods to estimate trait level, assuming that item parameters are known. For routine applications of standardized tests, assuming known item parameters is practical because item calibration occurs during test standardization. However, for new tests and measures, item parameters must be estimated from the data. In many research applications, the same data are also used to estimate trait levels.

Item parameters for IRT models are usually estimated by a maximum likelihood (ML) method. The most frequently used methods are (a) joint maximum likelihood (JML), (b) marginal maximum likelihood (MML), and (c) conditional maximum likelihood (CML). If prior information about the item parameters is available, Bayesian estimation methods are possible for JML or MML. Before elaborating these methods, two heuristic estimation methods will be introduced. These methods can provide insights into how some basic IRT model properties are accomplished.

All methods will be illustrated on data for 10 items from the Abstract Reasoning Test (ART; Embretson, 1995d). ART has a bank of 150 matrix completion items. Each item has eight response alternatives, so that guessing is minimal. The ART item bank shows reasonably good fit to the Rasch model (Embretson, 1998a). The data used to estimate the ART item parameters were obtained from 818 young adult participants.

ASSUMPTIONS

Two major assumptions required for estimating item parameters for IRT models are (a) local independence and (b) appropriate dimensionality (i.e., number of traits) in the IRT model. The various estimation methods for IRT models may require additional assumptions; for example, CML estimation requires that total score is a sufficient statistic for estimating trait level (and so is restricted to Rasch models). Here, we will elaborate the two major assumptions.

Local independence means that the response to any item is unrelated to any other item when trait level is controlled. The items may be highly intercorrelated in the whole sample; however, if trait level is controlled, local independence implies that no relationships remain between the items. Local independence may be partially understood by comparing its implications for factor analysis. Under certain assumptions, an IRT model with item discrimination parameters, such as the two-parameter normal ogive model, is identical to a factor analysis model (see Takane & deLeeuw, 1987). In this case, local independence would be achieved if a single factor fits the data. That is, the factor accounts for the correlations, so that the residual correlations do not differ from zero. It should be noted, however, that local independence is a broader assumption than zero correlations; local independence also includes nonlinear or higher-order relationships between the items.

To illustrate, the correlations between the 10 ART items are highly significant as a set ($\chi^2_{45} = 550.154$; $p < .000$). An ML factor analysis with one factor fits the data. Specifically, after controlling for the common factor, the residual correlations between the items are not significant ($\chi^2_{35} = 41.980$; $p = .194$).

Practically, local independence is violated when item responses are linked. In a cognitive test, several conditions can result in local dependence. For example, if a correct response to one item is necessary for another item or if the content of one item provides relevant information for answering another item, local independence is violated. For another example, items that contain common wording or refer to a common stem, as in paragraph comprehension tests may be locally dependent. In personality and attitude testing, local dependence also can result from interactive effects of item context. For example, a person may be more willing to endorse a moderately negative item if the item is preceded by very extreme negative statements.

To apply an IRT model, local independence must be assumed because the response pattern probability is the simple product of the individual item probabilities. If local independence is violated, then the response pattern probabilities will be inappropriately reproduced in standard IRT models. Special methods to include locally dependent items in a test have been developed, however. For example, Jannarone (1986) developed a model that included interaction terms, which is particularly applicable to personality items. Thissen and Steinberg (1988) elaborate methods for blocking locally dependent items into a single set, or "testlet," which can then treated as a unit in a model. Estimation methods for these models have also been developed (e.g., Gibbons & Hedeker, 1992). Such methods should be considered for locally dependent items.

Appropriate dimensionality means that the IRT model contains the right number of trait level estimates per person for the data. Ultimately, appropriate dimensionality is determined by how well IRT models of varying dimensionality fit the data. If a standard IRT model, such as the 1PL, 2PL, or 3PL model fits the test data reasonably well, then the appropriate dimensionality is specified by one trait level estimate per person. However, if these models do not fit, then either an IRT model with additional dimensions or a locally dependent IRT model may be needed (see chap. 4). In any case, if local independence is fully met, then appropriate dimensionality has been specified in the IRT model. Failing to estimate a dimension that is important in the items will lead to local dependency.

HEURISTIC ESTIMATION METHODS

In this section, two heuristic estimation methods are explicated: (a) Rasch's (1960) approximation with the basic data matrix and (b) logistic regression on known abilities. Neither method is suitable for routine application; the logistic regression method requires the unrealistic assumption that abilities are known, while the basic data matrix approximation does not have optimal properties as compared to the maximum likelihood methods. Nevertheless, both methods provide some insights about the advantages of IRT item parameter estimates, such as population invariance.

Rasch's Basic Data Matrix

If the data fit the Rasch model, calculations from the basic data matrix provide a reasonable approximation of item and person parameters. For the Rasch model, sufficient statistics are available to estimate the parameters. A sufficient statistic exists when no other information from the data is needed to estimate a parameter. For the Rasch model, total score is a sufficient statistic for estimating a person's ability, and the number of persons passing an item is a sufficient statistic for estimating item difficulty. Stated in another way, persons with the same total score are assumed to have the same ability, regardless of which specific items are passed or failed. Furthermore, the specific persons who passed or failed a particular item do not influence item-difficulty estimates.

Rasch (1960) showed how item parameters could be estimated by hand calculations from a basic data matrix. The rows represent items and the columns represent groups of persons with equal abilities. Table 8.1 presents the basic data matrix obtained for the 10-item ART form. Although the total sample is 818 persons, 31 persons had extreme scores, leaving 787 persons to be classified into the 9 ability score groups. Extreme scores that result from passing all items or failing all items are not useful for estimating item parameters in this approach. Extreme scores provide no information about differences between the items because the person has the same outcome on each item. The columns of Table 8.1 show that the number of persons in the various total score groups varies substantially. For example, relatively few persons scored only one item correct, but many persons scored five items correct.

Items are ordered by easiness on Table 8.1. Each item is labeled by its item-bank identification number. For each item (row), it can be seen that the probability of solution increases with ability. The score groups are ordered by total score, which represents ability. Within each ability group (column), the probabilities decrease with item difficulty. Thus, persons in the low scoring groups (e.g., score = 2), have lower probabilities for passing each item than persons in higher scoring groups (e.g., score = 5).

Figure 8.1 plots the probability of solving the various items in the test for three score groups. Notice that the probabilities are higher on each item for the higher ability groups. Notice also that the gap between ability groups varies considerably across items. The varying gaps between ability groups results partly from the nonoptimal scaling of performance in the raw data (see chap. 6 for further elaboration).

Rasch (1960) estimated item and person parameters for his simple IRT model by averaging across the rows and columns. However, to obtain es-

TABLE 8.1
Basic Data Matrix for ART ($n = 787$)

					Score/Ability Group				
Item	1	2	3	4	5	6	7	8	9
(N)	(18)	(40)	(96)	(101)	(132)	(133)	(111)	(88)	(68)
7	.39	.40	.69	.81	.89	.86	.94	.98	1.00
10	.22	.57	.63	.75	.85	.91	.91	.97	.96
13	.11	.18	.28	.46	.62	.79	.86	.90	.99
08	.00	.13	.38	.52	.61	.74	.87	.93	.97
27	.00	.15	.34	.39	.52	.69	.82	.85	.93
19	.11	.18	.14	.30	.34	.54	.60	.80	.91
16	.01	.15	.19	.21	.32	.56	.64	.67	.87
33	.01	.01	.16	.25	.39	.32	.54	.61	.87
22	.00	.01	.15	.23	.27	.34	.49	.73	.85
28	.00	.10	.01	.01	.19	.24	.32	.57	.66

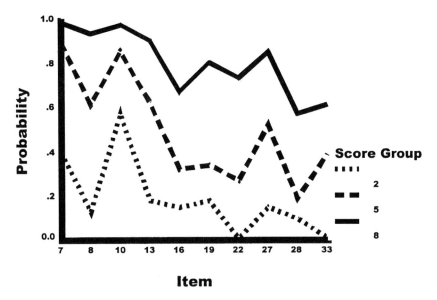

FIG. 8.1. Item-solving probabilities for three ability groups.

timates that are consistent with his model (a) the cell entries in the basic data matrix first must be transformed into log odds ratios before averaging, and (b) the estimates must be adjusted to reflect item deviations. Table 8.2 shows the log odds ratios for all cells, as well as the marginal means to represent ability and item easiness. For example, for Item 7, for persons with a score of 5, the log odds are given as follows:

$$\log \text{odds}_{75} = \log_n(P_{75}/1 - P_{75}) = \log_n(.89/.11) = 2.09 \quad (8.1)$$

Also shown in Table 8.2 are row and column marginal means. A marginal statistic corresponds to a row or column. Here, a row marginal is the mean log odds for solving a particular item across the ability groups. Each cell mean has an equal weight in determining the overall item mean, so that the number of persons in the groups does not influence the mean for an item. A column marginal is the mean log odds for a score group across the items.

An adjusted item mean is computed as the deviation of the item from the overall item mean. The overall item mean, averaged across items, is −.05. For Item 7, for example, the deviation from the item mean is 1.91. Easy items have large positive deviations. To convert the deviation to estimate Rasch item *difficulty* (rather than easiness) the deviation is multiplied by −1. The mean of the Rasch item difficulties will be zero because they are based on item deviations. This adjustment anchors the solution by setting the mean item parameter to zero, which is a popular anchoring method in

TABLE 8.2
Log Odds Data Matrix for ART With Marginal Means and Simple Rasch Item Difficulty Estimate

Item	Score/Ability Group									Mean	Rasch Difficulty β_i
	1	2	3	4	5	6	7	8	9		
7	-.45	-.41	.80	1.45	2.09	1.82	2.75	3.89	4.84	1.86	-1.91
10	-1.27	.28	.53	1.10	1.73	2.31	2.31	3.48	3.18	1.52	-1.57
13	-2.09	-1.52	-.94	-.16	.49	1.32	1.82	2.2	4.6	.63	-.68
8	-3.48	-1.90	-.49	.08	.45	1.05	1.90	2.59	3.48	.41	-.46
27	-3.48	-1.73	-.66	-.45	.08	.80	1.52	1.73	2.59	.04	-.09
19	-2.09	-1.52	-1.82	-.85	-.66	.16	.41	1.39	2.31	-.30	.25
16	-3.48	-1.73	-1.45	-1.32	-.75	.24	.58	.71	1.90	-.59	.54
33	-3.48	-4.60	-1.66	-1.10	-.45	-.75	.16	.45	1.90	-1.06	1.01
22	-3.48	-4.60	-1.73	-1.21	-.99	-.66	-.04	.99	1.73	-1.11	1.06
28	-3.48	-2.20	-4.60	-4.60	-1.45	-1.15	-.75	.28	.66	-1.92	1.87
Mean	-2.68	-1.99	-1.20	-.71	.05	.51	1.06	1.77	2.72	-.05	.00
Rasch Ability θ	-2.73	-2.04	-1.25	-.76	.00	.46	1.01	1.72	2.67		

applications of the Rasch IRT model. See chapter 6 for other ways of anchoring the solution.

Like the item parameters, person abilities may be estimated by averaging log odds ratios. Table 8.2 shows the ability means for each score group. These means are adjusted to correspond to Rasch item difficulties by adding −.05.

Figure 8.2 plots the log odds ratios for the same three ability groups as in Fig. 8.1. Analogous to Fig. 8.1, the higher ability groups have higher log odds on all items. However, notice that the gap between groups is now more uniform. For example, the group differences on Item 7 are now more similar to the group differences on Item 16.

The basic data matrix also can provide insights about the meaning of fitting the Rasch model to the data. If viewed as a contingency table, finding that the row and column marginal means that are sufficient to reproduce the data implies that ability level does not interact with specific items. The prediction for the basic data matrix cells can be given as a log linear model by the sum of the appropriate row and column means. The log odds predicted for the first score group on Item 7 is −.82 (i.e., −2.68 + 1.86 = −.82). An identical prediction is given from the Rasch model as follows:

$$\ln(P_{is}/1 - P_{is}) = \theta_j - b_i \qquad (8.2)$$

in which the log likelihoods for success is given as the simple difference of ability and item difficulty (not easiness). So, using the estimates on Table

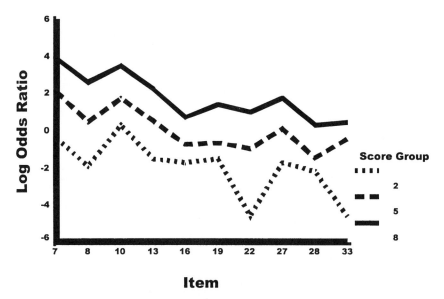

FIG. 8.2. Item log-odds ratios for three ability groups.

8.2 for ability and item difficulty, the log odds for the first ability group on Item 7 is also predicted as −.82 (i.e., −2.73 − (−1.91) = −.82).

The Rasch model is supported if the cell entries are well reproduced by predictions from Eq. 8.2. For example, the ability for a score of 7 is 1.01, and the Rasch item difficulty estimate for Item 16 is .54. The difference between these values is .47, which yields a residual of .11 from the observed log odds ratio (on Table 8.2) of .58. Table 8.3 shows the residual and predicted log odds for each cell in the basic data matrix.

Rasch (1960) examined the magnitude of the residuals, as shown in Table 8.3, to check the fit of the IRT model for the data. For the ART data on Table 8.3, the residuals are small to moderate for most cells. The average squared residual is .23, which yields a root mean square error (RMSE) of .48. Significance tests can be formulated from the residuals (see chap. 9 on fit).

The basic data matrix illustrates how certain properties of an IRT model are achieved. First, the item parameter estimates are population invariant because the ability distribution does not influence the estimates. The estimates are an *unweighted average*, such that each score group, regardless of

TABLE 8.3
Predicted and Residual[a] Log Odds Ratios
From Rasch Estimates for ART Data

	Score/Ability Group								
Item	1	2	3	4	5	6	7	8	9
7	−.82	−.13	.66	1.15	1.91	2.37	2.92	3.63	4.58
	(.37)	(−.28)	(.14)	(.30)	(.18)	(−.56)	(−.17)	(.26)	(.25)
10	−1.16	−.47	.32	.81	1.57	2.03	2.58	3.29	4.24
	(−.10)	(.75)	(.21)	(.29)	(.17)	(.29)	(−.26)	(.19)	(−1.06)
13	−2.05	−1.36	−.57	−.08	.68	1.14	1.69	2.40	3.35
	(−.04)	(−.16)	(−.38)	(−.08)	(−.20)	(.18)	(.12)	(−.21)	(1.24)
8	−2.27	−1.58	−.79	−.30	.46	.92	1.47	2.18	3.13
	(−1.20)	(−.32)	(.30)	(.38)	(−.01)	(.13)	(.43)	(.41)	(.35)
27	−2.64	−1.95	−1.16	−.67	.09	.55	1.10	1.81	2.76
	(−.84)	(.21)	(.49)	(.22)	(−.01)	(.25)	(.41)	(−.08)	(−.18)
19	−2.98	−2.29	−1.50	−1.01	−.25	.21	.76	1.47	2.42
	(.89)	(.77)	(−.32)	(.16)	(−.42)	(−.05)	(−.36)	(−.09)	(−.11)
16	−3.27	−2.58	−1.79	−1.30	−.54	−.08	.47	1.18	2.13
	(−.21)	(.85)	(.34)	(−.02)	(−.21)	(.32)	(.11)	(−.47)	(−.23)
33	−3.74	−3.05	−2.26	−1.77	−1.01	−.55	.00	.71	1.66
	(.26)	(−1.55)	(.60)	(.67)	(.56)	(−.21)	(.16)	(−.26)	(.24)
22	−3.79	−3.10	−2.31	−1.82	−1.06	−.60	−.05	.66	1.61
	(.31)	(−1.50)	(.58)	(.61)	(.07)	(−.06)	(.01)	(.33)	(.12)
28	−4.60	−3.91	−3.12	−2.63	−1.87	−1.41	−.86	−.15	.80
	(1.12)	(1.71)	(−1.48)	(−1.97)	(.42)	(.26)	(.11)	(.43)	(−.14)

[a]Residual values in parentheses.

number of persons, has equal impact on the item mean. The log odds are averaged across score groups without regard to size. Second, the ability estimates are not biased by the easiness of the items. Adjusting abilities to an anchoring value for the items (e.g., zero) allows comparable estimates to be obtained from different item sets. For example, the item mean for an easy set can be anchored to a lower value than the item mean for a harder item set. Third, the reproduction of the basic data matrix from the adjusted marginal means indicates appropriateness of the Rasch model for the data. The Rasch model fits when items and persons do not interact; that is, the log odds ratios are well reproduced by the corresponding item and person means.

It should be noted that the population trait distribution and the item properties do influence the standard errors for parameter estimates. More statistical information is available when the trait levels and item difficulties are similar to each other. If the population has generally high trait levels, for example, difficult items will be estimated more precisely than easy items. Similarly, if the items are hard, persons with high trait levels will be estimated more precisely than persons with lower trait levels.

Logistic Regression

An important meaning of the item parameters concerns the regression of item responses on ability. Assume that the abilities for the 787 participants are known (actually, they were estimated using MML item parameter estimates). Figure 8.3 shows how the probability of success increases with trait level for four ART items. Although the responses to an ART item are scored dichotomously, these responses can be regressed on trait level. The boxplots on Fig. 8.4 shows how responses to Item 22 is related to trait level on ART. Obviously, the distribution of trait level when Item 22 is failed is much lower level than when it is passed.

A slope and an intercept can be estimated by regressing responses to Item 22 on trait level. Because the item response is a dichotomous variable, a logistic regression is more appropriate than a simple linear regression. In a logistic regression, the probability of passing a dichotomous variable (i.e., the item) is predicted. An intercept, b_0, and a slope, b_1, for trait level are estimated. However, these parameters are contained in the exponent of a logistic function, x, as follows:

$$P(x_{is} = 1) = \exp(y)/(1 + \exp(y)) \tag{8.3}$$

and $y = b_0 + b_1\theta_s$. Table 8.4 shows the logistic regression estimate, b_0, as well as the Rasch basic data estimates.

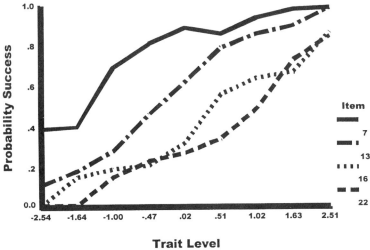

FIG. 8.3.   Item-solving probabilities for four items by known trait levels.

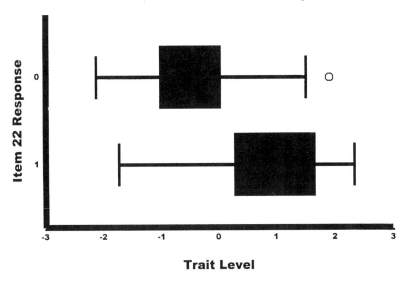

FIG. 8.4.   Box plots of ability distributions for passed versus failed items.

196

TABLE 8.4
Heuristic Item Estimates

Item Bank	P Value	Basic Data Matrix	Logistic Regression
7	.84	−1.91	−1.65
10	.82	−1.57	−1.50
13	.65	−.68	−.50
8	.66	−.46	−.45
27	.60	−.09	−.17
19	.47	.25	.46
16	.45	.54	.55
33	.40	1.01	.90
22	.38	1.06	.91
28	.26	1.87	1.57

The meaning of an item-characteristics curve as a regression becomes clear if the logistic regression model is compared to the 2PL IRT model. In fact, by reparameterizing y, the two 2PL model is obtained, with $y = \alpha_i(\theta_s - \beta_i)$, where α_i is item discrimination and β_i is item difficulty. Comparing models, the item discrimination parameter α_i equals the slope b_1 and item difficulty, β_i, equals a transformation of the intercept, $-b_0/b_1$.

To illustrate the empirical similarity of logistic regression to the 2PL IRT model, the responses to ART items were regressed separately on the known trait levels. Figure 8.5 shows two items, with the following probabilities plotted by trait level: (a) the observed probability of item solving, (b) the predicted probability from the logistic regression estimates of intercept and slope, and (c) the predicted probability from MML estimates for the 2PL model (described later in this chapter). Consider Item 13, where the MML predictions shadow the logistic regression predictions. Furthermore, both predictions are close to the observed probabilities, which supports the fit of the model to the item.

Last, consider Fig. 8.6. Here, the logistic regression estimates for all ten items were transformed into estimates of item discrimination and item difficulty, as described earlier, and then regressed on MML estimates for the 2PL. Notice the strong similarity of these estimates.

A logistic regression is also appropriate for describing how the changes in item probabilities relate to ability for the Rasch model. The Rasch model contains no item discrimination parameter, or equivalently, assumes that the item discrimination parameter is a constant value of 1.00. So, for logistic regression, the slopes must be constrained to 1.00. A generalized linear modeling approach to applying these constraints, with adjustments for anchoring, yielded the item difficulties shown on Table 8.4. Also shown in Table 8.4 are the item difficulties from the Rasch basic data matrix. Notice the similarity of these values, except at the extremes. Figure 8.7 shows the

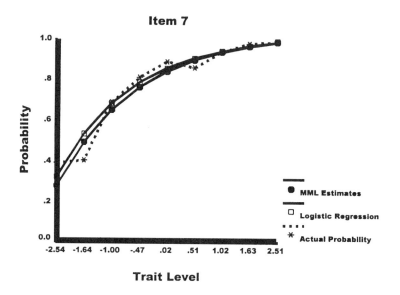

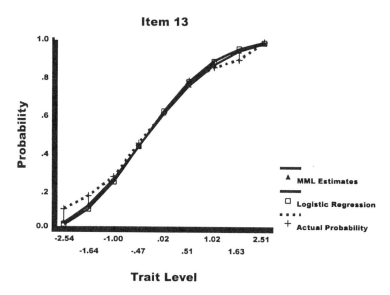

FIG. 8.5. Actual and predicted item probabilities for two items.

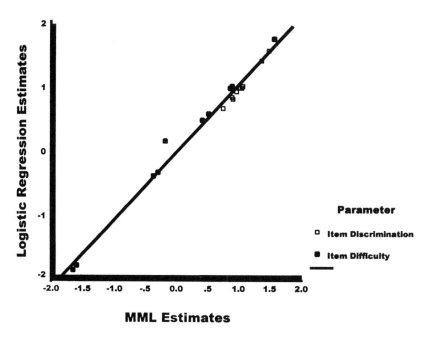

FIG. 8.6.   Regression of logistic item estimates on MML 2PL estimates.

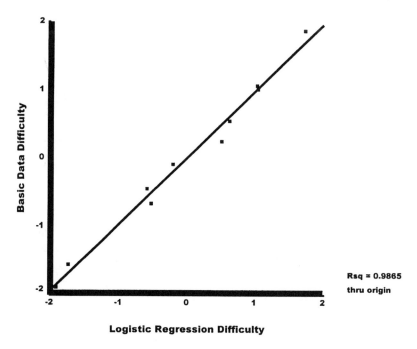

FIG. 8.7.   Regression of basic data matrix estimates on logistic estimates for the Rasch model.

regression of the basic data matrix item difficulties on the logistic item difficulties. The fit is high, $r^2 = .99$, and the slope of the regression line, through the origin, is close to 1.00 (i.e., slope = 1.12).

MAXIMUM LIKELIHOOD ESTIMATION

Three popular estimation methods for IRT item parameters are based on the maximum likelihood (ML) principle. The ML principle specifies how model prediction errors are quantified. Errors must be quantified because the parameters in a model are estimated to minimize error. For an ordinary least squares estimation method, such as those typically used in multiple regression and other general linear models, *error* is defined as the squared difference between the observed and the predicted value of the dependent variable. In contrast, for ML estimation, *error* is defined as unlikely observed data. Error definitions are implemented in the estimation equations for the model parameters (given later in this chapter).

Under large sample conditions, ML estimates of parameters have several optimal properties: (a) consistency, convergence to the true value with increasing sample size, (b) efficiency, the relatively smallest standard error, and (c) normally distributed estimation error. Furthermore, the overall likelihood of the data has a known relationship to the chi-square distribution, which permits models to be compared by the ratio of their likelihoods.

Although ML parameter estimates generally have desirable properties, some properties may not hold for a particular IRT model under a certain ML estimation method. A special difficulty in estimating IRT model parameters is that person parameters, as well as item parameters, are unknown. For example, although consistency is a general ML property, some IRT item parameter estimators can be inconsistent. An estimator is inconsistent when the precision does not increase with the number of observations. Under some ML methods, increasing the number of observations (i.e., persons) also increases the number of person parameters to be estimated. Person parameters are thus incidental or nuisance parameters, which complicate estimation of item or structural parameters (see Neyman & Scott, 1948) for certain models and methods.

Maximum Likelihood Estimation
With Known Person Parameters

Prior to elaborating some popular ML methods for estimating item parameters, we will begin with estimation assuming known person parameters. Although this method is not appropriate for practical applications, there are two advantages to presenting it. First, the development given later mirrors the description of person-parameter estimation described in chapter 7. Thus, the reader may be provided some continuity between the estimation chapters. Second, JML estimation is closely related to estimation with known person parameters.

Expressing the Likelihood of Item Response Data

ML estimation defines model prediction error in a special way; namely, error is an unlikely observation, given the model. Thus, we begin by defining the probability of a person's response to a particular item and end by defining the full data likelihood, the responses of all persons to all the items.

Probability of an Item Response. For dichotomous items (e.g., Pass-Fail; Yes-No), two response probabilities, P_{is} for passing and Q_{is} for failing, are predicted from the IRT model. So, for example with the Rasch model, the following equations give the two probabilities, conditional on the parameters for persons and items:

$$P(X_{is} = 1 \mid \theta_s, \beta_i) = \frac{\exp(\theta_s - \beta_i)}{1 + \exp(\theta_s - \beta_i)}$$

$$(8.5)$$

$$P(X_{is} = 0 \mid \theta_s, \beta_i) = \frac{1}{1 + \exp(\theta_s - \beta_i)}.$$

Suppose that a person fails a particular item ($X_{is} = 0$). If the probability of failing the item was quite small for the person (e.g., .07), then this observation is quite unlikely. On the other hand, if the predicted probability for failing was high (e.g., .98), then the observation is very likely. The formulation for representing the likelihood of observations may be generalized readily to other models and other distributional forms. That is, the Rasch model logit could be replaced by other models such as 2PL or 3PL. Or, other distributional forms, such as the normal ogive, may also be substituted in Eq. 8.5.

The probabilities for a correct and an incorrect response in Eq. 8.5 can be combined into a single expression for the probability of the observed response, X_{is}, whether it is 0 or 1, as follows:

$$P(X_{is}) = P_{is}^{X_{is}} Q_{is}^{1 - X_{is}}$$

$$(8.6)$$

Notice how the exponent controls whether the probability of passing or the probability of failing, Q_{is}, is used. That is, if the person passes the item, X_{is} is 1, so the probability of the response is modeled as $P_{is}^1 Q_{is}^{1-1}$, or just P_{is}. The term Q_{is}^0 falls out because it is defined as 1. If the person fails the item, X_{is} is 0, and then the probability of the response is modeled by Q_{is}.

Equation 8.6 models dichotomous data because a probability is given for each possible response, 0 and 1. Equation 8.6 generalizes to multiple category data (e.g., rating scales). In this case, a probability is predicted for the observed category response, X_{isx}.

It is convenient to express the probabilities in logarithmic form in the estimation process. Thus, the probability for a response to a particular item, from Eq. 8.6 can be given as

$$\ln(P(X_{is})) = X_{is}\,(\ln P_{is}) + (1 - X_{is})\,\ln Q_{is} \tag{8.7}$$

As in Eq. 8.6, X_{is} again controls whether the probability is given as passing or failing, but it is now given in logarithms.

The Likelihood of a Response Pattern.   The likelihood the response pattern of person s to I items, $(X_{1s}, \dots, X_{Is})$, conditional on trait level θ_s and the vector of item parameters, β, is simply the product of their response probabilities, as follows:

$$P(X_{1s}, \dots, X_{is} \mid \theta_s, \underline{\beta}) = \Pi_i\ P_{is}^{X_{is}} Q_{is}^{1-X_{is}} \tag{8.8}$$

For notational convenience, we will now denote the response pattern likelihood, $P(X_{1s}, \dots, X_{is} \mid \theta_s, \underline{\beta})$, as $P(\underline{X}_s \mid \theta_s, \underline{\beta})$.

The Data Likelihood.   The data likelihood, $P(\mathbf{X})$, may be obtained by multiplying Eq. 8.8 for response patterns across persons, as follows:

$$P(\mathbf{X}) = \Pi_s\ P(\underline{X}_s \mid \theta_s, \underline{\beta}) \tag{8.9}$$

Usually this probability is expressed as a log likelihood, which is the sum of the log likelihoods for response patterns (Eq. 8.9) across persons as follows:

$$\ln(P(\mathbf{X})) = \sum_s \ln P(\underline{X}_s \mid \theta_s, \underline{\beta}) \tag{8.10}$$

Search Procedures

For nonlinear models, such as IRT models, ML estimation typically involves a search process to find values that maximize the data likelihood.

ML estimation procedures capitalize on the relative changes in the data log likelihood under various possible values for a parameter.

In this section, we begin by showing how changes in item parameter estimates influence the data log likelihood. These changes provide diagnostic information about how to search for the ML estimate. Practically, however, the search procedure is applied to a set of *item estimation equations*. The item estimation equations define a set of numerical conditions that are fulfilled when the ML estimates have been reached. Estimation equations are shown for the Rasch model (other models are shown in the technical appendix at the end of this chapter). Last, a popular search procedure, Newton–Raphson, is elaborated and then illustrated on the ART data. The Newton–Raphson method was also elaborated in chapter 7 for ability estimation, so this chapter provides continuity.

Changes in Data Likelihoods.   Changes in the data log likelihood under various possible values for the item parameter guides the estimation search process. Figure 8.8 plots the log likelihood of the ART data under varying estimates of difficulty for Item 8 (using Eq. 8.10, holding constant the other item parameters). The data likelihood curve is an inverted U-shaped curve.

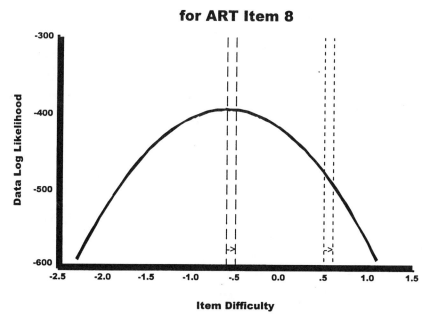

FIG. 8.8.   Data likelihood under various values of an item parameter.

The quality of a particular item-difficulty estimate is related to the shape of the curve. Two general points are worth noting. First, the curve peaks at the maximum likelihood value. In Fig. 8.8, the curve peaks at the ML estimate of –.55. Notice that only one peak occurs, which means that no other maxima exist for this function. Second, the data likelihood changes more slowly near the point of maximum likelihood. For example, as shown on Fig. 8.8, the data log likelihood changes more slowly between the values –.40 and –.50, which are close to the peak, than between the values .50 and .60.

This diagnostic information can be formalized by computing the instantaneous rate of change in the log likelihood at various points. A tangent to the curve represents the instantaneous rate of change. The *value* of the instantaneous rate of change can diagnose if a particular item difficulty value is at, above, or below the ML value. For the item shown in Fig. 8.8, a tangent to the curve for the item difficulty of 1.00 would have a negative slope. The instantaneous rate of change at the item difficulty value 1.00 is a large negative value, which means that it is greater than the ML estimate. The instantaneous rate of change for an item difficulty of –1.50 is a large positive value, which indicates that it is less than the ML estimate. The *relative change* in the instantaneous rates of change diagnoses the distance from the ML estimate. The changes in slopes are smaller near the peak.

Formulas for the instantaneous rate of change and the relative changes can be derived by differential calculus. The first symbolic partial derivative of the log likelihood, with respect to an item parameter, gives the instantaneous rate of change. The second symbolic partial derivative gives the rate of change of the *slopes* at a particular point. Table 8.6 in the Technical Appendix to this chapter presents the first and second derivatives of the item parameters for three standard IRT models for dichotomous data. Although item difficulty parameters are contained in all three models, notice that the derivatives depend on the particular model. Similar derivatives could be presented for multiple-category and rating-scale IRT models.

Estimation Equations.   Estimation equations express a set of conditions that are fulfilled when the ML estimates have been found. Because the point of maximum likelihood is reached when the instantaneous rate of change is zero, this defines conditions that are reached by the ML estimates. The estimation equations are the instantaneous rate of change formulas set to zero.

For example, in the Rasch model, the estimation equations for the item difficulties are the following:

$$0 = \Sigma_s X_{1s} - \Sigma_s P(X_{1s} = 1 \mid \theta_s, \underline{\beta})$$

$$0 = \Sigma_s X_{2s} - \Sigma_s P(X_{2s} = 1 \mid \theta_s, \underline{\beta})$$
$$\vdots \qquad \vdots \qquad \qquad \vdots$$
$$0 = \Sigma_s X_{Is} - \Sigma_s P(X_{Is} = 1 \mid \theta_s, \underline{\beta}) \qquad \qquad (8.11)$$

where $\Sigma_s X_{is}$ is the sum of the responses to item i over persons (i.e., the number of persons passing the item) and $\Sigma_s P(X_{is} = 1 \mid \theta_s, \underline{\beta})$ is the sum of the probabilities predicted over persons. The estimation equations define the ML estimate as the value for the item parameter that makes the sum of the item probabilities over persons equal to the number of persons who pass the item. For 2PL and 3PL models, these sums are weighted by the item discriminations (see the technical appendix to this chapter).

Newton–Raphson Search Procedure

The Newton–Raphson method is an iterative search process in which the parameter estimates are successively improved. The search process under Newton–Raphson estimation requires (a) defining the conditions that are fulfilled when the best estimate has been obtained, (b) finding improved estimates for the item parameters, and (c) defining a criterion to determine when to stop the search process.

Conditions Fulfilled. The Newton–Raphson procedure requires that the likelihood function has both a first and a second derivative. The first derivative defines the conditions that are fulfilled when the ML estimates have been obtained (i.e., the estimation equations). Figure 8.9 shows the value of the estimation equation for Item 8 under various item difficulty estimates. The ML estimate (shown) is reached when the estimation equation value is zero (also shown).

Improving Parameter Estimates. The Newton–Raphson procedure starts with some initial values for the item-difficulty estimates (sometimes started at 0.00). An improved parameter estimate is then computed by subtracting a value, h, from the current parameter estimate. The constant h is computed as the value of the estimation equation (first derivative times -1) divided by the second derivative. The first derivative determines the direction (positive or negative) to move from the current estimate in searching for a more likely estimate. The second derivative determines how quickly the estimation equation is changing and thus provides information about how drastically to modify the old estimate. If the slopes are changing slowly at the current estimate, the point of maximum likelihood is close. Thus, a small change is needed. The improved value of the item-difficulty estimate is given as follows:

$$\beta_{improved} = \beta_{current} - h \qquad \qquad (8.12)$$

Newton Raphson Procedure

ART Item 8

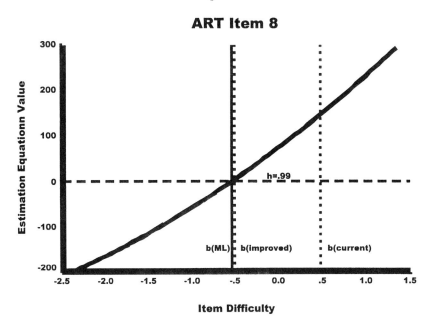

FIG. 8.9.   Estimation equation values under various values of an item parameter.

Figure 8.9 plots the value of the estimation equation at various possible values of item difficulty. In Fig. 8.9, the current item difficulty estimate is .47. The value of h is .99, which is subtracted from the current value to yielding an improved of $-.52$. Notice that the improved estimate is very close to the maximum likelihood estimate of $-.55$.

Stopping the Search: Convergence Criterion.   When the difference between the item parameter estimates from two successive stages becomes very small, the search process is stopped. The convergence criterion specifies the value that is so small that further improvements will be regarded as meaningless. The criterion may be applied to each item or to a summary function for the set.

Standard Errors for Item Parameter Estimates

The standard errors of item parameters reflect how rapidly the data likelihood changes around the parameter value. The more rapidly the likelihood changes, the smaller the standard error.

The formulas for standard errors are derived from the second partial derivatives. Recall that the second derivative reflects how rapidly the slopes are changing around a particular value. The rate of change at the ML estimate (i.e., the peak of the log likelihood) determines the standard error. In practice, an information matrix is calculated from the second partial derivatives and cross products (see Hambleton & Swaminathan, 1985). Under large sample theory, the inverse of this matrix is interpreted as the parameter covariance matrix. The square root of the diagonal values are the expected standard errors for the parameters. The technical apprendix to this chapter presents the first and second derivatives for the 1PL, 2PL, and 3PL models. For polytomous and multidimensional models, the reader should refer to the papers by the original developers.

To illustrate, the standard error for the Rasch model is relatively simple. The square root of the reciprocal of the probabililty of passing times the probability of failing each item, $P_{is}Q_{is}$, summed over persons, gives the standard error, σ_β, as follows:

$$\sigma_\beta = (1/\Sigma_s P_{is}Q_{is})^{1/2} \qquad (8.13)$$

Notice that the standard error for item difficulty is smallest when the denominator is large. This occurs when the probability of passing is close to the probability of failing (i.e., $P_{is} = Q_{is} = .50$) for many persons in the calibration sample. Stated another way, when an item is near the threshold level for many persons in the calibration sample (i.e., $P_{is} = Q_{is} = .50$), the standard error for a Rasch model item difficulty is small.

Three Maximum Likelihood Estimation Methods
for Unknown Trait Levels

In typical IRT applications, both item parameters and trait levels are unknown and must be estimated from the same data. Estimating item parameters with unknown trait levels is analogous to performing a logistic regression with unknown predictor values. Joint maximum likelilhood (JML), marginal maximum likelihood (MML), and conditional maximum likelihood (CML) are three popular methods for estimation with unknown trait levels. The three ML methods handle the problem of unknown trait levels differently. The three methods differ in how the probability of the observed response patterns is conceptualized.

Holland (1990) compared the sampling theory foundations of the three ML methods. Holland (1990) noted two general interpretations of response pattern probabilities that differ qualitatively. In the *stochastic subject* interpretation of probability, the persons who were observed are regarded as fixed. The probability represents the inherent unpredictability of specific events; that is, the encounter of a person with a particular item. The stochastic subject probability refers to repeatability over conditions,

such as the expected relative frequency of a response over repeated presentation of the same or equivalent items. Both JML and CML implicitly
employ stochastic subject interpretations in their conceptualization of response-pattern probabilities. In the *random sampling* interpretation of
probability, the persons who were observed are regarded as a random
sample from a population. The probability of observing the sample depends on the relative frequency of their trait levels in the population. That
is, the probability of observing the particular response patterns in the
sample depends jointly on the distribution of trait level and the IRT model
prediction from item parameters. Thus, a specific distribution of trait level
must be assumed to interpret the probability. MML interfaces well with
the random sampling interpretation, although MML is also compatible
with much weaker interpretations, such as exchangeability of examinees
with equivalent trait levels (Mislevy, 1999, personal communication).

Holland (1990) also analyzed the three ML methods for their expression of the data likelihoods. Results of his analysis are included in the
evaluation of each method.

Joint Maximum Likelihood (JML)

In JML estimation, unknown trait levels are handled by using provisional trait level estimates as known values. The provisional trait level estimates themselves are improved by using subsequently estimated item
parameters, which also are successively improved. To understand JML,
we first consider the data likelihood that is maximized. Then, we outline
an iterative two-stage process that produces improved estimates for items
and persons.

Response Pattern Likelihood.   The likelihood of a response pattern is
modeled exactly as shown in Eq. 8.8 for known person parameters except
provisional trait level estimates are substituted to compute the individual
response probabilities. Then, the data likelihood may be computed by
multiplying across persons, as in Eq. 8.9. However, the likelihood must be
interpreted differently since the response pattern probabilities depend on
estimated trait levels. These trait level estimates are best estimates at a certain iteration in the JML procedure. The JML estimates of item parameters
consequently rest on the quality of the person parameter estimates.

Estimation Equations.   The estimation equations are the same equations derived for ML estimation with known trait levels except that provisional estimates replace known trait levels in the computation of the
model probabilities. For the Rasch model, Eq. 8.11 defines the estimation
equations. Standard errors for the item parameters may also be estimated

by inserting the parameter estimates into the appropriate formulas, such as Eq. 8.13 for the Rasch model item difficulties. For 2PL and 3PL models, see the technical appendix to this chapter.

Procedure.   JML estimation is an iterative procedure that typically involves sequential estimates of person and item parameters. The sequential procedure is widely applicable, and it illustrates most clearly how provisional estimates replace known parameters. In the first stage, person parameters are estimated, and in the second stage item parameters are estimated. The first iteration of the two-stage procedure involves specifying starting values for the item parameters (e.g., a common value such as zero) so that ML estimates of person parameters can be obtained. Then, item parameters are estimated using the first person-parameter estimates. In the second iteration, person parameters are estimated using the improved item parameter estimates. Then, item parameters are estimated again, using the improved person-parameter estimates, and so forth. The iterations continue until the item parameters change very little between successive iterations. A convergence criterion is applied to the differences in item parameters between successive iterations. Most programs allow the user to specify a convergence value but also contain a default convergence criterion as well.

Illustration.   Table 8.5 presents results on JML estimates for the 10-item ART data. Shown are both the item parameter estimates and their estimated standard errors.

Evaluation.   JML has been used fairly extensively, especially in the early IRT programs. JML has several advantages. First, the algorithm is

TABLE 8.5
Maximum Likelihood Estimates for the 10–Item ART Data

Item Bank	JML Estimates		MML Estimates		CML Estimates	
	Difficulty	SE	Difficulty	SE	Difficulty	SE
7	−1.596	.102	−1.591	.108	−1.586	.105
10	−1.414	.097	−1.442	.103	−1.440	.102
8	−.460	.084	−.470	.087	−.473	.085
13	−.422	.083	−.419	.087	.000	.085
27	−1.51	.082	−.153	.084	−.155	.082
19	.452	.081	.437	.083	.438	.081
16	.531	.081	.531	.083	.532	.081
33	.752	.082	.776	.084	.778	.083
22	.863	.082	.868	.085	.870	.083
28	1.445	.088	1.462	.091	1.457	.090

easily programmable. Second, JML is applicable to many IRT models. Both 2PL and 3PL can be estimated with JML, for example. Third, JML is computationally efficient (however, with increasingly powerful computers this is less advantageous). However, JML has several disadvantages. First, the item parameter estimates do not have desirable properties. For example, it is well known that JML item parameter estimates are biased, although correction factors can remove most of the bias. Further, JML item parameter estimates are inconsistent for fixed length tests. Adding more persons for most IRT models does not result in improved estimates because more parameters are estimated. Second, and linked to the first disadvantage, the meaning of the JML standard errors is questionable. Because the item parameter estimates are biased and inconsistent, they do not provide optimal estimates to use in calculating the standard errors. Holland (1990) notes that JML standard errors are probably too small due to the handling of the unknown person parameters. Third, the JML likelihoods have questionable utility for hypotheses about IRT models, such as the comparative fit of different IRT models. Holland (1990) notes that the likelihoods for JML are probably too high. Fourth, estimates are not available for items or persons with perfect scores (all passed or all failed). When no constraints are placed on the solution, perfect scores provide no information about the parameters.

Marginal Maximum Likelihood (MML)

In MML estimation, unknown trait levels are handled by expressing the response pattern probabilities as expectations from a population distribution. In MML, the observed data are regarded as a random sample from a population (Bock & Lieberman, 1970). However, a practical estimation procedure was not available until Bock and Aiken (1981) developed an expectation/maximization (EM) algorithm (discussed later in this chapter) to estimate expectations. The EM algorithm for MML is an iterative procedure, like JML. For MML, however, the iterations successively improve the expected frequencies for correct responses and trait level. The following sections elaborate the Bock and Aitken (1981) procedure for MML estimation.

Response Pattern Likelihood. MML models the probability of observing a response pattern in the population. A probability can be modeled for each unique response pattern, $\underline{X}_p$. The persons who produce the pattern are regarded as replicates. The number of persons with the pattern is noted as n_p. For a particular trait level θ_q the probability of a response pattern can be computed from the IRT model as in Eq. 8.8. Although trait levels are not known for the persons who are observed, it is assumed that the probabilities of the various trait levels, $P(\theta_q)$, are specified. It may be known, in advance, that the distribution is normal with a certain mean and variance. Or, a distribution may be estimated empirically from the test data (see de Leeuw & Verhelst, 1986). In either case, the probabilities for the various trait levels can be specified.

For example, assume that the probability of each trait level can be specified from a population distribution. Then, the probability of observing a certain response pattern in a random sample from the population, $P(\underline{X}_p \mid \underline{\beta})$, involves (a) the probability of the pattern under $\underline{\theta}_q$, (b) the probability of observing the trait level in the population, $P(\theta_q)$, and then (c) summed over the possible discrete trait levels, as follows:

$$P(\underline{X}_p \mid \underline{\beta}) = \Sigma_q^Q P(\underline{X}_s \mid \theta_q, \underline{\beta}) P(\theta_q) \qquad (8.14)$$

This is also known as the *marginal* probabiity of response pattern.

Suppose that the population distribution consisted of five discrete trait levels, -2.00, -1.00, $.00$, 1.00, and 2.00, with probabilities of $.055$, $.244$, $.403$, $.244$, and $.055$, respectively. Then, the likelihood of a particular response pattern (e.g., an ART response pattern where $\underline{X}_s = 1,1,1,1,1,0,1,0,0,0$) in the population is the following:

$$P(\mathbf{X}(_p \mid \underline{\beta}) = .055(P(\underline{X}_p \mid \theta_q = -2, \underline{\beta}) + .244(P(\underline{X}_p \mid \theta_q = -1, \underline{\beta}) +$$
$$.403(P(\underline{X}_p \mid \overline{\theta}_q = 0, \underline{\beta}) + .244(P(\underline{X}_p \mid \overline{\theta}_q = 1, \underline{\beta}) + .055(P(\underline{X}_p \mid \theta_q = 2, \underline{\beta}) \qquad (8.15)$$

where each response pattern probability, $(P(\underline{X}_p \mid \theta_q, \underline{\beta})$, is computed from the IRT model, as in Eq. 8.8.

Of course, it is more reasonable to assume that trait level is a continous variable with a specific shape distribution in the population, such as a normal distribution, rather than a set of discrete values. Thus, for a continous variable, the expected value for a response pattern requires integrating across the range of trait level values. Practically, a procedure known as Gaussian quadrature is applied to find the expectation.

Gaussian quadrature is analogous to dividing a normal distribution into segments, with a representative value (i.e., the quadrature point), and a probability of occurrence (i.e., the weight). Figure 8.10 shows a normal distribution of trait level that is segmented into five regions. The five discrete trait levels that were calculated earlier are now shown as quadrature points to represent trait level values in the regions, and the weights are identical to the probabilities used before. The likelihood of the response pattern in the population may be computed from the quadrature points and weights exactly as in Eq. 8.15.

Notice that the quadrature points are equally spaced in this example. The probability associated with a quadrature point is the normal curve

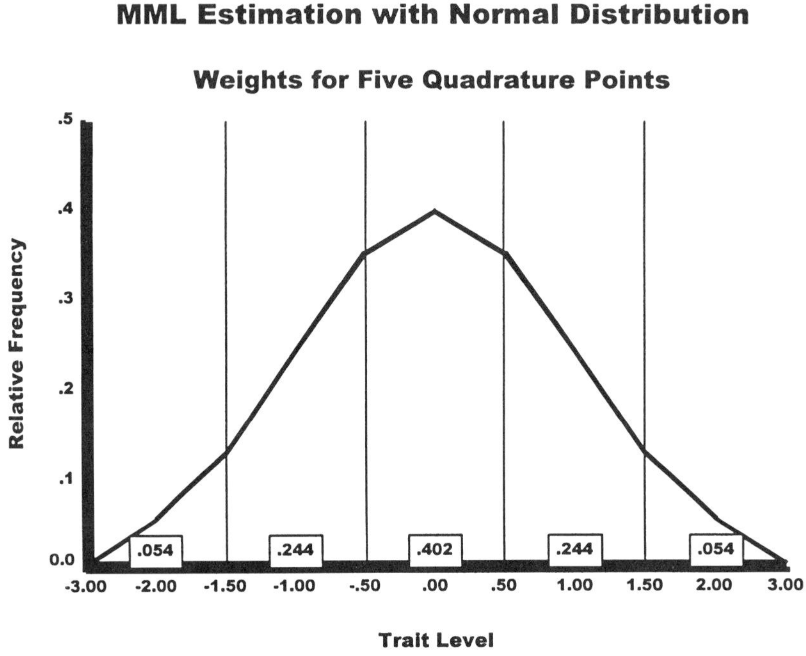

MML Estimation with Normal Distribution

Weights for Five Quadrature Points

FIG. 8.10.   Guassian quadrature with five points.

frequency density at the point, adjusted so that the sum over the regions is 1.00. If the limits of the intervals define the region, as shown in Fig. 8.10, the normal curve probabilities associated with five regions of .067, .241, .383, .241, and .067, respectively, approximate the quadrature weights. As the number of quadrature points increases, the weights more closely approximate the probabilities in the standard normal distribution. More formally, the probability of obtaining a particular response vector, $\underline{X}_p$ in a random sample from the population, is given by integrating the IRT model prediction over the range of trait level, as follows:

$$P(\underline{X}_p) = \int \Pi_i P^{x_{ip}} Q^{1-x_{ip}} \, g(\theta) d\theta \qquad (8.16)$$

where $g(\theta)$ is the probably density of θ, the latent ability.

The quadrature points need not be equally spaced, however. Bock and Aitken (1981), for example, use Gauss–Hermite quadrature with unequal spacing to give more optimal results for integrating a normal distribution.

Data Likelihood.   The data likelihood may be obtained by multiplying the response pattern likelihoods across the persons observed. MML is a full population model for the particular response patterns that are observed. The log likelihood of the data in MML is the sum of the marginal probabilities of the response patterns (from Equation 8.14), weighted by their frequency, n_p, as follows:

$$\ln L(\mathbf{X}) = \Sigma_p n_p \ln P(\underline{X}_p \mid \underline{\beta}) \tag{8.17}$$

MML requires the distribution of trait levels to be specified. Typically, the distribution is specified as normal. However, the distribution need not be known in advance. If sufficient sample size is available, the trait distribution may be estimated from the data. Or, other nonnormal distributions, if appropriate, can be specified (see Mislevy, 1984).

Estimation Equations. The MML estimation equations involve expected frequencies rather than observed frequencies as in JML. The expected frequencies are based on the probabilities of the response patterns, given the item parameters and the assumed trait level distribution. For example, to estimate item difficulty for the Rasch model, the expectations are summed over q trait levels (i.e., quadrature values), as follows:

$$
\begin{aligned}
0 &= \Sigma_q x'_{1.q} - \Sigma_q N'_q \left(P(X_{1j} = 1 \mid \theta_q, \underline{\beta}) \right) \\
0 &= \Sigma_q x'_{2.q} - \Sigma_q N'_q \left(P(X_{2j} = 1 \mid \theta_q, \underline{\beta}) \right) \\
&\vdots \\
0 &= \Sigma_q x'_{I.q} - \Sigma_q N'_q \left(P(X_{Is} = 1 \mid \theta_q, \underline{\beta}) \right)
\end{aligned}
\tag{8.18}
$$

where $x'_{i.q}$ is the expected number of persons in the sample to pass item i at θ_q, $P_i(\theta_q)$ is the IRT model prediction for passing item i at θ_q and N'_q is the expected number of persons with trait level θ_q. In contrast to the JML estimation equations (Eq. 8.11), the observed number correct is replaced by an expectation, $\Sigma_q x'_{i.q}$, which depends on the probability of observing various response patterns (see the Technical Appendix to this chapter). Also, model predictions, $P_i(\theta_q)$, are weighted by the expected number of persons at a trait level, N'_q, rather than computed for each person observed as in JML.

Procedure. The Bock and Aitken (1981) MML procedure applies the EM algorithm to estimate the item parameters. The EM algorithm is so named because it has an expectation (E) stage and a maximization (M) stage. In the expectation stage, the expected number of persons at each trait level (represented by the quadrature points) is computed as well as the expected number of persons passing each particular item. Then, using these expectations in the estimation equations, item parameter estimates are found to maximize the likelihoods in the maximization stage. A second expectation stage then uses the item parameters to compute updated expectations, which is by another maximization stage to maximize the data likelihood based on the updated expectations. Then, when the values converge, a Newton–Gauss procedure is employed to find the final item parameter estimates and standard errors.

Illustration. Table 8.5 shows MML estimates for the 10-item ART data, along with their associated standard errors. It can be seen that these values are similar to the JML estimates.

Evaluation. MML has several advantages. First, MML is readily applicable to all types of IRT models, including multidimensional models. Second, MML is efficient for both long and short tests. Third, the MML estimates of item standard errors may be justified as good approximations of expected sampling variance of the estimates. Fourth, estimates are available for perfect scores. No loss of information occurs for persons because perfect responses also have an expected relative frequency. Items need not be trimmed, particularly if a distribution of item parameters can be specified as well. Fifth, MML data likelihoods can be justified as useful for hypothesis testing and fit indices. If one model is a subset of a larger model, then a likelihood ratio chi-square test can determine whether the models differ significantly. For example, the likelihood ratio test may be applied to determine whether the 2PL model fits significantly better than the 1PL model. See Bock and Aitkin (1981) and Mislevy (1986) for further details on these advantages.

MML also has some disadvantages. First, an effective algorithm for MML estimation is difficult to program. Effective computer programs must be both computationally and numerically sophisticated. However, despite this disadvantage, IRT programs for the newer, more complex models, are increasingly employing MML (e.g., Adams, Wilson, & Wang, 1996; Wilson, 1989). Second, a distribution must be assumed for trait level, thus making the parameter estimates contingent on the appropriateness of the assumed distribution. It is not clear that this is a great disadvantage, however. The assumed distribution need not be normal, and in fact can be estimated from the data. Various trait level distributions with skew or nonnormal kurtosis can be accommodated by specifying weights. Furthermore, item parameter estimates appear to be not strongly influenced by moderate departures from normality, so inappropriately specified distributions may not be very important.

Conditional Maximum Likelihood (CML)

In CML estimation, unknown trait levels are handled by expressing the response pattern probability without including the trait level parameters.

This is possible if a sufficient statistic is available in the data for estimating trait level. In the Rasch model, persons item total scores are sufficient statistics for estimating trait level. A sufficient statistic means that no other information is needed from the data for estimating the parameters. Thus, persons with the same total score (i.e., the sufficient statistic), regardless of which items are passed, will receive the same trait level estimate. In more complex models, such as 2PL and 3PL, total score is not a sufficient statistic for estimating trait level. Trait level estimates depend on which items are passed. Thus, since CML requires sufficient statistics for trait level, CML is applied only to the Rasch model and its extensions. Similar to JML estimation, the person parameters are regarded as fixed values.

Response Pattern Likelihood.   In CML, the likelihood of a response pattern, $P(\underline{X}_s|\theta_s,\underline{\beta})$, is reformulated to include total score instead of the unknown person trait level, $\underline{\theta}_s$. Now, implicit in the response pattern $\underline{X}_s$ is two kinds of information; a certain number of items are passed, which gives a total score, r_s, and the specific items that are passed or failed. For CML, the second kind of information from the response pattern is irrelevant to the estimation of trait level; total score is a sufficient statistic.

CML estimation is based on factoring the probability of the response vector $P(\underline{X}_s|\theta_s,\underline{\beta})$ into two terms: (a) the probability of the total score, given the trait level and the item parameters, $\underline{P}(r_s|\theta_s,\underline{\beta})$, and (b) the probability of the specific response pattern, given total score and the item parameters, $\underline{P}(\underline{X}_s|r_s,\underline{\beta})$. The relationship is expressed as follows:

$$P(\underline{X}_s|\theta_s,\underline{\beta}) = P(r_s|\theta_s,\underline{\beta})\, P(\underline{X}_s|r_s,\underline{\beta}) \tag{8.19}$$

The probability of the response pattern in terms of r_s and the item parameters results from rearranging Eq. 8.19 gives, as follows:

$$P(\underline{X}_s|r_s,\underline{\beta}) = P(\underline{X}_s|\theta_s,\underline{\beta})\big/P(r_s|\theta_s,\underline{\beta}) \tag{8.20}$$

The numerator of the right side of Eq. 8.20 may be readily computed from the IRT model. For the Rasch model, for example (see also Eq. 8.5), the probability of the response pattern is given as follows:

$$P(\underline{X}_s|\theta_s,\underline{\beta}) = \Pi_i P_i^{x_{is}}\, Q_i^{(1-x_{is})} = \Pi_i \frac{e^{x_{is}(\theta_s-\beta_i)}}{1+e^{(\theta_s-\beta_i)}} \tag{8.21}$$

On the far right, the response of Person s to item i, x_{is}, in the numerator controls whether the Rasch model predicts passing, P_i, or failing, Q_i.

The denominator is in Eq. 8.20, however, is new. The raw score r_s can result from several different response patterns, depending on which specific items are passed or failed. The probability of each *specific* response pattern that yields total score r_s for a particular trait level θ_s can be computed readily from Eq. 8.21. These probabilities are then summed over all possible response patterns yielding total score r_s as follows to give the probability of total score r_s for a particular trait level:

$$P(r_s | \theta_s , \underline{\beta}) = \Sigma_{\Sigma x_{is} - r_s} \, \Pi_i \, \frac{e^{x_{is}(\theta_s - \beta_i)}}{1 + e^{(\theta_s - \beta_i)}} \qquad (8.22)$$

where $\Sigma_{\Sigma x_{is} - r_s}$ means the summation over all patterns that yield the score r. In this way, CML partials θ out of the likelihood equation.

Obviously, both the numerator and denominator on the right of Eq. 8.20 contain trait level parameters. However, it can be shown with some algebra (see the technical appendix to this chapter) that the terms involving trait level will cancel out. Thus, the response pattern likelihood involves only the item parameters, as follows:

$$P(\underline{X}_s | r_s , \underline{\beta}) = \Pi_i e^{-\beta_i x_{is}} / \gamma_r \qquad (8.23)$$

where γ_r represents the likelihood of r_s from the various combinations of items that can yield total score r_s. The term γ_r involves only item parameters. See the technical appendix to this chapter for details.

Data Likelihood.   Collecting the response pattern probabilities across persons gives the data likelihood, as follows:

$$P(\mathbf{X}_s | \underline{r} , \underline{\beta}) = \Pi_s \Pi_i e^{-\beta_i x_{is}} / \gamma_{rs} \qquad (8.24)$$

where x_{is} is the response of person j to item i and γ_{rs} is the appropriate elementary symmetric function for person s. The elementary symmetric function represents the probability of obtaining score r_s, given the item difficulties and all the possible response patterns for obtaining the score.

Proofs show that the log likelihood, $\ln P(\mathbf{X})$, of the data can be given as the sum of two components, if total score is a sufficient statistic

$$\ln P(\mathbf{X}) = - \Sigma_i x_{i.} \beta_i - \Sigma_s \ln \gamma_{r_s} \qquad (8.25)$$

where $x_{i.}$ is the number of persons passing item i, β_i is item difficulty, and γ_{rj} is defined earlier.

Estimation Equations.   The CML estimation equations for the Rasch model appear similar to the JML estimation equations except that the probability of a correct item response, $P(X_{1s}{=}1 \,|\, r_s, \, \underline{\beta})$, is expressed from total score rather than the unknown trait level. The CML estimation equations thus are the following:

$$0 = \Sigma_s x_{1s} - \Sigma_s \ P(X_{1s} = 1 \mid r_s, \beta)$$
$$0 = \Sigma_s x_{2s} - \Sigma_s \ P(X_{2s} = 1 \mid r_s, \beta)$$
$$\vdots \qquad \vdots \qquad \vdots$$
$$0 = \Sigma_s x_{Is} - \Sigma_s \ P(X_{Is} = 1 \mid r_s, \beta) \tag{8.26}$$

The probability $P(X_{is} = 1 \mid r_s, \beta)$ involves a stochastic person interpretation. That is, given that a person has a certain number of items correct in the test, r_s, what is the conditional probability that a particular item i is passed? The calculation of this probability involves elementary symmetric functions to represent the various combinations of correct items that result in score r_s, and relatively easier items will have higher conditional probabilities. Elementary symmetric functions are elaborated in the technical appendix to this chapter.

Like JML, the standard errors are based on the second derivatives of the likelihood function. The estimated item parameters are inserted as the true values.

Procedure. Item parameters are estimated by an iterative search process, such as Newton–Raphson, in CML estimation. After solving iteratively for the item parameters, trait levels are estimated for persons *post hoc*, assuming that the estimated item difficulties are now known parameters.

Illustration. The CML item parameter estimates and associated standard errors for the 10-item ART test are presented in Table 8.5. It can be seen that these values are similar to MML.

Evaluation. CML estimation has several advantages. First, no assumed distribution of trait level is required. The unknown person parameters are factored out of the estimation equations for items. Second, and following from the first advantage, CML item parameter estimates reflect the principle of invariant item parameters. That is, the estimates are invariant because they are not directly influenced by the trait level of the sample. Third, CML estimators have desirable properties under many conditions. That is, Andersen (1970) shows that they are consistent, normally distributed, and (under some weak assumptions) efficient. Fischer (1981) elaborates conditions for the existence and uniqueness of the CML estimates. Fourth, standard errors for the item parameters are more justifiable as representing sampling error as compared to JML. However, the meaning of sampling error for stochastic person probabilities has been questioned (see Holland, 1990). Fifth, the CML data log likelihood may be justified as useful for hypothesis testing. For example, the Rasch model can be compared to a model with constraints placed on the item parameters by a likelihood ratio chi-square test. The constraints can represent substantive hypotheses about the source of item difficulty. Examples are presented in chapter 11.

However, CML has several disadvantages. First, the most salient disadvantage is that it applies only to the Rasch model and its generalizations. Parameters for IRT models with item discrimination parameters, such as 2PL, 3PL, and many multidimensional models, cannot be estimated with CML because total score is not a sufficient statistic for estimating trait level in these models. Second, some loss of information occurs with CML. No estimates are available for items or persons with perfect scores (i.e., all passed or all failed). Third, numerical problems often develop for long tests. Precision in evaluating the elementary symmetric functions becomes difficult for long tests because the product term values (i.e., see Eq. A8.12) becomes extremely small. For the early computer programs, estimation often failed at about 30 items. Although newer CML programs can handle longer tests, numerical failure can occur for very long tests, complicated patterns of missing data, or polytomous data with many response categories. Last, the CML conditional probability is sometimes regarded as incomplete. Holland (1990) notes that the stochastic person probabilities in CML do not consider the probability of observing these particular persons. However, the various properties of CML estimates for the Rasch model (invariance, elimination of person parameters, and no assumptions about trait distribution) are regarded by many psychometricians as negating this criticism.

Thus, given the sufficient statistics for items and persons (i.e., the marginals in the basic data matrix) and the estimated item parameters, the likelihood of the data can be readily computed. Notice that neither the raw data nor the cell entries in the basic data matrix are needed for this computation.

OTHER ESTIMATION MODELS

A complete outline of estimation methods is beyond the scope of this introductory chapter, but some other estimation methods should be at least mentioned. Two methods in particular have a long history. Least-squares estimation procedures were extended to IRT models with discrimination parameters. McDonald (1962) developed methods for estimating parameters in nonlinear factor analysis, which readily extends to normal ogive IRT models. A conditional pairwise estimation (Chopin, 1968, 1983) was developed for the Rasch model as an efficient alternative to JML. This method uses responses of persons to pairs of items. Like CML, the trait levels cancel out of the estimation for item difficulties. Andrich (1988b) presents data showing good approximation to other methods, such as JML. Bayesian methods for estimating IRT parameters have also been developed. In a Bayesian method, prior probabilities are stated for the parameters, based on either theoretical or empirical considerations. Bayesian estimation methods have been developed in conjunction with MML and JML (Mislevy, 1986; Swaminathan & Gifford, 1985). For example, Mislevy (1986) places prior constraints on item discrimination values for MML estimation. Recently, repeated sampling methods have been developed to incorporate prior information into estimating item parameters. Repeated sampling, which is similar to the brute force estimation shown in chapter 3, may become practical with high speed computers. Albert (1992), for example, shows how Gibbs sampling can be used to simulate draws from distributions of item and ability parameters.

SUMMARY

This chapter examines several methods for estimating item parameters. To illustrate more clearly certain properties of IRT item parameters, two heuristic method are elaborated. The basic data matrix approach for estimating Rasch model parameters shows how the impact of the trait level distribution is removed from item difficulty estimates. The logistic regression approach shows how item parameters reflect the regression of item responses on trait level.

Prior to discussing the three major procedures for item estimation, some general features of ML estimation are discussed. The probability of a response pattern and the data likelihood are elaborated. Furthermore, estimation procedures were elaborated for the special case when trait level is known to show the generality of the method. Of course, trait levels typically are not known.

Three popular ML estimation procedures, JML, MML, and CML, are elaborated. The three procedures differ in handling the problem of unknown trait levels. JML models the response pattern probabilities using provisional estimates of trait level estimates. MML models the response-pattern probabilities as arising from random sampling from a population with a known distribution of trait level. CML models the response-pattern probabilities from the probabilities of the various response patterns that lead to the same total score.

The advantages and disadvantages of the three procedures are elaborated. MML has the most desirable features; not only do the estimators have desirable properties, but MML applies to many models and provides estimates for extreme values. In contrast, JML is limited by failing to achieve some desirable properties, such as unbiasedness and consistency. Although CML has many desirable features, it applies only to the Rasch model and is thus somewhat limited in applicability.

Item parameters for a 10-item test of abstract reasoning were estimated by each procedure to illustrate the method. For this particular example, however, neither the estimates nor their standard errors differ drastically among the three ML methods.

TECHNICAL APPENDIX

JML Estimation

The first and second derivatives of the log likelihood functions, conditional on trait level, are shown in Table 8.6 for the 1PL, 2PL, and 3PL models. Setting the first derivatives of the item parameters to zero yields the set of simultaneous equations required for estimation.

An inspection of the first derivatives, as shown in Table 8.6, clarifies the properties of the maximum likelihood estimate. For example, for the Rasch model, the maximum likelihood estimate occurs when sum across persons of the differences between the item response (X_{is}) and the probability predicted by the IRT model (P_{is}) is zero. In the 3PL model, in contrast, notice how this difference depends on a factor involving the lower asymptote (i.e., $[P_{is} - \gamma_i]/P_{is}]$).

An inspection of the second derivatives can explicate what contributes to the error variance of parameter estimates. A major contributor to the second derivative is the probability of passing times the probability of failing. This value is at a maximum if probability of passing equals the probability of failing (i.e., 50). For the Rasch model, under certain assumptions, the error variance for item difficulty may be estimated by the reciprocal of the second derivative. Thus, error variance for the parameter will be smallest when the probability of passing the item is .50 for many persons in the sample.

MML Estimation

Estimation Equations

The estimation equations for item i in MML involve the differences between two expectations, as follows:

$$0 = \Sigma_q n'_{iq} - \Sigma_q N'_q P_i(\theta_q) \tag{A8.1}$$

Both expectations involve predictions from the model and from the assumed distribution of trait level. First, the expected number of persons passing an item at a particular trait level, n'_{iq}, is obtained by summing across the observed response patterns p as follows:

TABLE 8.6

Derivatives for 1PL, 2PL, and 3PL IRT Models

Parameter	First Derivatives	Second Derivatives
3PL Model		
Discrimination	$\partial \ln L/\partial \alpha_i = (1-\gamma_i)^{-1} \Sigma_s[x_{is} - P_{is}][\theta_s - \beta_i][(P_{is} - \gamma_i)/P_{is}]$	$\partial^2 \ln L/\partial \alpha^2_i = -(1-\gamma_i)^{-2} \Sigma_s[1 - P_{is}][\theta_s - \beta_i]^2[P_{is} - \gamma_{is}][1 - (x_{is}\gamma_i)/P^2_{is}]$
Difficulty	$\partial \ln L/\partial \beta_i = -\alpha_i(1 - \gamma_i)^{-1} \Sigma_s[(P_{is} - \gamma_i)/P_{is}][x_{is} - P_{is}]$	$\partial^2 \ln L/\partial \beta^2_i = -\alpha^2_i(1 - \gamma_i)^{-2} \Sigma_s[1 - P_{is}][P_{is} - \gamma_i][1 - (x_{is}\gamma_i)/P^2_{is}]$
"Guessing"	$\partial \ln L/\partial \gamma_i = (1 - \gamma_i)^{-1} \Sigma_s(x_{is} - P_{is})/P_{is}$	$\partial^2 \ln L/\partial \gamma^2_i = -(1 - \gamma_i)^{-2} \Sigma_s[1 - P_{is}][x_{is}/P^2_{is}][1 - (x_{is}/P_{is})]$
2PL Model		
Discrimination	$\partial \ln L/\partial \alpha_i = \Sigma_s[(\theta_s - \beta_i)(x_{is} - P_{is})]$	$\partial^2 \ln L/\partial \alpha^2_i = -\Sigma_s[P_{is}(1 - P_{is})][\theta_s - \beta_i]^2$
Difficulty	$\partial \ln L/\partial \beta_i = -\alpha_i\Sigma_s[x_{is} - P_{is}]$	$\partial^2 \ln L/\partial \beta^2_i = -\alpha^2_i\Sigma_s[P_{is}(1 - P_{is})]$
1PL (Rasch Model)		
Difficulty	$\partial \ln L/\partial \beta_i = -\Sigma_s[x_{is} - P_{is}]$	$\partial^2 \ln L/\partial \beta^2_i = -\Sigma_s[P_{is}(1 - P_{is})]$

$$n'_{iq} = \Sigma_p \, n_p \, x_{ip} \, [P(\underline{X}_p|\theta_q)P(\theta_q)/P'(\underline{X}_p)] \qquad (A8.2)$$

where n_p is the number of persons with response pattern p, x_{ip} is the actual item response in pattern p (i.e., 0 or 1 for binary data), and the term in brackets is the relative probability of response pattern p at a particular trait level.

Second, an expectation for the number of people at a particular trait level (i.e., a quadrature point), N'_q, is given by the following:

$$N'_q = \Sigma_p \, n_p \, [P(\underline{X}_p|\theta_q)P(\theta_q)/P'(\underline{X}_p)] \qquad (A8.3)$$

Combining Eqs. A8.2 and A8.3 with the probability of the item response at a trait level $P_i(\theta_q)$ gives the estimation given by Eq. A8.1.

CML Estimation

As noted earlier, in CML the data likelihood and the estimation equations involve only the item parameters and total score. The unknown person parameters are not involved in this likelihood. This technical appendix shows how the person parameters are factored out of the likelihood equations.

Response Pattern Likelihood

The probability of a particular response vector $\underline{X}_s$ given a certain raw total score, x_s (also noted as r_s), and the item difficulty parameters β can be given by the ratio of two probabilities: (a) the probability of the response pattern, given trait level and item parameters are known, $\underline{P}(\underline{X}_s|\theta_s, \beta)$, and (b) the probability of the raw score given the trait level and the item parameters, $P(r_s|\theta_s, \beta)$. This ratio is expressed as follows:

$$P(\underline{X}_s \mid r_s, \underline{\beta}) = P(\underline{X}_s \mid \theta_s, \underline{\beta})/P(r_s \mid \theta_s, \underline{\beta}) \qquad (A8.4)$$

where $P(\underline{X}_s|\theta_s, \underline{\beta})$ is the probability of the vector with a known trait level and $\underline{P}(r_s|\theta_s, \beta)$ is the probability of the raw score, given the ability and item parameters.

Several proofs show that terms with the unknown trait levels on the right side of Eq. A8.4 cancel out (e.g., Andersen, 1972; Fischer, 1974; Gustafsson, 1980); thus, the response-pattern likelihood can be computed with only the item parameters and observable statistics from the data. For convenience, these proofs usually are developed with the antilogs of trait level ($\xi_s = e^{\theta_s}$) and item difficulty (item easiness $\varepsilon_{i_{=}} = e^{-\beta_i}$).

Both terms on the right side of Eq. A8.4 must be rewritten to accomplish the cancellation. The first term, the probability of a response pattern conditional on trait level (scaled as ξ_s) and the item-easiness parameters (scaled as ε rather than β), may be given as the product of predicted probabilities over items, as follows:

$$P(\underline{X}_s | \theta_s, \underline{\varepsilon}) = \Pi_i P_i^{x_{is}} Q^{(1-x_{is})} = \Pi_i \frac{(\xi_s \varepsilon_i)^{x_i}}{1 + \xi_s \varepsilon_i} \tag{A8.5}$$

In Eq. A8.5 for the likelihood of a response pattern, the parameters are expressed in the antilog scale. The exponent x_{is} is the observed response of person s to item i, which controls whether the probability of passing, P_i, or failing, Q_i, enters the response pattern probability. It can be shown that Eq. A8.5 may be simplified into the following equation:

$$P(\underline{X}_s | \theta_s, \underline{\varepsilon}) = \frac{\xi_s^{x.s} \Pi_i \varepsilon_i^{x_{is}}}{\Pi_i (1 + \xi_s \varepsilon_i)} \tag{A8.6}$$

where x_s is the total score of person s.

The probability that total score $x._s$ equals a particular value r may be calculated by summing the model predictions across all ways in which total score r could be obtained from the I items, as follows:

$$P(x._s = r | \xi_s, \underline{\varepsilon}) = \Sigma_{\Sigma_i x_i = r_s} \Pi_i \frac{(\xi_s \varepsilon_i)^{x_i}}{1 + \xi_s \varepsilon_i} \tag{A8.7}$$

where $\Sigma_{\Sigma_i x_i = r_s}$ indicates the summations across response patterns with total score r and the other terms are defined as before. Now Eq. A8.7 simplifies into a form similar to Eq. A8.6, as follows:

$$P(x._s = r | \xi_s, \underline{\varepsilon}) = \frac{\xi_s^{x.s} \Sigma_{\Sigma_i x_i = r_s} \Pi_i \varepsilon_i^{x_{is}}}{\Pi_i (1 + \xi_s \varepsilon_i)} \tag{A8.8}$$

Now, Eq. A8.6 divided by Eq. A8.8 gives the target probability; that is, the likelihood of the response pattern, given total score and the item parameters. Notice that the denominators are identical, which means that they cancel in the ratio. Also notice that one term in the numerator, $\xi^{x_{is}}$, is also identical, and it also will cancel. Thus, the probability of the response pattern can be expressed without terms involving the unknown trait levels, as follows:

$$P(\underline{X}_s | r_s, \underline{\varepsilon}) = \frac{\Pi_i \varepsilon_i^{X_{is}}}{\Sigma_{\Sigma_i x_i = r_s} \Pi_i \varepsilon_i^{X_{is}}} \tag{A8.9}$$

Noting the denominator of Eq. A8.9 as γ_r, where

$$\gamma_r = \Sigma_{\Sigma_i x_i = r_s} \Pi_i \varepsilon_i^{X_{is}} \tag{A8.10}$$

leads to writing the response pattern likelihood as follows:

$$P(\underline{X}_s | r_s, \underline{\varepsilon}) = \frac{\Pi_i \varepsilon_i^{X_{is}}}{\gamma_r} \tag{A8.11}$$

The denominator γ_r is an elementary symmetric function that represents the combinatorial aspect of the probability of total score r. These are elaborated next.

Elementary Symmetric Functions

The term γ_r, derived earlier, represents an elementary symmetric function of order r in the item parameters. A symmetric function is associated with each total score r to represent the combinatorial aspect of the probability of obtaining r, given the item parameters. In each elementary symmetric function, all possible ways of obtaining a score r are represented with the products of the item parameters.

To illustrate the meaning of the elementary symmetric functions, consider a test of four items. The complete elementary symmetric functions for all scores on the test is given as follows:

$$\begin{aligned}
\gamma_0 &= 1 \\
\gamma_1 &= \varepsilon_1 + \varepsilon_2 + \varepsilon_3 + \varepsilon_4 \\
\gamma_2 &= \varepsilon_1\varepsilon_2 + \varepsilon_1\varepsilon_3 + \varepsilon_1\varepsilon_4 + \varepsilon_2\varepsilon_3 + \varepsilon_2\varepsilon_4 + \varepsilon_4\varepsilon_3 \\
\gamma_3 &= \varepsilon_1\varepsilon_2\varepsilon_3 + \varepsilon_1\varepsilon_2\varepsilon_4 + \varepsilon_1\varepsilon_3\varepsilon_4 + \varepsilon_2\varepsilon_3\varepsilon_4 \\
\gamma_4 &= \varepsilon_1\varepsilon_2\varepsilon_3\varepsilon_4
\end{aligned} \tag{A8.12}$$

Thus, for γ_3, all possible ways of passing three items are represented by products of item-easiness values.

In the estimation equations, the probability that a particular item i is correct given a certain total score has been obtained, $P(X_{is} = 1 | r_s, \underline{\varepsilon})$, may also be computed from the elementary symmetric functions, as follows:

$$P(X_{is} = 1 | r_s, \underline{\varepsilon}) = \varepsilon_i(\gamma_{r-1}^{(i)}/\gamma_r) \tag{A8.13}$$

where $\gamma_{r-1}^{(i)}$ is the elementary symmetric function of $r - 1$ arguments where the easiness value for item i is omitted.

Data Likelihood

The response pattern likelihoods from Eq. A8.11 may be multiplied across persons for the likelihood of the data, as follows:

$$P(\mathbf{X}|\underline{r}, \underline{\varepsilon}) = \Pi_s \Pi_i \varepsilon_i^{x_{is}} / \gamma_r \qquad (A8.14)$$

A relatively simple equation for the data log likelihood may be derived from Eq. 8.14 by taking the logarithm. Thus, the log likelihood of the data depends only on the item easiness, the observed total scores, and the number of persons passing each item, as follows:

$$\ln P(\mathbf{X}|r, \underline{\varepsilon}) = \Sigma_i x_{i.} \ln\varepsilon_i - \Sigma_s \ln\gamma_{rs} \qquad (A8.15)$$

where $x_{i.}$ is the number of persons passing item i, and γ_{rs} is an elementary symmetric function. Notice that the first term on the right contains item difficulty ε_i, weighted by the number of persons passing an item, $x_{i.}$, and the second term represents the log likelihood of the persons' total scores computed from the elementary symmetric functions, $\ln\gamma_{r_s}$.

The data log likelihood also may be expressed directly in terms of item difficulty, as follows:

$$\ln P(\mathbf{X}|r, \underline{\beta}) = -\Sigma_i x_{i.} \beta_i - \Sigma_s \ln \gamma_{r_s} \qquad (A8.16)$$

Estimation Equations

The estimation equations used for computation are expressed in terms of the elementary symmetric functions, as follows:

$$
\begin{aligned}
0 &= \Sigma_s x_{1s} - \Sigma_s \exp(-\beta_1)(\gamma_{r-1}^{(i)} / \gamma_r)) \\
0 &= \Sigma_s x_{2s} - \Sigma_s \exp(-\beta_2)(\gamma_{r-1}^{(i)} / \gamma_r)) \\
\vdots \quad &\quad \vdots \qquad\qquad \vdots \\
0 &= \Sigma_s x_{Is} - \Sigma_s \exp(-\beta_I)(\gamma_{r-1}^{(i)} / \gamma_r))
\end{aligned}
\qquad (A8.17)
$$

where $\gamma_{r-1}^{(i)}$ is the first partial derivative with respect to the item-easiness parameter, which was described earlier.

9

Assessing the Fit of IRT Models

As with any model-based approach to interpreting psychological data, the advantages of IRT models (e.g., item-free examinee trait level estimates, test information curves) are obtained in direct proportion to the degree to which the data are consistent with the assumptions underlying their application. This chapter focuses on ways to assess and evaluate the adequacy of IRT model applications and is divided into two sections. First, we discuss the principles of unidimensionality and local independence that underlie IRT-based measurement and describe several methods of determining whether these criteria are met in the context of a particular model being applied to a particular data set. In the second section, we describe several approaches to assessing the goodness-of-fit of IRT models at the item, person, and model levels. Note that the topic of model-fit is an active area of current research and that to date, no definitive answers exist in this area. We conclude this chapter with recommendations and discussion of additional issues that need to be considered in applying IRT models.

ASSESSING IRT MODEL ASSUMPTIONS

Most commonly employed IRT models make relatively simple but strong assumptions about the relationship between item responses and the latent trait(s). There are two major and interrelated assumptions that have been described in numerous sources. First, all commonly employed IRT models assume "appropriate" dimensionality. In the overwhelming majority of applications, IRT models assume unidimensionality, that is, a single latent trait variable is sufficient to explain the common variance among item responses. When this condition is met, test scores (i.e., trait level estimates) are unambiguous indicators of a single construct.

Second, and consistent with the first assumption, is the concept of local (statistical) independence. Local independence means that, controlling for examinee trait level(s), the test items are not correlated (i.e., are independent). An alternative way of stating this is that the probability of endorsing an item is strictly determined by an examinee's trait level(s), not by his or her responses to other test items or unaccounted-for sources of common variance. The local independence assumption is analogous to the CTT assumption of uncorrelated errors conditional on examinee true scores. Later in this chapter, we draw a distinction between strong and weak versions of local independence. For now, note that although conceptually distinct, unidimensionality and local independence are related because, by definition, a data set is unidimensional when item responses are locally independent based on a single latent variable (see McDonald, 1981 for an extended description).

Now that we have briefly described the two main criteria by which the applicability of IRT models is judged, two issues are important to review. First, what methods exist for evaluating dimensionality and local independence, and second, what are the consequences of applying IRT models when these conditions are not met? In what follows, we attempt to address these questions by introducing recent research that has tackled these issues.

EVALUATING DIMENSIONALITY

Although developments continue to accrue in multidimensional IRT modeling (e.g., Ackerman, 1994; Reckase, 1997), most commonly employed IRT models assume that a single latent-trait dimension underlies the probability of an item response, and it is these models that are of primary concern in this chapter. Numerous studies have proposed and investigated methods of assessing the dimensionality (i.e., the number of latent factors) of data matrices. Even in the application of multidimensional IRT models, the correct number of latent factors must be identified a priori, and hence, determining dimensionality is a critical issue in IRT modeling regardless of whether unidimensional or multidimensional models are being considered.

Numerous heuristic approaches and statistical procedures for assessing dimensionality have been proposed and investigated. Research on dimensionality is plagued by misunderstandings of the concept, and the fact that a number of approaches to ostensibly assess dimensionality are essentially irrelevant to the issue. Hattie (1984; 1985) reviewed dozens of proposed approaches to assessing the dimensionality of a data matrix including procedures that are based on (a) the consistency of examinee answer patterns (e.g., Guttman scalability), (b) test score reliability, (c) statistical output from principal components analyses (e.g., the number of eigenvalues greater than 1.0 or the ratio of first to second eigenvalue), (d) output from linear and nonlinear factor analyses, and (e) statistics derived from fitting latent trait models (e.g., residual analyses after fitting a particular model).

Hattie's review is relatively simple to summarize, namely, he found most approaches to dimensionality assessment to be either irrelevant to the issue or extremely wanting. Among the central problems he identified were that many of the statistical procedures proposed to assess dimensionality: (a) cannot reliably distinguish between a one- and two-dimensional data set, (b) have no known sampling distribution, (c) their performance under various testing conditions is undemonstrated, and ultimately, (d) few if any guidelines exist for researchers who wish to use particular procedures to judge the number of dimensions with any degree of accuracy.

Given these findings, it is fair to ask whether commonly encountered procedures for arguing for unidimensionality, such as the comparison of the ratio of the first to second eigenvalues from a tetrachoric correlation matrix (e.g., Reise & Waller, 1990) are completely worthless. In a sense, the answer is "yes" because with this index, like numerous others, there is no strong rationale for judging the obtained values and their ability to distinguish the number of factors question remains unproved. The answer is "no" in the sense that there is some utility in these heuristic indices in that they may provide supporting "evidence" that a data set is reasonably dominated by a single common factor. This evidence may be useful in conjunction with more formal procedures for assessing dimensionality that, as described subsequently, have yet to be fully developed.

Although the tone was mostly negative, some positive findings were revealed in the Hattie studies (Hattie, 1984, 1985). For example, he recommends the use of nonlinear factor analysis as a possible dimensionality-assessment tool, in particular the analyses of residual covariance terms after fitting a particular nonlinear factor model using programs like NOHARM (Fraser, 1988). Hambleton and Rovinelli (1986) also report nonlinear factor analyses to be a promising technique for assessing dimensionality. Furthermore, there have been important developments since Hattie's (1985) study. Two in particular strike us as important to review. These are the suggestions presented in McDonald and Mok (1995) and the line of research that developed from Stout's (1987; 1990) articulation of the "essential" dimensionality concept.

NEW APPROACHES TO ASSESSING DIMENSIONALITY

As numerous authors have made clear, all statistical models of psychological processes (e.g., an IRT model) are false, and we only need a large enough sample size to prove it. Because of this fact, in covariance structure analysis (CSA) researchers have been turning away from interpreting chi-square model fit statistics as indicators of model adequacy and have moved toward a greater reliance on so-called practical, or goodness-of-fit, indices. Analogously, McDonald and Mok (1995) point out that two general types of models (i.e., full and bivariate information) may be fit to item-response data, and that these may in turn provide researchers with methods of evaluating dimensionality, as well as assessing the goodness-of-fit of both unidimensional and multidimensional IRT models.

These two models are based on slightly different versions of local independence. If we let X be a vector of item responses ($x = 1 \ldots I$), θ be a k-dimensional vector of latent trait scores, and P_i be the probability of a particular item response under a given IRT model, then the strong form of local independence can be written as

$$P\{X = x \mid \theta\} = \Pi_{i=1}^{I} P_i \{X_i = x \mid \theta\} \tag{9.1}$$

This equation indicates that the test items are completely independent once the vector of latent traits has been accounted for. Knowing that a person passes a particular item does not change the conditional probability of some other item response. The weak form of local independence may be written as $\mathrm{Cov}\{X_j, X_k \mid \theta\} = 0$ $j \neq k$, which indicates that pair-wise, items share no covariance once that latent trait(s) have been accounted for. This is a weaker form of local independence because higher order dependencies among items are allowed here but not in Equation 9.1.

These two forms of local independence are the foundation for model-fitting algorithms that can provide goodness-of-fit indices and residual covariance terms. Specifically, full-information (because it is based on analyzing the entire item response pattern) parameter estimation routines (Bock & Aitken, 1981; Bock, Gibbons, & Muraki, 1988) and bivariate information (based on analyses of item means and covariances) methods (Chrisoffersson, 1975; Muthen, 1978; McDonald, 1985) assume the strong and weak versions of local independence, respectively.

Application of these IRT/factor models by means of programs such as TESTFACT (Wilson, Wood, & Gibbons, 1991), NOHARM (Fraser, 1988), or LISCOMP (Muthen, 1987) presents researchers with the possibility of developing confirmatory item-response models as well as the capacity to assess dimensionality by developing goodness-of-fit indices such as are found in many programs that are used for covariance structure modeling, and the ability to inspect covariance residual terms after fitting models of one or more dimensions (see also Hattie, 1984). Clearly, the methods of evaluating model-fit in covariance structure models have relevance to critical questions of fit in IRT models. At this time, however, more research and development in this area is needed.

With increasing recognition that real-world data will never be strictly unidimensional, it is important to develop statistics that inform researchers when a data matrix is so "essentially" unidimensional that the resulting parameter estimates (e.g., trait level estimates) derived from application of an IRT model will be reliable and consistent. The research of Stout (1987; 1990), Nandakumar and Stout (1993) and Nandakumar (1993), represents a relatively simple approach for assessing exactly this issue.

The IRT/factor models used to assess dimensionality proposed in McDonald and Mok (1995) depend on having a computer program (e.g., TESTFACT) to estimate model parameters. The technique for assessing essential dimensionality developed by Stout (1987; 1990) and enhanced in Nandakumar and Stout (1993) requires no estimation of IRT model parameters. Basically, Stout (1987; 1990) developed a procedure by which to judge whether a data set is essentially unidimensional. In other words, is the dominant factor so strong that examinee trait level estimates are unaffected by (or are "robust to") the presence of smaller specific factors and influences?

Under the Stout framework, a test is considered essentially unidimensional when the average between-item residual covariances after fitting a one-factor model approaches zero as the length of the test increases. This perspective is derived from the "weak" form of local independence described earlier. The Stout procedure is used to identify the number of "major" common dimensions in a test, and it ignores the minor factors. Consequently, a test can be considered essentially unidimensional if local independence approximately holds in a sample of test takers who are approximately equal on the latent trait. Because several steps are involved in actually testing the hypothesis of one dominant factor, we do not present the step-by-step technical details involved in implementing the Stout procedure. Interested readers should see the original research and obtain a copy of the DIMTEST (Stout, 1987) computer program. In closing this section, we note that research by Nandakumar (1994) found Stout's procedure and nonlinear factor analyses implemented with NOFA (Etazadi-Amoli & McDonald, 1983) to be about equally effective in detecting unidimensionality, but DIMTEST was more powerful in terms of detecting the presence of multidimensionality. Further demonstration of DIMTEST's ability to evaluate unidimensionality can be found in Hattie, Krakowski, Rogers, and Swaminathan (1996).

RECOMMENDATIONS

It is tiresome to continuously recommend more research, but at this time in regard to testing dimensionality researchers know more about what not to do than what to do. For example, it is known that the size of an internal consistency index (e.g., coefficient alpha) is irrelevant to dimensionality and so are any indices based on components analysis. The future outlook is very bright, however, especially in terms of developing goodness-of-fit indices rather than statistical tests of strict dimensionality. The techniques described earlier seem especially promising in providing researchers with firm guidelines by which to judge the applicability of unidimensional IRT models. Ultimately, the search for a test of dimensionality may be misleading on several fronts. First, all models are strictly wrong and are only approximations to reality. Second, the effect on parameter estimation of small departures from unidimensionality remains undemonstrated. In fact, some research indicates that IRT model parameter estimation is fairly robust to minor violations of unidimensionality, especially if the latent-trait dimensions (factors) are highly correlated or if secondary dimensions are relatively small (Drasgow & Parsons, 1983; Reckase, 1979).

EVALUATING LOCAL INDEPENDENCE

A violation of local independence, called *local dependence* (LD), occurs when examinee item responses depend not just on their trait level but on their responses to other test items (or combinations of items) or other common factors. This phenomena may occur in testing situations that are relatively common in both educational and personality assessment contexts. In this section, we describe the consequences of LD and identify several testing contexts in both educational and personality measurement where LD is especially likely to occur. In addition, we describe two statistical techniques for identifying LD and offer some suggestions for dealing with its occurrence.

The presence of LD can have serious consequences in regard to the applicability of unidimensional IRT models. First, and most important, the key equation by which the likelihood of an examinee answer pattern is computed, Eq. 9.2, has diminished validity under conditions of LD.

$$L(X \mid \theta_s) = \Pi_{i=1}^{I} (P_{si} \mid \theta_s)^{x_i} (1 - P_{si} \mid \theta_s)^{(1-x_i)} \qquad (9.2)$$

where, $L(X \mid \theta_s)$ represents the conditional probability of an item response pattern X, and $P_{si} \mid \theta_s$ is the probability of an endorsement for item i determined from the IRT model.

For Eq. 9.2 to be valid, the condition of local independence must be met. Thus, when LD occurs, a researcher is left with no reliable way of computing the basic values through which all other IRT features work. In empirical studies, Yen (1993) demonstrated that the presence of LD effects the estimation of test information and item discrimination parameters, making both larger than they should be. The presence of LD can also result in IRT computer programs identifying the wrong (not desired) latent trait dimension (Steinberg & Thissen, 1996). It is thus fair to state that basically all aspects of the IRT modeling process and application, such as computerized adaptive testing, are disturbed by the presence of local dependence.

In educational assessment, several testing factors may influence the occurrence of violations of local independence. For example, when multiple questions are embedded within the context of a single word passage, responses on latter items may be influenced unduly by responses on earlier items. Focusing on the context of so-called performance assessments, Yen (1993) catalogued a list of testing features that may lead to local dependence. Some examples of testing contexts listed by Yen are (a) speeded testing situations, (b) situations where there is differential practice or exposure to material among students, and (c) if items are chained together so that answering one item affects the answers to other items.

Yen (1993) proposed use of the Q3 (Yen, 1984) statistic as a means of identifying pairs of test items that display LD. The Q3 index represents the correlation between items after partialling out the latent trait variable. Once item parameters and examinee trait levels have been estimated, it is relatively easy to compute an examinee's expected response to each test item. All a researcher need do is plug in item parameter and trait level estimates into the equation for the IRC and compute the most likely response. A residual is calculated by taking the difference between an observed raw item response and the expected item response under the IRT model. Finally, the Q3 statistic is then calculated by correlating the residual scores among item pairs. The expected value of Q3 under the hypothesis of local independence is $-1/(N-1)$. Thus, in large samples a researcher would expect Q3 to be around zero and large positive values indicate item pairs that share some other factor that may be a cause of concern.

The occurrence of LD is not just a problem in aptitude or achievement-assessment contexts. Steinberg and Thissen (1996) demonstrated that LD can occur in personality assessment contexts as well. For example, in personality assessment it is fairly common to observe subsets of scale items that are near replicates of each other. Furthermore, some research (e.g., Knowles, 1988) indicates that on personality questionnaires, examinee responses become more consistent as the test progresses — apparently as people clarify their self-concepts. This latter phenomena, as well as having near replicate items, will lead to LD and should be guarded against. Chen and Thissen (1997) developed a G^2 statistic for identifying local dependence. This statistic provides researchers with a way to formally analyze the residuals after fitting an IRT model. The statistic evaluates pairs of items looking for unexpected covariance given the covariance among the other items in the test.

RECOMMENDATIONS

The best way of dealing with local dependence is to prevent its occurrence in the first place. Yen (1993) provided a list of suggestions for how testing situations may be arranged to minimize the chances of local dependencies occurring. In some contexts, however, the problem of LD may be unavoidable, such as when content facets are required for substantive validity purposes. In such cases, Yen (1993) and Steinberg and Thissen (1996) suggest that items displaying LD be combined into "testlets" (Wainer & Kiely, 1987). Testlets are sets of items (e.g., true/false) that are treated (i.e., scored) as a single test question. Although the use of testlets can greatly alleviate problems associated with LD, it should be noted that it is difficult to form testlets when items are not dichotomous.

ASSESSING MODEL-DATA FIT

The prior section was devoted to methods for assessing unidimensionality and local independence, which are the main assumptions of commonly employed IRT models. In the following section, we focus on methods used to assess the goodness-of-fit of particular IRT models. These techniques, which always require parameter estimation, are used to judge how well an IRT model represents data at the item, person, or model level. As stated previously, there are no procedures that result in a researcher stating *definitively* that a particular model does or does not fit, or is or is not appropriate. Much like the assessment of "practical" fit in covariance structure modeling, judging fit in IRT models calls for a variety of procedures to be implemented, and ultimately, a scientist must use his or her best judgment.

JUDGING ITEM FIT

In applications of IRT models, there is no need for the same model to be applied to all items in a test. For example, a test may consist of a combination of dichotomous and polytomous items, and some items may be represented by a two-parameter logistic and others by the graded-response model. Because separate IRT models are estimated for each test item, much research has been devoted to the topic of judging the fit of a particular IRT model on an item-by-item basis, as opposed to judging general or overall model-data fit. Reckase (1997) provides some historical reasons for the emphasis on item fit in IRT modeling. Although analysis of item-fit is an important part of the IRT model application process, our treatment will be rather sparse. Interested readers may wish to see Hambleton and Swaminathan (1985), which provides fuller examples of detailed item-fit analysis. Furthermore, literally dozens of potential methods of assessing fit are described in the various chapters of van der Linden and Hambleton (1996).

There are basically two general approaches to evaluating item fit (i.e., how well the IRT model explains or predicts the responses to a particular item). We begin by describing what may be called heuristic or graphical procedures in that no statistical tests are actually performed. Specifically, we describe judging item-fit on the basis of a comparison between an estimated IRC and what is called an "empirical" IRC. We then describe more formal statistical procedures that attempt to assess item-fit.

Several researchers have pointed to the utility of examining how well an estimated item response curve (IRC) accounts for or represents observed test data. One way to approach this issue is to compare an estimated IRC with an "empirical" IRC derived from actual data. There are a number of ways in which an empirical IRC may be created. One common method is as follows. The parameters of an IRT model are estimated for a set of test items, and in turn, examinee trait levels are estimated based on these item parameters. Examinees are then sorted by their trait level estimates and divided up into, say, 10 trait level groups with an equal number of examinees within each group. For a single test item, within each of the trait level groups, the actual or "observed" percentage of item endorsements is computed. Using the within-group median trait level estimate and the proportion endorsed within a trait level group as coordinates, these values are then plotted along with the estimated IRC.

These plots can reveal areas along the trait level continuum where there are discrepancies between the empirical IRC and the IRC estimated by means of some computer program. The discrepancies (residuals) indicate problems in item fit that may be due to one or more of many possible causes. For example, poor item fit may be due to (a) unaccounted for multidimensionality, (b) a failure to estimate enough item parameters (e.g., when a 1PL is fit to 2PL data), (c) nonmonotonicity of item-trait relations (all parametric IRT models assume that as trait levels increase, the probability of endorsement also increases), (d) a subgroup of examinees may be drawn from a different population and display poor person-fit, or (e) poor item construction.

By means of example, in Table 9.1 are displayed residuals based on 2,000 responses to 5 items from a measure of Stress Reaction (Tellegen, 1982). These results are taken from Reise and Waller (1990). To create these residuals, 2PL (i.e., discrimination and difficulty) item parameters were estimated for all scale items. Then, based on these item parameter estimates, all examinees were scored on the scale. Examinees were then ordered by their trait level estimates and grouped into 10 theta intervals. For each interval, the proportion endorsing a particular item was computed. Then, the predicted proportion was computed by taking the median trait level estimate within each interval and plugging this number and the item parameters into the formula for the 2PL function. Finally, the residual was computed by taking the difference between the expected (i.e., from the IRC) and observed (i.e., from the data) proportion endorsed. As one can see from these residuals, the estimated IRC do an excellent job of capturing the observed proportions endorsed on these particular items. In fact, the largest residual is 0.06, which occurs for ST3 around the middle of the trait scale.

Moving beyond this visual/graphical technique for exploring item-fit, several researchers have attempted to formalize the comparison of empirical IRCs with model-based IRCs by developing statistics that test for the significance of residuals. As with the graphical technique described earlier, these statistics also require estimating an IRC, scoring examinees, and then grouping them into a fixed number of trait level intervals. For example, the Bock (1972) chi-square index is:

$$BCHI = \sum_{g=1}^{G} \frac{N_g(O_{ig} - E_{ig})^2}{E_{ig}(1 - E_{ig})} \qquad (9.3)$$

In Equation 9.3, O_{ig} is the observed proportion-correct (proportion endorsed) on item i for interval g, E_{ig} is the expected proportion correct based on evaluating the estimated IRC at the within interval median trait level estimate, and N_g is the number of examinees with ability estimates falling within interval g. Ostensibly, this test of residuals is distributed as a chi-square variable with degrees of freedom equal to $G - m$, where m is the number of item parameters estimated. Values of this chi-square for the five example items are given in Table 9.1. McKinley and Mills (1985) compared the relative power of several of the statistical indices for assessing item fit. However, note that like many chi-square statistics, these tests of fit are very sensitive to sample size and should probably not be treated as solid decision-making tools.

A somewhat new chi-square item-fit approach is implemented in the BILOG 3 (Mislevy & Bock, 1990) and BILOG-MG (Zimowski, Muraki,

TABLE 9.1

Residuals for Five Stress-Reaction Items, Chi-Square Tests of Item-Fit
and Item Discrimination, and Difficulty-Parameter Estimates ($N = 2,000$)

Midpoints of Theta Intervals	χ^2										8 DF	α	β
	-2.10	-1.15	-0.70	-0.40	-0.10	0.10	0.40	0.70	1.10	1.80			
ST1	0.00	0.03	-0.02	0.01	0.01	-0.01	0.02	0.02	0.01	-0.01	5.04	2.062	-.494
ST2	0.02	-0.04	0.01	-0.04	0.01	0.04	0.04	-0.02	-0.02	0.01	9.36	1.330	-.685
ST3	-0.02	0.02	-0.03	-0.02	0.05	0.01	0.06	0.02	0.00	-0.02	10.96	1.215	.701
ST4	0.00	0.02	-0.01	0.04	-0.05	0.00	-0.00	0.02	-0.03	0.00	6.60	1.299	-.631
ST5	-0.01	0.00	-0.04	-0.01	-0.03	-0.05	0.05	0.04	-0.04	0.00	15.12	1.643	-.675

Note. Original analyses reported in Reise & Waller (1990).

Mislevy, & Bock, 1996) programs. This test was designed specifically for scales with more than 20 items. The procedure is as follows. First, item parameters are estimated. Then, based on these parameters, EAP scores are calculated for each examinee. Examinees are then assigned to score-group intervals, and the proportion of examinees endorsing the item within each interval is computed. The likelihood ratio chi-square is computed by comparing these observed frequencies with those expected on the basis of the estimated model as in Eq. 9.4.

$$\chi^2 = 2 \Sigma [R_g \log \frac{R_g}{N_g P(\theta_M)} + (N_g - R_g) \log \frac{R_g}{N_g (1 - P(\theta_M))}] \quad (9.4)$$

In Eq. 9.4, the summation is performed over the G theta groups, and R_g is the proportion endorsed (correct) within group g, N_g is the number of examinees in group g, and $P(\theta_M)$ is the model predicted proportion based on evaluating the estimated IRC at the mean within group trait level estimate. Because these residuals are not under linear constraints, there is no loss of degrees of freedom due to parameter estimation. Thus, the degrees of freedom is equal to the number of theta groups. In the BILOG 3 and BILOG-MG programs, theta groups are collapsed to avoid expected values of less than 2. Further discussion and extension of this approach to polytomous items can be found in Muraki (1996).

Finally, some researchers, especially in the context of Rasch models, have found it useful to compute standardized residuals to judge item fit. Because standardized residuals are computed within each cell of the persons by items matrix, they can be added together and used as an index of item or person fit. As described in Masters and Wright (1996), given an estimated IRT model the expected response $E[x_{si}]$ for a particular person s responding to item i is described by

$$E[x_{si}] = \sum_{k=0}^{K-1} kP_i(\theta_s) \quad (9.5)$$

Where K is the number of response categories ($K = 2$ for dichotomous items, and $K = 5$ for a 5-point Likert rating scale) and $P(\theta_s)$ is the model-derived probability. The variance of x_{si} is

$$V[x_{si}]E = \sum_{k=0}^{K-1} (k - [x_{si}])^2 P_i(\theta_s) \quad (9.6)$$

The standardized residual of an observed response x_{si} is then

$$z_{si} = (x_{si} - E[x_{si}]) / \sqrt{V[x_{si}]} \quad (9.7)$$

As noted, this value can be computed for each and every cell of the persons by items response matrix. A mean square-fit statistic can then be computed for either an item (Eq. 9.8) or person (Eq. 9.9).

$$\text{Item fit} = \Sigma \frac{z_{si}^2}{N} \tag{9.8}$$

$$\text{Person fit} = \Sigma \frac{z_{si}^2}{I} \tag{9.9}$$

In Eq. 9.8, for each item the summation is performed over the N persons and in Eq. 9.9 for each person the summation of the squared residuals is performed over the i items.

PERSON FIT

A second approach to evaluating fit has gained increasing currency of late. Specifically, significant research has been devoted to the development of so-called person-fit indices (Meijer & Sijtsma, 1995). These are statistics that attempt to assess IRT model-fit at the level of the individual examinee. In a way, person-fit indices attempt to assess the validity of the IRT measurement model at the individual level and the meaningfulness of a test score derived from the IRT model.

There are several dozen published and researched person-fit statistics that go by various names such as appropriateness measures (Levine & Rubin, 1979), caution indices (Tatsuoka, 1984; 1996), and scalability indices (Reise & Waller, 1993). Despite the differences in the names, all person-fit indices are based, in some way, on the consistency of an individual's item response pattern with some proposed model of valid item responding. It should be noted that some person-fit indices were developed within the context of specific models and are applicable only to specific IRT models such as the Rasch and nonparametric models (Meijer, 1994). Further, person-fit statistics differ in the extent to which they are applicable across different item response formats — most are designed for dichotomous item responses.

Space precludes a thorough review of this topic area and a detailed description of all the various person-fit statistics. Interested readers seeking more details may wish to review the special issue on person-fit in *Applied Measurement in Education* (1996) and the citations to be found therein. To facilitate discussion, we present a simple example of person-fit analysis. In Table 9.2 are listed all possible response patterns with a raw score of 2

TABLE 9.2
Descriptive Statistics for the 15 Hypothetical
Examinees Who Responded to the Six–Item Test

Examinee	Response Pattern	θ	$T\text{-}INFO\,\vert\,\theta$	$SEM\,\vert\,\theta$	Z_L
1	0 0 0 0 1 1	−0.96	0.99	1.006	−4.10
2	0 0 0 1 0 1	−0.96	0.99	1.006	−3.68
3	0 0 1 0 0 1	−0.96	0.99	1.006	−2.83
4	0 0 0 1 1 0	−0.96	0.99	1.006	−2.83
5	0 1 0 0 0 1	−0.96	0.99	1.006	−2.41
6	0 0 1 0 1 0	−0.96	0.99	1.006	−1.99
7	1 0 0 0 0 1	−0.96	0.99	1.006	−1.57
8	0 0 1 1 0 0	−0.96	0.99	1.006	−1.57
9	0 1 0 0 1 0	−0.96	0.99	1.006	−1.57
10	0 1 0 1 0 0	−0.96	0.99	1.006	−1.15
11	1 0 0 0 1 0	−0.96	0.99	1.006	−0.73
12	1 0 0 1 0 0	−0.96	0.99	1.006	−0.31
13	0 1 1 0 0 0	−0.96	0.99	1.006	−0.31
14	1 0 1 0 0 0	−0.96	0.99	1.006	0.53
15	1 1 0 0 0 0	−0.96	0.99	1.006	0.95

for a six-item test. Hypothetically, the six test items all have discrimination parameters of $\alpha = 1.0$, and the item difficulties (β) from left to right are
−2.0, −1.0, −0.5, 0.5, 1.0, and 2.0. In other words, the items are ordered according to difficulty and the first examinee in Table 9.2 is the most model
inconsistent (he gets the two most difficult items correct and the easy ones
wrong), and the last examinee has the most consistent response pattern
(he gets the two easiest items correct and the most difficult ones wrong).

In the second column of Table 9.2 it is shown that each of these hypothetical examinees has a maximum likelihood $\hat{\theta}$ of −0.96. They are exactly the
same because the item discrimination parameters are constant across the
items. Note that if there was variation among the item discrimination parameters, examinees who endorsed the most discriminating items would
receive the highest $\hat{\theta}$ estimates (see chap. 7). For this six-item test, the
amount of test information is 0.99 at $\hat{\theta} = -0.96$. Because the standard error
for estimating $\hat{\theta}$ equals one divided by the square root of test information,
all examinees receive the same standard error of measurement of 1.006.
Now something is clearly odd with the results in Table 9.2 because it is
strange to think that these examinees are equally scalable on this trait dimension.

Rather than describing the details of several statistics for assessing person-fit, we describe a single index and its use in practice. Specifically, we
describe a person-fit statistic called Z_L originally proposed in Drasgow,
Levine, and Williams (1985). Like most person-fit statistics, the goal of Z_L

is to identify a pattern of item responses that is relatively unlikely given some normative model of item responding.

The Z_L statistic is based on the log-likelihood of an item response vector. Given the parameters of an estimated IRT model (i.e., estimates of all person and item parameters), the log-likelihood (LogL) of any particular cell, x_{si} in an item response matrix is given by

$$LogL \mid \theta_s = [x_{si} \times \log(P_i \mid \theta_s)] + [(1 - x_{si}) \times \log(1 - P_i \mid \theta_s)] \qquad (9.10)$$

where x_{si} is an item response (e.g., 0,1), and log is the natural logarithm.

It may appear as if the *LogL* of an item response pattern would make a good index of person-fit, however, there is a major problem in interpreting raw likelihoods. Specifically, under any realistic testing conditions, the expected value of the raw likelihood will change depending on examinee-estimated trait level. Thus, some method is needed by which to "standardize" the log-likelihoods conditional on examinee trait level. This can be accomplished as follows. Given the log-likelihood of an item response pattern, found by summing values in Eq. 9.10 over the rows of a data matrix, one can compute its expected value as:

$$E(\log L \mid \theta_s) = \Sigma \{P_i \mid \theta_s \times \log(P_i \mid \theta_s) + Q_i \mid \theta_s \times \log(Q_i \mid \theta_s)\} \qquad (9.11)$$

The expected value in Eq. 9.11 simply gives the average log-likelihood value for the sampling distribution of log-likelihoods conditional on a particular trait level. The variance of this conditional distribution can be calculated by Eq. 9.12.

$$V(\log L \mid \theta_s) = \Sigma (P_i \mid \theta_s)(Q_i \mid \theta_s)[\log(P_i \mid \theta_s) / Q_i \mid \theta_{is})]^2 \qquad (9.12)$$

Combining these terms, Dragsow, Levine and Williams (1985) define the standardized Z_L fit index as:

$$Z_L \mid \theta_s = \Sigma[LogL \mid \theta_s - \Sigma E(LogL \mid \theta_s)] / (\Sigma V(LogL \mid \theta_s))^{1/2} \qquad (9.13)$$

The conditional null distribution for the Z_L statistic is the standard normal (Dragsow, Levine, & Williams, 1985). Thus, Z_L scores have an expected value of zero and variance of 1.0 when examinees respond according to the estimated IRT model parameters. Large negative Z_L values (e.g., those two standard errors below 0.0) indicate misfit. Large positive Z_L values indicate response patterns that are higher in likelihood than the model predicts. These Z_L values are computable for both dichotomous and polytomous items (Dragsow, Levine, & Williams, 1985) and have multitest extensions (Dragsow, Levine, & McLaughlin, 1991).

In the last column of Table 9.2 are displayed the Z_L statistic values for each of the response patterns. Now, as clearly indicated by the large negative Z_L values, many of these patterns are extremely unlikely given the model parameters. In a real-world situation, researchers may consider, somewhat arbitrarily, only examinees with Z_L values above some threshold value, say $Z_L > -2.0$, as being scalable and as having interpretable trait level estimates. Alternatively, researchers may forgo the referencing of a person-fit statistic against a null distribution, and simply set aside a fixed proportion of bad person-fit scores for further scrutiny.

Person-fit statistics are engaging to both researchers and test practitioners because they offer the possibility of identifying interesting test taking phenomena (Meijer & Nering, 1997). For example, some researchers are interested in the ability of person-fit indices to identify abnormal test behavior like cheating, fumbling, response carelessness, or, response dissimulation (Birenbaum, 1986; Harnisch, 1983; Wright & Stone, 1979). Other researchers may be interested in identifying examinees who are aberrant in order to clean up a data matrix (Tatsuoka & Tatsuoka, 1982). In personality assessment contexts, Reise and Waller (1993) used person-fit statistics to identify individual differences in personality trait structure — traitedness (Baumeister & Tice, 1988). Finally, several researchers have demonstrated the use of person-fit indices as a method of diagnosing specific skill deficits or cognitive errors in achievement tests (Tatsuoka & Tatsuoka, 1983).

Although the area of person-fit research represents an exciting domain for future development, several researchers have identified problems in this area. For example, person-fit indices ostensibly can detect a wide-range of deviant test behaviors if such behaviors are manifested in the response pattern. Yet, there is no way of interpreting what the causes of misfit are or to meaningfully interpret the origins of a poor person-fit index score (Meijer, 1996; Nering & Meijer, 1998). Another major problem is the appropriateness of the sampling distribution used to evaluate hypotheses of person fit. Several researchers have indicated that the sampling distributions are not as claimed by some researchers (see Liou & Chang, 1992). Molenaar and Hoijtink (1990; 1996) and Reise (1995), for example, indicated that the Z_L may not actually have a normal null distribution under real-world testing conditions. However, note that given the ease of simulating data under IRT models, there is no reason why empirical null-distributions should not be generated and used as a null hypothesis distribution.

Perhaps of greater concern is the issue of statistical power (Drasgow et al., 1987; Meijer, 1994; Meijer, Muijtjens, & Van Der Vlueten, 1996; Reise, 1995; Reise & Due, 1991). In this context, power is defined as the ability of a person-fit statistic to identify response aberrance (of any particular form) when it is present. Drasgow, Levine and McLaughlin (1987) developed "optimal" statistical procedures (Levine & Drasgow, 1988) that indicate the best (most power) any "practical" person-fit index (e.g., Z_L) could have to identify a specific form of response aberrance (Drasgow, Levine, & Zickar, 1996). In our judgment, results from this line of research leave us cautious regarding the potential application of person-fit statistics.

Other research, conducted on the power of various person-fit statistics under a 1PL, 2PL, or 3PL models does not strike us as very encouraging either (Liou, 1993; Reise, 1995; Reise & Due, 1991). It seems that for a person-fit statistic to function effectively, tests must be designed with the intention of detecting response aberrance. Specifically, responses that improve the power of person-fit indices are longer tests (e.g., more than 30 items), a wide range of item difficulty parameters, and highly discriminating test items (Meijer, Molanaar, & Sijtsma, 1994; Reise & Flannery, 1996).

Even with these concerns about the power of person-fit indices, most of the previously cited research was in the context of applied educational assessment where the emphasis was on identifying cheaters. In this context, certain legal concerns that are irrelevant to basic day-to-day psychological research come into play. We would like to encourage use of person-fit statistics as a potential tool for researchers to identify generalized "faulty" responding examinees within their data sets and to consider estimating item parameters after removal of poorly fitting examinees. Also, there are applications of person-fit indices, such as in assessing the importance of DIF, that we would like to see further developed (see Reise & Flannery, 1996). Finally, it is critically important that validity research be conducted to demonstrate that test scores associated with lack of person-fit are not as good as predictors in real-life situations. That is, researchers need to demonstrate that protocols deemed invalid by person-fit statistics are truly invalid.

MODEL COMPARISON APPROACH

After examining fit at the level of the item or person, it is appropriate to ask whether there are methods that seek to judge the fit at the level of the entire model. Note that some person-fit or item-fit indices may be aggregated across examinees or items to obtain a general indication of model fit. For example, the components of the Z_L index (Eqs. 9.11–9.13) may be aggregated across all cells in a person by items matrix to gain an overall index of fit. However, generally speaking, IRT analysis is not like covariance structural modeling, which routinely produces a chi-square index of model-fit.

Most IRT models are estimated with "marginal" maximum likelihood routines that use a multiway contingency table as their basis. This is not a problem in terms of deriving a fit index because the general multinomial model may be used as a null. However, this is only possible when there is a small number of dichotomous items and a sample size large enough so that all possible response patterns will be observed. Thus, in any real data set, there is bound to be unobserved response patterns and a sparse contingency table. Under these conditions, the resulting chi-square would have no ready interpretation. In a nutshell, there is no general fit index in IRT as there is in CSM.

As alluded to earlier, it is well known that the fit of covariance structure models can be evaluated by use of a chi-square statistic that reflects the discrepancy between the observed covariance matrix and that predicted from the estimated model. Furthermore, it is also well known that covariance models that are nested may be compared in terms of the change in chi-square caused by constraining certain parameter estimates to be fixed. The research of Thissen, Steinberg and Gerrard (1986) illustrate a model comparison approach to judging relative IRT model fit that is analogous to procedures used in structural modeling. In structural modeling, a model is said to be a good representation to the data when it can recover an observed covariance matrix. In IRT models, a model can be considered appropriate to the extent to which it can reproduce the observed item responses.

Given this, Thissen et al. (1986) described a procedure through which nested models can be compared through the use of the log-likelihood of the data given the model. Specifically, consider a five-item true-false personality scale. Now, a researcher might wish to decide between a 2PL model and a 1PL (all slopes are equal). It is possible to estimate the 2PL model and compute the log-likelihood of the data given the model (note: this is given in MULTILOG [Thissen, 1991] output). The number of parameter estimates would be five-item discriminations and five-item difficulties, plus the mean and variance of the latent distribution, for a total of 12. Now placing the constraint that the item discriminations are equal means that only one "common" item discrimination parameter will be estimated, and thus the number of parameters estimated is one discrimination, five difficulties, plus the mean and variance of the latent distribution for a total of eight. A researcher could then compare the log-likelihoods for Model 1 versus Model 2. This change should be distributed as chi-square on $DF_1 - DF_2$ degrees of freedom. Large and significant differences in this chi-square–distributed statistic would indicate that imposing constraints (e.g., all discrimination parameters are equal) resulted in significant worsening of the model.

The model comparison strategy is a developing technique, see Reise, Widaman, and Pugh (1993) for an application, and many points of controversy remain. Foremost, in any realistic type of data set, there will be no way to judge the adequacy of the baseline model, indeed, the procedure is only meant for model comparisons not absolute judgments of fit. More importantly, it is not clear that under conditions of sparse contingency tables that the change in G^2 will always be distributed as chi-square with the change in degrees of freedom equal to the difference in the number of parameter estimates between models. However, see Cohen, Kim, and Wollack (1996), who evaluate the likelihood ratio test in the context of differential item functioning assessment. Despite their positive findings, we still regard this issue as being in need of more research.

The model comparison approach is interesting, but its role in data analyses appears more important in structural modeling than it does in IRT. In structural models, a variety of representations of the relationships among a set of observed variables are possible. In IRT a researcher's choices are somewhat more restricted. If a researcher has a multiple-choice test where examinees can obtain correct answers by guessing, he or she pretty much knows that the 3PL model is the right one, and if a researcher has personality data, he or she can then choose between a 1PL or 2PL model. The most interesting use of the model comparison strategy is not so much in picking an appropriate model but rather, as illustrated in Thissen, Steinberg, and Gerrard (1986), in exploring differential item functioning.

Maydue-Olivares, Drasgow, and Mead (1994) presented an alternative procedure for comparison of the fit of competing IRT models. Their procedure can be used even to compare the fit of models with the same number of parameter estimates (i.e., non-nested models). Specifically, their approach is called the "ideal" observer method, and it can be used to compare different parameterizations of the same data set under different IRT models. The method is based on observing the likelihoods of the item response patterns under various models and conducting a likelihood ratio test to assign the response patterns to one model versus another (see Levine et al., 1992). When the likelihoods are near equivalent across different models, it really makes no difference which model is ultimately selected. Research findings thus far indicate that in polytomous data sets that varied in test length, there were essentially no differences in fit under a partial credit model and a graded response model. Whether these findings are generally true across a range of data sets remains to be explored.

FUTURE DIRECTIONS AND CONCLUSIONS

In the beginning of this chapter, we state that the topic of model-fit is currently an active area of research. As the state of the art currently stands, we do have some general recommendations to make regarding IRT model-fit assessment. First, it is suggested that any considered application of IRT models begin with an evaluation of the construct being measured and conceptual model underlying the measurement of that construct. More specifically, researchers should ask themselves whether the construct is to be assessed by an emergent measurement model or a latent variable model.

As Bollen and Lennox (1991) described, an emergent variable is one that is defined by its indicators. Constructs like "economic strength" may be measured by an aggregate of stock prices called the Dow-Jones industrial average, "health" may be measured by absence of heart disease and low blood pressure, or "social class" may be measured by job prestige rating and preferences for beer versus wine. With these types of variables, the construct is defined by the indicators or, stated differently, the direction of causation goes from item to construct. On the other hand, some constructs are better represented as latent variables. It is arguable that constructs like intelligence or extroversion are variables that cause variation in test items and, thus, cause two or more items to be intercorrelated.

Many measurement implications of this distinction between latent variable and emergent variable measurement models are well articulated in the Bollen and Lennox (1991) article. For our purposes, we raise this issue because of its implications for the applicability of IRT testing models. Namely, IRT models are "latent" variable models and assume that the direction of causation goes from latent trait to indicator (i.e., test item). It simply makes no sense to fit IRT models to emergent variables, and such applications are bound to lead to trouble. Thus, we encourage researchers to consider the nature of what it is they are trying to assess and to build their measurement models appropriately — IRT is not the answer for all measurement problems.

That said, a good exploration of model-fit will include some type of formal assessment of dimensionality and local independence. We maintain that researchers should now be starting to move away from reporting heuristic indices such as "variance accounted for by the first factor" or "ratio of first to second eigenvalue" and start implementing the new procedures that tackle these issues in a much more sophisticated manner. Specifically, as described in this chapter, we recommend more application of Stout's procedure for determining essential dimensionality and/or the application of appropriate techniques such as are found in TESTFACT (Wilson, Wood, & Gibbons, 1991), POLYFACT (Muraki, 1993b), NOHARM (Fraser, 1988), and LISCOMP (Muthen, 1987). What is especially needed are methods of examining residual covariance terms after a one-factor model has been estimated for a data set. In addition to explorations of dimensionality and local independence, researchers may wish to consider plots of residuals (either raw or standardized). We also suggest that one or more item- and person-fit statistics be considered. In this regard, the concern should not necessarily be on formal hypotheses testing of item- or person-fit, but rather on using these indices to direct the researcher to items and examinees that are extremely aberrant relative to the assumed measurement model. For example, large item-fit statistics may lead the researcher to find and correct a poorly worded item or to eliminate it from the test altogether. Identifying examinees with poor fit may allow the investigator to clean up the data set to derive better item-parameter estimates.

Finally, many authors in the IRT literature view choice of IRT model and the evaluation of alternative models as a central issue in IRT investigations. We are more skeptical in this regard for several reasons. First, we think that in many cases the model choice is going to be rather obvious. For example, with dichotomous items, if there is guessing and the items are not all related to the latent trait with exactly the same strength, then the 3PL is called for, or if personality assessment data is used, then the 2PL seems a rather obvious choice. Second, for the majority of research applications (i.e., where examinees are not charged to take the test and no important life decisions are based on the test), assuming the data is strongly unidimensional and one has a large sample, then it probably doesn't make much difference which particular IRT model is actually used. For example, the research reviewed previously showed little or no differences in fit among competing polytomous IRT models (Maydeu-Olivares, Drasgow, & Mead, 1994). However, we caution that in a related context Goldstein (1980) explicitly argued that different models can have large consequences in terms of the relative scaling of individuals on the latent-trait continuum.

IV

APPLICATIONS OF IRT MODELS

10

IRT Applications: DIF, CAT, and Scale Analysis

In this chapter we present an overview of several ways that IRT modeling is or could be used in the analysis of psychological test data. In what follows, three applications of IRT methods are presented: (a) using IRT modeling to identify differential item functioning (DIF), (b) how IRT models are used to form the basis of computerized adaptive testing (CAT), and (c) how IRT methods might be used in the scale construction, analysis, and refinement process. The main goal of this chapter is to provide a general overview of each of these three applications; where relevant, we cite research literature for more information and fuller treatment of these topics. Also, in keeping with the general theme of this book, we severely limit discussion of statistical procedures and methods that are mostly relevant to large-scale educational or aptitude testing contexts. Although we realize that DIF assessment and computerized adaptive testing are primarily used in large-scale aptitude testing, we focus our discussion on the general underlying principles of these applications that are relevant to psychological researchers.

ASSESSMENT OF ITEM AND TEST BIAS

In the last several decades measurement specialists, substantive researchers, and the general public have become increasingly concerned with the possibility that psychological measures may "work differently" or be biased either for or against a particular group of examinees (e.g., men or women). For this reason, a rather large research base has accumulated regarding how to scrutinize psychological measures for item bias. In any discussion of how a psychological measure functions across different groups of examinees, a researcher must distinguish between two types of bias (Drasgow, 1982; 1987). External bias occurs when test scores have different correlations with nontest variables for two or more groups of examinees. This results in differential predictive validity of the measure. This differential validity or lack of structural invariance may or may not be of concern depending on the context of test use. In many research contexts, the differential predictiveness of a measure is anticipated by a substantive theory, and may form the heart of a research program.

A second form of bias occurs when a test's internal relations (e.g., the covariances among item responses) differs across two or more groups of examinees. This is called *measurement bias* and in turn, measurement bias leads to a measurement scale not being invariant or equivalent across groups. This section is solely concerned with item-level methods of detecting measurement invariance and its lack thereof. The study of a scale's item-level measurement invariance is of fundamental importance in psychometric research. For test scores—either observed raw scale scores or latent trait level estimates—to be comparable across different groups of examinees, those scores must be on the same measurement scale. That is, the items must display measurement invariance across different groups of examinees. This begs the question, when are test scores on the same measurement scale across two or more groups of examinees?

Working under a CTT framework, many researchers have investigated measurement invariance at the item level (i.e., item bias) by examining the comparability of classical item statistics such as the item-test correlation or the item-means (proportions endorsed) between groups. Of course, these statistics are not sample invariant because item means are confounded by valid group differences on the measured trait and item-test correlations are affected by group variability on the measured trait. Because of this, and the fact that it is often difficult to place traditional item statistics computed in two or more samples onto comparable scales (i.e., equating is difficult), traditional approaches for investigating item bias, such as comparing item-means and item-test correlations between groups, are mostly unsatisfactory in measurement invariance studies and are seldom used in modern research.

Because of the problems in studying a scale's measurement invariance with classical procedures, researchers have been turning toward latent variable modeling. Within a modeling framework, a test item is measurement invariant when it has the same relationship with a latent variable across groups. When a set of scale items displays the same relationship to a latent variable across two or more groups, then the measurement scale is said to be "invariant" across those groups. As a consequence, examinee scores on the latent variable are comparable and mean differences between groups in raw scores legitimately reflect real mean differences on the latent variable and cannot be attributed to a measurement artifact. Under a modeling framework, one method of investigating measurement invariance is to use multiple-group covariance structure analytic (CSA) techniques. These procedures are extremely useful, but they are limited in that CSA procedures are typically geared toward the analysis of small sets of normally distributed continuous variables. These conditions do not hold when a researcher wants to study the invariance of a 48-item dichotomously scored measure. Under conditions of dichotomous or polytomous observed variables (i.e., items), IRT methods may offer more promise in detecting item bias and measurement invariance.

In the IRT literature, the term item bias has been essentially replaced by a new rubric, called *differential item functioning* (DIF). Analogous to measurement invariance investigations under a CSA paradigm, DIF is said to occur when a test item does not have the same relationship to a latent variable (or a multidimensional latent vector) across two or more examinee groups. Concretely, an item displays DIF if the IRC differs across groups, or equivalently, when any item parameter differs across groups. Millsap and Everson (1993) recently reviewed the literature on testing for DIF. These authors exhaustively cover a variety of topics and procedures. In this chapter, we restrict discussion to the logic of IRT-based DIF-detection approaches. Note, however, it can be argued that the most commonly used DIF-detection procedures are not IRT based and are not based on latent-variable analysis at all (see Clauser & Mazor, 1998, for a review). For example, one extremely popular DIF-detection procedure is the Mantel and Haenszel (1959) statistic (see, Holland & Thayer, 1988 for fuller treatment). Also, the highly flexible logistic regression approaches to detect DIF (Swaminathan & Rogers, 1990) have been used successfully in several studies. Nevertheless, the following discussion is focused entirely on IRT-based procedures and readers interested in these other approaches are directed to the review articles cited earlier and the references contained therein.

DETECTING DIFFERENTIAL ITEM FUNCTIONING WITH IRT

In this section, we assume the existence of two distinct groups of examinees (e.g., men and women), typically called the reference and focal group in the DIF detection literature. Depending on the research context, these groups may differ from each other in their mean and standard deviation on a latent variable. Note that group differences in mean and standard deviation on a latent variable are not signs of DIF, but they do complicate DIF investigations. We also assume that a researcher is interested in deciding whether the items on a particular instrument provide "invariant" measurement across these two groups. In other words, the researcher is interested in studying whether trait level estimates are comparable or on the same scale for the reference and focal group examinees. In real-world contexts there may be many distinct and definable examinee populations. However, the methods presented here are easily generalizable beyond the two-group situation.

As mentioned, under an IRT framework a test item is defined as showing DIF if the IRC is not the same for the reference and focal group. If an item displays DIF, then examinees from the reference and focal groups who are equal in level on the latent trait do not have the same probability of endorsing a test item. Therefore, using a common set of item parameter estimates to score examinees in the presence of DIF can distort trait level estimates and cause them to be either relatively too high or too low for members of one of the groups. The basic IRT definition of DIF suggests a very simple way in which DIF can be investigated. Namely, collect a large sample of examinees from both reference and focal group populations, administer the scale of interest, estimate item parameters separately in the two groups, and then compare the IRCs visually or use a more complex statistical procedure (see following).

Generally speaking, this obvious approach is not adequate for the study of DIF. The major problem is that in IRT modeling there is an indeterminacy between the scale of the item and person parameters. In each separate item parameter calibration, the scale of the latent variable is typically arbitrarily defined to have a mean of 0 and a standard deviation of 1 for identification purposes. This fixing of the latent trait scale identifies and fixes the scale of the item parameters. As a consequence, the item parameter estimates calibrated separately in two groups are not on the same scale and cannot be compared directly. The only case in which it would be appropriate to compare item parameters (or resulting trait level scores) estimated separately in two or more groups is when the researcher can assume the groups have the same distribution on the latent trait variable. It is usually not safe to make this assumption in DIF investigations, so before comparing item parameters estimated separately in different groups, the item parameters must be placed on the same scale. This process is known in the IRT literature as "linking" scales (Vale, 1986). Linking is the modern analogue to traditional test equating procedures.

LINKING SCALES

Item parameter linking is typically discussed in the context of large-scale ability or aptitude assessment. In these contexts, examinees are administered two different tests of the same construct (call them Test A and Test

B), but the tests share a common set of items. The common set of items is known as an "anchor" set. The item parameters are then estimated separately in the two groups of examinees and the parameter estimates of the anchor items are used, through finding an appropriate linking transformation (see following), to place the item (and person) parameters of Test A and Test B onto a common scale. Note that it does not matter if the two groups of examinees differ in mean or standard deviation on the latent trait. The goal of a linking study in this context is to place the item parameters from Test A and Test B onto a common scale so that scores from the two exams are comparable. An example would be a testing firm attempting to maintain comparability of scores on a test of verbal ability across years and across different test forms administered within the same year.

A more common situation in psychological research is that the exact same set of items has been administered in two groups of examinees and the researcher is interested in studying DIF. The motivation for studying DIF might be substantive (e.g., to study qualitative differences in trait manifestation) or for more technical reasons (e.g., to simply eliminate items from a scale). For example, both substantive and technical concerns may be of interest in a study where a researcher was interested in determining whether the items from a popular depression measure work equivalently (i.e., are measurement invariant) for male and female examinees. In this kind of situation, where each group of examinees receives the exact same measure, a researcher can think of every item on the scale as being a potential "anchor" item to be used in estimating an appropriate linking transformation.

To illustrate the issues involved in item parameter linking, we generated three Monte Carlo data sets, called Set-1, Set-2, and Set-3. For each data set, we specified that the true generating item parameters were exactly the same — the test contains *no DIF*. Thus, any differences in an IRC estimated for these sets would be due to differential scaling and estimation error. In particular, we created a 10-item test that fit the 2PL model, and all items had a constant α (discrimination) parameter of 1.0 and β parameters (difficulty) were $\beta = [-2.0, -1.5, -1.0, -0.5, 0.0, 0.0, 0.5, 1.0, 1.5, 2.0]$. Although the item parameters used to generate the data were the same across the three data sets, the data sets were generated to differ in mean and standard deviation on the latent trait. Specifically, the mean and standard deviation of θ used to generate responses was 0 and 1 for Set-1; 0.2 and 1 for Set-2; and 0 and 1.5 for Set-3. For each data set, 5,000 examinees were simulated, and the classical item statistics are shown in Table 10.1.

BILOG-3 (Mislevy & Bock, 1990) was used to estimate item parameters for each of the three data sets, and the results are shown in Table 10.2. Note that in each calibration it is assumed that the latent trait distribution is normal with a mean of 0 and a standard deviation of 1. Examining Table

TABLE 10.1
Classical Item Statistics for the Three Simulated
Data Sets as Output From BILOG-3

ITEM	NAME	TRIED	RIGHT	%	LOGIT/1.7	r	Item–Test BISERIAL
Set 1							
1	0001	5000.0	4593.0	0.919	1.43	0.309	0.560
2	0002	5000.0	4309.0	0.862	1.08	0.340	0.532
3	0003	5000.0	3750.0	0.750	0.65	0.435	0.593
4	0004	5000.0	3146.0	0.629	0.31	0.477	0.609
5	0005	5000.0	2496.0	0.499	0.00	0.496	0.621
6	0006	5000.0	2450.0	0.490	−0.02	0.497	0.623
7	0007	5000.0	1755.0	0.351	−0.36	0.477	0.615
8	0008	5000.0	1225.0	0.245	−0.66	0.433	0.593
9	0009	5000.0	696.0	0.139	−1.07	0.368	0.574
10	0010	5000.0	393.0	0.079	−1.45	0.296	0.544
Set 2							
1	0001	5000.0	4670.0	0.934	1.56	0.270	0.523
2	0002	5000.0	4421.0	0.884	1.20	0.345	0.566
3	0003	5000.0	3983.0	0.797	0.80	0.417	0.594
4	0004	5000.0	3469.0	0.694	0.48	0.461	0.605
5	0005	5000.0	2776.0	0.555	0.13	0.490	0.617
6	0006	5000.0	2789.0	0.558	0.14	0.485	0.610
7	0007	5000.0	2091.0	0.418	−0.19	0.486	0.613
8	0008	5000.0	1454.0	0.291	−0.52	0.465	0.617
9	0009	5000.0	952.0	0.190	−0.85	0.402	0.581
10	0010	5000.0	548.0	0.110	−1.23	0.344	0.574
Set 3							
1	0001	5000.0	4298.0	0.860	1.07	0.463	0.721
2	0002	5000.0	4007.0	0.801	0.82	0.525	0.752
3	0003	5000.0	3583.0	0.717	0.55	0.578	0.769
4	0004	5000.0	3008.0	0.602	0.24	0.616	0.781
5	0005	5000.0	2492.0	0.498	0.00	0.636	0.797
6	0006	5000.0	2513.0	0.503	0.01	0.628	0.787
7	0007	5000.0	1970.0	0.394	−0.25	0.610	0.775
8	0008	5000.0	1481.0	0.296	−0.51	0.572	0.755
9	0009	5000.0	1026.0	0.205	−0.80	0.507	0.720
10	0010	5000.0	681.0	0.136	−1.09	0.435	0.683

10.2, it is clear that in Set-1, the item parameter estimates are very close to the true generating values. In Set-2, the item discriminations are all estimated to be around 1.0, and the item difficulties are all smaller than the true generating item difficulties on average by 0.241. Finally, in Set-3 we see that on average the item discriminations are too large and the difficulty parameters appear to be shrunk toward zero. The bottom line of these results is that if these data sets where assumed to be drawn from different examinee populations and the item parameters were to be com-

TABLE 10.2
Item–Parameter Estimates for the Three Simulated Data Sets

Item Number	True α	True β	α	β	α	β	α	β
1	1.0	-2.0	1.060	-1.956	0.906	-2.301	1.550	-1.315
2	1.0	-1.5	0.887	-1.658	0.968	-1.746	1.568	-1.026
3	1.0	-1.0	0.988	-0.964	0.983	-1.191	1.481	-0.703
4	1.0	-0.5	0.987	-0.470	0.964	-0.730	1.408	-0.322
5	1.0	0.0	0.999	0.003	0.974	-0.197	1.472	0.007
6	1.0	0.0	1.008	0.036	0.952	-0.208	1.411	-0.007
7	1.0	0.5	0.997	0.544	0.985	0.297	1.410	0.339
8	1.0	1.0	0.974	0.995	1.067	0.761	1.437	0.665
9	1.0	1.5	1.004	1.549	1.021	1.238	1.416	1.029
10	1.0	2.0	0.987	2.055	1.121	1.670	1.408	1.376
Mean			0.989	0.013	0.994	-0.241	1.456	0.004
SD			0.043	1.318	0.061	1.282	0.061	0.875

pared, a researcher would almost certainly conclude that the items contained DIF. However, the researcher would be absolutely wrong.

To compare IRCs the item parameter estimates calibrated in different groups have to be placed onto the same scale. Assuming that there is no DIF operating in the items and that the item parameters have been well estimated, placing two sets of item parameters onto a common scale is possible because of the IRT model invariance property. Most linking procedures hinge on the following set of transformations that leave the IRCs invariant (i.e., $P^* \mid \theta^*,\alpha^*,\beta^*,c^* = P \mid \theta,\alpha,\beta,c$):

$$\theta^* = x\theta + y \tag{10.1}$$

$$\beta^* = x\beta + y \tag{10.2}$$

$$\alpha^* = \alpha/x \tag{10.3}$$

$$c^* = c \tag{10.4}$$

The goal of finding a linking transformation is to find the values of x and y, called "linking constants," that place the item parameters estimated separately from two groups onto the same scale. In the present example, if we wanted to place the item parameters onto a common 0,1 trait scale we know what the correct linking constants are because we simulated the data. Each of the separate calibrations assumed a 0,1 distribution for the latent trait. Thus, no changes are needed to the item parameters in Set-1. The only difference between the assumed latent trait distribution and

Set-2 was that the mean for Set-2 was 0.20 rather than zero. This resulted in the estimated item difficulties to be shifted to the left. To adjust for this, we have to multiply those difficulty parameters by $x = 1$ and add $y = 0.2$, and the item discriminations are divided by $x = 1$ and, thus, stay the same. In Set-3, the true generating latent trait had a mean of zero and standard deviation of 1.5. To transform to the 0,1 metric, the discrimination parameters must be divided by $x = 1.5$ and difficulties must be multiplied by $x = 1.5$, and then $y = 0$ is (trivially) added.

In Table 10.3 are shown the item parameter estimates after performing the transformations described in the preceding paragraph. These results introduce a complexity researchers often encounter when analyzing items for DIF. Specifically, even when the true generating values are known, and thus the true linking constants are known, estimation error results in differences among the IRCs. There are two types of estimation error, that for the item parameters and that for the person parameters. Estimation of item parameters was kept relatively small here by generating 5,000 cases, but in practice such sample sizes are rare. On the other hand, there are only 10 items and there may be substantial error in estimating the mean and standard deviation of the latent-trait distribution within a given examinee group. In real-world linking situations, basing a linking transformation on small item sets could be a source of problems.

In practice, the linking constants (x and y) are unknown and must be estimated through some method. It is commonly the case that the linking constants are not estimated using all the items on a test. Rather, in DIF investigations it is more typical that a subset of items, which on the basis of prior research are assumed to have no DIF, are used as a basis for estimating the linking constants. The items used to estimate the linking constants must not have any DIF because DIF invalidates the invariance assump-

TABLE 10.3
Item–Parameter Estimates for the Three
Simulated Data Sets, after Transformations

Item Number	True α	True β	α	β	α	β	α	β
1	1.0	-2.0	1.060	-1.956	0.906	-2.101	1.033	-1.972
2	1.0	-1.5	0.887	-1.658	0.968	-1.546	1.045	-1.539
3	1.0	-1.0	0.988	-0.964	0.983	-0.991	0.987	-1.054
4	1.0	-0.5	0.987	-0.470	0.964	-0.530	0.938	-0.483
5	1.0	0.0	0.999	0.003	0.974	0.017	0.981	0.010
6	1.0	0.0	1.008	0.036	0.952	-0.008	0.940	-0.010
7	1.0	0.5	0.997	0.544	0.985	0.497	0.940	0.508
8	1.0	1.0	0.974	0.995	1.067	0.961	0.959	0.997
9	1.0	1.5	1.004	1.549	1.021	1.438	0.944	1.543
10	1.0	2.0	0.987	2.055	1.121	1.870	0.970	2.064

tion, which, in turn, invalidates the procedures for estimating the linking constants (see following).

That said, there are two main methods for estimating linking constants, and, in turn, the accuracy of any linking depends on the accuracy of estimating these x and y values. The first common approach is called "mean and sigma" methods because they use the mean and standard deviation of the item parameters. These methods assume a set of common anchor items or that two groups of examinees have answered the exact same tests. One example of a mean and sigma method is to identify the linking constants so that the mean and standard deviation of the item difficulty parameters from Test B are the same as those from Test A. Let

$$\bar{\beta}_A \text{ and } \bar{\beta}_B \text{ be the mean item difficulty}$$
$$\text{estimated in Group A and Group B} \qquad (10.5)$$

$$\sigma_A \text{ and } \sigma_B \text{ be the standard deviation of item difficulty}$$
$$\text{estimated in Group A and B} \qquad (10.6)$$

Then, to place the item parameters in Group B to the metric of Group A

$$B_B^* = x\beta_B + y \qquad (10.7)$$

$$x = \frac{\sigma_A}{\sigma_B} \qquad (10.8)$$

$$y = \bar{\beta}_A - x\left(\bar{\beta}_B\right) \qquad (10.9)$$

For example, to transform the item parameters from Set-2 to the scale of Set-1, the x value would be $1.318/1.282 = 1.028$, and the y value would be $0.013 - (1.028 * -0.241) = 0.260$. These values would then be plugged into Eqs. 10.1–10.3 to derive the appropriate estimates for each item and person parameter.

Over the years, a number of enhancements and modifications have been made to this very basic procedure (e.g., see Mislevy & Bock, 1990, pp. 1–20). A central problem with the mean and sigma method described earlier is that the estimation of the linking constants can be adversely impacted by outliers and the differential standard errors of the item difficulty estimates. "Robust" procedures developed in Bejar and Wingersky (1981) and Linn, Levine, Hastings, and Wardrop (1980) attempt to adjust for these problems. Another potential problem with the mean and sigma method illustrated earlier is that only information about the item difficulty parameters is used to derive the linking constants. An alternative set of linking procedures are called *characteristic curve* methods (Divgi, 1985;

Stocking & Lord, 1983). (Note that Baker [1992, 1993, 1997] developed characteristic curve methods for graded-response and nominal-response IRT models.) In these procedures, a set of linking constants is estimated so that the test characteristic curves derived from two different groups of examinees are as similar as possible. Characteristic curve procedures, therefore, make use of all the estimated item parameters in finding appropriate linking constants. The drawback is that these procedures are more computationally intensive. Although in theory characteristic curve methods should outperform mean and sigma methods, empirical research does not demonstrate great differences (Baker & Al-Karni, 1991). As noted in Millsap and Everson (1993, p. 310), the superiority of one method over the other across all testing conditions has not been clearly demonstrated.

In sum, IRT linking involves estimating IRCs separately for two or more groups of examinees. After finding a common set of items that contain no DIF, statistical methods are implemented to identify a set of linking constants that can be used to place item parameters onto equivalent scales. Once on a common scale, it is legitimate to then compare IRCs across groups in order to identify DIF. Thus, in practice, linking is really a two-stage process because a researcher must identify a set of no-DIF anchor items and then estimate the linking constants using just these DIF-free items. Herein lies a major problem in DIF studies, namely, for the linking constants to be estimated correctly, the items must contain no DIF. To address this concern, some researchers have developed "iterative" linking/DIF procedures. For example, a researcher may estimate linking constants based on all the items, then link scales and test for DIF. Items displaying DIF are eliminated from the anchor, and new linking constants are estimated based on only the no-DIF items. After linking, the items are again tested for DIF. This process is repeated until the same items are identified as containing DIF each time (e.g., Candell & Drasgow, 1988; Drasgow, 1987). An alternative iterative procedure has been developed by Park (see Lautenschlager & Park, 1988; Park & Lautenschlager, 1990). The major difference between Park's method and previous iterative linking/DIF detection procedures is that Park's method does not require the estimation of linking constants.

SPECIFIC IRT PROCEDURES FOR INVESTIGATING DIF

Now that we have introduced the concept of metric linking, we examine some specific methods that have been proposed for studying DIF in the IRT literature. Note that most of the linking procedures introduced earlier were developed before computer programs were available for conducting "multiple-group" IRT parameter calibrations (e.g., MULTILOG [Thissen, 1991] or BILOG-MG [Zimowski, Muraki, Mislevy, & Bock, 1996]). In a multiple-group IRT calibration, item parameters for two or more groups are estimated simultaneously as well as group mean differences on the latent variable.

Multiple-group IRT modeling parallels multiple-group covariance structure analysis in significant ways (Reise, Widaman, & Pugh, 1993). Importantly, in each methodology a set of "anchor" items must be identified that contain no DIF. Specifically, in a multiple-group calibration item parameters for the anchor items are estimated on the basis of data from both the reference and focal groups. That is, for the anchor items, one set of item parameters is assumed to apply to both reference and focal groups. The item parameters for the remaining items are then freely estimated for each group separately (but simultaneously). Item parameter values can then be inspected for the presence of DIF. In this context the anchor items serve to identify the metric of the latent trait scale, and thus item parameters from the nonanchor items are directly comparable. In short, with modern multiple-group IRT programs, the process of estimating linking constants described earlier can be circumnavigated. However, note that Kim and Cohen (1988) compared linking results based on the procedures described previously (i.e., mean and sigma methods, test characteristic curve methods) and "concurrent calibration" methods and did not find any particular method to yield superior results.

Thissen, Steinberg, and Gerrard (1986) describe how multiple-group IRT modeling can be used to investigate DIF on a personality measure (see also Thissen, Steinberg, & Wainer, 1988; 1992). Their approach to DIF assessment is generalizable to any type of measure and IRT model and analogous to procedures used in CSA for testing measurement invariance in a multiple-group factor-analysis context. Basically, their likelihood ratio model comparison procedure consists of two parts. First, a model is estimated in which one or more item parameters are freely estimated within the reference and focal groups, and a log-likelihood is obtained. Second, a model is estimated in which these item parameters are constrained to equality in the reference and focal groups, and again, a log-likelihood value is obtained. Negative two times the difference in the log-likelihoods for the two models is distributed as chi-square with degrees of freedom equal to the difference in the number of parameters estimated in each model. If the resulting chi-square is large, this would indicate that constraining the parameters resulted in a significantly worse model fit. This is tantamount to saying that the item with the freely estimated parameters contains DIF (see, Cohen, Kim, & Wollack, 1996 for research findings).

In practice, the model comparison approach depends on finding a set of items that contain no DIF to be used as an anchor to identify a common latent trait metric between groups. When such a set has not been identified on the basis of prior research, a researcher may use a one-item-at-a-time approach. For example, if there was a 10-item test, a researcher might begin by estimating a model constraining all item parameters across groups to be equal while simultaneously estimating the group mean difference on the latent variable. Then, a new model might be estimated using items 1–9 as an anchor and allowing the item parameters for Item 10 to be freely estimated within groups. In this case, Item 10 would be the "studied" item to be evaluated for DIF. If DIF is found then on all subsequent calibrations, the researcher would allow the item parameters for Item 10 to be freely estimated. If DIF was not found, then Item 10 would go back into the anchor, and the process repeated but this time allowing the parameters for Item 9 to be freely estimated across groups.

Although multiple-group IRT modeling represents an improvement over the methods described in the previous section, there are some drawbacks. First, it must be assumed that some IRT model fits the data for both groups. More importantly, in long tests when there is no previously identified anchor set to define the scale, the one-item-at-a-time process will be labor-intensive and unwieldy. Also, there is a really limited data base to guide practitioners regarding how many anchor items are needed to ensure parameters are on the same scale. If many items on a test are found to display DIF, then it is possible to run out of anchor items. Another potential problem, not specific to this technique, however, is that statistically significant DIF may not be practically important. That is, a difference in item discrimination of 0.20 may be statistically significant, but the practical impact, in terms of estimating a person's latent trait score may be minimal. Nevertheless, it is at least arguable that the presence of DIF on an IRT-based test is not as great of a concern as it would be on a CTT-based test because it is possible to create a "partial" measurement invariance IRT model by allowing some of the items to have different IRCs across examinee groups.

An alternative procedure for investigating DIF is available in the BILOG-MG (Zimowski et al., 1996) program. This program was specifically designed for multiple-group IRT modeling, and, therefore, the detection of DIF is one of its main features (see chap. 13 for more details). The BILOG-MG program allows researchers to test for DIF in the form of different item-difficulty parameters for two groups, but it does not allow for testing group differences in item discriminations. Let us illustrate the BILOG-MG approach by using data Set-1 and Set-2. Let us assume that these data sets come from different examinee populations, and we call the data Set-1 group the reference and the Set-2 group the focal group. Given this, in BILOG-MG DIF would be investigated in the following three-step procedure.

First, item parameters are estimated separately in the two groups of examinees with the constraint that the item discrimination parameter for each item is equivalent across groups. It is not assumed by the program that the groups have the same mean and standard deviation on the latent variable. In fact, the program fixes the reference group mean on the latent variable to 0 and the standard deviation to 1. The mean and standard deviation on the latent variable are estimated parameters for the focal group. In this example, the mean for the focal group was estimated to be 0.229, and the standard deviation was estimated to be 0.998. The first set of columns in Table 10.4 gives the results of the first stage of BILOG-MG for this example problem.

In Stage 2, the mean item difficulty is computed for the reference and focal groups, respectively, and the difference in these values is computed. The item-difficulty parameters in the focal group are then "adjusted" by subtracting this mean difference from every item difficulty parameter. Finally, in Stage 3, a contrast is set up by taking the difference between the reference group item difficulties and the "adjusted" focal group item difficulties. These values, which are shown in Table 10.4, can be evaluated for statistical significance. Large values indicate relative DIF—the item is more or less difficult for one of the groups after accounting for group mean differences on the latent variable. In the present case, no item was identified as displaying DIF, which is a good result because there is none.

Beyond these two computer-program specific approaches to exploring DIF, there are a wide variety of statistical procedures for evaluating whether two IRCs are different. All of these procedures assume that the IRCs are on the same scale first, so the tests are only as good as the linking allows. We will not provide mathematical formulas for each of these sta-

TABLE 10.4
DIF Analysis Output from BILOG-MG

Item	Reference		Focal		Adjusted		DIF
	α	β	α	β	α	β	
01	0.977	-2.048	0.977	-2.209	-2.048	-1.987	0.061
02	0.917	-1.637	0.917	-1.797	-1.637	-1.575	0.062
03	0.975	-0.975	0.975	-1.197	-0.975	-0.975	0.000
04	0.960	-0.476	0.960	-0.730	-0.476	-0.508	-0.032
05	0.971	0.007	0.971	-0.191	0.007	0.031	0.024
06	0.963	0.040	0.963	-0.201	0.040	0.021	-0.019
07	0.976	0.557	0.976	0.310	0.557	0.532	-0.025
08	1.012	0.986	1.012	0.796	0.986	1.018	0.032
09	1.015	1.549	1.015	1.259	1.549	1.481	-0.069
10	1.072	1.976	1.072	1.719	1.976	1.942	-0.034

tistics. Rather, here we merely introduce the reader to one commonly cited approach. Specifically, among the best-known procedures for deciding whether two IRCs are different from each other are the signed and unsigned area measures (Raju, 1988, 1990). These statistics indicate the area (both unsigned and signed) between two IRCs. For example, in the 2PL model the formulas for the signed and unsigned areas are

$$\text{Signed Area} = \beta_2 - \beta_1 \tag{10.10}$$

$$\text{Unsigned Area} = \left| \frac{2(\alpha_2 - \alpha_1)}{D\alpha_1\alpha_2} \ln\left\{ 1 + \exp\left[\frac{D\alpha_1\alpha_2(\beta_2 - \beta_1)}{\alpha_2 - \alpha_1} \right] \right\} - (\beta_2 - \beta_1) \right| \tag{10.11}$$

And if $\alpha_1 = \alpha_2$ (i.e., no DIF in item discriminations) then the unsigned area reduces to

$$\text{Unsigned Area} = |\beta_2 - \beta_1| \tag{10.12}$$

MULTIDIMENSIONALITY AND DIF

The leading cause of DIF (lack of measurement invariance) is most likely multidimensionality caused by subsets of items that are highly similar in content (Ackerman, 1992; Merideth, 1993; Roussos & Stout, 1996, p. 367). That is, although all items on a scale might be good markers of a single common factor, some items might be influenced by smaller "nuisance" dimensions. In turn, differential group mean differences on these nuisance factors can lead to the identification of DIF when the items are studied as a whole under a unidimensionality framework (Oshima & Miller, 1992). This type of situation is rather common in psychological testing, where it is rare that a substantively interesting scale can be found that truly measures one and only one latent trait. It is arguable that purely unidimensional scales can only be created for the narrowest of constructs (e.g., self-esteem in eighth-grade math class). This fact of psychological measurement calls into question the use of unidimensional IRT models in general, and unidimensional IRT-based DIF detection procedures in particular.

For this reason, we believe that an exciting development in DIF analysis is the Shealy-Stout multidimensional model for DIF (MMD; Shealy & Stout, 1993a; 1993b). This nonparametric procedure explicitly allows for smaller nuisance dimensions to be incorporated into the analysis of DIF. Roussos and Stout (1996) describe how the procedure can be integrated with substantive theory and the resulting advantages (see also Douglas,

Roussos, & Stout (1996) for more details) and computer programs, called SIBTEST and MULTISIB are available to implement this class of procedures (see, Stout & Roussos, 1995; Stout, Hsin-Hung, Nandakumar, & Bolt, 1997). Although we do not review the logic of the SIBTEST procedure here, we note that research results thus far have been very promising. Most important, the theory underlying the model is more in line with real-world tests, and we expect that over the years this framework will see more research attention.

COMPUTERIZED ADAPTIVE TESTING

One of the chief potential applications of IRT models lies in the realm of computerized adaptive testing (CAT). A computerized adaptive test is a measurement instrument that is administered to examinees via the computer rather than in conventional paper-and-pencil format. Perhaps the chief goal of CAT is to use the IRT invariance property to create an algorithm by which each examinee receives a test that is a "good" measure for that particular individual. In other words, the test is "tailored" to the individual examinee so that the questions are neither too difficult or too easy. As a by-product, IRT-based CAT exams usually contain fewer items than conventional paper-and-pencil measures. Other advantages will be described in a later section.

As is well known, conventional testing rests on the assumption that all examinees receive the exact same items or parallel items. It is also well known that most paper-and-pencil psychological measures are not efficient in that many items do not provide useful information in distinguishing among examinees in certain ranges of the latent trait. For example, on a typical exam, high trait level examinees may receive several easy items for which they have little chance of answering wrong, and thus such items provide almost no information about their relative trait standing. Conversely, low trait level examinees may receive several items that are much too difficult for them, and, thus, their incorrect responses tell us very little about their relative trait standing. IRT-based CAT addresses this inefficiency issue directly by attempting to administer each examinee a test for which their proportion correct will be around 0.50.

IRT-based CAT algorithms have been researched for several decades and much is known about their functioning in comparison to paper-and-pencil measures (Wainer, 1990; Weiss, 1982; 1985). In the following sections, we do not provide an exhaustive historical review of this literature. Rather, our objective is to highlight the main steps in CAT and point out relevant issues that need to be considered within each phase.

The Item Bank

The basic goal of CAT is to administer a set of items that are in some sense maximally efficient and informative for each examinee. To accomplish this, different examinees will receive different sets of items, and their scores on the latent trait are estimated on the basis of their responses to these different item subsets. Clearly, the capacity to implement IRT-based CAT rests on having an "item bank" that contains a large set of items for which IRT item parameter estimates are known (Millman & Arter, 1984). The item bank may contain mixtures of any type of item response format such as dichotomously scored multiple-choice items, true/false questions, or questions with polytomously scored graded response formats (Dodd, De Ayala, & Koch, 1995; Master & Evans, 1986). Because of the primary importance of the item bank in determining the efficiency of CAT, much thought and research has gone into issues involving the creation and maintenance of item banks.

It is generally agreed that if the goal of testing is to measure well across the entire trait range, then ideally an item bank should contain a sufficient number of highly discriminating items with difficulty parameters spread widely across the trait range (Weiss, 1982). When an item bank meets this objective all examinees, regardless of their location on the latent trait, can be administered an appropriately tailored exam and all examinees can be measured accurately. No precise number can be given regarding how many items this requires, but a rough estimate is around 100. (Note that if the items are polytomously scored, many fewer items are needed in the bank [Dodd, De Ayala, & Koch, 1995].) In some domains, such as personality and attitude assessment, there are no existing scales with 100 items. Furthermore, it is difficult to conceive of a large number of highly discriminating items with a wide range of difficulty values being written to assess some personality constructs (e.g., aggression, paranoia).

In other domains, such as eighth-grade mathematics, it is easy to conceive of an almost infinite domain of potential items with varying difficulties. This may be one reason why adaptive testing has been implemented in cognitive performance but has not found much application in personality assessment (however, see Balasubramanian & Kamakura, 1989; Waller & Reise, 1989). Sometimes in special circumstances, creating a large pool of items is simplified because the items can be written by the computer (Hornke & Habon, 1986). However, implementing this procedure assumes a good knowledge of the psychological factors that influence item parameter values. Computerized item-writing applications are beginning to emerge in cognitive testing and haven't been tried in typical performance assessments. See Embretson (1985) for a discussion of the ideas underlying theory-based item construction and also see chapter 11.

In some testing contexts, the goal of computerized adaptive testing is not to scale people with equal precision across the entire latent trait range. Rather, the objective of testing is to make a dichotomous decision regarding whether an examinee is above or below some threshold value. For example, mastery or competency testing (Lewis & Sheehan, 1990; Sheehan & Lewis, 1992) is one such class of assessment situations. The type of item bank required to make mastery decisions is quite different from the one in the previously described testing situation. In mastery testing, it is conceivable that an item pool consist entirely of items with item difficulty parameters around the cut-score. This will lead to the test information peaking around the cut-score. Beyond the educational setting, another example of mastery testing is a clinical assessment, where the researcher is interested only in deciding whether a person is high on the trait (e.g., above $\theta = 2.0$) or not. Waller and Reise (1989) labeled this *clinical decision adaptive testing.*

A critical concern in CAT relevant to the item bank is with the original derivation of the item parameter estimates to be used in CAT (Hetter, Segall, & Bloxom, 1994). Specifically, significant research has been extended toward the issue of whether item parameters estimated on paper-and-pencil tests are translatable into computerized test versions (Green et al., 1984; Lee, Moreno, & Sympson, 1986; Mead & Drasgow, 1993; Neuman & Baydoun, 1998; Sykes & Ito, 1997; Spray, Ackerman, Reckase, & Carlson, 1989). For example, Divgi (1986) and Divgi and Stoloff (1986) found that the estimated IRCs differed for a test depending on whether it was administered as a CAT or in paper-and-pencil versions. Note that serial order or item context effects are not an issue in conventional paper-and-pencil testing because the order of items is typically a fixed constant. However, in CAT, a researcher must assume no presentation-order effects on the item parameter estimates.

Before moving on to the next section, we note that prior to implementing IRT-based CAT, a researcher needs to pay sufficient attention to the technical aspects and details involved when examinees are administered an adaptive exam via the computer rather than the more familiar paper-and-pencil version (Mills & Stocking, 1996). For example, in typical applications, a training module must be created to teach unfamiliar examinees how to use the computer and how to respond to the questions (e.g., mouse click vs. touch screen). Examinees also must be informed of their response options, such as whether they can go back and review and change their responses later (see, Lunz, Bergstrom, & Wright, 1992; Wise, Barnes, Harvey, & Plake, 1989), how to change their responses while the item is still on the screen, and so on. Even when these issues are fully resolved, there remains the issue concerning how to best communicate test results to examinees, which come in the form of scores on the latent trait metric. This issue, and issues of item bank security, go beyond our current purposes and should not be discussed.

Administering the First Several Items

Once a sufficient pool of items has been assembled, the next issue that arises is how should the computerized adaptive exam begin? This is sometimes referred to as the "starting point for entry" problem. If it can be assumed that the examinee population is normally distributed, then a reasonable choice for starting a CAT is with an item of moderate difficulty, such as one with a difficulty parameter of between –0.5 and 0.5. If some prior information is available regarding the examinee's position on the trait continuum, then such information might be used in selecting the difficulty level of the first item. Also, the pool of items should be of sufficient size so that random selection of items can occur within a difficulty range so that not every examinee receives the same first couple of items. Finally, some testers like to begin their CATs with an "easy" item so that the examinee has a success experience which may, in turn, alleviate some problems such as test anxiety.

ITEM SELECTION PROCEDURES/SCORING EXAMINEES

After the examinee responds to the first item, then the CAT algorithm officially begins. The computer, in conjunction with the parameters of the IRT model, is used to select the next item to administer based on the examinee's previous pattern of correct and incorrect responses. Therefore, examinees need to be scored on the latent trait metric after every item response. The relevant issues are (a) how should each response be scored, and (b) based on the examinee's previous item response, how should the computer decide what item to administer next?

As described in chapter 7, there are three main methods for estimating an examinee's position on the latent trait continuum: (a) ML, (b) MAP, and (c) EAP. However, a ML estimate is not available until an examinee has endorsed and not endorsed at least one item. Thus, in the early stages of a CAT, ML scoring is often not possible. To avoid this problem, EAP scoring can be used to score examinees in adaptive testing contexts (Bock & Mislevy, 1982). This scoring algorithm makes use of prior information and thus examinees can be estimated on the latent trait after only a single-item response. Some researchers do not endorse the use of priors because they potentially affect scores. For example, if few items are administered, then trait level estimates may be pulled toward the mean of the prior distribution. For this reason, some researchers have implemented a "step-size" procedure to assigning scores at the beginning of a CAT (see Dodd, 1990). For example, starting with a trait level estimate of 0, if an examinee endorses the first item, the algorithm then raises his or her trait level estimate by a fixed step size such as 0.25. When an item is not endorsed, the examinee's trait level estimate is reduced by a fixed step size. This process might continue until an ML estimate was computable, and then ML scoring would be used for scoring all subsequent responses.

Corresponding to these two scoring strategies are two major ways in which to select the next item to administer. First, select the next item to administer that provides the most psychometric information at the examinee's current estimated trait level. This strategy usually corresponds to ML scoring. The most informative items will be those for which the examinee has a 50% chance of endorsing in the 2PL or 1PL models and around a 60% chance of endorsing in the 3PL model. Alternatively a researcher can randomly select among a subset of items all containing approximately the same information. This latter approach is less efficient of course. A second strategy is to select the item that minimizes the examinee's expected posterior standard deviation. That is, select the item that makes the examinee's standard error the smallest. This typically corresponds to the Bayesian scoring procedures and does not always yield the same results as the maximum information strategy.

Some researchers have indicated that other factors should be used in conjunction with item information in deciding what item to administer next (Stocking 1993). In fact, over the years several authors have proposed enhancements to the basic "maximize information" or "lower standard error" decision rules for item selection (e.g., Theunissen, 1986). In these enhancements, the way items are selected in CAT depends on more than just the conditional item information. For example, Stocking and Swanson (1993) describe an algorithm to place content constraints on the items administered within CAT. In some testing contexts, it may not be desirable to administer an examinee multiple reading passages with similar content (e.g., science; see also Kingsbury & Zara, 1991).

TERMINATING THE ADAPTIVE TEST

In CAT, after every item response an examinee's trait level and standard error is reestimated and the computer selects the next item to administer. But this cannot go on forever, and the CAT algorithm needs to have a stopping rule (see review in Hambleton, Zaal, & Pieters, 1991). The most commonly employed stopping rule for CAT is to repeat administering items until the standard error of measurement is below some acceptable value. Implementing this requires that the item bank contain items that, when considered in aggregate, provide sufficient test information to make this possible. A second alternative is to administer a fixed number of items. This procedure is known as fixed-length adaptive testing (e.g., De Ayala, 1992). Generally speaking, the standard error stopping rule makes the best use of the CAT algorithm and is therefore preferred.

APPLICATIONS OF CAT

Although CAT has been researched for several decades, real-world applications are only now starting to emerge. For example, this decade has seen the advent of the Computerized Placement Tests program (College Board, 1990; Ward, 1988); computerized adaptive math, reading, and writing exams (American College Testing, 1993); the CAT version of the Armed Services Vocational Aptitude Battery (Curran & Wise, 1994; McBride, 1997; Moreno & Segall, 1992; Moreno, Wetzel, McBride, & Weiss, 1984), and a CAT-adaptive version of the Graduate Record Examination (Educational Testing Service, 1993). Also, CAT has been implemented in at least one large school district (Kingsbury & Houser, 1993) and several licensure boards are at least in the process of evaluating CAT (Zara, 1988). Finally, it should be noted that CAT will not become popular in psychology unless there are programs available that facilitate implementation. For this reason we alert readers to the MICRO-CAT (Assessment Systems Corporation, 1991) program, which can be used for a wide variety of IRT-CAT applications.

ADVANTAGES OF CAT

The major advantage of CAT, relative to traditional paper-and-pencil exams, is that it is efficient. Research has repeatedly demonstrated that on average a CAT exam is 50% shorter than a paper-and-pencil measure with equal or better measurement precision. Thus, researchers have more time to assess relevant constructs. Beyond this main feature, CAT offers the researcher other advantages as well. For example, the computer can continuously monitor the psychometric properties of the items, the examiner can easily record reaction time if this is of interest, and the computer administration opens up a wide array of alternative item formats to be included in the same exam (e.g., multimedia graphic displays). Furthermore, the computer can immediately score examinees and save that score to a database, and there is no need to buy answer sheets or number 2 pencils. There is a need to hire someone to constantly supervise the testing station, however. With networking and the rapid growth of the Internet, it is conceivable that computerized testing may open up a new world for assessment researchers.

USING IRT METHODS FOR SCALE CONSTRUCTION

In psychology, there is no single set of rules to follow in creating a psychological measure. Rather, different authors have taken different approaches depending on the construct to be assessed and the goals of the assessment. For example, some of the most popular and successful measures, such as the Minnesota Multiphasic Personality Inventory (MMPI) and Strong Vocational Interest Bank (SVIB), used an empirical keying approach to psychological scale development. Ostensibly, such measures are often explicitly not designed to be unidimensional, factor-pure "latent-trait" measures, but rather were designed to make predictions about people. Although there are good psychometric principles to follow in designing empirically keyed scales (e.g., cross-validate, have a diverse sample), these principles are not easily extended to an IRT framework. In fact, it is difficult to conceive how these types of scales might be translated into IRT terms because IRT models, by their very nature, assume the existence of one or more latent traits by which people can be scaled on. In short, the empirical keying strategy of scale construction has no analogue in IRT terms.

Another approach to scale construction, perhaps the most common, is what might be called the "construct" approach (Wiggins, 1972) — usually associated with factor analysis. In this method, a set of items that have been demonstrated to share some common variance and meet other types of psychometric criteria is selected. For example, select items for the scale that are not too highly correlated with items on another scale that measures a different construct; select items that have high item-test correlations and load highly on a single factor dimension; and select sets of items so that responses are internally consistent (i.e., highly intercorrelated), which results in high coefficient alpha reliability coefficients. Most researchers have some familiarity with this traditional approach to scale construction and test analysis. In what follows, we describe how IRT procedures might be used alternatively to construct a scale and/or analyze the psychometric properties of an existing instrument.

We begin by assuming that a large pool of dichotmously scored items has already been written that are potentially good indicators of some trait construct. Furthermore, this item pool has been administered to a large sample of examinees. It is critically important, especially in IRT modeling, that the sample be heterogeneous with respect to the latent trait variable. It is *not* important that the sample be "random" or "stratified random" or "representative" of any defined examinee population. Examinee heterogeneity is important to achieve good estimates of the item parameters, especially the discrimination and guessing (if multiple-choice test) parameters.

Let us ignore discussion of preliminary item-level factor analyses, which are described elsewhere, and jump right into the IRT analysis. Given the responses from this large and heterogeneous calibration sample, the first step is to estimate the parameters for an appropriate IRT model. For example, if a personality trait is being measured with dichotomous items, the 2PL model could be estimated. Alternatively, a competing model, such as the 1PL could be estimated and the fit compared to the 2PL. Given the item parameter estimates from some model, the next step is to explore the issue of item fit as described in chapter 9. Specifically, a researcher may compute one or more chi-square item-fit statistics and inspect graphs of the empirical versus estimated IRCs. Items that display poor fit to the estimated model parameters are the first candidates for elimination from the scale.

The second step is inspection of the estimated item parameters. The estimated item parameters are used to generate item information curves that can be added together to form a test information curve. Recall from chapter 7 that the conditional standard error of measurement is equal to 1 divided by the square root of the conditional information value. After formation of the test information curve, the researcher needs to decide what type of measure he or she wants to create. Let us assume testing time is limited and only a few items can be retained in the final paper-and-pencil measure. The main issue is whether the researcher wants to create a peaked test or a more or less equal-precise test. That is, is it more important to measure extremely well within a limited range of the latent trait or is it more important to measure examinees at all ranges of the latent trait equally well? The choice critically affects which items are included in the final version of the scale.

For an equal-precise measure, items must be selected so that the test information curve is relatively flat across the trait range. This means that a set of highly discriminating items with a broad range of difficulty parameters must be identified. If there are certain trait ranges where the test information is not high enough, new items will need to be written specifically for that purpose, and these new items will again have to be administered to a heterogeneous calibration sample. How much information is high enough? Well, if the conditional information is around 10, then the conditional standard error is about 0.31. To place this in more conventional terms, a standard error of 0.31 corresponds to a reliability coefficient of 0.90.

On the other hand, let us make the highly reasonable assumption that the trait is normally distributed such that the majority of the examinee population is between plus and minus 1 standard deviation from the mean. In this situation it may be reasonable to try to maximize the information in the middle of the trait range where most people are, and to deemphasize measurement precision in the extremes. This would be accomplished by identifying highly discriminating items that had difficulty values in the middle of the trait range. Items with large positive and negative difficulties would be eliminated from the final version of the test. In this situation, the test created by IRT methods would be highly similar to the test created by traditional item analysis.

Judging by the preceding discussion, the concept of item and test information is clearly critical to analyzing the psychometric properties of existing scales and in the creation of new measures. Because of this emphasis on information, as opposed to item test correlations or the average item intercorrelations, the type of item selected in an IRT-based measure may be different than one selected by traditional item-analysis procedures. For example, in a traditionally constructed test, items might be selected that have proportions endorsed around 0.50 so that examinee variability is maximized and internal consistency estimates are correspondingly increased. On the other hand, as is clear from the preceding discussion, with IRT methods the notion of internal consistency is superceded by the concepts of test and item information. The usefulness of the concept of information goes beyond the construction and analysis of single measures. Specifically, under an IRT framework two competing measures of the same construct could be compared on the basis of the information function. It is possible that two tests with the same reliability coefficient can provide information in different trait ranges. The choice between these tests then becomes one of deciding where on the trait continuum smaller standard errors are most important.

SUMMARY

In this chapter we focus on how IRT models are applied in order to address real-world testing problems. We explore how IRT methodologies are used to identify differential item functioning. We illustrate how IRT item parameters estimated on the basis of separate groups of examinees are not comparable. The logic of linking transformations is introduced and examples are provided. However, as we noted, at some point, these linking procedures may be superceded by developments in multiple-group IRT modeling. The likelihood ratio procedure for DIF testing and the procedure implemented by BILOG-MG are described. IRT applications in computerized adaptive testing and in scale analysis and development are also described. The critical role that item and test information play in both these endeavors is emphasized. Specifically, in CAT item and test information considerations determine (a) the adequacy of the initial item pool, (b) which items are going to be administered next, and (c) when a CAT is to be terminated. In scale construction, item and test information considerations are critical in determining which items to include on a final version of a scale. Also, of course, these values would play a critical role analyzing the psychometric properties of any existing scale. It should be noted, however, that all applications described in this chapter assume the data can be appropriately modeled by IRT methods. To the extent that this is not true, these applications become less viable.

11

IRT Applications in Cognitive
and Developmental Assessment

Applications of IRT-based methods are becoming more common in research on cognitive abilities and lifespan development. Several substantive issues relevant to the meaning and nature of many constructs have
been addressed using IRT-based methods. New aspects of individual differences, such as information processing, also can be measured with some
IRT models. Furthermore, IRT is useful for solving many applied issues in
cognitive and developmental measurement, such as linking measurement
results across samples, handling missing data, and adaptive testing. In
this chapter, we focus on how IRT can contribute to substantive issues,
such as construct validity and the nature and amount of lifespan changes
in cognitive performance. A few elaborated applications are presented as
models for the reader in several areas. Applied measurement issues, such
as linking and adaptive testing, are covered in chapter 10.

ISSUES IN CONSTRUCT VALIDITY

Although substantive research on abilities has a long history, many issues
remain unresolved. The nature of abilities remains elusive. One reason for
this is that modern ability testing originated outside of psychological theory. Although Galton (1883) attempted to apply psychological principles
to testing, the low-level cognitive processes represented in his tasks (i.e.,
sensation and perception) had no predictive validity for important social
indicators of intelligence. Wissler's (1901) study on similar tasks showed
that the various measures were relatively uncorrelated with each other

and with school grades. In contrast, Binet and Simon's (1905) complex tasks required judgment and reasoning but were not linked explicitly to the low-level processes studied in psychology at the time. However, performance on these complex tasks did predict school grades and teachers' judgments and so provided the foundation for intelligence testing. Consequently, most ability tests were constructed with little explicit attention to operationalizing substantive theories. But, because theory is central to construct validity, substantial validation issues remain to be solved.

This section reviews four major areas in which IRT applications address issues in construct validity: (a) assessing dimensionality, (b) decomposing cognitive processes on ability test items, (c) identifying qualitative differences between examinees in the basis of test performance, and (d) enhancing ability interpretations with item-referenced meaning. Implications for measuring new aspects of individual differences are also considered within each topic. The reader is referred back to chapter 4 and chapter 5 for more detailed presentation of the IRT models in the examples that appear in this chapter.

Assessing Dimensionality

Elaborating the number and the nature of the dimensions underlying an ability test is an important aspect of construct validation. Does the score derived from an ability test represent a single construct or a composite of several constructs? In contemporary ability measurement, dimensionality assessment is often a by-product of estimating a psychometric model. Effective applications of unidimensional IRT models require that the test or item bank is essentially unidimensional. So, if a unidimensional IRT model is applied, then model fit indices implicitly evaluate how well a single dimension accounts for test data (see chap. 9).

Multidimensional item response theory (MIRT) models can identify multiple dimensions that are involved in item responses. In this section, applications of compensatory MIRT models for elaborating construct validity will be considered. The traditional factor-analytic approach is not appropriate for evaluating dimensionality for dichotomous ability test items. A linear factor analysis of correlations between dichotomous items leads to factor structures that are confounded by item difficulty (see Carroll, 1945). Applying a compensatory MIRT model circumvents this problem because correlations are not modeled. Compensatory MIRT models predict individual item responses. The number of dimensions is analogous to the number of factors. Furthermore, like factor analysis, the construct is elaborated from the pattern of item discriminations. Like factor loadings, item discrimination parameters represent the impact of a dimension on an item. In fact, compensatory MIRT models are identical to factor-analysis models under certain assumptions (see Takane & deLeeuw, 1987).

Compensatory MIRT models are applied less often to elaborate construct validity in cognitive measurement than in personality and attitude measurement. Interpreting the dimensions requires that meaningful substantive features may be gleaned from the items. Ability test items often are not regarded as substantively meaningful. Many ability test items are novel tasks that do not represent practically important domains. Furthermore, the stimulus features of items that influence difficulty are often unknown. Typical item specifications are too global (e.g., abstract versus concrete content) to enhance substantive meaning. In contrast, many personality and attitude items have more direct interpretability. For example, self-reported behaviors, feelings, or attitudes can be interpreted with respect to the constructs.

Compensatory MIRT models are most useful for elaborating ability constructs when the stimulus features of items represent skills and knowledge (as for some achievement items) or cognitive processes. Some research examples are presented next.

Applications of Exploratory MIRT Models. Zwick (1987) applied an exploratory MIRT model to identify the dimensions behind the reading items on the National Assessment of Educational Progress (NAEP). Items were classified by reading experts on several variables that reflected passage type, decision task and content. The results suggested that a single factor adequately characterized patterns of item responses in reading. Items on comprehending fictional stories had the highest loadings, whereas items on comprehending documents, such as phone books and bus schedules, had the lowest loadings.

Reckase and McKinley (1991) supported two dimensions underlying a mathematics usage test by applying a MIRT model. Most interestingly, their results suggested that the mathematics usage construct shifts with increased item difficulty. A linear regression of item easiness on the two item discriminations yielded a high multiple correlation coefficient ($R = .80$), but item discrimination on the two dimensions had opposing relationships to item easiness. Figure 11.1 is a three-dimensional scattergram of item discriminations by item easiness that was produced from their results. For easy items, Dimension 1 is most important, whereas for hard items, Dimension 2 becomes increasingly important. These results suggest that the construct shifts with increased item difficulty because the hardest items involve a second dimension.

Construct-shift may apply to many ability tests, and it may be involved when either easy or hard items have relatively lower discriminations. The interpretation of construct shift could be substantively interesting. For

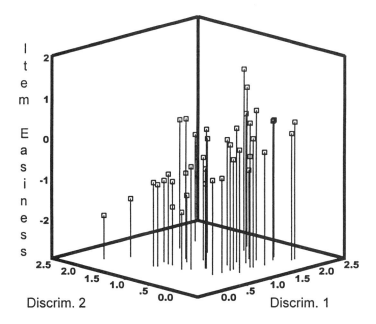

FIG. 11.1.   Three dimensional scatterplot of item easiness by item discriminations on two dimensions.

Reckase and McKinley's (1991) analysis, for example, the difficult mathematics usage items may require higher levels of linguistic or factual knowledge but not increased knowledge of mathematical problem-solving methods.

Applications of Confirmatory MIRT Models. · Confirmatory MIRT models permit a specific dimensional structure to be evaluated. For example, McKinley and Way (1992) evaluated the potential of specific secondary dimensions to account for performance on the Test of English as a Foreign Language (TOEFL). Although a strong general dimension was supported by their results, significant secondary dimensions were also found.

Similarly, Embretson (in press) evaluated a specific secondary dimension for impact on the Abstract Reasoning Test (ART; Embretson, 1995d), a measure of fluid intelligence. ART contains matrix-completion problems that were constructed to reflect analytic processes (see Carpenter, Just, & Shell's [1990] cognitive processing theory). However, one type of matrix relationship, figure addition/subtraction, may involve holistic rather than analytic processing. Confirmatory MIRT models were compared to evaluate the impact of holistic processing. A model with a single dimension, postulated to be analytic processing, was compared to a two-dimensional model, consisting of a general factor and a secondary factor. For the two-dimensional model, all items loaded on the general factor, whereas the 12 items with figure addition/subtraction relationships also loaded on the secondary dimension. The two-dimensional model fit the data significantly better than the one-dimensional model ($\chi^2 = 156.22$, $df = 12$, $p < .01$). Table 11.1 shows that most holistic items discriminate at least modestly on the general dimension and that their discriminations on the secondary dimension range widely. These results suggest that the holistic items can be solved by analytic processing like the other items, but that a few items are solved primarily by holistic methods.

TABLE 11.1
Item Discriminations and Difficulties for Two MIRT
Models of the Abstract Reasoning Test

Item	1 Dimension		2 Dimensions		
	Discrimination	Difficulty	Discrimination 1	Discrimination 2	Difficulty
1	.29	.13	.32	.00	.03
2	.60	1.24	.78	.00	1.06
3	.43	.12	.57	.00	−.06
4	.43	.05	.63	.00	−.15
5	.91	2.20	1.05	.16	1.87
6	.71	.16	.71	.62	−.16
7	.61	1.13	.74	.00	.93
8	.57	.39	.69	.00	.18
9	.64	.46	.69	.00	.24
10	.67	1.02	.81	.00	.80
11	.60	1.03	.67	.00	.83
12	.99	1.54	1.05	.47	1.12
13	.67	.60	.86	.00	.35
14	.69	.44	.69	.62	.14
15	1.24	1.43	1.33	.68	.90
16	.91	.85	.96	.79	.47
17	.48	−.14	.53	.00	−.30
18	1.30	1.11	1.50	1.45	.61
19	.93	1.01	1.11	.00	.70
20	.68	−.15	.84	.22	−.46
21	.66	−.10	.64	.64	−.41
22	.68	.78	.73	.00	.54
23	1.06	.97	1.16	1.08	.56
24	.40	−.37	.52	.00	−.54
25	.51	−.33	.64	.00	−.54
26	.80	−.20	.92	.54	−.59
27	.71	.16	.74	.56	−.16
28	.78	.07	.78	.70	−.28
29	.52	−.11	.72	.00	−.34
30	.24	−.71	.27	.00	−.79

New Measures of Individual Differences.   Applying MIRT models can help refine tests to measure the targeted constructs. For example, finding secondary ability dimensions on a test is valuable information for test equating. These separate dimensions or processes cannot be ignored if multiple test forms or adaptive tests are to be administered. The construct may shift across forms if the multiple dimensions are ignored.

Several different approaches may be applied when secondary dimensions exist in the item bank. If the secondary dimensions are irrelevant to the goals of measurement, items loading on secondary dimension should be omitted from the test bank if possible. For example, one could consider eliminating the figure addition/subtraction items from ART because they load on a secondary dimension. If items with the secondary dimensions must be retained, another approach is balancing secondary dimensions across tests. In Fig. 11.1, for example, items can be selected to balance the relative impact of the two factors. Reckase (1997) has employed this strategy with high-dimensional IRT models to balance item content on the several tests from the American College Testing (ACT) Program.

MIRT models can permit information about multiple abilities, rather than a single ability, to be extracted from a single set of items. Methods to apply MIRT models in adaptive testing are now being developed (e.g., Segall, 1996). However, individual differences measured from MIRT models do not necessarily reflect any *new* aspects of individual differences. Dimensions that are identified from exploratory MIRT models may differ little from traditional factors. Furthermore, even when multiple dimensions yield better fit, test developers may opt to select the items to measure each trait separately.

Applications of confirmatory MIRT models do have *potential* for measuring new aspects of individual differences. When the postulated secondary ability dimensions are closely related to cognitive theory, for example, new dimensions of individual differences can be measured. The confirmatory MIRT models are useful for measuring processes on which persons differ quantitatively. More qualitative aspects of processing, such as differing knowledge or strategies, require models that can assess class membership. These models are considered later in this chapter.

Decomposing Cognitive Processes on Items

Do paragraph-comprehension items on a particular test depend more on reading comprehension processes or on decision processes? Do mathematical word problems depend more on how the problem is represented or on the methods used to isolate the unknown quantity? Elaborating the processes that are involved in successful item performance is a major aspect of construct validity. The construct representation aspect of construct validity is supported by explicating the processes, strategies, and knowledge structures that underlie item solving (Embretson, 1983).

Many complex tasks found on ability tests have been studied by contemporary cognitive psychology methods. Complex tasks involve multiple processes for solution. Sources of processing difficulty vary across items, depending on their particular stimulus features. In cognitive psychology, the task features are explicitly designed to reflect processes. In ability testing, however, item features that influence processing usually are not explicitly specified. Thus, for testing, the impact of specific processes on test performance is largely unknown, but it could be determined by applying process decomposition methods from cognitive psychology.

The methods for process decomposition of items are quite removed from the compensatory MIRT models that assess dimensionality. Although in a sense, the item discriminations in compensatory MIRT models decompose items, the dimensions often do not represent processes for several reasons. First, items that involve the same processes may not correlate very highly under certain conditions. For example, individuals may vary little on some processes; hence, the contribution of such processes to item correlations will be small. Second, the difficulty of separate processes may be confounded in the items. Item features that produce difficulty on one process may be associated invariably with features that produce difficulty on another process. Thus, a factor dimension may correspond to confounded composites of processes rather than to single processes. Although the items could be designed to separate the processes, the rather global item specifications for most tests lead to confounded processes. Third, processing competencies may be highly correlated among examinees in a particular population. Conditions in a population, such as common patterns of experiences, educational prerequisites, and even genetics, can influence correlations of processing competencies. The result of such influences again implies that the processes will not correspond to separate dimensions.

A popular method for decomposing processes is mathematical modeling of item responses. Applications of two types of IRT models for process decomposition will be considered: (a) models for decomposing sources of item difficulty and (b) noncompensatory MIRT models for measuring processing components.

Applications of Models for Decomposing Sources of Item Difficulty

Item difficulties for both verbal and nonverbal abilities have been decomposed with compensatory MIRT models. In this approach, item difficulty is modeled or replaced by a linear combination of item-stimulus features that are postulated to control processing. Nonverbal items have been particularly amendable to process decomposition, due to their objectively scorable stimulus features. Geometric analogies, for example, contain relatively simple figures with stimulus features that change systematically to define an analogical relationship. Whitely and Schneider (1981) decomposed processes on geometric analogy items from the Cognitive Abilities Test. Their model operationalized two processes, encoding and relational comparisons, the number of figure elements and the number of transformations between figures, respectively, which were scored for each item. Whitely and Schneider's (1981) results indicated that items differed substantially in their primary source of difficulty.

Some examples of other nonverbal items that have been decomposed include abstract reasoning (Hornke & Habon, 1986; Embretson, 1998a), spatial visualization (Green & Smith, 1987; McCollam, 1997; Pellegrino, Mumaw & Shute, 1985; Smith & Kramer, 1992), and developmental balance problems (Spada & McGaw, 1985). Some examples of verbal items that have been decomposed include paragraph comprehension (Embretson & Wetzel, 1987; Sheehan, 1997), literacy (Sheehan & Mislevy, 1990), vocabulary (Janssen & DeBoeck, 1995) and mathematical word problems (Embretson, 1995b; Fischer, 1973; Medina-Diaz, 1993; Mitchell, 1983; Sheehan, in press). To illustrate how IRT models are applied to decompose processes, two examples are elaborated next.

Linear Logistic Latent-Trait Model (LLTM). As noted before, ART was designed to reflect Carpenter, Just and Shell's (1990) theory of processing. The two major sources of analytic processing difficulty are working memory demand and abstraction. Working memory demand can be scored for each ART item by the number of rules required for the correct answer. Abstraction can be scored as a binary variable by the type of rules in ART items. Figure 11.2 shows an ART item that contains three rules (change of number, change of orientation, and Latin Square distribution of shapes) and no abstract correspondence. Encoding difficulty also varies between ART items; the objects within the matrix may be distorted (yes or no), fused (yes or no), or overlaid (yes or no). The item in Fig. 11.2 has no distorted or fused objects, but it does have overlaid objects (i.e., the sticks inside the shapes). Thus, five variables — the number of rules, abstraction, distortion, fusion and overlay — were scored for the 150 items in the ART item bank.

A sample of about 750 participants were administered blocks of ART items (see Embretson, 1998a). LLTM (see chap. 4) was operationalized as follows:

$$P(X_{is} = 1 \mid \theta_s, \underline{\tau}_i) = \frac{\exp(\theta_s - (\tau_1 q_{i1} + \tau_2 q_{i2} + \tau_3 q_{i3} + \tau_4 q_{i4} + \tau_5 q_{i5}))}{1 + \exp(\theta_s - (\tau_1 q_{i1} + \tau_2 q_{i2} + \tau_3 q_{i3} + \tau_4 q_{i4} + \tau_5 q_{i5}))} \quad (11.1)$$

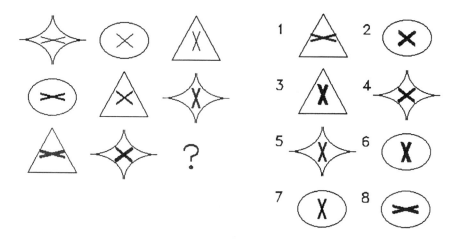

FIG. 11.2.   Item from ART.

where q_{ik} are the scored features of ART item i (q_{i1} = number of rules, q_{i2} = abstraction, q_{i3} = distortion, q_{i4} = fusion, q_{i5} = overlay), τ_k are the weights of the scored features in ART item difficulty, and θ_s is the ability for person s.

Table 11.2 presents the LLTM estimates, standard errors, and t values that were obtained for modeling item difficulty. The most significant variable is the number of rules, which operationalizes working memory. However, abstract correspondence and two drawing principles are also significant. The information in the data predicted by of LLTM (as compared to the Rasch model) was moderately high ($\Delta^{1/2}$ = .76, which is similar in magnitude to a multiple correlation coefficient). Thus, the results indicate that moderately good explanation of item difficulty has been obtained.

Each item can be decomposed into its processing contributions by multiplying the value of the stimulus features in an item, q_{ik}, times its weight. Thus, for the item in Fig. 11.2 with three rules (3), no abstract correspond-

TABLE 11.2
LLTM Estimates for Cognitive Model on ART[a]

Processing Variable	Scored Variable	LLTM		
		Weight τ_m	$SE\tau_m$	t
Working Memory Load	Number of Rules	.67	.09	7.14
Abstraction	Abstract Correspondence	1.49	.25	5.99
Drawing Principles	Distortion	.88	.29	3.05
	Fusion	−.31	.24	−1.31
	Overlay	.96	.20	4.73

[a]The model also included dummy variables to represent key position.

ence (0), no distortion (0), no fusion (0), and overlay (1), item difficulty is decomposed as follows, using the weights given in Table 11.2:

$$b_i' = .67(3) + 1.49(0) + .88(0) - .31(0) + .96(1) - 2.39$$
$$= 2.01 + 0 + 0 + 0 + .96 - 2.39$$
$$= 1.58. \tag{11.2}$$

Thus, the item is predicted to be moderately difficult (1.58), and the primary source of difficulty is working memory load. Other items, in contrast, could be difficult primary from other factors, such as abstraction.

Figure 11.3 plots ART item difficulty by process contributions from working memory load and abstraction. Notice that few items requiring abstraction have low working memory loads. Furthermore, notice the positive relationships between item difficulty and the contribution of each process. Information on this plot could be used to select items to involve a specified combination of working memory and abstraction.

An Example With Multiple Regression.   If item difficulties are calibrated by any IRT model, multiple regression analysis provides an alternative to an LLTM analysis. The item difficulties are the dependent vari-

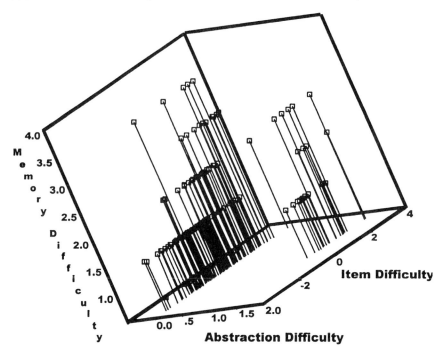

FIG. 11.3.   Item difficulty by memory difficulty and abstraction difficulty.

ables, whereas the scored item features are the independent variables. The number of observations equals the number of items. Green and Smith (1987) show that multiple regression yields results similar to LLTM. The regression method can be applied to item difficulties that are calibrated from complex IRT models, such as the 2PL or 3PL models, as well as from the Rasch model. However, the standard errors for the regression weights, unlike the LLTM weights, are based on composite data, which is a disadvantage.

Tree-based regression is especially useful for parsimonious interpretations of item difficulty. Tree-based regression is similar to linear multiple regression, but the independent variables are hierarchically organized for strength of prediction. A forward stepwise procedure can select variables according to importance in predicting IRT item difficulty.

Figure 11.4 shows results from Sheehan's (1997) tree-based regression analysis of SAT-V reading passage items. At the highest level is reading comprehension, which is parsed into four categories: vocabulary in context, main ideas, inference, and apply extrapolation. These categories are further subdivided; for example, inference is divided into specific purpose versus attitudes. The mean difficulty of items within any category, at any level, can be determined by dropping a perpendicular to the horizontal axis. Below this level are the individual items, which span the horizontal axis of IRT item difficulty. For example, that the difficulties of items concerning inferences about specific purposes and items concerning infer-

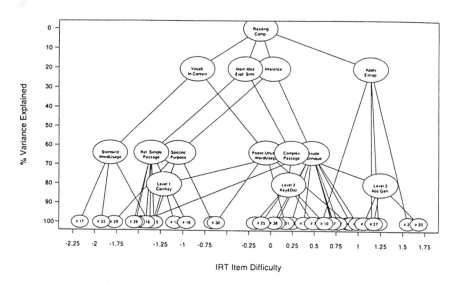

FIG. 11.4. Tree-based regression analysis of reading passage items (Reprinted from Sheehan, 1997).

ences about attitudes are rather close to the category mean. For other categories (e.g., complex passages), the item difficulties are more widely dispersed. The item difficulties in the more widely dispersed categories are less well predicted by the category mean. Tree-based regression has also been applied to decompose mathematics word problems (see Sheehan, in press).

Applications of Models for Measuring Processing Components

Processing components have noncompensatory impact if the item is failed when just one component is not completed accurately. High performance on the other components cannot compensate for the missed component. LLTM and the regression approaches are not appropriate because item difficulty is modeled by a linear combination of component difficulties; low values on one component are compensated by high values on another component.

Noncompensatory models have been applied to decompose cognitive processes on several different types of ability test items, including verbal analogies (Whitely, 1980), verbal classifications (Embretson, 1985), synonym items (Janssen & DeBoeck, 1997; Maris, 1995), spelling items (Hoskens & DeBoeck, 1997) and abstract reasoning items (Embretson, 1995d).

Multicomponent Latent-Trait Model (MLTM).   As mentioned in chapter 4, MLTM (see chap. 4) can be applied to items for which subtasks are available to identify the components. Maris (1995) applied MLTM to estimate two components that were postulated to underlie success on synonym items: generation of a potential synonym and evaluation of the potential synonym. Subtasks for the generation and evaluation components, as well as the standard synonym items, were administered to a large sample. The estimated component difficulties decomposes the items. Although Maris (1995) does not present individual item data, a scatter plot of component difficulties would probably be quite similar to Fig. 11.5, which shows uncorrelated component difficulties. Notice that items in which difficulty stems primarily from only one component can be identified. That is, such items are so easy on one component that item difficulty depends only on the other component (see labeled regions on Fig. 11.5).

The component decomposition had two implications for construct validity. First, the construct representation of synonym items was further elaborated by Maris' (1995) results. The two-component model had good fit to the synonym item responses, thus supporting the importance of both components. Furthermore, the nature of the task was elaborated by com-

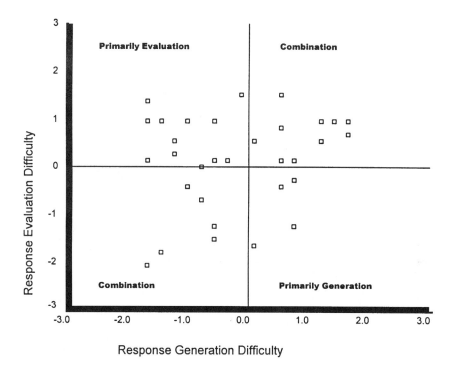

FIG. 11.5.   Scatter plot of item difficulties for response generation and response evaluation components from MLTM.

paring the relative strength of the components; success on the generation component was far more crucial to item solving. Second, a related study indicated that the relative strength of the generation and evaluation components in synonym items influenced nomothetic span. Janssen, DeBoeck and Van der Steene (1996) found that generation is primarily related to verbal fluency, whereas evaluation is primarily related to verbal comprehension.

New Measures of Individual Differences

Applications of the compensatory MIRT models of item difficulty do not directly yield new measures of individual differences. LLTM, as shown in Eq. 11.1, contains only one ability parameter. A Rasch model applied to the data would measure approximately the same ability. However, applications of LLTM can have indirect impact on the construct that is measured. LLTM provides important information to design tests to operationalize cognitive constructs. Items can be selected to reflect primarily one source of processing difficulty or to reflect a specified combination of processing difficulties. Consider the two-dimensional plot of working memory difficulty by abstraction difficulty for ART items in Fig. 11.3. Abstraction difficulty could be eliminated as a source of processing difficulty by selecting only items that do not involve this source. Or, selecting items to involve a combination of difficulty sources would retain both working memory demand and abstraction as important processes. Recently, Smith (1996) demonstrated that component balancing not only can equate constructs across tests, but also can equate difficulty levels when different samples take different test forms with no common items.

Results from noncompensatory MIRT models can guide item selection in a similar manner. Selecting on the values of component item difficulty can yield tests to measure primarily one component or to measure some specific combination of components. For example, a synonym test that measures only the generation component could be developed by selecting very easy items on the response evaluation component (see Fig. 11.5). Or, items could be selected to measure a combination of processes. For example, if both the generation and the evaluation component are desired in the ability construct, then comparable levels of each processing source should appear across forms.

Importantly, however, noncompensatory MIRT models such as MLTM also can define new measures of individual differences. Abilities on the underlying processes, such as generation ability and evaluation ability in the Maris (1995) study, are measured by separate trait levels in the MLTM model (see chap. 4). MLTM can identify the separate abilities through the subtasks that represent the underlying processes.

Recently, a new estimation algorithm (Maris, 1995) significantly extends the usefulness of noncompensatory MIRT models for measuring new aspects of individual differences. For most tests, the subtask data that is required by MLTM are not available. However, with the Maris' (1995) algorithm, the general component latent trait model (GLTM, an extension of MLTM; see chap. 4) can estimate multiple abilities from standard item response data. Figure 11.6 is a scatter plot of two component abilities, working memory capacity and general control processes, that were extracted from standard ART items using GLTM (Embretson, 1995d). GLTM can estimate separate component abilities if values for component item difficulties can be specified. For ART, the number and level of rules in the items (as shown in Table 11.2) strongly predicted the working memory component. General control processes, on the other hand, often are assumed to be of equal difficulty across items. The differing patterns of item difficulty on the two components permitted working memory capacity to be separated from general control processing ability. Differing correlations of these two abilities with reference tests further supported their validity (see Embretson, 1995).

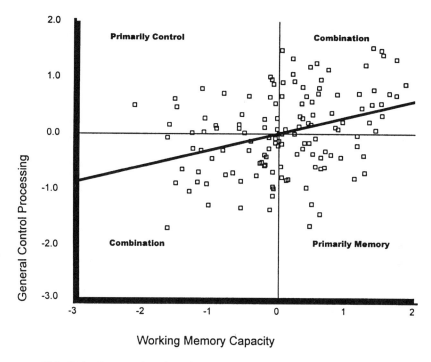

FIG. 11.6.   Scatter plot of working memory capacity by general control processes from GLTM on abstract reasoning.

Identifying Qualitative Differences in Test Performance

Cognitive psychology also emphasizes qualitative differences between persons that can influence responses. Persons can vary in the knowledge structures or strategies that they apply to items. If a person applies atypical knowledge structures or strategies to item solving, then item difficulties may not have the expected pattern. Such a person may fail easy items yet pass more difficult items. Three approaches exist to analyzing a test for qualitative differences between persons: (a) assessing differential item functioning (DIF) for externally defined populations, (b) analyzing the fit of individual persons to the IRT model underlying the test, and (c) identifying latent classes. The relevancy of these approaches to construct validity depends on assumptions about the nature of the item domain and the persons who differ qualitatively.

Population Differences

Population differences in experiences or conditions — such as those associated with gender, ethnicity, and age — are often believed to have qualitative impact on item responses. Many studies have shown, for example, that the content of verbal ability and achievement test items often show characteristic patterns of DIF across populations (see chap. 10). DIF is typically applied to evaluate equity issues in testing.

Results from DIF are relevant to construct validity under some conditions. If populations differ systematically on certain types of items or if the number of biased items is substantial, then the results from DIF are pertinent to construct validity. In this case, DIF results imply that the construct is not generalizable across populations. Thus, DIF is also an important tool for studying individual differences in construct meaning. If only a few items are biased, however, construct generality is supported. The particular items showing DIF may be regarded as "flawed" and thus eliminated from an item bank.

Person Fit

The validity of an ability score for a person may be evaluated by IRT-based fit statistics (see chap. 9). Both systematic and idiosyncratic differences between examinees may be revealed by person-fit statistics. For example, a cognitive construct may be poorly measured or inapplicable to certain persons. Daniel (1999) notes that diverse conditions, such as physical or cultural handicaps, as well as sporadic testing conditions, may lead to low person fit indices.

Both the amount and the nature of person misfit may have implications for construct validity. If relatively few persons do not fit, such cases can be regarded as random errors that have no special implications for construct validity. However, if many persons do not fit the predicted pattern of item responses, then either important subclasses of persons or additional dimensions may exist. If misfit is related to other variables, such as gender, race-ethnicity, or age, then the results are pertinent to the generality of the construct across groups.

Latent Classes

For some item types, two or more different knowledge structures or strategies may result in successful performance. Systematic differences between persons in knowledge structure or strategies differences may not be strongly associated with observable population differences; thus, DIF cannot be applied. If a particular strategy or knowledge structure results in a characteristic pattern of item difficulties, latent classes of people may be identified.

To give some examples, Rost (1990) identified two latent classes that reflected knowledge states on a physics achievement test. For one class, items that concerned textbook knowledge were relatively more difficult than items that reflected practical experience. For the other class, the opposite pattern was observed. Further analysis revealed that the amount of formal physics training differed substantially between classes, which further supported knowledge structures differences. Similarly, Tatsuoka (1985) studied children's knowledge states in arithmetic problems. Tatsuoka identified several knowledge states that represented specific improper or incomplete knowledge.

Qualitative differences in strategies also may characterize ability test items. Several studies (e.g., McCollam, 1997; Mislevy & Verhelst, 1990) concern strategy differences in performance on spatial visualization tests. Although the goal of spatial visualization tests is measuring spatial processing, many items may be solved by verbal-analytic strategies. McCollam (1997), for example, identified two latent classes on a spatial visualization test that represented persons who applied primarily spatial processes versus verbal-analytic processes in item solving. Similarly, other studies have identified strategy differences on other nonverbal ability tests (Tatsuoka, Solomonson & Singley, in press), as well as on verbal tests (Buck, Tatsuoka & Kostin, in press).

Identifying latent classes is pertinent to validity in two ways. First, construct representation is elaborated. If only one class exists, then the construct is supported as involving the same strategies or knowledge structures across persons. When two or more classes exist, the nature of the construct depends on the class to which the person belongs. Second, class membership may be a moderator variable that has importance for criterion-related validity. Ability may be more prognostic of criterion performance for one class than for another. As yet, little research has concerned this potentially important issue.

Two different approaches to identifying latent calsses, an exploratory approach and a confirmatory approach, will be reviewed here. The mixed Rasch model (MIRA; Rost, 1990) is an exploratory approach because latent classes are identified empricallly on the basis of similar response patterns. The rule space method (Tatsuoka, 1985) is a confirmatory method that classifies a person into substantively meaningful strategies or knowledge states.

Mixed Rasch Model (MIRA). MIRA identifies latent classes, each with distinct item difficulty patterns, that are required to fit item response data. The classes are mixed in the observed sample. MIRA parameters include class proportions and class-specific item difficulties to maximize the likelihood of the item response data.

To illustrate how MIRA identifies classes of persons, consider again the role of holistic processing on the ART. This example was elaborated earlier to illustrate compensatory MIRT models. Items with figure addition/subtraction relationships reflected a combination of holistic and analytic processing. However, figure addition/subtraction items may be much more difficult if solved by analytic processes because the most difficult rule in Carpenter et al. (1990) hierarchy must be applied.

Embretson (in press) applied MIRA to the same data and identified two latent classes. Figure 11.7 plots the item difficulties in the two classes. Items are labeled on the plot to show if they contain figure addition/subtraction relationships. Items near the 45° line are equally difficult in the two classes. Interestingly, the holistic items are relatively more difficult for Class 2. This suggests that holistic items are solved by a different (and more difficult) strategy in Class 2, such as the more difficult analytic strategy. These results suggest differing knowledge states about rules in the items. Hence, the ability estimates reflect somewhat different processes in the two classes. Should abilities be interpreted equivalently for the two classes? The issue of adjusting scores for deficient knowledge states is an interesting issue for future research.

Rule Space Analysis. The rule space methodology (Tatsuoka, 1983, 1984, 1985) also classifies persons into classes that reflect knowledge states or strategies. Rule space analysis is a confirmatory method because identi-

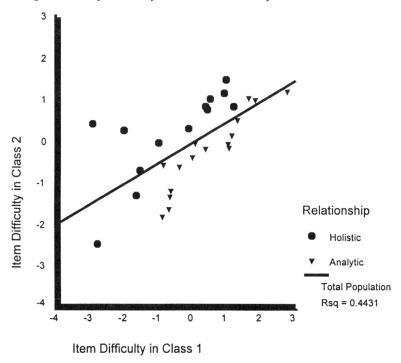

FIG. 11.7. Scatter plot of item difficulties in two classes of persons identified by MIRA.

fying the classes depends on the theory about how item stimulus features are related to knowledge states.

A basic rule space is defined by two dimensions, an IRT ability and an IRT-based person fit index. Ability, of course, represents overall performance, and the fit index measures the typicality of the person's response pattern. Figure 11.8 plots both persons and knowledge states into the rule space from ability level and fit. Person are classified into knowledge states by the distances of their response patterns from the locations of the knowledge states. Although persons can be located in the rule space directly from their abilities and fit indices, locating a knowledge state requires some intermediate steps. First, an attribute incidence matrix is scored to reflect which attributes are required to solve each item. Second, knowledge states are defined from patterns of attributes by applying a clustering algorithm to the attribute incidence matrix. Third, an ideal response pattern is generated for each knowledge state; that is, the ideal response pattern specifies which items are passed and failed by someone in the knowledge state. To locate a knowledge state in the rule space, the ideal response pattern is scored for ability (i.e., from total number of items passed) and for fit.

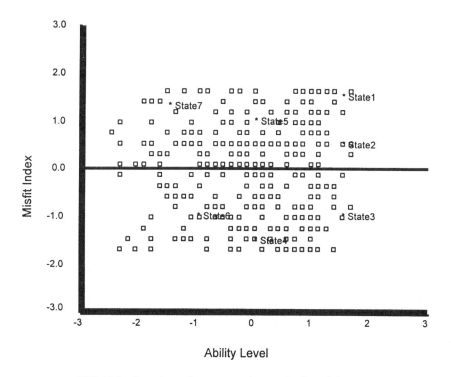

FIG. 11.8. Locations of persons and states in the rule space.

To illustrate the rule-space analysis, consider Tatsuoka's (1985) application to a mathematics test. A person's score indicates overall performance levels but does not usually diagnose processes or knowledge structures that need remediation. The rule-space methodology additionally can classify the person into a knowledge states that reflects which mathematical operations are not yet mastered.

New Measures of Individual Differences

Several approaches reviewed earlier can provide new measures of individual differences. First, person-fit indices may have diagnostic value. Although person-fit indices probably do not define a trait continuum, extreme values may be identify persons for whom a test poorly diagnoses potential Thus, person-fit indices may have potential as moderator variables. Second, the latent-class analyses, MIRA, and rule-space analysis indicate a person's likelihood of belonging to a particular latent class. These classes may reflect knowledge states or strategies which are involved in item solving. In MIRA, a person's class membership can be identified by comparing the relative likelihood of a person's response pattern within the various classes. The person is assigned to the class in which the response pattern has the highest likelihood. In a rule-space analysis, class membership is estimated from the person's distance to a knowledge state or strategy class. Class membership also may be an important moderator variable for predicting various criteria from test scores.

Enhancing Ability Interpretations With Item-Referenced Meaning

Norm-referenced interpretations of ability and competency scores have long been viewed as limited. Norm-referenced interpretations compare the person's performance to a reference group but do not describe what the person can do. With IRT, increased meaning for ability or competency is possible because persons and items are placed on a common scale. Thus, a person may be characterized by the items that are relatively difficult or easy. Item-referenced meaning for cognitive tests is possible when substantively meaningful features describe the skills or processes that the items represent. Such features could be represented in the compensatory MIRT models for decomposing processes, as described earlier.

Applications of item-referenced meaning are now appearing in the literature. In this section, we begin by showing how the probability that a person passes any item in the domain may be assessed. Then, two examples of item-referenced ability interpretations, enhanced person characteristics curves and diagnostic assessments, are given.

Person Characteristics Curves

The meaning of a person's ability for the probability of solving items at various difficulty levels is easily shown by a person characteristics curve (PCC; see Lumsden, 1977). Suppose that three persons are selected from the sample, with abilities of –1.0, .00, and 1.0, respectively, with all parameters based on the Rasch model. Figure 11.9 shows the PCCs for the three persons. Item difficulty is represented on the horizontal axis, and item-solving probability is represented on the vertical axis. The point of inflection occurs at the probability of .50, where the person is as likely to pass as to fail an item. Notice that the threshold item difficulties for each person equals their ability.

Several meanings for an ability level are shown in Fig. 11.9 by matching specific items with the predictions. First, items at the person's threshold may be identified. An inspection of their content may provide additional meaning for ability. Second, diagnostic information about the person's relative success on other items may be readily obtained. For example, If a person's ability exceeds item difficulty, then the difference is positive and a probability of success greater than .50.

For more complex data, IRT models such as the 2PL permit item-solving probabilities to depend on both item discrimination and item diffi-

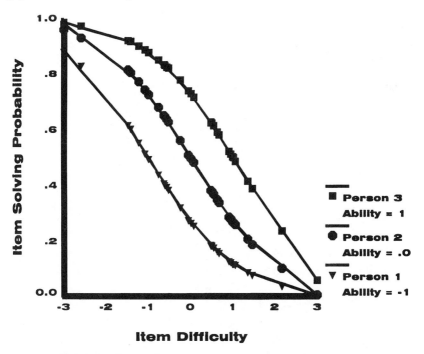

FIG. 11.9. Person characteristics curves with uniform slopes.

culty. A more complex figure for the PCC is required. Another way to handle more complex data is to allow PCC's to differ in slope. Probabilities of item solving may be more responsive to changes in task difficulty for some persons than for other persons (see Lumsden, 1977).

Of course, the person's actual responses to items is known. In what ways do PCCs provide additional information? If the IRT model fits the data well, the advantages of PCCs for diagnosing performance include (a) more accurate description of performance because actual item responses have only two values, pass or fail, (b) implicit inclusion of error in the prediction, a probability rather than a response is given, and (c) predictions for items that the person has not been presented, if their item difficulties are known.

Enhanced Person Characteristics Curves. More interestingly, the probability that a person solves particular *types* of items links ability more directly to construct validity. One method is to describe the features of items on the horizontal axis of the PCCs. To provide meaningful interpretations, these item features must have at least two characteristics: (a) high correlations with item difficulty and (b) substantive meaning, such as operationalizing item-solving processes or major content divisions in the item domain.

To illustrate, consider the cognitive model for ART items that was presented in Table 11.2. The two major processes were working memory load and abstraction, which were represented by number of rules and abstract relationships, respectively. To link these processes to a PCC, ART item difficulty was regressed on these two variables in a general linear model with interactions. In Fig. 11.10, the number of rules (2, 3, or 4) are nested within abstraction ("no" versus "yes"). The vertical lines from each abstraction level show the mean item difficulty, which is .5 for "no" and 1.75 for "yes." Item difficulties for various number of rules within abstraction level are also shown by vertical lines. The PCC links item-solving probabilities directly to processing operations. For example, the probability for the PCC shown for an ability level of –1.0 solves items involving abstract relationships with two rules is only about .10. However, for items with no abstract relationship, then the probability that the person solves an item with two rules is about .30. Thus, the person's ability is referenced to the types of items that can be solved.

It should be noted that these enhanced interpretations for ability are expectations for a population. A PCC may not appropriately describe a particular person's response pattern if the person has poor fit to the IRT model. Thus, person-fit to the IRT model should be evaluated in conjunction with any PCC interpretation.

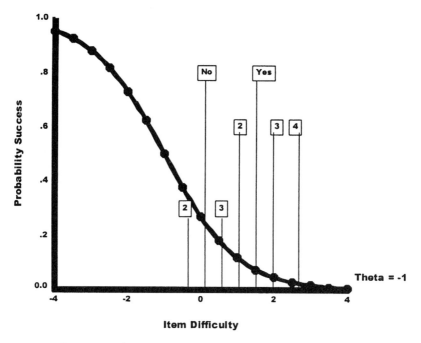

FIG. 11.10.   Enhanced meaning for a person characteristics curve.

Diagnostic Assessment.   Sheehan (1997) enhances test meaning by scoring persons on the clusters that are obtained from tree-based regression, such as shown in Fig. 11.4. Scores are reported on bar graphs that show "typical percent correct score range" for each cluster, based on their IRT trait level score. A range of probabilities, rather than a single value, is shown to represent error fluctuations in the IRT trait level estimates. The actual proportion of items the examinee solved in the cluster is also shown. Presumably, accuracy scores that fall outside of the predicted range provides meaningful diagnostic information.

New Measures of Individual Difference

PCCs enhance score meaning but not do provide any new measures of individual differences. However, using cluster scores for diagnostic assessment does provide new measures of individual differences. Sheehan's (1997) cluster scores may have diagnostic meaning about the types of skills that the person has mastered. However, some cautions are needed in applying diagnostic assessment technique. More research is needed to determine the amount of information about separate item bundles that may be reliably and validity decomposed from unidimensional tests, such as the SAT. If significant multidimensionality does not exist in the data, the diagnostic assessments based on clusters may represent mostly measurement errors.

ISSUES IN LIFESPAN DEVELOPMENT

Lifespan cognitive development concerns the amount and nature of age-related changes in cognitive performance. Special problems in measuring and analyzing change have created difficulties for the area. We begin by explicating these problems. Then, applications of IRT models to study continuous and discontinuous changes are reviewed.

Problems in Measuring and Analyzing Change

Many psychometric problems exist in studying change. So many, that at least two national conferences have devoted to measuring and analyzing change (Harris, 1963; Collins and Horn, 1991). In this section, we will consider a few problems that can be addressed by applying IRT-based methods.

Measuring Individual Change.   Traditionally, individual change has been measured by a simple change score, the difference between raw scores on two repeated measures. Bereiter (1963) noted three problems in using individual change scores. First, the reliability of change scores is paradoxical. As the correlations between the two measures decreases, the reliability of change scores increases. However, low correlations between two measures of the same trait also indicates low reliability. Second, change has a spurious negative correlation with initial status. With a few simple assumptions, it can be shown that correlation of change scores with initial status has a negative bias. Third, the scale units for change do not have a constant meaning. That is, the meaning of change depends on the initial score level. For example, a small change from an extremely high score may imply greater psychological impact than the same small change from a moderate score.

Many recommendations for improved change scores have been made (e.g., residualized gain scores, Cohen & Cohen, 1975), but all remain controversial (see Ragosa, Grant, & Zimowski, 1982). Perhaps most fundamentally, the third problem remains unresolved by any classical test theory approach. That is, if interval level measurement has not been achieved, then identical change scores, if obtained from different initial levels, will not necessarily have the same implications for true change.

This problem is potentially solvable, however, by using IRT-based approaches that have justifiable interval scale properties.

Analyzing Trends. Due to the complexities of individual change scores, many researchers apparently heed Cronbach and Furby's (1970) recommendation to avoid using them. Rather than compute individual change scores, the research question is refocused. For example, mean scores can be compared across varying conditions. Unfortunately, unequal scale units (i.e., Bereiter's third problem) also influences comparisons between means. Maxwell and Delaney (1985) show that even a simple *t*-test on classical test scores can be biased under certain conditions.

Consider a popular design to assess lifespan trends in ability levels, comparing means across age groups. Often, the same test is administered to each group and the means plotted to show a trend. Trends are highly influenced by test difficulty when classical raw scores (or their linear transformation) are used. For example, a Monte Carlo study (Embretson, 1994b) demonstrated that if classical raw scores are used to study growth, the age group for which the test difficulty level was most appropriate (i.e., item probabilities of about .50) changes the most. To illustrate, suppose that the true latent trait increased linearly with age. Classical total scores would not be linearly related to age if a single test were administered to all age levels. If test difficulty was focused for 10-year-olds (i.e., item probabilities at about .50), then the means would increase more sharply for 10-year-olds than for either younger or older children. However, if test difficulty was most appropriate for older children, then the greatest change would be observed for these children. Thus, the form of the growth curve depends on test selection.

Analyzing Developmental Discontinuities. Cognitive development is often hypothesized to occur in identifiable stages (i.e., Brainerd, 1978). A period of relative stability is followed by rapid changes in competency. Developmental discontinuities can be studied with a factorial analysis of variance in which age group is crossed with type of task or treatment. For the method of multiple tasks (Fischer, Pipp & Bullock, 1984), an interaction of task type with age provides evidence for developmental stages. For example, performance on two tasks may differ greatly for young children but not for older children. Such patterns imply that the older children had mastered the operations required for both tasks, whereas the younger children had mastered only the operations for one task. For the method of treatment differences, an interaction of treatment (e.g., treatment versus control) with age provides evidence for developmental stages as well. For example, younger children may perform at a much lower level than older children except when given the treatment, but older children may perform equally under treatment and control. These results would suggest that the younger children have not mastered the operations that were represented in the treatment.

Unfortunately, interaction effects also may be biased if based on classical test scores. Spurious interactions of treatment or task effects with populations can be obtained when test difficulty levels are biased (see Embretson, 1994b, 1996a). If age represents a population factor in the design, greater treatment or task differences can be found for one age group, even when no true interaction exists. That is, the age group for whom the test difficulty level is most appropriate will show greater effects. Employing measures based on IRT can help avoid these spurious interactions. A full correction of spurious interactions, however, requires that adaptive testing be applied to measure each person to the same degree of precision.

If developmental stages have substantial impact on different *types* of tasks within a test, standard IRT models will not fit the data very well. If competency on a certain type of task develops in a stage, item solving probabilities will change quite dramatically for that task, but not for other tasks. When several types of tasks are mixed in the test, each developing at different developmental stages, a single ability estimate will not adequately reproduce item solving probabilities. As noted later and also in chapter 4, several alternative IRT models have been developed to handle this type of data.

Analyzing developmental discontinuities is also important in assessing competency. Mislevy (1993) noted that new foundations for test theory are needed to provide information about learners that is relevant to teaching. Modern cognitive psychology emphasizes that learners' competency does not develop just by acquiring facts but instead "by reconfiguring their knowledge structure, by automating procedures and chunking information to reduce memory load, and by developing strategies and models that tell them when and how facts and skills are relevant" (Mislevy, 1993, pp. 19–20). Thus, qualitative differences between learners should be assessed.

Modeling Continuous Changes in Performance Levels

Some developmental changes are continuous; gradual increases or decreases in cognitive performance are observed. In this case, IRT models that provide an S-shaped ogive can be applied directly. Applications of IRT for assessing growth curves or individual change are now appearing in the literature.

Developmental Trends.   Successfully estimating the growth of ability or competency depends on using measures with two properties. First, performance should be assessed with interval level scales. Second, performance should be assessed with the same precision at each level. Fixed content standardized tests typically fall short on both properties. However, abilities measured with computerized adaptive testing can fulfill both properties.

Andrich and Styles (1994) study on abstract reasoning illustrates how IRT, with computerized adaptive testing, can examine growth spurts in cognitive ability. Andrich and Styles (1994) developed an interval scale measure of abstract reasoning by scaling the Raven's Progressive Matrices Test for Children with the Rasch model. Approximately equal precision throughout the ability range was obtained by adding many new items. The augmented item bank was then administered adaptively to maximize precision at each developmental level. It was postulated that larger variances indicate a growth spurt because some children have entered the new stage while others have not. Using IRT abilities to estimate variances is important because, without interval level measurement and equal precision, a large variance for a particular age level will reflect test appropriateness rather than a growth spurt. Andrich and Styles (1994) results supported a growth spurt in abstract reasoning starting around age twelve.

Measuring Individual Change: MRMLC.   In lifespan development, the possible modifiability of age-related declines in ability is an important issue. For example, Willis and Nesselroade (1990) report success in modifying spatial ability scores in a sample of elderly adults. However, to determine who changes the most, an individual score is needed. Justifiable interval scale measurement is required to assure comparable meaning for change from each initial level, as noted before.

McCollam (1997) employed a training design to study the modifiability of spatial ability in elderly adults. Elderly and young adults were measured initially for spatial visualization ability and then measured again after short training segments. The multidimensional Rasch model for learning and change (see chap. 4) was applied to the three spatial ability measurements to estimate initial ability and modifiability. Substantial, but nearly equal, modifiability was found for both elderly and young adults. Although these results seemingly suggest that age is unrelated to modifiability, structural equation modeling of ability and modifiability revealed that training had qualitatively different effects for young versus elderly adults.

Developmental Scaling of Cognitive Tasks.   The developmental level at which various cognitive skills are mastered is also an important educational issue. However, interfacing age or grade level with cognitive skills requires measuring on an interval level scale. Some interesting applications of developmental scaling with IRT models are now appearing.

Educational Testing Service (1998) reports a scaling of the mathematics achievement items for the National Assessment of Educational Progress (NAEP) using IRT. Figure 11.11 presents the resulting scale values, which are linear transformations of IRT parameter estimates. On the left, the properties of items that fall at various difficulty levels are listed. These properties were determined from an inspection of the item clusters at the various scale points. Notice that items in which drawings are used to calculate areas are hard, while items requiring subtraction of whole numbers with regrouping are easy. Other mathematical operations fall between these extremes. On the right, the mean competency for various popula-

FIG. 11.11.   Map of selected items on the NAEP mathematics scale and average scale scores of fourth and eighth graders, 1996 (Reprinted from Educational Testing Service, 1998).

tions are shown. Because items and persons are scaled jointly, the population means can be referenced to characteristic operations. For example, the mean for all eighth graders is at 274. The type of operations that correspond to this level are "Find difference of two distances" and "Find area of figure on a grid."

Developmental scaling of cognitive abilities by IRT also is important in lifespan development. In accordance with the neo-Piagetian view, different types of cognitive operations appear at different age levels. If trait level represents cognitive development, scale can be anchored by the characteristic cognitive operations that can be performed.

For example, the developmental balance task can be constructed to represent different combinations of cognitive operations required for solution. Spada and McGaw (1985) applied LLTM to estimate the impact of eight cognitive operations in item difficulty. Similarly, Pennings and Hessels (1996) operationalized Pascual-Leone's (1970) theory, which states that mental attentional capacity increases linearly with age. To examine this hypothesis, the items on two figural reasoning tests were scored for mental demand from their stimulus properties. Two issues were addressed: (a) predicting item difficulty from mental demand and (b) the relationship of age to mental demand. A Rasch model scaling of the two tests generally indicated that mental demand had the hypothesized effects, thus supporting Pascual-Leone's theory.

Sheehan's (1997) study on reading comprehension illustrates developmental scaling of achievement. Items were clustered by their stimulus content to represent homogenous combinations of skills and processes and then scaled by a standard IRT model. A cluster characteristic curve (CCC) plots the predicted probability of item success for the cluster by competency level. The clusters may be compared for expected proficiencies at a particular competency level. For example, Sheehan (1997) found that "Inference-author's Purpose" was mastered at much lower competency levels than "Inference-Attitude or Technique."

Discontinous Changes in Performance Levels

Stage Effects: SALTUS. Many developmental theories specify stage effects in which qualitative differences in knowledge states, processes, or strategies have profound impact on cognitive performance. For example, learning hierarchies imply that the final task level cannot be completed without mastery of all subordinate tasks and, furthermore, that any subordinate task may be successfully completed if the final task is mastered (Gagne, 1962). Similarly, rule assessment theory (Siegler, 1981) postulates that the child learns an increasingly powerful set of rules for solving problems. Thus, like learning hierarchies, mastery of the most powerful rules implies that tasks involving lower-level rules also can be solved.

The SALTUS IRT model, reviewed in chapter 4, was developed to analyze and assess developmental stages. Item probability changes are not characterized by a single logistic function in SALTUS; instead, parameters to reflect the stage mastery of each type of item are included to boost the item solving probabilities for persons who have reached those stages. An important implication of the SALTUS model is that the ICC depends on the developmental stage.

To give an example, Wilson (1989) fit both SALTUS and the Rasch model to arithmetic data that was postulated to reflect learning hierarchy effects. An arithmetic test with two item types, subtraction without regrouping (A) and subtraction with regrouping (B), was administered to grade school children. SALTUS not only yielded significantly better fit than the Rasch model, but its parameter estimates more clearly showed the learning hierarchy. The upper section of Fig. 11.12 shows the range of Rasch model estimates for item difficulty on the two item types, A and B, as well as the correspondence of ability to total score, ranging from 1 to 11. It can be seen that ability is rather linearly related to total score. The lower section of Figure 11.12 shows the SALTUS estimates, which more clearly show the developmental discontinuity. The abilities that correspond to total score levels 1–6 are much lower than the abilities that correspond to total scores 7–11. Furthermore, the difficulty range for item type A, which involves no regrouping, is sharply distinguished from the difficulty range for item type B, which does involve regrouping. Thus, the learning hierarchy effects are reflected in SALTUS parameters but not in the Rasch model parameters.

Stage Effects: Assessment by DIF.   As noted in chapter 10, differential item functioning can occur for many substantive groups. In the lifespan development context, certain types of items may be less indicative of abil-

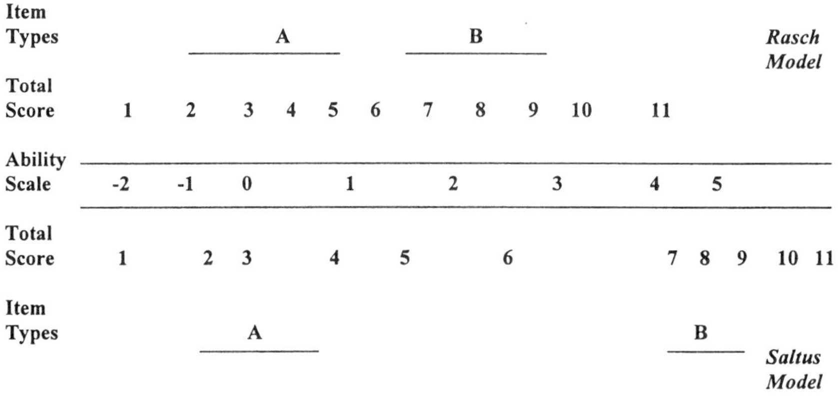

FIG. 11.12. Scaling of scores and items by SALTUS versus the Rasch model.

ity for elderly adults than for younger adults. For example, factors such as speed and perceived relevancy, may produce items that are biased against elderly adults. So, even at the same overall trait level, elderly adults may be less likely to be able to solve these items.

Kemtes and Kemper (1997) studied qualitative differences between young and elderly adults in cognitive intrusions while performing cognitive tasks. Kemtes and Kemper's (1997) DIF analysis indicated that elderly and younger adults differed in some thresholds at which they endorsed items about cognitive intrusions. Thus, their results indicated some qualitative differences in the meaning of the intrusion items across age groups.

Process Decomposition: GLTM. An important issue in lifespan development is understanding the source of ability differences. Although age-related decline on many abilities is well established (e.g., Schaie & Willis, 1993), their source remains controversial. Age-related decline is variously attributed to general slowing (White & Cunningham, 1987), reduced attention, reduced working memory capacity (Salthouse & Mitchell, 1989), and general control processing (Labouvie-Vief & Gonda, 1976). These sources are usually examined in separate studies by employing tasks that represent relatively unconfounded indicators of the source (e.g., pure speed tasks). However, this approach results in applying an indirect method to establish relevancy, namely, the correlations of the sources with ability.

An alternative method is to use a process-decomposition approach to the ability task. For example, McCollam (1997) applied the general component latent-trait model (GLTM; see chap. 4) to decompose working memory versus control processing resources on a spatial ability test. McCollam (1997) had administered the test to both younger and elderly adults and then applied GLTM to decompose processes. The results indicated significant age-related declines on both working memory capacity and control processes.

SUMMARY

This chapter examines applications of IRT to substantive issues about cognitive abilities and lifespan development. Construct validity continues to be a salient issue in ability measurement. Applications of IRT for elaborating construct validity are reviewed in four areas: (a) assessing dimensionality, (b) decomposing cognitive processes on items, (c) identifying qualitative differences in the basis of performance, such as knowledge structures or strategies, and (d) enhancing ability interpretations with item-referenced meaning. The issues within the areas are considered, and illustrative applications are elaborated. Also, implications for measuring new aspects of individual differences are elaborated.

Evaluating the dimensionality underlying test scores is an important aspect of construct validity. The number and the nature of the underlying ability dimensions is more appropriately evaluated with MIRT than with traditional factor analysis. Although ability tests are usually scored for a single dimension, secondary dimensions often exist. Several studies have applied MIRT models not only to assess secondary dimensions but also to guide-item selection and test equating. If applied in adaptive testing, MIRT models can lead to more efficient estimation of multiple abilities. Last, new aspects of individual differences can be assessed with the confirmatory MIRT models. An example on abstract reasoning is elaborated to show how cognitive theory provided the basis for identifying a secondary dimension.

Decomposing cognitive processes on items contributes to the construct representation aspect of construct validity. Applications of IRT models to decompose processes on both verbal and nonverbal items are reviewed. Several IRT models can estimate the relative contributions of various processes to item difficulty. Component-process difficulties are useful for guiding item selection and test equating to measure targeted cognitive constructs. Importantly, some component IRT models also can estimate new aspects of individual differences. Research that supported the differential validity of the new measures suggests that some component processing abilities have promise as new measures of individual differences.

The generality of construct meaning across persons is another important issue for construct validity. Ability test items often can be solved with different knowledge structures or strategies; thus, item solving may reflect different processes for different persons. Three approaches to identifying qualitative differences are reviewed: DIF, person-fit indices, and latent-class analyses. New aspects of individual differences are measured with person-fit indices and latent-class model estimates.

Enhancing ability interpretations with item-referencing provides a new basis for score meaning. Rather than rely on norm-referencing for interpreting ability, in several IRT applications have linked ability to the cognitive operations that are reflected in item solving. A person characteristics curve can predict the types of items that can be solved. Systems for parsing item content and linking predictions to a person's actual responses were also shown.

In lifespan development, several issues in measuring and assessing change have confounded clear substantive interpretations. Individual change measures have often been abandoned, due to well-known psychometric problems. Unfortunately, recent research indicates that the same problems extend to group comparisons that are used to estimate growth curves and developmental discontinuities. Some applications of IRT to these issues are reviewed.

Also considered are applications of IRT for developmental scaling of tasks. Both achievement and ability tasks have been scaled for developmental level. Last, discontinuous changes with age are also considered. Learning hierarchies, for example, are most effectively assessed with an IRT model that includes parameters for developmental stages.

The diverse studies presented here show that IRT can illuminate several issues about cognitive abilities and lifespan development that previously had been elusive with CTT methods. This chapter elaborates several examples to further acquaint the reader with the methods.

12

Applications of IRT in Personality and Attitude Assessment

In achievement and aptitude testing, IRT procedures are well established, and there is a history of applications by which a researcher can judge their own data against. The situation in terms of application of IRT models to typical performance (i.e., personality and attitude) measurement is different. In this context, there have been relatively few empirical explorations of how IRT modeling may enhance the understanding of assessment instruments and psychological constructs. There may be some compelling reasons for the relative lack of application of IRT procedures in the typical performance domain and these are reviewed in the last section of this chapter. The goal of the following sections is to describe some of the existing literature that has used IRT modeling in personality and attitude measurement. Our objective is not just to show that IRT models can be applied or that IRT models are useful for understanding psychometric properties of personality scales, but rather to show that IRT models can also be used to address substantive issues relevant to the assessment of typical performance constructs. In what follows, we classify the literature into two sections. First, studies that explore the applicability and utility of various IRT models to personality and attitude measures are described. Second, research that uses IRT procedures to address psychometric issues with substantive implications are highlighted. The latter section includes studies that investigate person-fit, differential item functioning, and item serial-order effects.

ANALYZING PERSONALITY AND ATTITUDE SCALES WITH IRT

As illustrated in this book, the application of IRT measurement models affords several advantages over traditional CTT-based psychometric procedures. With these advantages in mind, several authors have embarked on the application of IRT models to study the psychometric properties of particular personality and, to a limited degree, attitude scales. Among the main objectives of this line of research have been to establish the applicability of IRT models to typical performance data and to explore what benefits may be accrued by such applications. Most applications of IRT models to personality or attitude measures have been to previously created scales; to our knowledge, IRT methods have not been used to develop any widely used personality or attitude instruments. In what follows, we highlight several of these applications and describe how analyzing typical performance measures with IRT methods contrasts with traditional psychometric practices that fall under the rubric of CTT.

First, it is of fundamental importance to personality test users to know how a particular measurement instrument "works" in assessing a particular construct for a given examinee population. For this reason, several journals, such as the *Journal of Personality Assessment* and *Psychological Assessment*, are almost exclusively devoted to research describing psychometric properties of various personality scales and multiscale inventories. In addressing basic psychometric issues, among the salient issues are questions such as these: What is the dimensionality of the scale? Will the test create a ceiling or floor effect by being too easy or too difficult, respectively? Another way to ask the same question is, do the scale items span a broad range of difficulty? Finally, how precise or reliable are the resulting scale scores? As illustrated by the following research, IRT measurement models can be useful in addressing these questions.

ASSESSING DIMENSIONALITY

We begin the discussion with the investigation of the dimensionality of a personality or attitude measure. That is, how many latent factors are influencing the observed item responses to a particular test? Generally speaking, the more strictly unidimensional the scale items, the less ambiguous the interpretation of the resulting raw scale scores, and corrections for attenuation are legitimate (Schmitt, 1996). Also, the application of unidimensional IRT measurement models is more valid and reasonable. If item responses are influenced by two or more common factors, the researcher may wish to consider the creation and scoring of subscales or the application of multidimensional IRT models (Reckase, 1997).

The most popular tools used to address the dimensionality issue in personality and attitude assessment research are exploratory and confirmatory *linear* factor analysis. Unfortunately, the linear factor analysis model is often not appropriate for the study of item-level data because most personality and attitude scale items have dichotomous or polytomous (multicategory) response formats. As pointed out in numerous sources, traditional factor analysis assumes continuous ratings and normality; criteria that are often if not always violated in typical performance-assessment contexts. Violations of these assumptions can and do lead to underestimates of factor loadings and/or overestimates of the number of latent dimensions (Bock, Gibbons, & Muraki, 1988; Gibbons et al., 1985; Waller, Tellegen, McDonald, & Lykken, 1996). Note that the use of polyserial, polychoric, or tetrachoric correlations instead of Pearson correlations does not necessarily solve these problems.

What personality researchers should be using to analyze the dimensionality of scales, especially those with dichotomous item response formats, is nonlinear factor analysis or some related technique specifically designed for the analysis of dichotomous or polytomous items. Waller et al. (1996) describe the role and utility of nonlinear factor analysis in a personality-measurement context. Specifically, they used nonlinear factor analysis to create a psychometrically sound measure of a construct termed *negative emotionality*. Furthermore, they demonstrated how the application of standard linear factor analysis in scale construction would have led to potentially misleading and less than optimal results.

As an alternative to nonlinear factor analytic techniques, some of the problems with linear factor analysis can be avoided by using multidimensional IRT models to assess dimensionality. As described previously, some multidimensional IRT models, such as full-information item factor analysis available in TESTFACT (Muraki & Engelhard, 1985; Wilson et al., 1991), are essentially equivalent to nonlinear factor models (McDonald & Mok, 1995). The term *full-information* is derived from the fact that this factor-analysis technique is based on all the information available from the entire item-response matrix, in contrast to just the information available from the covariance or correlation matrix. Full-information item factor analysis has the advantage of being applicable to a large number of dichotomously scored items (Bock et al., 1988). Other alternative algorithms exemplified in the work of Christofferson (1975) and Muthen (1978; 1984) are more limited. Furthermore, the TESTFACT algorithm can handle items with guessing effects and missing data.

Essentially, full-information item-factor analysis with the TESTFACT program can be thought of as fitting a two- or three-parameter normal-ogive IRT model to the examinee response vectors. Accordingly, TESTFACT output includes not only estimates of factor loadings on one or more latent dimensions but estimates of IRT item-discrimination and difficulty (threshold) parameters. TESTFACT also provides researchers with a tool to assess the structure of binary data sets by conducting likelihood ratio chi-square tests of the number of latent factors. These tests do not depend on any stringent distribution assumptions.

Steinberg and Thissen (1995) describe positive features and provide brief summaries of several applications of full-information item-factor analysis, including analyses of a popular Minnesota Multiphasic Personality Inventory– (MMPI) derived scale known as the Cook and Medley (1954) Hostility scale. More elaborate explication regarding applying IRT to this scale is given in Steinberg and Jorgensen (1996). In other applications, Hendryx, Haviland, Gibbons, and Clark (1992) and Haviland and Reise (1996) used the TESTFACT program to fit multidimensional IRT models to investigate the dimensionality of the Toronto Alexithymia Scale (TAS; Taylor, Bagby, & Parker, 1992). Treating the TAS responses dichotomously, the objective of these studies was to use IRT modeling to investigate the feasibility of interpreting a global TAS score as an index of alexithymia severity. The results of both studies indicated that the TAS is multidimensional, and furthermore, the dimensions are not highly correlated with each other. Caution should therefore be used when interpreting global TAS scores, especially in clinical samples. Although at this time full-information item-factor analysis is applicable only to dichotomously scored scale items, extensions of the full-information model for polytomous responses have been developed (Muraki & Carlson, 1995) and a beta version of POLYFACT is undergoing testing (Muraki, 1993b).

SCALE ANALYSIS USING IRT

Beyond the assessment of dimensionality, IRT techniques provide a new way of assessing the psychometric properties of personality or attitude scales, which in turn has implications for scale construction and interpretation of examinee scores (Embretson, 1996c). For example, in traditional scale analysis, two item statistics play central roles. First is the item-test correlation coefficient, which is often used as an indicator of an item's acceptability as a trait indicator. Personality researchers often want item-test correlations to be as high as possible, but this can lead not only to a lack of measurement bandwidth but to violations of local independence (see Steinberg & Thissen, 1996). The second traditional index is the item mean (or proportion endorsed with dichotomous items). Often, personality researchers try to write dichotomously scored test items that have proportions endorsed around 0.50 within a particular population. This increases test score variance and leads to higher internal consistency indices. As pointed out previously, both of these CTT-based item indices are sample dependent; their values are dependent on the characteristics of the administered sample.

IRT offers analogues to the CTT item indices just described. Specifically, in the context of the 2PL model (Birnbaum, 1968), dichotomously scored personality test items can be judged by their item difficulty and item discrimination parameters. Neither of these indices are sample dependent within a linear transformation, and, thus, they provide less ambiguous interpretations than their CTT counterparts. Beyond the sample invariance property, an advantage of the IRT item parameters over the traditional item statistics lies in the ability to conduct advanced analyses based on the IRT item parameters. For example, with IRT the item difficulty is on the same metric as the latent trait variable, thus tests can be designed to make discriminations among examinees within particular trait ranges (see chap. 10). Also, as will be elaborated later in this chapter, the IRT item parameters facilitate the identification of item bias, computerized adaptive testing, and person-fit assessment—three advances in personality measurement that are each exceedingly difficult without IRT formulations. Furthermore, perhaps the chief advantage of the IRT item parameters and the corresponding item characteristic curve is their ability to be transformed into item information curves.

Traditionally, the precision of personality and attitude scales is judged by their internal consistency coefficients and all subjects receive the same standard error of measurement. As reviewed in chapter 10, under an IRT framework, personality test items are judged by the "information" they provide, and examinees at different trait levels receive different standard errors. In other words, IRT-based psychometrics acknowledges that personality tests perform differently for examinees with different trait levels. Two important consequences regarding item information are useful to test developers and ultimately for test interpretation. First, item information curves are additive across items measuring the same latent variable. Thus, a researcher can calculate how much information a test or subtest contains by adding together item information curves. Such a "test" information curve indicates exactly where on the latent-trait continuum the scale provides maximal information or, equivalently, the best discriminations among examinees. The second useful feature of item (or test) information is that it is inversely related to an examinee's error of measurement. The more information a test provides at a particular trait level, the smaller the standard error for examinees who score in that range.

Psychometric information analysis provides a different way of looking at personality tests than traditional psychometric techniques. For example, two competing personality scales would not necessarily be judged by their alpha coefficients, but rather by their test information curves. Two personality tests may have equal alpha coefficients but provide information in different ranges of the latent trait. Also, in terms of scale construction, item information curves can be used to create tests that target a specific type of examinee. For example, a researcher may want to make precise discriminations among examinees who are greater than one standard deviation from the mean on a given latent variable. Again, see chapter 10 for more details.

Finally, IRT models differ from CTT scale analysis in that the philosophy underlying scale score interpretation is different (see chaps. 6 and 7). Under traditional methods, raw scale scores are interpreted in relationship to norms. These norms are usually derived from some specific population such as males/females or clinical/nonclinical. In contrast, because the examinee trait parameter and the item-difficulty parameters are on the same scale, IRT modeling facilitates a more item-content–based interpretation of examinee standing on a latent trait. For example, an examinee with a trait level estimate of 1.0 is not just one standard deviation above the mean. If a researcher were to examine the difficulty parameters of the scale items, he or she could interpret which particular behaviors the examinee has a high or low probability of engaging in.

With these comments in mind, several researchers have explored the application of IRT models to personality scales to clarify psychometric properties. In a recent article, Steinberg and Thissen (1996, p. 81) describe ways that IRT methods can be used to "examine the source (or sources) of item covariance, focused on the distinction between covariation due to unintended features of the items or to a construct more narrow than we want to measure on the one hand, and covariation attributable to the intended underlying construct on the other." More specifically, they describe how IRT-based testlets can be used to assess constructs relevant to psychopathology. A testlet is a conglomerate of several scale items and can be useful for eliminating measurement disturbances caused by violations of local independence. In personality contexts, violations of local independence occur when pairs of items have highly similar content. When violations of local independence occur, the correlation between the items cannot be explained by the latent trait but rather must include shared specific variance as well. This in turn causes illusory high reliability and bogus multifactor solutions. Most important, as illustrated in the Steinberg and Thissen article, violations of local independence can systematically distort the measurement of the intended construct. Forming testlets on the basis of an IRT analysis is one way to overcome these problems. Finally, these researchers demonstrate how the use of traditional psychometric procedures may lead to less than optimal results.

If one does not consider factor analysis as a subclass of IRT model, then it is fair to state that there are few personality instruments developed solely by IRT methods (see Thissen, Steinberg, Pyszczynki, & Greenberg, 1983, for an exception). In fact, most applications of IRT models are to existing instruments. A prime example of this is Reise and Waller's (1990) application of the 2PL model to each of the eleven scales of the Multidimensional Personality Questionnaire (MPQ; Tellegen, 1982). Their findings regarding the relatively good fit of this IRT model to each of the 11 MPQ scales demonstrates that IRT can be used effectively to characterize dichotomously scored personality item responses. This is not surprising given that the original MPQ scales were developed with factor analytic methods, which tends to result in highly unidimensional scales. However, the examples provided in Steinberg and Thissen (1995) demonstrate that IRT modeling may also be useful in personality assessment contexts where the scales have not necessarily been created with factor analytic techniques. Other examples of IRT scale analyses have been conducted on the Meyers-Briggs Type Indicator (Harvey, Murry, & Markham, 1994; Harvey & Murry, 1994), the Beck Depression Inventory (Santor, Ramsay, & Zuroff, 1994), the Mississippi Scale for Combat-Related Posttraumatic Stress Disorder (King, King, Fairbank, & Schlenger, 1993), and the Trier Personality Inventory (Ellis, Becker, & Kimmel, 1993).

For illustrative purposes, we examine one research project in depth. Gray-Little, Williams, and Hancock (1997) applied the graded-response model (Samejima, 1969) to explore the psychometric properties of the 10-item Rosenberg Self-Esteem Scale (RSE; Rosenberg, 1965), a widely used instrument. Their stated objective was to provide a more refined psychometric analysis than is ordinarily offered. This is a particularly interesting application of IRT for a number of reasons. First, self-esteem is a commonly measured construct in which most existing measures are multidimensional; in fact, some researchers have suggested that the RSE is multidimensional. This might suggest that an IRT model would not fit the data very well. Second, the item content of most self-esteem scales is characterized by repetitiveness, perhaps in order to inflate alpha coefficients. It is possible that the IRT analysis will show this in the form of all items having similar item information curves. Finally, the RSE scale contains a five-point Likert rating format, and it should prove interesting to see whether so many discriminations can be made by examinees. It can be argued that people can't reliably distinguish between "a little true of me" or "somewhat true to me" in response to the kinds of questions that are asked on self-esteem items. This would be evidenced by category threshold parameters that are either clumped closely together or clumped within a small range of the latent trait. Recall that in the graded response model (chap. 5) with five response categories, there are four between-category threshold (β_{ij}) parameters for each item, and one item-slope (discrimination) parameter (α_i).

The findings of the Gray-Little et al. (1997) study indicated that the unidimensional IRT graded-response model fit the responses to the RSE scale very well. Thus, based on this study at least, there is no evidence that the RSE measure cannot serve as a global indicator of self-esteem. Furthermore, item parameter estimates revealed that 7 of the 10 items have almost identical category response curves, which would mean that they provide similar psychometric information. Generally speaking, although the RSE scale provides some psychometric information throughout the entire trait range, most of it is concentrated at the low end of the trait continuum. That is, the scale does a good job of differentiating low from high scoring examinees, but does not provide highly reliable distinctions among examinees who are high on the construct. This finding is consistent with Flannery, Reise, and Widaman (1995) who found similar results when another popular set of self-concept scales was analyzed with IRT methods.

Gray-Little et al. (1997) also found that the β_{i1} parameters (the threshold parameter for the lowest response category) was difficult to estimate, thus, indicating that few examinees select this extreme. We note from inspection of their graphed ICCs (p. 448) that for 7 of the 10 items, any examinee above the mean on the latent trait is most likely to select the highest response category (5) and that examinees between –1 and 0 standard deviations on the latent trait appear to be most likely to select response category (4). Only people who are extremely low on the latent trait select category 1, 2, or 3. To illustrate, we used their results (p. 447) to create plots of the category response curves for Item 1 ("I feel that I am a person of worth, at least on an equal plane with others") and Item 5 ("On the whole, I am satisfied with myself"), which are shown in Figs. 12.1 and 12.2, respectively. These curves suggest that anything other than a true/false response format is perhaps not necessary because individuals who are low in self-esteem include anyone who does not respond in the highest category. Note this is our interpretation, not that of the study authors. We also believe that such findings illustrate that even when using a polytomous response format, it is difficult to write items in certain construct domains that actually provide discriminations in all ranges of the underlying construct. This could be because the construct is quasi-categorical in nature, thus calling for a latent class analysis. Similar concerns have also been expressed historically in the attitude measurement literature (Nunnally, 1978). Interestingly, Gray-Little et al. (1997) identified that the items with the lowest discrimination tended to have an "at time" qualifier. For example "I certainly feel useless at times" or "at times I think I am no good at all." However, it was also argued that these items are worth having on the scale because responses to them are not as highly skewed.

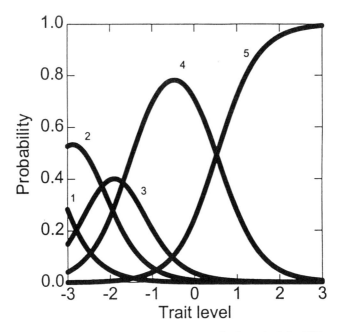

FIG. 12.1. The category response curves for Item 1 of the RSE.

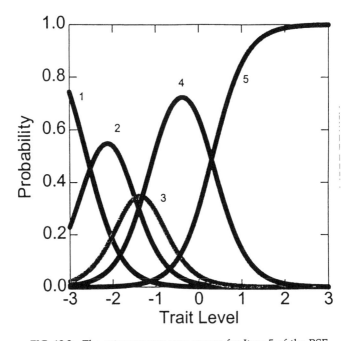

FIG. 12.2 The category response curves for Item 5 of the RSE.

This, in turn, assists in spreading psychometric information to the positive trait ranges.

ATTITUDE ASSESSMENT WITH IRT

The field of personality assessment dwarfs the field of attitude measurement and as might be expected, applications of IRT models in this domain are rare. Nevertheless, researchers have used existing attitude measures to demonstrate that the parameters for a new proposed IRT model may be estimated and how such parameters may be interpreted. For example, Roberts and Laughlin (1996) demonstrated how a graded unfolding model fits responses to a measure of attitudes toward capital punishment. Also, a measure of students' interest in physics and technology was analyzed to demonstrate the applicability of a generalized Rasch model (Rost, 1988).

One IRT technique that we believe is of particular interest to attitude (and personality) assessment can be found in Rost (1990), see also Rost (1991). As mentioned in chapters 4 and 11, Rost developed what can be termed a mixed-measurement IRT model that incorporates aspects of both latent-trait and latent-class analysis. More specifically, the model assumes that a Rasch IRT model (i.e., a one-parameter model) is applicable for all persons within a given latent class. In other words, the mixed-model assumes that there may be two or more latent classes of examinees for whom different IRT models hold. The mixed-measurement model thus allows for both qualitative and quantitative individual differences to be identified and examined. This model can be implemented by means of the Windows-Mixed Item Response Analysis (WIN-MIRA) (Davier, 1995) computer program, which can estimate mixed models for both dichotomous and polytomous item-response data.

When applied to responses from a particular attitude scale, the WIN-MIRA program searches for latent classes of examinees who are qualitatively different with respect to the latent trait. This is manifested by different item-response curves for different latent classes of examinees. The end result is that the estimated model parameters can be used to classify examinees into qualitatively different latent classes, and within each latent class, examinees can be scaled on a continuous latent-trait dimension. Note that the latent classes are not ordered.

Rost's (1990, 1991) mixed-measurement model has been applied to attitude-assessment questionnaires in a number of studies. Indeed, the capacity of the algorithm to handle multiple polytomous IRT models makes it ideally suited for such applications. For example, Rost and Georg (1991) analyzed a scale measuring "adolescent centrism." They found that there were two latent classes with respect to the responses to this scale, and 80%

of the population was estimated to be of one type and 20% to be of the other. However, the smaller class appeared to be "unscalable" in the sense that their responses to the questionnaire items made no psychological sense. That is, no consistent ordering of items along the trait continuum in terms of difficulty could be identified for this group. The use of mixed-measurement models to identify what may be termed poor "traitedness" in the attitude domain appears to be analogous to the person-fit approach in personality assessment adopted by Reise and Waller (1993), as described later in this chapter.

In the personality domain, there have been several applications of mixed-measurement (e.g., see Rost, Carstensen, & Davier, 1996). In a particularly interesting application, Davier and Rost (1996) used a mixed-measurement IRT model to explore both qualitative and quantitative variation on the Self-Monitoring scale (Snyder, 1974). Personality researchers are familiar with the theory that the self-monitoring construct is really a discrete taxon (i.e., a typology) as opposed to a continuous variable (Gangestad & Snyder, 1985; Snyder & Gangestad, 1986). In brief, Davier and Rost concluded on the basis of their mixed-measurement analyses that there are different types of people who differ qualitatively in regard to controlling expressive behavior. Interestingly, they identified two classes (types) of high–self monitors. Within each class there is quantitative variation (i.e., people who are higher or lower on the trait). The classes are qualitatively different from each other in that one group appears to employ "actor-like skills" in controlling expressive emotion, whereas the other group does not.

COMPUTERIZED ADAPTIVE TESTING

Another implication of IRT modeling, in contrast to traditional test theory, is that it lends itself nicely to computerized adaptive testing. With tests designed under a CTT framework, examinees can be compared if and only if they receive the *exact* same item set. That is, unless the tests are parallel, raw scores across different versions of a measure cannot be directly compared (Embretson, 1996c). This is a severe limitation, especially since many items within a scale are a waste of examinee time because their difficulty does not match an examinee's trait level. For instance, in a personality assessment context, it would be a waste of examinee time and psychometrically useless to ask an examinee who is high on sociability whether he or she "would enjoy the solitary life of a monk."

The problem of administering psychometrically uninformative test items can be overcome through a process of IRT-based computerized adaptive testing (see chap. 10). In turn, the ability to perform computerized adaptive testing is a direct result of the capacity of IRT models to scale examinees (and items) on a common latent trait metric, even if they have taken a completely different set of items. Computerized adaptive testing (CAT; Wainer, 1990) is a process by which test items are selected, via a computer, to match an examinee's trait level. Consequently, different examinees take different versions of a test, yet their scores are comparable on the same measurement scale.

There is a large literature on IRT-based CAT relevant to ability assessment and programs for item banking and test administration are available (Assessment Systems, 1991), yet few investigations of the procedure have occurred in personality testing. Waller and Reise (1989) used Monte Carlo and real-data simulations to study computerized adaptive testing with the 34-item Absorption scale from Tellegen's (1982) MPQ. Among their findings was that when items were tailored to match examinee trait level, 50% of the items could be eliminated with little loss of information. Furthermore, using real-data simulations, examinees who were high on the trait (e.g., greater than 2.0 standard deviations above the mean) could be identified with perfect accuracy using around eight items on average. Although such findings bode well for potential applications of CAT in personality assessment, there is a strong tradition of long personality tests that needs to be addressed.

Although a variety of IRT models may be applied to Likert-type attitude rating scales, Dodd (1990) argues that the Andrich (1978a) rating scale model (chap. 5) may be most easily transformed into a computerized adaptive attitude assessment procedure. Dodd examined the feasibility and psychometric properties of a computerized adaptive test of a teacher's attitudes toward communication skills of administrators, and attitudes toward the rights and roles of women. More specifically, real-data simulations were used to investigate types of CAT item-selection procedures and step size until the maximum likelihood could be estimated. Simulated data was also used for the sake of comparisons. Findings were very positive. For example, generally speaking, examinees could be reliably assessed using only around half the items in the full scale. Furthermore, examinee scores from the computerized adaptive tests were highly correlated with the known full-scale trait scores. As the author notes, this is quite good considering that one of the item pools contains just 24 items. It is not unusual to require fewer items in a pool when the items are polytomously scored in contrast to dichotomously scored. Further research and illustration of computerized adaptive attitude assessment can be found in Koch, Dodd, and Fitzpatrick (1990), Dodd and De Ayala (1994) and the summary of this research provided in a special issue on polytomous IRT models in *Applied Psychological Methods* (Dodd, De Ayala, & Koch, 1995).

As we noted earlier, IRT facilitates CAT because IRT models allow for examinee position on a latent trait continuum to be estimated from any subset of test items that have been calibrated onto the same scale. We close this section by mentioning that related to this property is the fact that IRT models place few restrictions on item formatting (Thissen, 1993). Most personality and attitude measures consist of items of the same response format. This is not a necessity of CTT, but most researchers want to maintain similar variances across items lest some items affect the total score more than others. With IRT modeling, there is no compelling reason to maintain similar item-response formats (except to avoid respondent confusion) because there is no need to produce a reliability coefficient. Thus, in the future, IRT-based personality tests can be constructed with some true/false and some Likert ratings, and the Likert rating items may even have a different numbers of options (see Thissen, 1993).

EXPLORING SUBSTANTIVE ISSUES WITH IRT

Thus far, we have examined how IRT has been applied to understand the psychometric properties of existing scales and to create new types of assessment procedures such as computerized adaptive testing. In what follows, we describe the application of IRT models to explore more substantive issues in the personality field. We begin by describing research that has explored differential item functioning, or, how a test may function differently between two or more groups of examinees. Within this context we describe application of IRT methods to explore item serial order effects. Finally, we wrap up the following section by describing applications of "person-fit" statistics in personality testing contexts.

Differential Item Functioning

IRT-based techniques can be used to create a common latent-trait metric by which the psychometric properties of items from different tests, or items that have been given to different samples of examinees, may be compared. As covered more extensively in chapter 13, the BILOG-MG program (Zimowski et al., 1996) was specifically designed to facilitate such comparisons. For example, assume that a researcher has two self-report instruments that ostensibly measure the same construct, say, agreeableness. Using IRT-based linking procedures, which are available in both BILOG-MG and XCALIBRE (Assessment Systems Corporation, 1996), a researcher could link the latent-trait scales of these tests. That is, a researcher could place the item response curves from each test on the same scale, which in turn would allow researchers to compare the two instruments more readily. All that is needed to accomplish this objective is a set of examinees that responded to several of the items (called an "anchor" set in IRT jargon) on both measures; the examinees can be drawn from different populations.

This capacity to calibrate items onto a common metric with IRT has led to some interesting studies. Steinberg (1994), for example, implemented IRT methods to study item-position effects. In both personality and attitude assessment, there is evidence that an item's location within an inventory significantly affects its relationship with the construct being measured (Knowles, 1988; Tourangeau & Rasinski, 1988); items placed toward the end of questionnaires tend to have higher item-test correlations. One proposed explanation is that level of self-awareness is increased as a respondent completes a measure (Hamilton & Shuminsky, 1990). Unfortunately, this research on item serial-order effects is based on traditional psychometric procedures that do not permit clear and unambiguous interpretation of the phenomena. Using IRT-based procedures, Steinberg (1994) was able to clarify how item content and serial-order affect item-trait relations. In particular, when her data were analyzed with the methods used in previous studies, she was able to replicate previous findings. However, when examined from an IRT perspective, she found little if any evidence of a general serial-order effect in personality item responses. In fact, only 1 of 20 items "I feel secure" drawn from a commonly used anxiety scale was found to display a context effect; it had a higher item-discrimination parameter when presented 11th rather than 1st in an inventory. That is, the item probably derived a meaning more consistent with the other items when it was 11th, rather than 1st.

Another derivative outcome of the ability to place items onto a common metric in IRT is the study of differential-item functioning (DIF) or item/test bias (Thissen, Steinberg, & Gerrard, 1986). In IRT terms, a scale item displays DIF if examinees with the same latent-trait level have different probabilities of endorsing an item. In other words, in IRT terms, a personality or attitude item is biased if the IRCs are not the same across two groups of examinees. This is an important issue because for test scores to be comparable across groups, the items must work in the same way. Accordingly, several statistical procedures for comparison of ICCs across different examinee groups have been developed (Raju, 1988, 1990; Thissen, Steinberg, & Wainer, 1988, 1992).

Although the topic of DIF is important in psychological testing, especially for large-scale testing programs, little if any work on the topic has occurred in personality assessment. Traditionally, this issue has been addressed by investigating the factorial invariance (i.e., equality of loadings) of a measure across two or more groups using confirmatory factor analytic (CFA) methods. Reise, Widaman, and Pugh (1993) compared confirmatory factor analyses and IRT methods of testing measurement invariance in the context of a personality measure. Specifically, they investigated the invariance of a five-item mood measure across samples of American and Chinese subjects. They concluded that the IRT and CFA analyses produced similar results. Note that an IRT item-discrimination parameter is analogous to a factor loading, and thus when researchers test for factorial invariance with CFA, this can be thought of as testing whether the items are equally discriminating in an IRT sense. However, although invariance of factor loadings or item discriminations is important, differences in item difficulty can also be substantively interesting. That is, items can be equally discriminating across groups — indicating that the item is a viable trait indicator in both samples — but can have different item-difficulty parameters.

For example, Smith and Reise (in press) investigated differential item functioning between gender groups on the 23-item Stress Reaction scale of the MPQ (Tellegen, 1982). To study DIF they divided their sample into two groups: men and women. The BILOG-MG (Zimowski et al., 1996) program was then used. First, assuming that the items are equally discriminating across groups, the BILOG-MG program estimates a common set of item discrimination parameters for each group but freely estimates separate item difficulties for each group. That is, for each item, separate IRCs are estimated for each examinee group with the constraint that they have the same slope across groups. Note that in classical test theory, the item difficulties (proportion endorsed) could be different across groups because of group mean differences on the latent trait. With BILOG-MG, however, group mean differences on the latent trait are explicitly taken into account by setting up contrasts that compare item-difficulty parameters across groups after taking into account the best estimate of group mean differences on the latent trait.

Smith and Reise's (in press) findings indicated that there was significant DIF between gender groups on several Stress Reaction scale items. Interestingly, the DIF on the Stress Reaction scale was not all in the same direction; some items were easier to endorse (i.e., required a lower trait level) for men, and some of the items were easier to endorse for women. The direction of the DIF appeared related to item content. It appeared to these authors that items that are easier to endorse for men come from a cluster of items described as "easily upset and irritable," and the items that are easier for women to endorse come from a cluster of items characterized as "is sensitive or vulnerable."

Perhaps more potentially interesting than the investigation of gender differences is the application of IRT-based DIF procedures to study cross-cultural differences in personality and attitude (e.g., Ellis, Becker & Kimmel, 1993; Ellis, Minsel, & Becker, 1989; Hulin, Drasgow, & Komocar, 1982). In this context, IRT procedures might be used to study the adequacy of a translation, the measurement equivalence of an item set across different cultural groups, or, if invariance cannot be established, IRT methods might be used to explore how different cultural groups may be compared on the same scale while allowing some items to have different ICCs across groups. Most important, as in the previous example, IRT techniques can be used to identify and highlight interesting substantive issues in the area of cross-cultural measurement and personality.

Recently, Huang, Church, and Katigbak (1997) used IRT procedures to compare items from the Neuroticism Extraversion Openness Personality Inventory (NEO-PI) (Costa & McCrae, 1985) across Filipino and American college students. Among their findings were that many items contained significant DIF (ranged from 30 to 79 out of 176 items depending on the particular DIF detection statistic used). When the scales were purified of such DIF, many mean comparisons between groups were no longer statistically significant. The authors did not elaborate, however, on the content of biased and unbiased items and the impact of item content on the particular form of DIF observed. This is unfortunate because such knowledge is extremely useful in drawing inferences about cultural differences in personality trait manifestation. Furthermore, the DIF that was identified was characterized as small, and there was no case where an NEO-PI item was highly discriminating in one culture but not in the other.

Person-Fit

Regardless of whether a researcher is working from a maximum or typical performance assessment framework, most response factors (e.g., carelessness) that undermine the validity of psychological measurements manifest themselves in the inconsistency of an individual's item response pattern. By consistency, we mean the degree to which a subject's item response pattern is congruent with some model of normative item responding (i.e., valid responding). Because IRT models are formal (statistical) models, they lend themselves readily to the examination of the consistency of an individual's item response pattern with respect to a set of estimated IRT model parameters. In other words, IRT models lend themselves nicely to the evaluation of examinee person-fit.

IRT-based person-fit assessment involves the evaluation of the consistency of an examinee's item response pattern with a set of estimated IRT model parameters. Many educational psychologists have discussed response factors that decrease the interpretability of examinees' "scores" (i.e., theta estimates) on psychological measures. For example, an examinee may cheat or mismatch an answer sheet due to carelessness. In personality and attitude assessment contexts, researchers have also suggested response factors that may diminish the ultimate interpretability of scale scores. For example, socially desirable responding, malingering, random responding, poor reading skills, or a unique interpretation of item content may bias item responses. Furthermore, some researchers have even suggested that responses to personality measures may be inconsistent because the construct being assessed is not applicable to the individual examinee (Baumeister & Tice, 1988; Tellegen, 1988). Reise and Flannery (1996) reviewed how IRT-based person-fit indices might be used to identify such response factors in personality assessment.

To our knowledge, only a few studies have focused specifically on person-fit in typical performance assessment contexts. Most recently, Zickar and Drasgow (1996) investigated the ability of an IRT-based likelihood ratio model comparison strategy to identify faking good on personality instruments (see also, Drasgow, Levine, & Zickar, 1996). Their study was based on real examinees, some of whom were instructed to fake their responses to look good on a particular instrument, while others were instructed to respond normally. Findings indicated that the IRT-based procedures outperformed, in terms of correct identifications and fewer false positives, more traditional methods such as a social desirability scale. Clearly, the results of this study call for more directed research aimed at clarifying the relative strengths and weaknesses of IRT-based invalidity assessment versus the legion of techniques (e.g., lie scales, k corrections, semantic consistency scales, social desirability scales) that have been historically used in applied personality assessment contexts.

A study by Reise and Waller (1993) examined the ability of an IRT-based person-fit index called Z_L (see Chapter 9; Drasgow et al., 1985) to identify poor person-fit on the 11 scales of the Multidimensional Personality Questionnaire (MPQ; Tellegen, 1982). More specifically, they attempted to use person-fit statistics to show that although the MPQ scales are univocal measures for most examinees, for some examinees, the items did not hold together in a univocal manner. They showed that some examinees with poor person-fit were responding inconsistently to the scale items as a whole, but when considered within specific facets of item content, responses made sense. Also, Reise and Waller (1993) showed that person-fit scores are modestly correlated across different scales of the MPQ, suggesting that person-misfit is a more general characteristic. To further clarify this point, when person-fit scores were aggregated across the 11 MPQ scales, the resulting aggregate was found to correlate with impulsivity and stress reaction as measured by the MPQ scales.

Finally, Reise (1995) conducted a series of Monte Carlo studies that examined various psychometric properties of the above referenced Z_L index on three MPQ scales. Basic findings were that Z_L was not well standardized under these testing conditions. For example, after estimating item parameters for one of the MPQ scales, data were simulated to fit an IRT model under these conditions. When the Z_L statistic was computed, it did not have a normal distribution. This would be problematic if one were to use Z_L to conduct strict hypothesis tests of fit. Furthermore, in the Reise (1995) study, the effects of different scoring strategies (e.g., maximum likelihood, expected a posteriori) on the power of the Z_L statistic was explored. Findings indicated that power was low regardless of scoring strategy. This means that examinees that were simulated not to fit the IRT model were not identified with high accuracy as such by the Z_L statistic. Of course, person-fit statistics have different power for different types of response deviance, and in the Reise study, only one method was used to simulate poor-fitting examinees.

THE DISADVANTAGES OF IRT

This chapter highlights what we believe are several key applications of IRT in the personality and attitude assessment domains. We have purposely stayed away from in-depth discussion of which models are most appropriate for typical performance data, how many subjects are needed for good parameter estimates, or how should model fit be judged. There are no pat answers to any of these questions, but judging from the literature, it appears that the 2PL model (Birnbaum, 1968) and the graded-response model (Samijima, 1969) are receiving the most use. The number of subjects necessary will, of course, depend on a variety of factors, including the number of response options and the spread of responses across categories. Probably the best way to judge the adequacy of parameter estimation is to inspect the standard errors of parameter estimates. Finally, issues of IRT model fit and model selection are covered extensively in chapter 9, and we refer the reader there.

The research reviewed here highlights the promise IRT models have for advancing the fields of personality and attitude assessment. As we also state, however, application of IRT in these domains is relatively rare, and there may be some good reasons why. In what follows, we briefly address some of the stumbling blocks that may limit the potential usefulness of IRT in the typical performance assessment domain. First, IRT modeling can have the negative consequence of limiting the type of constructs assessed by personality psychologists. By this we do not simply mean that the unidimensionality assumption required by most available IRT models is too restrictive but rather that, conceptually speaking, some of the constructs we wish to assess do not lend themselves to an IRT type of analysis.

Bollen and Lennox (1991) elaborated on an important distinction between emergent variable and latent variable measurement models. In a latent variable measurement model, the construct causes the indicators and thus explains the item covariances (analogous to a factor model), whereas in an emergent-variable measurement model, the construct is defined by the indicators (analogous to a components model). IRT modeling is clearly a latent variable measurement model, and attempting to fit constructs that don't fit this mold is bound to lead to problems. It is easy to think of important personality variables and their associated measures that do not easily fit an IRT measurement framework. For example, Gough's folk constructs as measured by the CPI would be problematic. Furthermore, many arguably important constructs in personality (e.g., hardiness) do not refer to unidimensional variables but are by definition multifaceted constructs. In short, in personality assessment a wide variety of constructs are conceptualized on different theoretical levels (see Ozer & Reise, 1994), and not all of them are appropriately assessed by an IRT measurement framework. It would be unwise if typical performance assessment was limited to constructs and associated scales that absolutely meet "fundamental measurement criteria" or "fit Rasch models." After all, perhaps the most well-validated scale ever is Gough's socialization measure (Gough, 1994), an explicitly nonhomogeneous or factorally pure scale.

Another technical problem in IRT is scoring. Estimating someone's position on a latent-trait continuum using his or her pattern of item responses requires advanced numeric methods, and is no where near as easy as adding up raw item responses. Also, it is unclear at this time the extent to which the added complexity is worth the trouble in terms of test score validity or in correctly evaluating statistical hypotheses based on scale scores. Our observations are that raw scores and trait level estimates always correlated greater than 0.95, and no one has shown that in real data a single psychological finding would be different if IRT scores were used rather than raw scale scores. Without such demonstrations, arguments of IRT supporters will fall on deaf ears. Finally, the issue of model-fit is a concern in IRT, whereas researchers usually don't consider the issue of model fit under traditional testing theory. At this time there is no "agreed upon" method of assessing IRT model fit, and it is not entirely clear what the effects of violating model assumptions are.

In sum, IRT modeling definitely offers advantages over traditional procedures, but it is clearly not the solution to all measurement problems in personality or attitude assessment. The chief strengths of IRT, in terms of personality assessment, appear to lie in the capacity to address interesting psychometric and substantive issues that would otherwise be very difficult with traditional procedures. In particular, we cite the study of item-positioning effects, the study of cultural differences in item functioning, and the assessment of person-fit as prime examples of IRT's advantages. Furthermore, IRT is also valuable as an alternative way of studying the psychometric characteristics of a test and in interpreting the meaning of examinee scale scores. IRT modeling doesn't make good items bad or questionable constructs legitimate, but it might help expose poorly functioning items and bad concepts (Steinberg & Thissen, 1996). On the other hand, some of the advantages of IRT may ultimately be of little interest to personality assessment researchers. For example, computerized adaptive testing seems perhaps more crucial to large-scale testing programs like the Educational Testing Service (ETS) and American College Testing (ACT) than to the basic personality researcher.

13

Computer Programs for Conducting IRT Parameter Estimation

In this chapter, computer software programs that assist in the application of IRT modeling are reviewed. First we describe TESTFACT (Wilson, Wood, & Gibbons, 1991), a program that can be used to evaluate the dimensionality of a set of dichotomously scored items and to estimate unidimensional or multidimensional normal-ogive IRT item parameters. Seven stand-alone commercial programs that provide solely for estimating unidimensional IRT model parameters are then reviewed. These software packages vary in the types of models that can be estimated, the options available to estimate parameters, their ability to handle multiple examinee subgroups, the type of fit statistics provided, and on numerous other dimensions. All programs described in this chapter are available for IBM-clone machines, require at least a 386 microprocessor, and 2MB of free RAM.

To facilitate the discussion, analyses of two Monte Carlo simulated data sets are used throughout this chapter. The first data set consists of 1,000 simulated examinees responding to a five-item dichotomously scored test. The 1PL item parameters used to simulate responses are shown in Table 13.1. Responses to this scale are scored 0 (not keyed) and 1 (keyed), and all examinees were simulated assuming a normal distribution for the latent trait. The $D = 1.7$ scaling constant was used in the simulations. The second data set is 1,000 simulated examinees responding to a five-item polytomously scored test. Each item was specified to have five response options, and item parameters from the graded response model were used to generate the data. Again, the exact item parameter values are shown in Table 13.1. The first data is used to illustrate the dichotomous

TABLE 13.1
True Item Parameters Used to Generate Monte Carlo Data Sets

	Dichtomous 1PL		Polytomous Graded-Response Model				
Item	Discrimination	Difficulty	Slope	β_1	β_2	β_3	β_4
1	1.0	−1.5	1.0	−2.00	−1.00	0.00	1.00
2	1.0	−0.5	1.0	−1.75	−0.75	0.25	1.25
3	1.0	0	1.0	−1.50	−0.50	0.50	1.50
4	1.0	0.5	1.0	−1.00	−0.50	0.50	1.00
5	1.0	1.5	1.0	−0.75	−0.25	0.25	0.75

Note. $D = 1.7$ scaling factor used in all data simulations.

IRT programs, and the second data set is used to illustrate the polytomous IRT programs. In the analyses that follow, default conditions are used in running the various programs, and any departures from this standard are noted.

TESTFACT

With the TESTFACT 2 (Wilson, Wood, & Gibbons, 1991) program, a researcher can conduct full-information item-factor analyses (Bock, Gibbons, & Muraki, 1988; Muraki & Engelhard, 1985) on questionnaire data with dichotomous item response formats. Equivalently, the program allows researchers to estimate two- or three-parameter normal-ogive multidimensional IRT model parameters. However, in the three-parameter normal-ogive model, the guessing parameters must be set to fixed values and are not actually estimated. Data sets that contain polytomous item response formats may not be currently analyzed, however; see Muraki and Carlson (1995) for psychometric developments. Furthermore, Muraki (1993b) has developed a beta version of POLYFACT.

TESTFACT is a batch program run in DOS mode, where commands are typed into a text file (e.g., filename.TSF) and then submitted. The TESTFACT program is particularly useful for three major research objectives, and we address each of these applications in turn. The TESTFACT command file for the analyses to be presented in this section is given here.

```
>TITLE
 ITEM FACTOR ANALYSIS OF 5 MONTE CARLO SIMULATED ITEMS
 GENERATED UNDER THE 1PL MODEL (D = 1.7) FOR BOOK CHAPTER
>PROBLEM NITEM=5,RESPONSE=3;
>NAMES D01,D02,D03,D04,D05;
>RESPONSE ' ','0','1';
>KEY 11111
>RELIABILITY ALPHA;
```

```
>TETRACHORIC  RECODE,NDEC=2,LIST;
>FACTOR  NFAC=2,NROOT=2,NIT=(5,0.001),NDEC=2,RESIDUAL;
>FULL  QUAD=10,ITER=(3,5,0.005),IQUAD=2,STEPWISE;
>SAVE  TRIAL;
>INPUT  NIDW=1,SCORES,FILE='TRUED.DAT';
 (4A1,1X,5A1)
>STOP
```

This command file instructs the program to conduct both a one- and two-factor full-information item-factor analysis, to output basic item descriptive statistics, including coefficient alpha, the tetrachoric correlation matrix, and the residual correlation matrix, and to save the resulting item parameter estimates in a text file.

The first application of TESTFACT is as a tool for conducting psychometric analyses of tests and subtests. As part of the standard output, the program provides a wealth of basic descriptive statistics about test items. As shown in Table 13.2, for each item the following statistics are provided: (a) the mean test score for individuals endorsing the item, (b) the item facility, (c) item difficulty (delta scale), (d) item-test biserial, and (e) the point-biserial correlation. Beyond these descriptive statistics, the user has the following options: (a) viewing a fractile table for each item, (b) viewing a graph of test scores versus the item discrimination estimates, and (c) computing item psychometric properties against an external or criterion variable.

The second important application of TESTFACT is that it allows a researcher to explore the dimensionality of a dichotomously scored data set — something that is notoriously problematic with standard linear factor analytic routines (see, Bock, Gibbons, & Muraki, 1988; Waller, Tellegen, McDonald, & Lykken, 1996). TESTFACT fits the full-information item-factor model by making use of a marginal maximum likelihood (MML) routine implemented by means of an EM algorithm (Bock & Aitken, 1981). As noted in chapter 6, MML routines integrate out the latent

TABLE 13.2
Item Statistics for Five-Item Dichotomous
Data Set Output From TESTFACT

ITEM	RMEAN	FACILITY	DIFF	BIS	P.BIS
D01	2.75	0.83	9.05	0.79	0.53
D02	3.15	0.62	11.78	0.85	0.67
D03	3.45	0.47	13.22	0.88	0.70
D04	3.71	0.36	14.40	0.89	0.70
D05	4.40	0.12	17.58	0.86	0.54

Note. RMEAN is the average raw score for people endorsing this item, FACILITY is the proportion endorsed, DIFF is the item difficulty on the delta scale, BIS is the biserial correlation, and P. BIS is the point-biserial correlation.

trait parameter by specifying a number of quadrature points (nodes) and a series of quadrature weights (see also Baker, 1992).

At the heart of full-information item-factor analysis lies the estimation of a "smoothed" (i.e., Grammian) tetrachoric correlation matrix. For the present data set, the average inter-item tetrachoric correlation was 0.47, and the first two eigenvalues from this correlation matrix were 2.88 and 0.69. In Table 13.3 is displayed the TESTFACT output from a one-factor model. Specifically for each test item, estimates of six item parameters are important: intercept, threshold, item slope, difficulty, communality, and the factor loading (see chap. 4 for details). Note that in multidimensional solutions, one slope and one factor-loading parameter are estimated for each test item on each of the latent factors. Furthermore, although the rotation is not necessary for the unidimensional solution, both Varimax and Promax options are provided to rotate factor loadings in the multifactorial case.

To judge model fit, the TESTFACT program provides a G^2 statistic (see chap. 9 on assessing model fit). This statistic evaluates the likelihood of the data under the model versus the general multinomial alternative. This G^2 statistic is not appropriate for judging the fit of a single-factor model because of problems resulting from sparse contingency tables. However, models of increasing dimensionality may be evaluated by examining the change in G^2 values relative to the change in degrees of freedom. For example, in the current data set, going from a one- to two-factor model did not produce a significant increase in chi-square, and, thus, a second factor is not significant. Specifically, the change in G^2 was 4.95 on four degrees of freedom ($p = 0.292$).

This result is not surprising given that the ratio of the eigenvalues for the first and second factors was $2.88/0.69 = 4.17$, which by conventional standards most people would judge that this data matrix has a very strong dominant first factor. Nevertheless, we warn readers about relying heavily on any particular statistical approach to evaluating dimensionality or fit, especially with large samples. Also, caution should be used in

TABLE 13.3
Item Parameters for the Five-Item Dichotomous
Data Set Output From TESTFACT

	Invariant			Dependent		
	INTERCEPT	THRESHOLD	SLOPE	DIFFICULTY	COMMUNALITY	LOADING
D01	1.23	−1.63	0.75	−0.98	0.36	0.60
D02	0.40	−0.46	0.86	−0.30	0.42	0.65
D03	−0.07	0.07	1.00	0.05	0.50	0.70
D04	−0.52	0.47	1.10	0.35	0.54	0.74
D05	−1.65	1.58	1.04	1.14	0.52	0.72

TABLE 13.4
Correlation Matrix and Residual Correlations
After Fitting the One-Factor Model

| Item | Original Tetrachoric Correlations | | | | | Residual Correlations After One-Factor | | | | |
	D01	D02	D03	D04	D05	D01	D02	D03	D04	D05
D01	1.00					0.00				
D02	0.39	1.00				−0.00	0.00			
D03	0.40	0.47	1.00			−0.03	0.00	0.00		
D04	0.52	0.49	0.51	1.00		0.07	−0.00	−0.03	−0.02	
D05	0.36	0.46	0.57	0.52	1.00	−0.07	−0.00	−0.02	0.05	−0.01

comparing different factor structures if the number of quadrature nodes used differs across solutions, which happens by default in TESTFACT. Perhaps more valuable than the G^2 statistic, the TESTFACT program also provides the residual correlations produced after fitting models of different dimensionality. Table 13.4 displays the original correlation matrix and the residual correlations after fitting a one-factor model. In this simulated unidimensional data set, almost no residual common variance is left unaccounted for by the first factor.

This brings us to the third use of TESTFACT, namely, parameter estimates output from the full-information item-factor analysis can be converted into normal-ogive unidimensional or multidimensional IRT model parameters. In turn, these parameter estimates can be used to scale examinees on the latent trait dimension(s) using EAP scoring. Before concluding this section it is important to mention a few of the other options available with the TESTFACT program. First, when estimating a factor model, prior distributions can be placed on intercept parameters (normal prior) or on factor slopes (beta prior). Second, an additional useful feature of TESTFACT is the ability to supply the program with known item-parameter estimates, and it can then generate vectors of simulated item responses.

BILOG AND BILOG-MG

The BILOG 3 (Mislevy & Bock, 1990) program allows researchers to estimate 1PL, 2PL, and 3PL IRT models on questionnaire data with dichotomous item response formats. An option is provided where the user may estimate parameters using $D = 1.7$ (i.e., in the normal metric) or with the $D = 1.0$ scaling factor (i.e., in a logistic metric). Parameter estimates are derived using a marginal maximum likelihood method (Bock & Aitkin, 1981). As discussed before, MML estimation of a two- or three-parameter

IRT model is essentially equivalent to performing a unidimensional full-information item-factor analysis. However, because BILOG 3 is specifically designed for item parameter calibration and examinee scoring, it naturally contains many more options and features than the TESTFACT program.

BILOG 3 is a Windows 95 program with drop-down menus where commands are typed into a text file and then submitted for analysis. A very extensive help file menu is also provided within the BILOG environment. The command file for the analyses presented in this section is given here.

```
FIVE  ITEM  EXAMPLE  TEST  N  =  1000
ONE-PARAMETER  MODEL
>COMMENT
 THIS  IS  AN  EXAMPLE  RUN;  NORMAL  METRIC,  D  =  1.7
>GLOBAL  NPARM=1,  DFNAME='TRUED.DAT';
>LENGTH  NITEMS=  5;
>INPUT  NTOTAL=5,  NIDCH=4,  SAMPLE=1000;
(4A1,1X,5A1)
>TEST  TNAME=TRUED;
>CALIB  FLOAT;
```

This command file instructs the program to estimate a 1PL test model (i.e., all discriminations equal) with item parameters reported in the normal metric (i.e., $D = 1.7$). By default, the number of quadrature points is set to 10, and priors are placed on the item parameters. Specifically, the priors have a mean of zero and $SD = 2.0$ for threshold (difficulty) parameters and a mean of 0 and $SD = 0.5$ for the log of the item discriminations. Also, in the current example, the priors for the item parameters are allowed to float (i.e., change) between estimation cycles. Note that in the command file the sample command was set equal to 1,000. This tells the program to use all the examinees in the item parameter calibration phrase.

BILOG can be run in three phases, and different options are available within each phase. The first phase is basic item descriptive statistics. In this phase, for each item the following values are provided: (a) the number of attempts, (b) the number correct, (c) proportion endorsed, (d) the point-biserial, and (e) the biserial correlation. In the second phase, the actual item calibration is produced. It is in this phase that the user has numerous options, all of which may importantly influence item calibration depending on a number of factors, such as the number of items, the number of examinees, and so forth. Among the more important and useful options are the following. First, default prior distributions for the item parameters may be changed and/or allowed to float (i.e., change) between estimation cycles. Second, besides being able to specify the number of quadrature points and quadrature weights, the program can be instructed to compute an empirical distribution for the latent trait. Third, graphs of item information, test information, or residuals can be requested. These plots are useful in terms of understanding how well a particular measure is working and for judging item fit.

Table 13.5 shows the output from Phase 2 of BILOG. For each item, an estimate and standard error is provided for the slope (discrimination), intercept, dispersion, threshold (difficulty), and asymptote (which equals zero for all items). If the test has more than 20 items, then a likelihood ratio chi-square item-fit statistic is produced (see chap. 9). In the present data with only five items, the BILOG output shows "standardized posterior residuals" that are calculated by comparing the posterior probability of an item endorsement with that predicted from the estimated model parameters at a given number of points on the latent trait continuum. A residual greater than 2.0 can be taken to mean that there is a problem in an item's fit at a specific trait level. In the present case, no items displayed a residual greater than 2.0. The values shown in the last column of Table 13.5 are the root mean square of the residuals for each item. Not shown in the table, but produced in the final output is –2 times the marginal log-likelihood of the solution, which in this data was 5,182. This value may be useful in judging the relative fit of nested models.

Finally, in Phase 3 of BILOG the user is presented with a variety of options in terms of scoring examinees. There are three main options for scoring examinees: (a) maximum likelihood (ML), (b) Bayes or expected a posteriori (EAP), and (c) maximum a posteriori (MAP). These techniques are described in chapter 7. The BILOG program also allows a researcher to transform scale scores and item parameters. Furthermore, item parameters from Phase 2 may be saved to a text file and used in future BILOG runs to score new samples of examinees. As with most programs reviewed in this section, no person-fit statistics are provided. BILOG does not provide a way to handle multiple group data and to test for invariance. That is, it is not possible to constrain specific item parameters to equality across groups or to fix item parameters at specific values. Further review of the BILOG program can be found in Kim (1997).

BILOG-MG (Zimowski, Muraki, Mislevy, & Bock, 1996) is a DOS-based program that does just about everything that BILOG does but also provides convenient ways of simultaneously handling multiple groups of examinees (Bock & Zimowski, 1996). The term *multiple groups* is broadly defined and can range from the analysis of different gender or ethnic groups, to the same sample of examinees across two or more time periods, to different examinee samples that have received slightly different forms of a particular test. Specifically, the BILOG-MG program facilitates studies of (a) the equating of test scores across equivalent or nonequivalent groups, (b) vertical equating, (c) differential item functioning (bias) detection, (d) the study of item parameter drift, (e) two-stage testing, and (f) estimation of ability distributions in aggregate samples. These capacities are

TABLE 13.5
Selected Output From Phase 2 of BILOG

ITEM	INTERCEPT S.E.	SLOPE S.E.	THRESHOLD S.E.	DISPERSN S.E.	ASYMPTOTE S.E.	RT MEAN SQUARE STD POSTERIOR RESIDUAL
0001	1.389	0.975	-1.424	1.025	0.000	0.799
	0.071*	0.048*	0.073*	0.051*	0.000*	
0002	0.431	0.975	-0.442	1.025	0.000	0.758
	0.057*	0.048*	0.058*	0.051*	0.000*	
0003	-0.072	0.975	0.074	1.025	0.000	0.642
	0.055*	0.048*	0.057*	0.051*	0.000*	
0004	-0.486	0.975	0.498	1.025	0.000	0.717
	0.058*	0.048*	0.059*	0.051*	0.000*	
0005	-1.624	0.975	1.664	1.025	0.000	0.861
	0.082*	0.048*	0.084*	0.051*	0.000*	

Note. Asterisks indicate standard errors.

important for large testing enterprises, such as school districts but also have their uses in more routine psychological research.

To provide a demonstration, we used the current data set to investigate a form of differential item functioning between groups. Specifically, we arbitrarily assigned the first 500 examinees to be in Group 1 and the second 500 examinees to be in Group 2. The analysis was accomplished by instructing the BILOG-MG program to conduct a DIF analyses (see Thissen, Steinberg, & Wainer, 1993). The command file used is shown here.

```
GROUP 1 (n=500) VS. GROUP 2 (n=500) DIFFERENTIAL ITEM FUNCTIONING
FIVE  ITEM  EXAMPLE  DATA  SET
>COMMENT
ITEM  DISCRIMINATIONS  ARE  FIXED  BUT  ITEM  DIFFICULITES  ARE  FREELY
 ESTIMATED
>GLOBAL  DFN='TRUED.DAT',NPARM=1,NSUBJECT=1000,SAVE;
>SAVE  PARM='TRUED.PAR',DIF='TRUED.DIF';
>LENGTH NITEMS=5;
>INPUT  NTOT=5,NGROUPS=2,SAMPLE=1000,DIF,NIDC=4;
>ITEMS  INAMES=(D1(1)D5),INUMBERS=(1(1)5);
>TEST  TNAME=TRUED;
>GROUP1  GNAME=GP1;
>GROUP2  GNAME=GP2;
(4A1,1X,I1,1X,5A1)
>CALIB  CYCLES=50,REFERENCE=1;
```

This command file shows that a 1PL model will be estimated, the two groups are Group 1 and Group 2, and the metric will be defined by setting the mean for Group 1 at 0 and the standard deviation at 1.0, whereas these values will be estimated in the Group 2 sample. The model assumes that the item discrimination parameters are equal across the two groups. Essentially, then, the program is looking for differences in item difficulty parameters that cannot be explained by group differences on the latent trait (i.e., by the test impact).

For each group, BILOG-MG outputs estimates and standard errors for item difficulty (threshold) and discrimination (slope), the latter being equivalent across groups. Also provided is the –2 times the log-likelihood of the solution, which in the present example was 5,173. By groups, the means and standard deviations for the parameter estimates output from BILOG-MG are shown in Table 13.6. Of special note is the adjusted value for the thresholds in Group 2. This value, 0.125, is subtracted from each threshold value in Group 2 to create a set of item difficulty parameter contrasts. For example, the contrast for items 1–5 are shown in the third column of Table 13.7. These results reveal that no item displays statistically significant DIF, as would be expected in this simulated data. If DIF was identified, a test of significance could be performed by calibrating the items again, this time treating them as a single group, and noting the log-likelihood value. As reported in the BILOG analysis, –2 (log-likeli-

TABLE 13.6
Summary Statistics Output From BILOG-MG

PARAMETER	MEAN	STN DEV

GROUP: 1 NUMBER OF ITEMS: 5
THRESHOLD   0.005   1.181
GROUP: 2 NUMBER OF ITEMS: 5
THRESHOLD   0.130   1.147

THRESHOLD MEANS

GROUP	ADJUSTED VALUE
1	0.000
2	0.125

TABLE 13.7
Item Difficulty Contrasts Output From BILOG–MG

| ITEM | GROUP | | 2 – 1 |
	1	2	
D1	−1.545	−1.468	0.077
	0.093*	0.087*	0.128*
D2	−0.560	−0.499	0.061
	0.076*	0.071*	0.104*
D3	0.009	−0.029	−0.029
	0.074*	0.074*	0.104*
D4	0.499	0.359	−0.140
	0.076*	0.078*	0.109*
D5	1.621	1.652	0.031
	0.101*	0.110*	0.149*

* indicates standard error.

hood) was equal to 5,182 when this data was analyzed as a single group. The difference between the two models is 9 on five degrees of freedom, which indicates that the DIF model is not a significant improvement over the single-group model. In other words, any observed DIF (i.e., differences in the difficulty parameter estimates) is not statistically significant. Finally, the BILOG-MG program estimated the mean on the latent variable for Group 2 to be −0.12 with a standard deviation of 0.99 (Group 1 was fixed to have a mean of 0.0 and a standard deviation of 1.0 on the latent-trait scale).

XCALIBRE

XCALIBRE (Assessment Systems Corporation, 1996) is produced by Assessment Systems Corporation and allows a researcher to estimate 2PL and 3PL IRT models. Thus, the program is relevant only for the analyses of dichotomous test items. This program is a Windows 95–based menu-driven system and is part of a larger package for conducting IRT-based test administration and psychometric analysis. For users that do not have Windows 95, a DOS batch-file version of the program is included. This is one of the easiest to use of all the programs reviewed herein and it certainly has one of the better manuals. A chief drawback is that the program does not provide as wide a range of calibration options as other IRT programs reviewed in this chapter nor are extensive examples provided in the manual.

Like almost all of the programs summarized in this chapter, XCALIBRE estimates item parameters using the MML method. By default, the latent-trait distribution is assumed standard normal with the number of quadrature nodes equaling 15, and prior distributions are placed on item parameters. These prior distributions on the item parameters can be changed either within the menu driven system or within a batch file that allows the user to permanently change program default values. Furthermore, a float option is provided for updating priors for the item parameters with each E-M cycle iteration. However, there appears to be no way to change the number of quadrature nodes and or their weights for the latent-trait distribution.

Item parameters are estimated in the "normal metric," that is, $D = 1.702$ is in the equation for the item characteristic curve — the user does not have the option of estimating parameters on either metric. Table 13.8 displays the results of a basic run with XCALIBRE. Note that a 2PL model was estimated because XCALIBRE does not estimate a Rasch model. In this run, the priors on the discrimination parameter (0.75, 0.12) and difficulty parameter (0.0, 2.0) were left at their default values and these priors were allowed to float. The likelihood of the data given the model is not displayed in the output, and, thus, it would not be possible to evaluate the relative fit

TABLE 13.8
Example Output From the XCALIBRE Program

Item	a	error	b	error	c	error	Resid
1	1.00	0.060	−1.66	0.064	0.00	N/A	1.19
2	1.27	0.063	−0.47	0.040	0.00	N/A	1.13
3	1.40	0.062	0.08	0.037	0.00	N/A	0.31
4	1.48	0.062	0.50	0.037	0.00	N/A	1.49
5	1.24	0.065	1.75	0.062	0.00	N/A	0.69

of nested models. As shown in Table 13.8, for each item estimates and standard errors are provided for the item discrimination and difficulty parameters, and a standardized residual term is provided by which to judge item-fit.

Not shown in Table 13.8 is that proportions endorsed, item-test biserials, and point-biserials are also provided for each item as standard output. A few more features should be mentioned before leaving this section. First, XCALIBRE is designed to facilitate the process of "linking" of item parameters from different measures, assuming there is an anchor test. This is an important capacity in educational testing situations, where different items may be administered to different classes, which in turn, may have different means on the latent variable. Note that the linking items must have known item parameter values and are treated as fixed parameters by XCALIBRE. As for scoring examinees, with a click of a button, examinees may be scored with either ML, EAP, or MAP methods. However, the options for scale transformations are not as extensive as those available in BILOG. Finally, graphical representations of the test information curve is provided, as well as an estimate of test score reliability and the average information a test provides. Further review and evaluation of XCALIBRE can be found in Gierl and Ackerman (1996).

MULTILOG 6

The MULTILOG 6 (Thissen, 1991) program allows the user to estimate item parameters for IRT models based on data sets that contain dichotomous or polytomous item response formats. Specifically, the program can estimate parameters of 1PL, 2PL, and 3PL test models, Samejima's graded response model, Master's partial credit model, or Bock's nominal response model (see chap. 5 on polytomous IRT models). All models estimated with MULTILOG are truly "logistic," which means that there is no $D = 1.7$ scaling factor. This means that resulting item-discrimination (slope) parameters will be approximately 1.7 times higher than they would be if reported in the normal metric.

The program command file is created by running the "INFORLOG" program, which requires typing in a series of commands. The INFORLOG program then creates a "filename.TEN" command file that is subsequently submitted to the MULTILOG program. Parameter estimation is carried out using the MML approach, and a large number of options are provided for the user that may affect parameter estimation. For example, among the options a user may (a) specify the number of quadrature nodes and their weights, (b) change the default prior distributions for the item parameters, (c) change the default number of estimation cycles, (d) fix item parameters to specific values, and (e) constrain various item parameters to equality. These latter features make IRT modeling with MULTILOG somewhat analogous to covariance structure modeling programs such as LISREL (Joreskog & Sorbom, 1996) or EQS (Bentler & Wu, 1995).

Table 13.9 displays example output from MULTILOG for a graded-response model estimated on the polytomous example data set. As can be seen in the table, the program does not provide a wealth of descriptive statistics regarding the test items, such as biserial or polyserial correlations. For each test item, an estimate is given for the slope and difficulty parameters and their respective standard errors. No statistical test of item fit is provided. However, the proportion of examinees who responded in each response category and that predicted by the estimated model parameters is provided. In turn, these values may be used to gauge item fit.

For each item, MULTILOG provides the psychometric information at 10 points along the trait level continuum. These values are useful for judging where an item is discriminating best. Furthermore, by summing across the item information curves, the test information at 10 points on the trait continuum is also routinely provided in the output. The test information values for the five example items are shown on the bottom of Table

TABLE 13.9
Selected Output From the MULTILOG Program

0ITEM 1: 5 GRADED CATEGORIES

P(#) ESTIMATE (S.E.)

A	1	1.56	(0.10)
B(1)	2	-2.02	(0.12)
B(2)	3	-0.94	(0.07)
B(3)	4	0.02	(0.06)
B(4)	5	1.09	(0.09)

@THETA:	-2.0	-1.5	-1.0	-0.5	0.0	0.5	1.0	1.5	2.0
I(THETA):	0.68	0.73	0.75	0.75	0.75	0.74	0.69	0.57	0.38

OBSERVED AND EXPECTED COUNTS/PROPORTIONS IN

CATEGORY(K):	1	2	3	4	5
OBS. FREQ.	92	175	241	259	233
OBS. PROP.	0.09	0.18	0.24	0.26	0.23
EXP. PROP.	0.19	0.17	0.24	0.26	0.23

TOTAL TEST INFORMATION

THETA:	-2.0	-1.5	-1.0	-0.5	0.0	0.5	1.0	1.5	2.0
I(THETA):	3.6	4.4	5.1	5.4	5.5	5.4	5.1	4.4	3.3
SE(THETA):	0.53	0.48	0.44	0.43	0.43	0.43	0.44	0.48	0.55

13.9. Note that a constant of 1.0 is added to these values because a standard normal prior for estimating trait level is assumed. Clearly, the example test provides peaked information, and, thus, the smallest standard errors occur for examinees around the middle of the trait continuum.

After the item parameter estimates have been derived, scoring examinees with MULTILOG requires a second run through the INFORLOG program. Two options are provided in terms of scoring: (a) ML and (b) MAP. One of the really nice features of the MULTILOG program is that it provides researchers with methods of handling multiple-group data and for estimating mean differences on the latent variable among groups. Finally, MULTILOG is the only program that allows for higher order moments of a latent-trait distribution to be estimated by means of Johnson curves.

PARSCALE 3.2

PARSCALE 3.2 (Muraki & Bock, 1993) is essentially an extension of the BILOG and BILOG-MG program that allows the estimation of item parameters for models based on data sets that contain dichotomous and/or polytomous item response formats. Specifically, the program can estimate parameters of 1PL, 2PL, and 3PL test models, the graded-response model, a rating scale version of the graded response model, the partial credit model and the generalized partial credit model (see chap. 5 for details). However, unlike MULTILOG, at this time the PARSCALE program does not allow estimation of item parameters for the nominal response model. PARSCALE does, however, contain several features the that MULTILOG does not. For example, for any model, PARSCALE allows the researcher to compute item information at numerous points across the trait range and then saves these values into an external text file for easy future use. Second, PARSCALE also provides more advanced chi-square item fit statistics (see Muraki, 1997).

In the most recent version of PARSCALE, options are provided for the analyses of data drawn from more than one group of examinees. Specifically, the program can be used to perform a DIF analyses of graded response data. The specific procedure used is highly similar to the DIF analysis routine in BILOG-MG. For example, a researcher may constrain slope parameters to equality across examinee groups and then test for group differences in item location while simultaneously estimating group differences on the latent trait. A second recent addition is that the PARSCALE program facilitates the analysis of "rater" effects. Essentially, examinees who are scored from different raters are treated as being sampled from different groups. In this way, a rater-effects analysis becomes analogous to a DIF-analysis model.

PARSCALE runs in DOS mode and a batch command file must be created just like in BILOG. In terms of parameter estimation, the user is given the choice of whether model parameters are to be estimated with $D = 1.7$ (normal metric) or $D = 1.0$ (logistic metric); the normal metric is the default. For example, the input commands for running a partial credit model on the polytomous example data set are shown here. Parameter estimation is conducted using a MML approach. However, unlike in the other programs, Newton cycles are not used in the EM algorithm, thus it is recommended to use a greater number of EM cycles (Note: beta version 3.5 includes Newton cycles).

```
EXAMPLE  POLYTOMOUS  DATA
PARTIAL  CREDIT  MODEL
>COMMENT  ;
 ALL  ITEMS  HAVE  5  CATEGORIES,  BLOCKS=5,  SCALE  =  1.0
>FILE  DFNAME='TRUEP.DAT',SAVE;
>SAVE  PARM='TRUEP.PAR',INF='TRUEP.INF',SCORE='TRUEP.SCO';
>INPUT  NIDW=2,NTOTAL=5,NTEST=1,LENGTH=(5),NFMT=1;
(2A1,1X,5A1)
>TEST1  TNAME=TRUEP,ITEM=(1(1)5),NBLOCK=5,SLOPE=(1(0)5);
>BLOCK1  BNAME=TRPBL1,NITEMS=5,NCAT=5,REPEAT=5,CAD=0.0,CLS;
>CAL  PARTIAL,LOGISTIC,SCALE=1.0,NQPTS=20,CYCLE=(100,2,2,2,2),
 ITEMFIT=5;
>SCORE  EAP,NQPTS=30,SMEAN=0.0,SSD=1.0;
```

A vast number of options that may affect item parameter estimation are provided for the user. For example, the user may: (a) specify the number of quadrature nodes and their weights (note that it is recommended to use a large number, perhaps 30, of quadrature points with polytomous items), (b) change the default prior distributions for the item intercepts, thresholds, or slopes, and/or (c) change the default number of estimation cycles. Other options do not affect parameter estimation, such as specifying the number of score groups used for the item-fit statistics but are extremely useful. The program also makes it easy to estimate item parameters within "blocks" of items. This is important when the items within a measure do not all have the same number of response categories. In these situations different models need to be applied to the different item types. As for scoring examinees, maximum likelihood, weighted maximum likelihood (a robust technique), and expected a posteriori scoring methods are provided.

Table 13.10 displays some of the basic descriptive statistics for Item 1 output from the first phase of PARSCALE. As shown in the top portion of the table, for each item the number of examinee responses and percentage endorsement in each response category is provided. Furthermore, as shown in the bottom potion of Table 13.10, the item means, initial slope estimates, and Pearson and polyserial item-test correlations are provided.

TABLE 13.10
Descriptive Statistics for Item 1 Output From PARSCALE Phase 1

ITEM NAME	TOTAL	NOT–PRESENT	OMIT	1	2	3	4	5
0001								
FREQ.	1000.00	0.00	0.00	92	175	241	259	233
PERCENT		0.00	0.00	9.2	17.5	24.1	25.9	23.3
CUM FREQ.				92	267	508	767	1000

BLOCK ITEM	RESPONSE MEAN (S.D.)	TOTAL SCORES MEAN (S.D.)	PEARSON POLYSERIAL	INITIAL SLOPES
SBLOCK1				
1 0001	3.366	15.364	0.717	1.000
	(1.265)	(5.115)	0.757	

Category	Scoring	Mean	S.D.	Parameter
1	1.00	8.804	3.194	0.000
2	2.00	11.491	3.628	1.338
3	3.00	13.988	3.620	0.674
4	4.00	17.181	3.633	–0.009
5	5.00	20.266	3.497	–0.707

Finally, the basic descriptive statistics include the raw total scale scores for examinees who responded in each of the categories. In this example item, people who responded in the first category had an average raw total score of 8.8 and people who responded in the fifth category had an average raw total score of 20.266. Table 13.11 displays some example output for Item 1 from the calibration phase (Phase 2) of PARSCALE. As shown, for each test item, an estimate and standard error is provided for the item step, slope (which is fixed to 1.0 in this example), and location parameters. On the bottom of Table 13.11 are displayed the chi-square item-fit statistics. Not shown in the tables but included in the output is the –2 times the log-likelihood values.

RUMM

The RUMM program (Sheridan, Andrich, & Luo, 1996) is a Windows 95 based menu-driven package that allows researchers to fit Rasch models to multiple-choice aptitude data or to multiple-category attitude or person-ality data. For Rasch modeling, the RUMM program is perhaps the most comprehensive system for analyzing psychometric test data that we have

TABLE 13.11
Output From Calibration Phase of PARSCALE

ITEM BLOCK 1	SBLOCK1					
SCORING FUNCTION	:	1.000	2.000	3.000	4.000	5.000
STEP PARAMTER	:	0.000	1.143	0.322	−0.392	−1.074
S.E.	:	0.000	0.134	0.103	0.093	0.095

ITEM BLOCK	2 BLOCK					
SCORING FUNCTION	:	1.000	2.000	3.000	4.000	5.000
STEP PARAMTER	:	0.000	0.885	0.673	−0.391	−1.168
S.E.	:	0.000	0.122	0.102	0.090	0.103

ITEM	BLOCK	SLOPE S.E.	LOCATION S.E.	GUESSING S.E.
0001	1	1.000	−0.415	0.000
		0.000	0.034	0.000
0002	2	1.000	−0.163	0.000
		0.000	0.033	0.000

BLOCK	ITEM	CHI-SQUARE	D.F.	PROB.
SBLOCK1	0001	16.79144	14.	0.267
BLOCK	0002	24.84439	14.	0.036
BLOCK	0003	32.19513	14.	0.004
BLOCK	0004	17.01120	13.	0.198
BLOCK	0005	23.44104	12.	0.024
TOTAL		114.28320	67.	0.000

encountered. The program is based on a hierarchical data-base system that makes it very easy to enter data and specify subject identification numbers, estimate the parameters of a model, examine both item- and person-fit, plot and inspect relevant distributions or item response curves, and then conduct another modified analysis. The program automatically saves all program and analysis specifications, so it is easy to go back and check previous results, and furthermore, the user does not have to go through a tedious set-up process every time he or she wants to run a new analysis on a previously examined data set.

There are five steps in analyzing a data set with RUMM, and we provide some detail on each so that the reader can get a feel for the program and its capacities. The first stage is creating a test project. All future analysis conducted on a particular test will be saved under the test project heading. In the second stage, the user must specify, using menus, the data file structure (e.g., single line per person or multiple-line per person). In the third stage, the data set is read into the program, and then menus are used to specify the file structure. It is in this stage that the user can specify as many as two unique subject identifiers, how many response categories each item has, how each item is to be scored, and whether the test is a multiple-choice or category rating scale. In the fourth stage, the researcher again uses menus and radio dial buttons to select an analysis name (each unique analysis must have its own name), determine the exact analysis specifications, and edit analysis specifications (e.g., delete particular items or persons). After the fourth stage, the estimated parameters and fit statistics are computed, and in the fifth stage the user is presented with a wealth of tools for graphically examining the output and/or saving it to a file.

Among the many options available in RUMM are basic descriptive statistics regarding item parameters, several tests of fit including item- and person-fit as well as a likelihood ratio test for nested models. The user can also graph, for any single item or group of items, category probability curves or item characteristic curves. Furthermore, the program can order and display subjects' item response patterns as to their degree of person-fit and display a listing, or the program can order items according to difficulty and display Guttman patterns.

Although the RUMM manual (which comes in zip files) is rich in concretely detailing how to do specific types of data analyses, it is a little sparse in technical details regarding which algorithms the program uses, how they are implemented, and what various output actually means. In other words, a user needs to have some background in Rasch modeling and parameter estimation to fully understand the program and all its output. A good selection of readings on various Rasch modeling topics is provided in the back of the RUMM manual.

A few more features should be mentioned before leaving this section. First, once a basic analysis is conducted, the RUMM program allows the user to go back and do a more targeted reanalysis. For example, the user may eliminate certain items or persons and reestimate item and person parameters. Furthermore, the user may wish to conduct analysis on separate groups of examinees such as men or women only. The RUMM program is also similar to the XCALIBRE program in that it is designed to facilitate the process of "linking" of item parameters from different measures, assuming there is an anchor test. Finally, we briefly list some of the other attractive program features. Specifically, the RUMM program facilitates distracter analysis, equating subgroups of items, rescoring an existing set of response vectors, appending a new set of data to an old set, and combining item sets that contain different item response formats. In sum, the program is a very comprehensive Rasch modeling package.

CONCLUSION AND SUMMARY

In this chapter a number of popular programs have been briefly introduced and summarized. Clearly, these current IRT programs vary tremendously on a number of dimensions such as type of models estimated, user friendliness, breath and scope of user's manual, fit statistics provided, examinee scoring options, graphical output features, and the specific numerical estimation algorithm used. In regard to this latter critical issue, although many programs use a marginal maximum likelihood procedure to estimate item parameters, a default run of the same data set through the various programs will generally not produce the exact same results. This is partially due to the specific numerical acceleration routines implemented by the various programs as well as numerous other factors. This is important to be aware of, and researchers should not assume the IRT parameters output from these programs are like OLS regression coefficients, where all software programs yield exactly the same results with the same data set.

Generally speaking, none of the currently available programs can be used with authority by researchers who are not well versed in the IRT literature. The user manuals are not really targeted at explaining the nuts and bolts of IRT methods to general audiences. There are many details not provided in this chapter that the applied researcher will need to become familiar with in order to use any of the reviewed programs effectively. Hence, it is advised that users become familiar with the existing literature surrounding the various programs and the various user options contained within. We also hope to see more research that investigates how various program options affect item- and person-parameter estimation. Currently, it is fair to state that some IRT programs contain user options that have unexplored empirical consequences. It should also be noted that many of these programs are currently being updated. For example, in a beta version, TESTFACT has been extensively revised and now allows up the estimation of up to 10 factors (5 was previous limit) and includes procedures to conduct bi-factor analyses. Other programs, such as MULTILOG, are being converted to Windows versions. Finally, in closing we note that a common feature of all the IRT software programs is that they are stand-alone packages. At present we are aware of no IRT programs available as part of commonly used mainframe statistical packages such as SAS or SPSS. We anticipate that IRT methods will see more widespread application when estimation routines are incorporated into these major packages.

References

Ackerman, T. A. (1992). A didactic explanation of item bias, item impact, and item validity from a multidimensional perspective. *Journal of Educational Measurement, 29,* 67–91.

Ackerman, T. A. (1994). Creating a test information profile for a two-dimensional latent space. *Applied Psychological Measurement, 18,* 257–275.

Adams, R. A., & Wilson, M. (1996). Formulating the Rasch model as a mixed coefficients multinomial logit. In G. Engelhard & M. Wilson (Eds.), Objective measurement III: Theory into practice. Norwood, NJ: Ablex.

Adams, R. A., Wilson, M., & Wang, W.-C. (1997). The multidimensional random coefficients multinomial logit model. *Applied Psychological Measurement, 21,* 1–23.

Albert, J. H. (1992). Bayesian estimation of normal ogive item response curves using Gibbs sampling. *Journal of Educational Statistics, 17,* 251–269.

American College Testing. (1993). *COMPASS user's guide.* Iowa City, IA.

Anastasi, A., & Urbina, S. (1997). *Psychological testing.* Upper Saddle River, NJ: Prentice-Hall.

Andersen, E. B. (1970). Asymptotic properties of conditional maximum likelihood estimators. *Journal of the Royal Statistical Society, Series B, 32,* 283–301.

Andersen, E. B. (1972). The numerical solution of a set of conditional estimation equations. *Journal of the Royal Statistical Society, Series B, 34,* 42–54.

Andersen, E. B. (1995). Polytomous Rasch models and their estimation. In G. H. Fischer & I. W. Molenaar (Eds.), *Rasch models: Foundations, recent developments, and applications.* New York: Springer-Verlag.

Andrich, D. (1978a). Application of a psychometric model to ordered categories which are scored with successive integers. *Applied Psychological Measurement, 2,* 581–594.

Andrich, D. (1978b). A rating formulation for ordered response categories. *Psychometrika, 43,* 561–573.

Andrich, D. (1982). An index of person separation in latent trait theory, the traditional KR 20 index and the Guttman scale response pattern. *Educational Research and Perspectives, 9,* 95–104.

Andrich, D. (1988a). A general form of Rasch's extended logistic model for partial credit scoring. *Applied Measurement in Education, 1,* 363–378.

Andrich, D. (1988b). *Rasch models for measurement.* Newbury Park, CA: Sage.

Andrich, D. (1995). Distinctive and incompatible properties of two common classes of IRT models for graded responses. *Applied Psychological Measurement, 19,* 101–119.

Andrich, D. (1996). Theoretical and empirical evidence on the dichotomization of graded responses. In G. Engelhard & M. Wilson (Eds.), *Objective measurement III: Theory into practice.* Norwood, NJ: Ablex.

Andrich, D. (1997). An hyperbolic cosine IRT model for unfolding direct response of persons to items. In W. J. Van der Linden & R. Hambleton (Eds.), *Handbook of modern item response theory* (pp. 187–208). New York: Springer-Verlag.

Andrich, D., & Styles, I. (1994). Psychometric evidence of growth spurts in early adolescence. *Journal of Early Adolescence, 14,* 328–344.

Angoff, W. (1982). Summary and derivation of equating methods used at ETS. In P. Holland & D. Rubin (Eds.), *Test equating.* New York: Academic Press.

Assessment Systems Corporation. (1991). *MicroCAT 3.0* [computer program]. St. Paul, MN: Assessment Systems Corporation.

Assessment Systems Corporation. (1996). *User's manual for the XCALIBRE marginal maximum-likelihood estimation program.* St. Paul, MN: Assessment Systems Corp.

Baker, F. B. (1992). Equating tests under the graded response model. *Applied Psychological Measurement, 16,* 87–96.

Baker, F. B. (1993). Equating tests under the nominal response model. *Applied Psychological Measurement, 17,* 239–251.

Baker, F. B. (1997). Empirical sampling distributions of equating coefficients for graded and nominal response instruments. *Applied Psychological Measurement, 21,* 157–172.

Baker, F. B., & Al-Karni, A. (1991). A comparison of two procedures for computing IRT equating coefficients. *Journal of Educational Measurement, 28,* 147–162.

Balasubramanian, S. K., & Kamakura, W. A. (1989). Measuring consumer attitudes toward the marketplace with tailored interviews. *Journal of Marketing Research, 26,* 311–326.

Baumeister, R. F., & Tice, D. M. (1988). Metatraits. *Journal of Personality, 56,* 571–598.

Bejar, I., & Wingersky, M. S. (1981). *An application of item response theory to equating the Test of Standard Written English (College Board Report No. 81-8).* Princeton, NJ: Educational Testing Service, 1981. (ETS No. 81-35).

Bentler, P. M., & Wu, E. J. C. (1995). *EQS for Windows User's Guide.* Encino, CA: Mulivariate Software, Inc.

Bereiter, C. (1963). Some persisting dilemmas in the measurement of change. In C. W. Harris (Ed.), *Problems in measuring change* (pp. 3–20). Madison: University of Wisconsin Press.

Binet, A., & Simon, T. (1905). Methodes nouvelles pour le diagnostic du niveau intellectuel des anormaux. *L'Annee Psychologique, 11,* 245–336.

Birenbaum, M. (1986). Effect of dissimulation motivation and anxiety on response pattern appropriateness measures. *Applied Psychological Measurement, 10,* 167–174.

Birnbaum, A. (1957). *Efficient design and use of tests of a mental ability for various decision-making problems.* Series Report No. 58-16. Project No. 7755-23, USAF School of Aviation Medicine, Randolph Air Force Base, Texas: January.

Birnbaum, A. (1958a). *Further considerations of efficiency in tests of a mental ability.* Technical Report No. 17. Project No. 7755-23, USAF School of Aviation Medicine, Randolph Air Force Base, Texas.

Birnbaum, A. (1958b). *On the estimation of mental ability.* Series Report No. 15. Project No. 7755-23, USAF School of Aviation Medicine, Randolph Air Force Base, Texas: January.

Birnbaum, A. (1968). Some latent trait models and their use in inferring an examinee's ability. In F. M. Lord & M. R. Novick (Eds.), *Statistical theories of mental test scores.* Reading, MA: Addison-Wesley.

Bock, R. D. (1972). Estimating item parameters and latent ability when responses are scored in two or more nominal categories. *Psychometrika, 37,* 29–51.

Bock, R. D. (1997). A brief history of item response theory. *Educational Measurement: Issues and Practice, 16*, 21–33.

Bock, R. D., & Aitken, M. (1981). Marginal maximum likelihood estimation of item parameters: Application of an EM algorithm. *Psychometrika, 46*, 443–459.

Bock, R. D., Gibbons, R., & Muraki, E. J. (1988). Full information item factor analysis. *Applied Psychological Measurement, 12*, 261–280.

Bock, R. D., & Lieberman, M. (1970). Fitting a response model for n dichotomously scored items. *Psychometrika, 35*, 179–197.

Bock, R. D., & Mislevy, R. J. (1982). Adaptive EAP estimation of ability in a microcomputer environment. *Applied Psychological Measurement, 6*, 431–444.

Bock, R. D., Thissen, D., & Zimowsky, M. F. (1997). IRT estimation of domain scores. *Journal of Educational Measurement, 34*, 197–211.

Bock, R. D., & Zimowski, M. F. (1996). Multiple group IRT. In W. J. van der Linden & R. K. Hambleton (Eds.), *Handbook of modern item response theory*. New York: Springer.

Bollen, K., & Lennox, R. (1991). Conventional wisdom on measurement: A structural equation perspective. *Psychological Bulletin, 110*, 305–314.

Brainerd, C. J. (1978). The stage question in cognitive-developmental theory. *The Behavioral and Brain Sciences, 2*, 173–213.

Buck, G., Tatsuoka, K., & Kostin, I. (in press). Exploratory rule space analysis of the Test of English for International Communication. *Journal of Language and Teaching*.

Candell, G. L., & Drasgow, F. (1988). An iterative procedure for linking metrics and assessing item bias in item response theory. *Applied Psychological Measurement, 12*, 253–260.

Carpenter, P. A., Just, M. A., & Shell, P. (1990). What one intelligence test measures: A theoretical account of processing in the Raven's Progressive Matrices Test. *Psychological Review, 97*.

Carroll, J. B. (1945). The effect of difficulty and chance success on correlations between items or between tests. *Psychometrika, 10*, 1–19.

Chen, W. H., & Thissen, D. (1997). Local dependence indices for item pairs using item response theory. *Journal of Educational and Behavioral Statistics, 22*, 265–289.

Chopin, B. (1968). An item bank using sample-free calibration. *Nature, 219*, 870–872.

Chopin, B. (1983). *A fully conditional estimation procedure for Rasch model parameters*. Report No. 196. Los Angeles, CA: University of California, Graduate School of Education Center for the Study of Evaluation.

Christoffersson, A. (1975). Factor analysis of dichotomized variables. *Psychometrika, 40*, 5–32.

Clauser, B. E., & Mazor, K. M. (1998). Using statistical procedures to identify differentially functioning test items. *Educational Measurement: Issues and Practice, 17*, 31–44.

Cohen, A. S., Kim, S., & Wollack, J. A. (1996). An investigation of the likelihood ratio test for detection of differential item functioning. *Applied Psychological Measurement, 20*, 15–26.

Cohen, J., & Cohen, P. (1975). Applied multiple regression/correlation analysis for the behavioral sciences. Hillsdale, NJ: Lawrence Erlbaum Associates.

College Board. (1990). *Coordinator's notebook for the computerized placement tests*. Princeton, NJ: Educational Testing Service.

Collins, L., & Horn, J. (1991). *Best methods for analyzing change* (pp. 184–197). Washington, DC: American Psychological Association Books.

Cook, W. W., & Medley, D. M. (1954). Proposed hostility and pharisaic-virtue scales for the MMPI. *Journal of Applied Psychology, 38*, 414–418.

Costa, P. T., Jr., & McCrae, R. R. (1985). *The NEO Personality Inventory manual*. Odessa, FL: Psychological Assessment Resources.

Costa, P. T., & McCrae, R. R. (1992). *The revised NEO personality inventory (NEO-PI-R) and NEO five-factor inventory (NEO-FFI) professional manual*. Odessa, FL: Psychological Assessment Resources.

Cronbach, L. (1988). Five perspectives on the validity argument. In H. Wainer & H. I. Brown (Eds.), *Test validity*. Hillsdale, NJ: Lawrece Erlbaum Associates.

Cronbach, L., & Furby, L. (1970). How should we measure change—Or should we? *Psychological Bulletin, 74*, 68–80.

Cronbach, L., Gleser, G. C., Nanda, H., & Rajaratnam, N. (1972). *The dependability of behavioral measurements: Theory of generalizability for scores and profiles*. New York: John Wiley and Sons.

Curran, L. T., & Wise, L. L. (1994). *Evaluation and implementation of CAT-ASVAB*. Paper presented at the annual meeting of the American Psychological Association, Los Angeles.

Daniel, M. H. (1999). Behind the scenes: Using new measurement methods on DAS and KAIT. In S. E. Embretson & S. L. Hershberger (Eds.), *The new rules of measurement*. Mahwah, NJ: Lawrence Erlbaum Associates.

Davison, M. L., & Sharma, A. R. (1990). Parametric statistics and levels of measurement: Factorial designs and multiple regressions. *Psychological Bulletin, 107*, 394–400.

De Ayala, R. J. (1992). The nominal response model in computerized adaptive testing. *Applied Psychological Measurement, 16*, 327–343.

DeLeeuw, J., & Verhelst, N. D. (1986). Maximum likelihood estimation in generalized Rasch models. *Journal of Educational Statistics, 11*, 183–196.

DiBello, L. V., Stout, W. F., & Roussos, L. (1995). Unified cognitive psychometric assessment likelihood-based classification techniques. In P. D. Nichols, S. F. Chipman, & R. L. Brennan (Eds.), *Cognitively diagnostic assessment*. Hillsdale, NJ: Lawrence Erlbaum Associates.

Divgi, D. R. (1985). A minimum chi-square method for developing a common metric in item response theory. *Applied Psychological Measurement, 9*, 413–415.

Divgi, D. R. (1986). *Determining the sensitivity of CAT-ASVAB scores to changes in item response curves with medium of administration* (Report No. 86-189). Alexandria, VA: Center for Naval Analyses.

Divgi, D. R., & Stoloff, P. H. (1986). *Effect of the medium of administration on ASVAB item response curves* (Report No. 86-24). Alexandria, VA: Center for Naval Analyses.

Dodd, B. G. (1990). The effect of item selection procedure and stepsize on computerized adaptive attitude measurement using the rating scale model. *Applied Psychological Measurement, 14*, 355–366.

Dodd, B. G., & De Ayala, R. J. (1994). Item information as a function of threshold values in the rating scale model. In M. Wilson (Ed.), *Objective measurement: Theory and practice* (Vol. 2, pp. 201–317). Norwood, NJ: Ablex.

Dodd, B. G., De Ayala, R. J., & Koch, W. R. (1995). Computerized adaptive testing with polytomous items. *Applied Psychological Methods, 19*, 5–22.

Dodd, B. G., & Koch, W. R. (1987). Effects of variations in item step values on item and test information in the partial credit model. *Applied Psychological Measurement, 11*, 371–384.

Douglas, J., Roussos, L. A., & Stout, W. F. (1996). Item bundle DIF hypothesis testing: Identifying suspect bundles and assessing their DIF. *Journal of Educational Measurement, 33*, 465–485.

Drasgow, F. (1982). Biased test items and differential validity. *Psychological Bulletin, 92*, 526–531.

Drasgow, F. (1987). Study of the measurement bias of two standardized psychological tests. *Journal of Applied Psychology, 72*, 19–29.

Drasgow, F., & Parsons, C. (1983). Applications of unidimensional item response theory models to multidimensional data. *Applied Psychological Measurement, 7*, 189–199.

Drasgow, F., Levine, M. V., & McLaughlin, M. E. (1987). Detecting inappropriate test scores with optimal and practical appropriateness indices. *Applied Psychological Measurement, 11*, 59–79.

Drasgow, F., Levine, M. V., & McLaughlin, M. E. (1991). Appropriateness measurement for some multidimensional test batteries. *Applied Psychological Measurement, 15,* 171–191.

Drasgow, F., Levine, M. V., & Williams, E. A. (1985). Appropriateness measurement with polychotomous item response models and standardized indices. *British Journal of Mathematical and Statistical Psychology, 38,* 67–86.

Drasgow, F., Levine, M. V., & Zickar, M. J. (1996). Optimal identification of mismeasured individuals. *Applied Measurement in Education, 9,* 47–64.

Educational Testing Service. (1993). *GRE 1993–94 guide to the use of the Graduate Record Examinations Program.* Princeton, NJ: ETS.

Educational Testing Service. (1998). *Grow in school: Achievement gains from the fourth to the eight grade.* Policy Information Center: Princeton, NJ: ETS.

Ellis, B. B., Becker, P., & Kimmel, H. D. (1993). An item response theory evaluation of an English version of the Trier personality Inventory (TPI). *Journal of Cross-Cultural Psychology, 24,* 133–148.

Ellis, B. B., Minsel, B., & Becker, P. (1989). Evaluation of attitude survey translations: An investigation using item response theory. *International Journal of Psychology, 24,* 665–684.

Embretson, S. E. (1983). Construct validity: Construct representation versus nomothetic span. *Psychological Bulletin, 93,* 179–197.

Embretson, S. E. (1984). A general latent trait model for response processes. *Psychometrika, 49,* 175–186.

Embretson, S. E. (1985). *Test design: Developments in psychology and psychometrics.* New York: Academic Press.

Embretson, S. E. (1988, June). *Psychometric models and cognitive design systems.* Paper presented at the annual meeting of the Psychometric Society, Los Angeles, CA.

Embretson, S. E. (1991). A multidimensional latent trait model for measuring learning and change. *Psychometrika, 56,* 495–516.

Embretson, S. E. (1994a). Application of cognitive design systems to test development. In C. R. Reynolds (Ed.), *Cognitive assessment: A multidisciplinary perspective* (pp. 107–135). New York: Plenum Press.

Embretson, S. E. (1994b). Comparing changes between groups: Some perplexities arising from psychometrics. In D. Laveault, B. D. Zumbo, M. E. Gessaroli, & M. W. Boss (Eds.), *Modern theories of measurement: Problems and issues.* Ottawa: Edumetric Research Group, University of Ottawa.

Embretson, S. E. (1995a). Developments toward a cognitive design system for psychological tests. In D. Lupinsky & R. Dawis (Eds.), *Assessing individual differences in human behavior.* Palo Alto, CA: Davies-Black Publishing Company.

Embretson, S. E. (1995b). A measurement model for linking individual change to processes and knowledge: Application to mathematical learning. *Journal of Educational Measurement, 32,* 277–294.

Embretson, S. E. (1995c, August). *The new rules of measurement.* Paper presented at the annual meeting of the American Psychological Association, New York.

Embretson, S. E. (1995d). The role of working memory capacity and general control processes in intelligence. *Intelligence, 20,* 169–190.

Embretson, S. E. (1995e, June). *Structured latent trait modes in measuring the modifiability of ability to stress.* Paper presented at the annual meeting of the Psychometric Society, Minneapolis, MN.

Embretson, S. E. (1996a). Item response theory models and inferential bias in multiple group comparisons. *Applied Psychological Measurement, 20,* 201–212.

Embretson, S. E. (1996b). The new rules of measurement. *Psychological Assessment, 8,* 341–349.

Embretson, S. E. (1997). Structured ability models in tests designed from cognitive theory. In M. Wilson, G. Engelhard, & K. Draney (Eds.), *Objective Measurement III* (pp. 223–236). Norwood, NJ: Ablex.

Embretson, S. E. (1998a). A cognitive design system approach to generating valid tests: Application to abstract reasoning. *Psychological Methods, 3,* 300–326.

Embretson, S. E. (1998b, August). *Modifiability in lifespan development: Multidimensional Rasch Model for learning and change.* Paper presented at the annual meeting of the American Psychological Association, San Francisco, CA.

Embretson, S. E. (1998c, October). *Multidimensional measurement from dynamic tests: Abstract reasoning under stress.* Presidential address for the Society of Multivariate Experimental Psychology, Mahwah, NJ.

Embretson, S. E. (in press). Generating abstract reasoning items with cognitive theory. In S. Irvine & P. Kyllonen (Eds.), *Item generation for test development.* Mahwah, NJ: Lawrence Erlbaum Associates.

Embretson, S. E., & McCollam, K. M. (in press). A multicomponent Rasch model for measuring covert processes. In M. Wilson & G. Engelhard. *Objective Measurement V.* In G. Engelhard & M. Wilson (Eds.), Objective measurement III: Theory into practice. Norwood, NJ: Ablex.

Embretson, S. E., & Wetzel, D. (1987). Component latent trait models for paragraph comprehension tests. *Applied Psychological Measurement, 11,* 175–193.

Engelhard, G., & Wilson, M. (1996). (Eds.). *Objective measurement III: Theory into practice.* Norwood, NJ: Ablex.

Etazadi-Amoli, J., & McDonald, R. P. (1983). A second generation nonlinear factor analysis. *Psychometrika, 48,* 315–342.

Feldt, L. S., & Brennan, R. L. (1989). Reliability. In R. L. Linn (Ed.), *Educational measurement* (3rd ed., pp. 105–146). New York: Macmillan.

Fischer, G. H. (1973). Linear logistic test model as an instrument in educational research. *Acta Psychologica, 37,* 359–374.

Fischer, G. H. (1974). *Einfuhrung in die Theorie psychologischer Tests* (Introduction to mental test theory.) Berne: Huber.

Fischer, G. H. (1981). On the existence and uniqueness of maximum-likelihood estimates in the Rasch model. *Psychometrika, 46,* 59–77.

Fischer, G. (1995). Derivations of the Rasch model. In G. Fischer & I. Molenaar (Eds.), *Rasch models: Foundations, recent developments, and applications.* New York: Springer-Verlag.

Fischer, K. W., Pipp, S. L., & Bullock, D. (1984). Detecting discontinuities in development: Methods and measurement. In R. N. Ende & R. Harmon (Eds.), *Continuities and discontinuities in development.* Norwood, NJ: Ablex.

Fitzpatrick, S. J., Choi, S. W., Chen, S., Hou, L., & Dodd, B. G. (1994). IRTINFO: A SAS macro program to compute item and test information. *Applied Psychological Measurement, 18,* 390.

Flannery, W. P., Reise, S. P., & Widaman, K. F. (1995). An item response theory analysis of the general and academic scales of the Self-Description Questionnaire II. *Journal of Research in Personality, 29,* 168–188.

Fraser, C. (1988). *NOHARM II: A Fortran program for fitting unidimensional and multidimensional normal ogive models of latent trait theory.* Armidale, N.S.W.: University of New England, Centre for Behavioral Studies.

Gagne, R. M. (1962). The acquisition of knowledge. *Psychological Review, 69,* 355–365.

Galton, F. (1883). *Inquiry into human faculty and its development.* London: Macmillan.

Gangestad, S., & Snyder, M. (1985). To carve nature at its joints: On the existence of discrete classes in personality. *Psychological Review, 92,* 317–349.

Gibbons, R. D., Clark, D. C., Cavanaugh, S. V., & Davis, J. M. (1985). Application of modern psychometric theory in psychiatric research. *Journal of Psychiatric Research, 19,* 43–55.

Gibbons, R. D., & Hedeker, D. R. (1992). Full information item bi-factor analysis. *Psychometrika, 57,* 423–436.

Gierl, M. J., & Ackerman, T. (1996). XCALIBRE Marginal maximum-likelihood estimation program, Windows version 1.10. *Applied Psychological Measurement, 20,* 303–307.

Goldstein, H. (1980). Dimensionality, bias, independence and measurement scale problems in latent trait test score models. *British Journal of Mathematical and Statistical Psychology, 33,* 234–246.

Gray-Little, B., Williams, V. S. L., & Hancock, T. D. (1997). An item response theory analysis of the Rosenberg Self-Esteem Scale. *Personality and Social Psychology Bulletin, 23,* 443–451.

Green, B. F., Bock, R. D., Humphreys, L. G., Linn, R. L., & Reckase, M. D. (1984). Technical guidelines for assessing computerized adaptive tests. *Journal of Educational Measurement, 21,* 347–360.

Green, K. E., & Smith, R. M. (1987). A comparison of two methods of decomposing item difficulties. *Journal of Educational Statistics, 12,* 369–381.

Guilford, J. P. (1954). *Psychometric methods.* New York: McGraw-Hill.

Gulliksen, H. (1950). *Theory of mental tests.* New York: Wiley.

Gustafsson, J. E. (1980). A solution of the conditional estimation problem for long tests in the Rasch model for dichotomous items. *Educational and Psychological Measurement, 40,* 337–385.

Hambleton, R. K., & Rovinelli, R. J. (1986). Assessing the dimensionality of a set of test items. *Applied Psychological Measurement, 10,* 287–302.

Hambleton, R. K., & Swaminathan, H. (1985). *Item response theory: Principles and applications.* Norwell, MA: Kluwer Academic Publishers.

Hambleton, R. K., Zaal, J. N., & Pieters, J. P. M. (1991). Computerized adaptive testing: Theory, applications, and standards. In R. K. Hambleton & J. N. Zaal (Eds.), *Advances in educational and psychological testing: Theory and applications.* Boston: Kluwer Academic Publishers.

Hamilton, J. C., & Shuminsky, T. R. (1990). Self-awareness mediates the relationship between serial position and item reliability. *Journal of Personality and Social Psychology, 59,* 1301–1307.

Harnisch, D. L. (1983). Item response patterns: Applications for educational practice. *Journal of Educational Measurement, 20,* 191–206.

Harris, C. W. (Ed.). (1963). *Problems in measuring change.* Madison: University of Wisconsin Press.

Harvey, R. J., & Murry, W. D. (1994). Scoring the Myers-Briggs Type Indicator: Empirical comparison of preference score versus latent-trait analyses. *Journal of Personality Assessment, 62,* 116–129.

Harvey, R. J., Murry, W. D., & Markham, S. E. (1994). Evaluation of three short-form versions of the Meyers-Briggs Type Indicator. *Journal of Personality Assessment, 63,* 181–184.

Hattie, J. (1984). An empirical study of various indices for determining unidimensionality. *Multivariate Behavioral Research, 19,* 49–78.

Hattie, J. (1985). Methodology review: Assessing unidimensionality of tests and items. *Applied Psychological Measurement, 9,* 139–164.

Hattie, J., Krakowski, K., Rogers, H. J., & Swaminathan, H. (1996). An assessment of Stout's index of essential unidimensionality. *Applied Psychological Measurement, 20,* 1–14.

Haviland, M. G., & Reise, S. P. (1996). Structure of the twenty item Toronto alexithymia scale. *Journal of Personality Assessment, 66,* 116–125.

Hendryx, M. S., Haviland, M. G., Gibbons, R. D., & Clark, D. C. (1992). An application of item response theory to alexithymia assessment among abstinent alcoholics. *Journal of Personality Assessment, 58,* 506–515.

Hetter, R. D., Segall, D. O., & Bloxom, B. M. (1994). A comparison of item calibration media in computerized adaptive testing. *Applied Psychological Measurement, 18,* 197–204.

Hoijtink, H. (1991). The measurement of latent traits by proximity items. *Applied Psychological Measurement, 15,* 153–169.

Holland, P. W. (1990). On the sampling theory foundations of item response theory models. *Psychometrika, 55,* 577–602.

Holland, P., & Rubin, D. (1982). *Test equating.* New York: Academic Press.

Holland, P. W., & Thayer, D. T. (1988). Differential item performance and the Mantel-Haenszel procedure. In H. Wainer & H. I. Braun (Eds.), *Test validity* (pp. 129–145). Hillsdale, NJ: Lawrence Erlbaum Associates.

Holland, P. W., & Wainer, H. (1993). *Differential Item Functioning.* Hillsdale, NJ: Lawrence Erlbaum Associates.

Hornke, L. F., & Habon, M. W. (1986). Rule-based item bank construction and evaluation within the linear logistic framework. *Applied Psychological Measurement, 10,* 369–380.

Hoskens, M., & DeBoeck, P. (1997). Componential IRT models for polytomous items. *Journal of Educational Measurement, 32,* 261–277.

Huang, D. C., Church, T. A., & Katigbak, M. S. (1997). Identifying cultural differences in items and traits: Differential item functioning in the NEO Personality Inventory. *Journal of Cross-Cultural Psychology, 28,* 197–218.

Hulin, C. L., Drasgow, F., & Komocar, J. (1982). Applications of item response theory to analysis of attitude scale translations. *Journal of Applied Psychology, 6,* 818–825.

Jannerone, R. J. (1986). Conjunctive item response theory kernels. *Psychometrika, 51,* 357–373.

Jansen, M. G. H., & Roshkam, E. E. (1986). Latent trait models and dichotomization of graded responses. *Psychometrika, 51,* 69–72.

Janssen, R., & De Boeck, P. (1997). Psychometric modeling of componentially designed synonym tasks. *Applied Psychological Measurement, 21,* 37–50.

Janssen, R., DeBoeck, P., & Van der Steene, G. (1996). Verbal fluency and verbal comprehension abilities in synonym tasks. *Intelligence, 22,* 291–310.

Jones, L. V. The nature of measurement. In R. L. Thorndike (Ed.), *Educational measurement* (2nd ed.). Washington, DC: American Council on Education.

Joreskog, K., & Sorbom, D. (1996). *LISREL 8: User's Reference Guide.* Chicago: Scientific Software Int.

Kelderman, H., & Rijkes, C. P. M. (1994). Loglinear multidimensional IRT models for polytomously scored items. *Psychometrika, 59,* 149–176.

Kemtes, K. A., & Kemper, S. (1997). Item response theory analysis of Sarason's Cognitive Interference questionnaire: A multiple group comparison of age. Presented at the *New Rules of Measurement Conference,* Continuing Education: Lawrence, KS.

Kim, S. (1997). BILOG 3 for windows: Item analysis and test scoring with binary logistic models. *Applied Psychological Measurement, 21,* 371–376.

Kim, S., & Cohen, A. S. (1998). A comparison of linking and concurrent calibration under item response theory. *Applied Psychological Measurement, 22,* 116–130.

King, D. W., King, L. A., Fairbank, J. A., & Schlenger, W. E. (1993). Enhancing the precision of the Mississippi Scale for Combat-Related Posttraumatic Stress Disorder: An application of item response theory. *Psychological Assessment, 5,* 457–471.

Kingsbury, G. G., & Houser, R. L. (1993). Assessing the utility of item response models: Computerized adaptive testing. *Educational Measurement: Issues and Practice, 12,* 21–27, 39.

Kingsbury, G. G., & Zara, A. R. (1991). A comparison of procedures for content-sensitive item selection in computerized adaptive tests. *Applied Measurement in Education, 4,* 241–261.

Knowles, E. S. (1988). Item context effects on personality scales: measuring changes the measure. *Journal of Personality and Social Psychology, 55,* 312–320.

Koch, W. R. (1983). Likert scaling using the graded response latent trait model. *Applied Psychological Measurement, 7,* 15–32.

Koch, W. R., Dodd, B. G., & Fitzpatrick, S. J. (1990). Computerized adaptive measurement of attitudes. *Measurement and Evaluation in counseling and Development, 23,* 20–30.

Labouvie-Vief, G., & Gonda, J. N. (1976). Cognitive strategy training and intellectual performance in the elderly. *Journal of Gerontology, 31*, 327–332.

Lautenschlager, G. J., & Park, D. G. (1988). IRT item bias detection procedures: Issues of model mispecificaiton, robustness, and parameter linking. *Applied Psychological Measurement, 12*, 365–376.

Lee, J. A., Moreno, K. E., & Sympson, J. B. (1986). The effects of mode of test administration on test performance. *Educational and Psychological Measurement, 46*, 467–474.

Levine, M. V., & Drasgow, F. (1988). Optimal appropriateness measurement. *Psychometrika, 53*, 161–176.

Levine, M. V., Drasgow, F., Williams, B., McCusker, C., & Thomasson, G. L. (1992). Distinguishing between item response theory models. *Applied Psychological Measurement, 16*, 261–278.

Levine, M. V., & Rubin, D. B. (1979). Measuring appropriateness of multiple-choice test scores. *Journal of Educational Statistics, 4*, 269–290.

Lewis, C., & Sheehan, K. (1990). Using Bayesian decision theory to design a computerized mastery test. *Applied Psychological Measurement, 14*, 367–386.

Linn, R. L., Levine, M. V., Hastings, C. N., & Wardrop, J. L. (1980). *An investigation of item bias in a test of reading comprehension (Technical Report no. 162)*. Urban, IL: Center for the study of Reading, University of Illinois, 1980.

Liou, M. (1993). Exact person tests for assessing model-data fit in the Rasch model. *Applied Psychological Measurement, 17*, 187–195.

Liou, M., & Chang, C. H. (1992). Constructing the exact significance level for a person-fit statistic. *Psychometrika, 2*, 169–181.

Lord, F. (1953). The relation of test score to the trait underlying the test. *Educational and Psychological Measurement, 13*, 517–548.

Lord, F. (1969). Statistical adjustments when comparing preexisting groups. *Psychological Bulletin, 72*, 336–339.

Lord, F. (1980). *Applications of item response theory to practical testing problems*. Hillsdale, NJ: Lawrence Erlbaum Associates.

Lord, F. N., & Novick, M. R. (1968). *Statistical theories of mental test scores*. Reading, MA: Addison-Wesley.

Luce, R. D., & Tukey, J. W. (1964). Simultaneous conjoint measurement: A new type of fundamental measurement. *Journal of Mathematical Psychology, 1*, 1–27.

Lumsden, J. (1977). Person reliability. *Applied Psychological Measurement, 1*, 477–482.

Lunz, M. E., Bergstrom, B. A., & Wright, B. D. (1992). The effect of review on student ability and test efficiency for computerized adaptive tests. *Applied Psychological Measurement, 16*, 33–40.

Mantel, N., & Haenszel, W. (1959). Statistical aspects of the analysis of data from retrospective studies of disease. *Journal of the National Cancer Institute, 22*, 719–748.

Marco, G. L. (1977). Item characteristic curve solutions to three intractable testing problems. *Journal of Educational Measurement, 14*, 139–160.

Maris, E. M. (1995). Psychometric latent response models. *Psychometrika, 60*, 523–547.

Masters, G. N. (1982). A Rasch model for partial credit scoring. *Psychometrika, 47*, 149–174.

Masters, G. N. (1984). Constructing an item bank using partial credit scoring. *Journal of Educational Measurement, 21*, 19–32.

Masters, G. N. (1985). A comparison of latent trait and latent class analyses of Likert-type data. *Psychometrika, 50*, 69–82.

Masters, G. N., & Evans, J. (1986). Banking non-dichotomously scored items. *Applied Psychological Measurement, 10*, 355–367.

Masters, G. N., & Wright, B. D. (1984). The essential process in a family of measurement models. *Psychometrika, 49*, 529–544.

Masters, G. N., & Wright, B. D. (1996). The partial credit model. In W. J. van der Linden & R. K. Hambleton (Eds.), *Handbook of modern item response theory*. New York: Springer.

Maxwell, S., & Delaney, H. (1985). Measurement and statistics: An examination of construct validity. *Psychological Bulletin, 97*, 85–93.

Maydeu-Olivares, A., Drasgow, F., & Mead, A. D. (1994). Distinguishing among parametric item response models for polychotomous ordered data. *Applied Psychological Measurement, 18*, 245–256.

McBride, J. R. (1997). Technical perspectives. In W. A. Sands, B. K. Waters, & J. R. McBride (Eds.), *Computer Adaptive Testing*. Washington, DC: American Psychological Association.

McCollam, K. M. Schmidt (1997). *The modifiability of age differences in spatial visualization*. Unpublished doctoral dissertation, University of Kansas, Lawrence, Kansas.

McCollam, K. M. Schmidt (1998). Latent trait and latent class models. In G. M. Marcoulides (Ed.), *Modern methods for business research*. Mahwah, NJ: Lawrence Erlbaum Associates.

McDonald, R. P. (1962). Nonlinear factor analysis. *Psychometric Monograph* No. 15.

McDonald, R. P. (1981). The dimensionality of tests and items. *British Journal of Mathematical and Statistical Psychology, 34*, 100–117.

McDonald, R. P. (1985). Comments of D. J. Bartholomew, Foundations of factor analysis: Some practical implications. *British Journal of Mathematical and Statistical Psychology, 38*, 134–137.

McDonald, R. P., & Mok, M. M. C. (1995). Goodness of fit in item response models. *Multivariate Behavioral Research, 30*, 23–40.

McKinley, R. L., & Mills, C. N. (1985). A comparison of several goodness-of-fit statistics. *Applied Psychological Measurement, 9*, 49–57.

McKinley, R. L., & Way, W. D. (1992). The feasibility of modeling secondary TOEFL ability dimensions using multidimensional IRT models. *TOEFL technical report TR-5*, Princeton, NJ: Educational Testing Service, February.

Mead, A. D., & Drasgow, F. (1993). Equivalence of computerized and paper-and-pencil cognitive ability tests: A meta-analysis. *Psychological Bulletin, 114*, 449–458.

Medina-Diaz, M. (1993). Analysis of cognitive structure using the lienar logistic test model and quadratic assignment. *Applied Psychological Measurement, 17*, 117–130.

Meijer, R. R. (1994). The number of Guttman errors as a simple and powerful person-fit statistic. *Applied Psychological Measurement, 18*, 311–314.

Meijer, R. R. (1996). Person-fit research: An introduction. *Applied Measurement in Education, 9*, 3–8.

Meijer, R. R., Molenaar, I. W., & Sijtsma, K. (1994). Influence of test and person characteristics on nonparametric appropriateness measurement. *Applied Psychological Measurement, 18*, 111–120.

Meijer, R. R., Muijtjens, A. M. M., & van der Vleuten, C. P. M. (1996). Nonparametric person-fit research: Some theoretical issues and an empirical example. *Applied Measurement in Education, 9*, 77–89.

Meijer, R. R., & Nering, M. L. (1997). Trait level estimation for nonfitting response vectors. *Applied Psychological Measurement, 21*, 321–226.

Meijer, R. R., & Sijtsma, K. (1995). Detection of aberrant item score patterns: A review of recent developments. *Applied Measurement in Education, 8*, 261–272.

Meiser, T. (1996). Loglinear Rasch models for the analysis of stability and change. *Psychometrika, 61*, 629–645.

Mellenbergh, G. J. (1994a). Generalized linear item response theory. *Psychological Bulletin, 115*, 300–307.

Mellenbergh, G. J. (1994b). A unidimensional latent trait model for continuous item responses. *Multivariate Behavioral Research, 29*, 223–236.

Merideth, W. (1993). Measurement invariance, factor analysis and factorial invariance. *Psychometrika, 58*, 525–543.

Michell, J. (1990). *An introduction to the logic of psychological measurement*. Hillsdale, NJ: Lawrence Erlbaum Associates.

Millman, J., & Arter, J. A. (1984). Issues in item banking. *Journal of Educational Measurement, 21*, 315–330.

Mills, C. N., & Stocking, M. L. (1996). Practical issues in large-scale computerized adaptive testing. *Applied Measurement in Education, 9*, 287–304.

Milsap, R. E., & Everson, H. T. (1993). Methodology review: Statistical approaches for assessing measurement bias. *Applied Psychological Measurement, 17*, 297–334.

Mislevy, R. (1984). Estimating latent distributions. *Psychometrika, 49*, 359–381.

Mislevy, R. (1986). Bayesian modal estimation I item response models. *Psychometrika, 51*, 177–195.

Mislevy, R. (1993). Foundations of a new test theory. In N. Frederiksen, R. Mislevy, & I. Bejar (Eds.), *Test theory for a new generation of tests*. Hillsdale, NJ: Lawrence Erlbaum Associates.

Mislevy, R. J., & Bock, R. D. (1990). *BILOG-3; Item analysis and test scoring with binary logistic models* [Computer software]. Mooresville, IN: Scientific Software.

Mislevy, R., & Verhelst, N. (1990). Modeling item responses when different subjects employ different solution strategies. *Psychometrika, 55*, 195–215.

Mitchell, K. (1983). *Cognitive processing determinants of item difficulty on the verbal subtests of the Armed Services Vocational Aptitude Battery and their relationship to success in Army training*. Unpublished doctoral dissertation, Cornell University.

Molenaar, I. W., & Hoijtink, H. (1990). The many null distributions of person fit indices. *Psychometrika, 55*, 75–106.

Molenaar, I. W., & Hoijtink, H. (1996). Person-fit and the Rasch model, with an application to knowledge of logical quantors. *Applied Measurement in Education, 9*, 27–45.

Moreno, K. E., & Segall, D. O. (1992). CAT-ASVAB precision. *Proceedings of the 34th annual conference of the Military Testing Association, 1*, 22–26.

Moreno, K. E., Wetzel, D. C., McBride, J. R., & Weiss, D. J. (1984). Relationship between corresponding Armed Services Vocational Aptitude Battery (ASVAB) and computerized adaptive testing (CAT) subtests. *Applied Psychological Measurement, 8*, 155–163.

Muraki, E. (1990). Fitting a polytomous item response model to Likert-type data. *Applied Psychological Measurement, 14*, 59–71.

Muraki, E. (1992). A generalized partial credit model: Application of an EM algorithm. *Applied Psychological Measurement, 16*, 159–176.

Muraki, E. (1993a). Information functions of the generalized partial credit model. *Applied Psychological Measurement, 17*, 351–363.

Muraki, E. (1993b). *POLYFACT* [Computer program]. Princeton, NJ: Educational Testing Service.

Muraki, E. (1996). A generalized partial credit model. In W. J. van der Linden & R. K. Hambleton (Eds.), *Handbook of Modern Item Response Theory* (pp. 153–164). New York: Springer-Verlag.

Muraki, E., & Bock, R. D. (1993). *PARSCALE: IRT based test scoring and item analysis for graded open-ended exercises and performance tasks*. Chicago: Scientific Software Int.

Muraki, E., & Carlson, J. E. (1995). Full-information factor analysis for polytomous item responses. *Applied Psychological Measurement, 19*, 73–90.

Muraki, E., & Engelhard, G. (1985). Full information item factor analysis: Application of EAP scores. *Applied Psychological Measurement, 9*, 417–430.

Muthen, B. (1978). Contributions to factor analysis of dichotomous variables. *Psychometrika, 43*, 551–560.

Muthen, B. (1984). A general structural equation model with dichotomous, ordered categorical and continuous latent variable indicators. *Psychometrika, 49*, 115–132.

Muthen, B. (1987). *LISCOMP: Analysis of linear structural equations with a comprehensive measurement model. Theoretical integration and user's guide*. Mooresville, IN: Scientific Software.

Nandakumar, R. (1993). Assessing essential dimensionality of real data. *Applied Psychological Measurement, 17,* 29–38.

Nandakumar, R. (1994). Assessing dimensionality of a set of items — Comparison of different approaches. *Journal of Educational Measurement, 31,* 17–35.

Nandakumar, R., & Stout, W. F. (1993). Refinement of Stout's procedure for assessing latent trait dimensionality. *Journal of Educational Statistics, 18,* 41–68.

Narens, L., & Luce, R. D. (1986). Measurement: The theory of numerical assignments. *Psychological Bulletin, 99,* 166–180.

Neuman, G., & Baydoun, R. (1998). Computerization of paper-and-pencil test: When are they equivalent? *Applied Psychological Measurement, 22,* 71–83.

Nering, M. L., & Meijer, R. R. (1998). A comparison of the person response function and the l_z person-fit statistic. *Applied Psychological Measurement, 22,* 53–69.

Neyman, J., & Scott, E. L. (1948). Consistent estimates based on partially consistent observations. *Econometrica, 16,* 1–32.

Nunnally, J. C. (1978). *Psychometric theory* (2nd ed.). New York: McGraw-Hill.

Oshima, T. C., & Miller, M. D. (1992). Multidimensionality and item bias in item response theory. *Applied Psychological Measurement, 16,* 237–248.

Ozer, D. J., & Reise, S. P. (1994). Personality assessment. *Annual Review of Psychology, 45,* 357–388.

Park, D., & Lautenschlager, G. J. (1990). Improving IRT item bias detection with iterative linking and ability scale purification. *Applied Psychological Measurement, 14,* 163–173.

Pascual-Leone, J. (1970). A mathematical model for the transition rule in Piaget's developmental stages. *Acta Psychologica, 32,* 301–345.

Pellegrino, J. W., Mumaw, R., & Shute, V. (1985). Analyses of spatial aptitude and expertise. In S. Embretson (Ed.), *Test design: Developments in psychology and psychometrics.* New York: Academic Press.

Pennings, A. H., & Hessels, M. G. P. (1996). The measurement of mental attentional capacity: A neo-Piagetian developmental study. *Intelligence, 23,* 59–78.

Peterson, N., Marco, G., & Steward, E. (1982). A test of the adequacy of linear score equating models. In P. Holland & D. Rubin (Eds.), *Test equating.* New York: Academic Press.

Ragosa, D., Brandt, D., & Zimowskyk, M. (1982). A growth curve approach to the measurement of change. *Psychological Bulletin, 92,* 726–748.

Raju, N. S. (1988). The area between two item characteristic curves. *Psychometrika, 53,* 495–502.

Raju, N. S. (1990). Determining the significance of estimated signed and unsigned areas between two item response functions. *Applied Psychological Measurement, 14,* 197–207.

Ramsey, J. O. (1991). Kernel smoothing approaches to nonparametric item characteristic curve estimation. *Psychometrika, 56,* 611–630.

Rasch, G. (1960). *Probabilistic models for some intelligence and attainment tests.* Chicago: University of Chicago Press.

Rasch, G. (1977). On specific objectivity: An attempt at formalizing the request for generality and validity of scientific statements. In M. Glegvad (Ed.), *The Danish Yearbook of Philosophy* (pp. 58–94). Copenhagen: Munksgaard.

Reckase, M. D. (1979). Unifactor latent trait models applied to multifactor tests: Results and implications. *Journal of Educational Statistics, 4,* 207–230.

Reckase, M. D. (1997). The past and future of multidimensional item response theory. *Applied Psychological Measurement, 21,* 25–36.

Reckase, M. D., & McKinley, R. L. (1991). The discriminating power of items that measure more than one dimension. *Applied Psychological Measurement, 15,* 361–373.

Reise, S. P. (1990). A comparison of item- and person-fit methods of assessing model-data fit in item response theory. *Applied Psychological Measurement, 14,* 127–137.

Reise, S. P. (1995). Scoring method and the detection of response aberrancy in a personality assessment context. *Applied Psychological Measurement, 19,* 213–229.

Reise, S. P., & Due, A. M. (1991). The influence of test characteristics on the detection of aberrant response patterns. *Applied Psychological Measurement, 15,* 217–226.

Reise, S. P., & Flannery, Wm. P. (1996). Assessing person-fit on measures of typical performance. *Applied Measurement in Education, 9,* 9–26.

Reise, S. P., & Waller, N. G. (1990). Fitting the two-parameter model to personality data: The parameterization of the Multidimensional Personality Questionnaire. *Applied Psychological Measurement, 14,* 45–58.

Reise, S. P., & Waller, N. G. (1993). Traitedness and the assessment of response pattern scalability. *Journal of Personality and Social Psychology, 65,* 143–151.

Reise, S. P., & Yu, J. (1990). Parameter recovery in the graded response model using MULTILOG. *Journal of Educational Measurement, 27,* 133–144.

Reise, S. P., Widaman, K. F., & Pugh, R. H. (1993). Confirmatory factor analysis and item response theory: Two approaches for exploring measurement invariance. *Psychological Bulletin, 114,* 352–566.

Roberts, J. S., & Laughlin, J. E. (1996). A unidimensional item response model for unfolding responses from a graded disagree-agree response scale. *Applied Psychological Measurement, 20,* 231–255.

Rosenberg, M. (1965). *Society and the adolescent self-image.* Princeton, NJ: Princeton University Press.

Roskam, E. E. (1997). Models for speed and time-limit tests. In W. J. Van der Linden & R. Hambleton (Eds.), *Handbook of modern item response theory* (pp. 187–208). New York: Springer-Verlag.

Roskam, E., & Jansen, P. G. W. (1984). A new derivation of the Rasch model. In G. Fischer & I. Molenaar (Eds.), *Rasch models: Foundations, recent developments, and applications.* New York: Springer-Verlag.

Roskam, E. E. (1997). Models for speed and time-limit tests. In W. J. Van der Linden & R. Hambleton (Eds.), *Handbook of modern item response theory* (pp. 187–208). New York: Springer-Verlag.

Rost, J. (1988). Measuring attitudes with a threshold model drawing on a traditional scaling concept. *Applied Psychological Measurement, 12,* 397–409.

Rost, J. (1990). Rasch models in latent classes: An integration of two approaches to item analysis. *Applied Psychological Measurement, 14,* 271–282.

Rost, J. (1991). A logistic mixture distribution model for polychotomous item responses. *British Journal of Mathematical and Statistical Psychology, 44,* 75–92.

Rost, J., Carstensen, C., & Davier, von, M. (1996). Applying the mixed Rasch model to personality questionnaires. In J. Rost & R. Langeheine (Eds.), *Applications of latent trait and latent class models in the social sciences.* New York: Waxmann Munster.

Rost, J., & Georg, W. (1991). Alternative Skalierungsmoglichkeiten zur klassischen Testtheorie am Beispiel der Skala "Jugendzentrismus." *Zerntral-Archiv-Information, 28.*

Rost, J., & von Davier, M. (1992). *MIRA: A PC-program for the mixed Rasch model.* Kiel, Federal Republic of Germany: IPN-Institute for science Education.

Roussos, L., & Stout, W. F. (1996). A multidimensionality-based DIF analysis paradigm. *Applied Psychological Measurement, 20,* 355–371.

Rozeboom, W. W. (1966). Scaling theory and the nature of measurement. *Synthese, 16,* 170–233.

Safrit, M. J., Costa, M. G., & Cohen, A. S. (1989). Item response theory and the measurement of motor behavior. *Research Quarterly for Exercise and Sport, 60,* 325–335.

Salthouse, T. A., & Mitchell, D. R. D. (1990). Effects of age and naturally occurring experience on spatial visualization performance. *Developmental Psychology, 26,* 845–854.

Santor, D. A., Ramsay, J. O., &, Zuroff, D. C. (1998). Nonparametric item analyses of the Beck Depression Inventory: Evaluating gender item bias and response option weights. *Psychological Assessment, 6*, 255–270.

Samejima, F. (1969). Estimation of latent ability using a response pattern of graded scores. *Psychometrika Monograph*, No. 17.

Samejima, F. (1996). The graded response model. In W. J. van der Linden & Hambleton, R. K. (Eds.), *Handbook of modern item response theory*. New York: Springer.

Schaie, K. W., & Willis, S. L. (1993). Age difference patterns of psychometric intelligence in adulthood: Generalizability within and across ability domains. *Psychology and Aging, 8*, 44–55.

Schmitt, N. (1996). Uses and abuses of coefficient alpha. *Psychological Assessment, 8*, 350–353.

Segall, D. O. (1996). Multidimensional adaptive testing. *Psychometrika, 61*, 331–354.

Shealy, R., & Stout, W. F. (1993a). An item response theory model for test bias. In P. W. Holland & H. Wainer (Eds.), *Differential item functioning* (pp. 197–239). Hillsdale, NJ: Lawrence Erlbaum Associates.

Shealy, R., & Stout, W. F. (1993b). A model-based standardization approach that separates true bias/DIF from group ability differences and detects test bias/DTT as well as item bias/DIF. *Psychometrika, 58*, 159–194.

Sheehan, K. M. (1997). A tree-based approach to proficiency scaling and diagnostic assessment. *Journal of Educational Measurement, 34*, 333–354.

Sheehan, K. M. (1998). *Understanding students' underlying strengths and weaknesses: A tree-based regression approach*. Technical Report. Princeton, NJ: ETS.

Sheehan, K., & Lewis, C. (1992). Computerized mastery testing with nonequivalent testlets. *Applied Psychological Measurement, 16*, 65–76.

Sheehan, K. M., & Mislevy, R. J. (1990). Integrating cognitive and psychometric models in a measure of document literacy. *Journal of Educational Measurement, 27*, 255–272.

Sheridan, B., Andrich, D., & Luo, G. (1996). *Welcome to RUMM: A windows-based item analysis program employing Rasch unidimensional measurement models*. User's Guide.

Siegler, R. S. (1981). Developmental sequences within and between groups. *Monographs of the Society for Research in Child Development, 46*, No. 2.

Smith, L. L., & Reise, S. P. (in press). Gender differences on negative affectivity: An IRT study of differential item functioning on the Multidimensional Personality Questionnaire Stress Reaction scale. *Journal of Personality and Social Psychology, 75*, 1350–1362.

Smith, R. M. (1996). Item component equating. In G. Engelhard & M. Wilson (Eds.), *Objective measurement: Theory into practice, Volume 3*. Norwood, NJ: Ablex.

Smith, R. M., & Kramer, G. A. (1992). A comparison of two methods of test equating in the Rasch model. *Educational and Psychological Measurement, 52*, 835–846.

Snyder, M. (1974). Self monitoring of expressive behavior. *Journal of Personality and Social Psychology, 30*, 526–537.

Snyder, M., & Gangestad, S. (1986). On the nature of self-monitoring: Matters of assessment, matters of validity. *Journal of Personality and Social Psychology, 51*, 125–139.

Spada, H., & McGaw, B. (1985). The assessment of learning effects with linear logistic test models. In S. Embretson (Ed.), *Test design: New directions in psychology and psychometrics* (pp. 169–193). New York: Academic Press.

Spearman, C. (1907). Demonstration of formulae for true measurement of correlation. *American Journal of Psychology, 18*, 161–169.

Spearman, C. (1913). Correlations of sums and differences. *British Journal of Psychology, 5*, 417–426.

Spray, J. A. (1997). Multiple-attempt, single-item response models. In W. J. Van der Linden & R. Hambleton (Eds.), *Handbook of modern item response theory* (pp. 187–208). New York: Springer-Verlag.

Spray, J. A., Ackerman, T. A., Reckase, M. D., & Carlson, J. E. (1989). Effect of the medium of item presentation on examinee performance and item characteristics. *Journal of Educational Measurement, 26*, 261–271.

Stegelmann, W. (1983). Expanding the Rasch model to a general model having more than one dimension. *Psychometrika, 48*, 259–267.

Steinberg, L. (1994). Context and serial order effects in personality measurement: Limits on the generality of "measuring changes the measure." *Journal of Personality and Social Psychology, 66*, 341–349.

Steinberg, L., & Jorgensen, R. (1996). Assessing the MMPI-based Cook-Medley Hostility scale: The implications of dimensionality. *Journal of Personality and Social Psychology, 70*, 1281–1287.

Steinberg, L., & Thissen, D. (1995). Item response theory in personality research. In P. E. Shrout & S. T. Fiske (Eds.), *Personality research, methods, and theory: A festschrift honoring Donald W. Fiske*. Hillsdale, NJ: Lawrence Erlbaum Associates.

Steinberg, L., & Thissen, D. (1996). Uses of item response theory and the testlet concept in the measurement of psychopathology. *Psychological Methods, 1*, 81–97.

Stevens, S. S. (1946). On the theory of scales of measurement. *Science, 103*, 221–263.

Stocking, M. L. (1993). *Controlling item exposure rates in a realistic adaptive testing paradigm (Research Report 93-2)*. Princeton NJ: ETS.

Stocking, M. L., & Lord, F. M. (1983). Developing a common metric in item response theory. *Applied Psychological Measurement, 7*, 201–210.

Stocking, M. L., & Swanson, L. (1993). A method for severely constrained item selection in adaptive testing. *Applied Psychological Measurement, 17*, 277–292.

Stout, W. (1987). A nonparametric approach for assessing latent trait unidimensionality, *Psychometrika, 52*, 589–617.

Stout, W. (1990). A new item response theory modeling approach with applications to unidimensional assessment and ability estimation. *Psychometrika, 55*, 293–326.

Stout, W. F., & Roussos, L. A. (1995). *SIBTEST users manual* (2nd ed.) [Computer program manual]. Urbana-Champaign: University of Illinois, Department of Statistics.

Stout, W., Hsin-Hung, L. Nandakumar, R., & Bolt, D. (1997). MULTISIB: A procedure to investigate DIF when a test is intentionally two-dimensional. *Applied Psychological Measurement, 21*, 195–213.

Swaminathan, H., & Gifford, J. A. (1985). Bayesian estimation in the two-parameter logistic model. *Psychometrika, 50*, 349–364.

Swaminathan, H., & Rogers, J. J. (1990). Detecting differential item functioning using logistic regression procedures. *Journal of Educational Measurement, 27*, 361–370.

Sykes, R. C., & Ito, K. (1997). The effects of computer administration on scores and item parameter estimates of an IRT-based licensure examination. *Applied Psychological Measurement, 21*, 57–63.

Takane, Y., & de Leeuw, J. (1987). On the relationship between item response theory and factor analysis of discretized variables. *Psychometrika, 52*, 393–408.

Tatsuoka, K. K. (1983). Rule space: An approach for dealing with misconceptions based on item response theory. *Journal of Educational Measurement, 20*, 34–38.

Tatsuoka, K. K. (1984). Caution indices based on item response theory. *Psychometrika, 49*, 95–110.

Tatsuoka, K. K. (1985). A probabilistic model for diagnosing misconceptions in the pattern classification approach. *Journal of Educational Statistics, 12*, 55–73.

Tatsuoka, K. K. (1996). Use of generalized person-fit indices, zetas for statistical pattern classification. *Applied Measurement in Education, 9*, 65–75.

Tatsuoka, K. K., Solomonson, C., & Singley, K. (in press). The new SAT I mathematics profile. In G. Buck, D. Harnish, G. Boodoo & K. Tatsuoka (Eds.), *The new SAT*.

Tatsuoka, K. K., & Tatsuoka, M. M. (1982). Detection of aberrant response patterns and their effect on dimensionality. *Journal of Educational Statistics, 7,* 215–231.

Tatsuoka, K. K., & Tatsuoka, M. M. (1983). Spotting erroneous rules of operation by the individual consistency index. *Journal of Educational Measurement, 20,* 221–230.

Tatsuoka, K. K., & Linn, R. L. (1983). Indices for detecting unusual patterns: Links between two general approaches and potential applications. *Applied Psychological Methods, 7,* 81–96.

Taylor, G. J., Bagby, R. M., & Parker, J. D. A (1992). The revised Toronto Alexithymia Scale: Some reliability, validity, and normative data. *Psychotherapy and Psychosomatics, 57,* 34–41.

Tellegen, A. (1982). *Brief manual for the Multidimensional Personality Questionnaire.* Unpublished manuscript, University of Minnesota, Minneapolis.

Tellegen, A. (1988). The analysis of consistency in personality assessment. *Journal of Personality, 56,* 621–663.

Thayer, R. E. (1989). *The biopsychology of mood and arousal.* New York: Oxford University Press.

Theunissen, T. J. J. M. (1986). Some applications of optimization algorithms in test design and adaptive testing. *Applied Psychological Measurement, 10,* 381–389.

Thissen, D. (1991). *MULTILOG user's guide: Multiple categorical item analysis and test scoring using item response theory.* Chicago: Scientific Software Int.

Thissen, D. (1993). Repealing rules that no longer apply to psychological measurement. In N. Frederiksen, R. J. Mislevy, & I. I. Bejar, (Eds.), *Test theory for a new generation of tests* (pp. 79–97). Hillsdale, NJ: Lawrence Erlbaum Associates.

Thissen, D., & Steinberg, L. (1984). A response model for multiple choice items. *Psychometrika, 49,* 501–519.

Thissen, D., & Steinberg, L. (1986). A taxonomy of item response models. *Psychometrika, 51,* 567–577.

Thissen, D., & Steinberg, L. (1988). Data analysis using item response theory. *Psychological Bulletin, 104,* 385–395.

Thissen, D., Steinberg, L., & Gerrard, M. (1986). Beyond group mean differences: The concept of item bias. *Psychological Bulletin, 99,* 118–128.

Thissen, D., Steinberg, L., Pyszczynksi, T., & Greenberg, J. (1983). An item response theory for personality and attitude scales: Item analysis using restricted factor analyses. *Applied Psychological Measurement, 7,* 211–226.

Thissen, D., Steinberg, L., & Wainer, H. (1988). Use of item response theory in the study of group differences in trace lines. In H. Wainer & H. I. Braun (Eds.), *Test validity* (pp. 147–169). Hillsdale, NJ: Lawrence Erlbaum Associates.

Thissen, D., Steinberg, L., & Wainer, H. (1992). Detection of differential item functioning using the parameters of item response models. In P. W. Holland & H. Wainer (Eds.), *Differential item functioning: Theory and practice* (pp. 67–113). Hillsdale, NJ: Lawrence Erlbaum Associates.

Tinsley, H. E. A. (1972). *An investigation of the Rasch simple logistic model for tests of intelligence or attainment.* Doctoral dissertation, University of Minnesota. Ann Arbor, MI: University Microfilms, No. 72-14387.

Tourangeau, R., & Rasinski, K. A. (1988). Cognitive processes underlying context effects in attitude measurement. *Psychological Bulletin, 103,* 299–314.

Townsend, J. T., & Ashby, G. (1984). Measurement scale and statistics: The misconception misconceived. *Psychological Bulletin, 96,* 394–401.

Vale, D. C. (1986). Linking item parameters onto a common scale. *Applied Psychological Measurement, 10,* 133–344.

van der Linden, W. J., & Hambleton, R. K. (1996). *Handbook of modern item response theory.* New York: Springer.

Verhelst, N. D., Verstralen, H. H. F. M., & Jansen, M. G. H. (1997). A logistic model for time-limit tests. In W. J. Van der Linden & R. Hambleton (Eds.), *Handbook of modern item response theory* (pp. 169–186). New York: Springer-Verlag.

von Davier, M. (1995). *WINMIRA: A Program System for Analyses with the Rasch Model, with the Latent Class Analysis and with the Mixed Rasch Model*. University of Kiel, Germany: Institute for Science Education.

von Davier, M., & Rost, J. (1996). Self monitoring—A class variable? In J. Rost & R. Langeheine (Eds.), *Applications of latent trait and latent class models in the social sciences*. New York: Waxmann Munster.

Wainer, H. (1990). *Computerized adaptive testing: A primer*. Hillsdale, NJ: Lawrence Erlbaum Associates.

Wainer, H., & Kiely, G. L. (1987). Item clusters and computerized adaptive testing: A case for testlets. *Journal of Educational Measurement, 24*, 185–201.

Wainer, H., & Thissen, D. (1987). Estimating ability with the wrong model. *Journal of Educational Statistics, 12*, 339–368.

Waller, N. G., & Reise, S. P. (1989). Computerized adaptive personality assessment: An illustration with the absorption scale. *Journal of Personality and Social Psychology, 57*, 1051–1058.

Waller, N. G., Tellegen, A, McDonald, R. P., & Lykken, D. T. (1996). Exploring nonlinear models in personality assessment: Development and preliminary validation of a negative emotionality scale. *Journal of Personality, 64*, 545–576.

Wang, W.-C., Wilson, M., & Adams, R. J. (1997). Rasch models for multidimensionality between and within items. In M. Wilson & G. Engelhard (Eds.), *Objective measurement: Theory into practice, Volume 4*, 139–156.

Ward, W. C. (1988). The College Board computerized placement tests: An application of computerized adaptive testing. *Machine-Mediated Learning, 2*, 217–282.

Weiss, D. J. (1982). Improving measurement quality and efficiency with adaptive testing. *Applied Psychological Measurement, 6*, 473–492.

Weiss, D. J. (1985). Adaptive testing by computer. *Journal of Consulting and Clinical Psychology, 53*, 774–789.

Whitely, S. E. (1980). Multicomponent latent trait models for ability tests. *Psychometrika, 45*, 479–494.

Whitely, S. E., & Dawis, R. V. (1976). The influence of test context on item difficulty. *Educational and Psychological Measurement, 36*, 329–337.

White, N., & Cunningham, W. R. (1987). The age comparative construct validity of speeded cognitive factors. *Multivariate Behavioral Research, 22*, 249–265.

Whitely, S. E., & Schneider, L. M. (1981). Information structure on geometric analogies: A test theory approach. *Applied Psychological Measurement, 5*, 383–397.

Wiggins, J. S. (1972). *Personality and prediction: Principles of personality assessment*. Malabor, FL.: Robert E. Kriger Publishing.

Willis, S. L., & Nesselroade, C. S. (1990). Long-term effects of fluid ability training in old-old age. *Developmental Psychology, 26*, 905–910.

Wilson, M. (1985). Measuring stages of growth: A psychometric model of hierarchical development. Occasional paper No. 19. Hawthorn, Victoria: Australian Council for Educational Research.

Wilson, M. (1989). Saltus: A psychometric model of discontinuity in cognitive development. *Psychological Bulletin, 105*, 276–289.

Wilson, M. (1992). The ordered partition model: An extension of the partial credit model. *Applied Psychological Measurement, 16*, 309–325.

Wilson, D. T., Wood, R., & Gibbons, R. (1991). *TESTFACT: Test scoring, item statistics, and item factor analysis*. Mooresville, IN: Scientific Software.

Wise, S. L., Barnes, L. B., Harvey, A. L., & Plake, B. S. (1989). Effects of computer anxiety and computer experience on the computer-based achievement test performance of college students. *Applied Measurement in Education, 2,* 235–241.

Wissler, C. (1901). The correlation of mental and physical tests. *Psychological Review, Monograph Supplement, 3*(6).

Woodcock, R. W., & Johnson, M. B. (1989). *Woodcock-Johnson Psycho-Educational Battery Revised.* Allen, TX: DLM Teaching Resources.

Wright, B. D., & Douglas, G. A. (1977). Best procedures for sample-free item analysis. *Applied Psychological Measurement, 1,* 281–294.

Wright, B. D., & Masters, G. N. (1982). *Rating scale analysis.* Chicago: MESA Press.

Wright, B. D., & Stone, M. H. (1979). *Best test design. Rasch measurement.* Chicago: Mesa Press.

Wu, M. L., Adams, R. J., & Wilson, M. R. (1995). *MATS: Multi Aspect Test Software.* Camberwell Victoria, Australia: Australian Council for Educational Research.

Yamamoto, K. (1987). *A model that combines IRT and latent class models.* Unpublished doctoral dissertation, University of Illinois, Champaign, IL.

Yen, W. M. (1984). Effects of local item dependence on the fit and equating performance of the three-parameter logistic model. *Applied Psychological Measurement, 8,* 125–145.

Yen, W. M. (1993). Scaling performance assessments: Strategies for managing local item dependence. *Journal of Educational Measurement, 30,* 187–213.

Zara, A. R. (1988). Introduction to item response theory and computerized adaptive testing as applied in licensure and certification testing. *National Clearinghouse of Examination Information newsletter, 6,* 11–17.

Zickar, M. J., & Drasgow, F. (1996). Detecting faking on a personality instrument using appropriateness measurement. *Applied Psychological Measurement, 20,* 71–88.

Zimowski, M. F., Muraki, E., Mislevy, R. J., & Bock, R. D. (1996). *BILOG-MG: Multiple-group IRT analysis and test maintenance for binary items.* Chicago: Scientific Software.

Zwick, R. (1987). Assessing the dimensionality of NAEP reading data. *Journal of Educational Measurement, 24,* 293–308.

Author Index

Subject Index

1PL model, (see Rasch model
2PL model, 51–53, 57–58, 70
3PL model, 70–73

A

Adaptive test, See Computerized adaptive test
Analyzing trends, 297, 298–299, 299
Anchoring IRT parameters, 129–131
Area measures,
    signed and unsigned, 262
Assumptions,
    dimensionality, 187–188, 227–231, 307–309
    essential dimensionality, 228, 230
    local independence, 48, 188, 231–233
    strong vs. weak, 229
    Q3 Index, 232
    testing IRT model, 226–233
Attitude models, 80
Attitude assessment, 315–316

B

Basic data matrix, 44–46, 189–195
Bias, item and test, see Differential item functioning

C

Category threshold parameters, 102–103
Category intersection parameter, 104–105, 111–112, 116

Category response curves,
    defined, 99
    in generalized partial credit, 113–114
    in graded response model, 99–100
    in nominal response model, 121
    in partial credit model, 106–109
    in rating scale model, 117
Change scores, 34–36
Change measurement, 296–297
Classical test theory, 126–127
    compared to IRT, 13–39
CML, See Maximum likelihood estimation, conditional maximum likelihood
Cognitive process decomposition, 278–285, 287–292, 303
Common scale measurement, 25–28, 125–129, 133–135
Computer programs, see Parameter estimation
Computerized adaptive testing, 263–269
    advantages, 268
    in personality assessment, 316–318
    item banks, 264–266
    item selection algorithms, 266–267
    stopping rules, 267–268
Continuous response models, 122

D

Developmental scaling, 299–301
Developmental discontinuities, 297–298, 301–303
Differential item functioning, 249–263

368